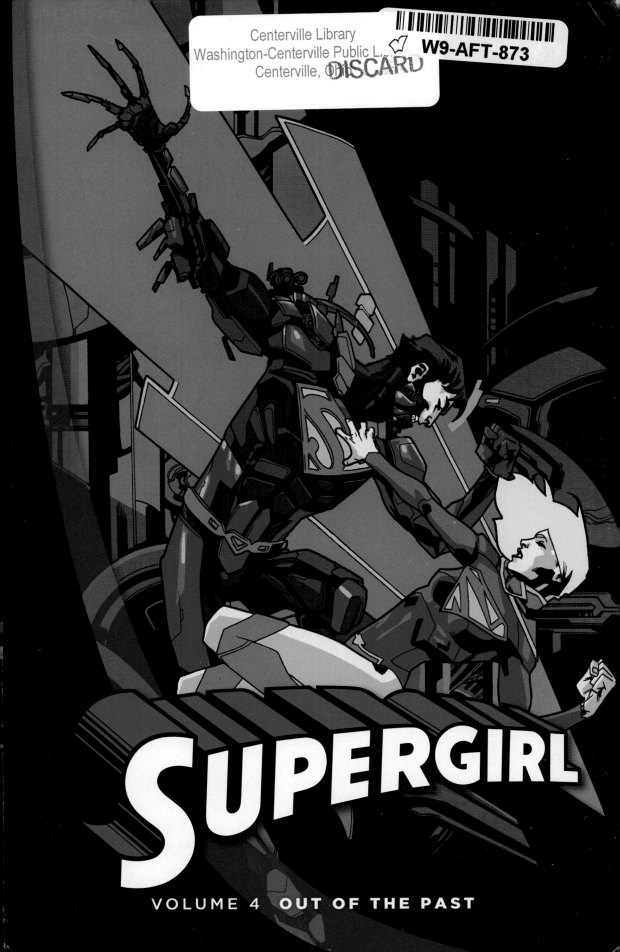

SUPERGIRL

VOLUME 4 OUT OF THE PAST

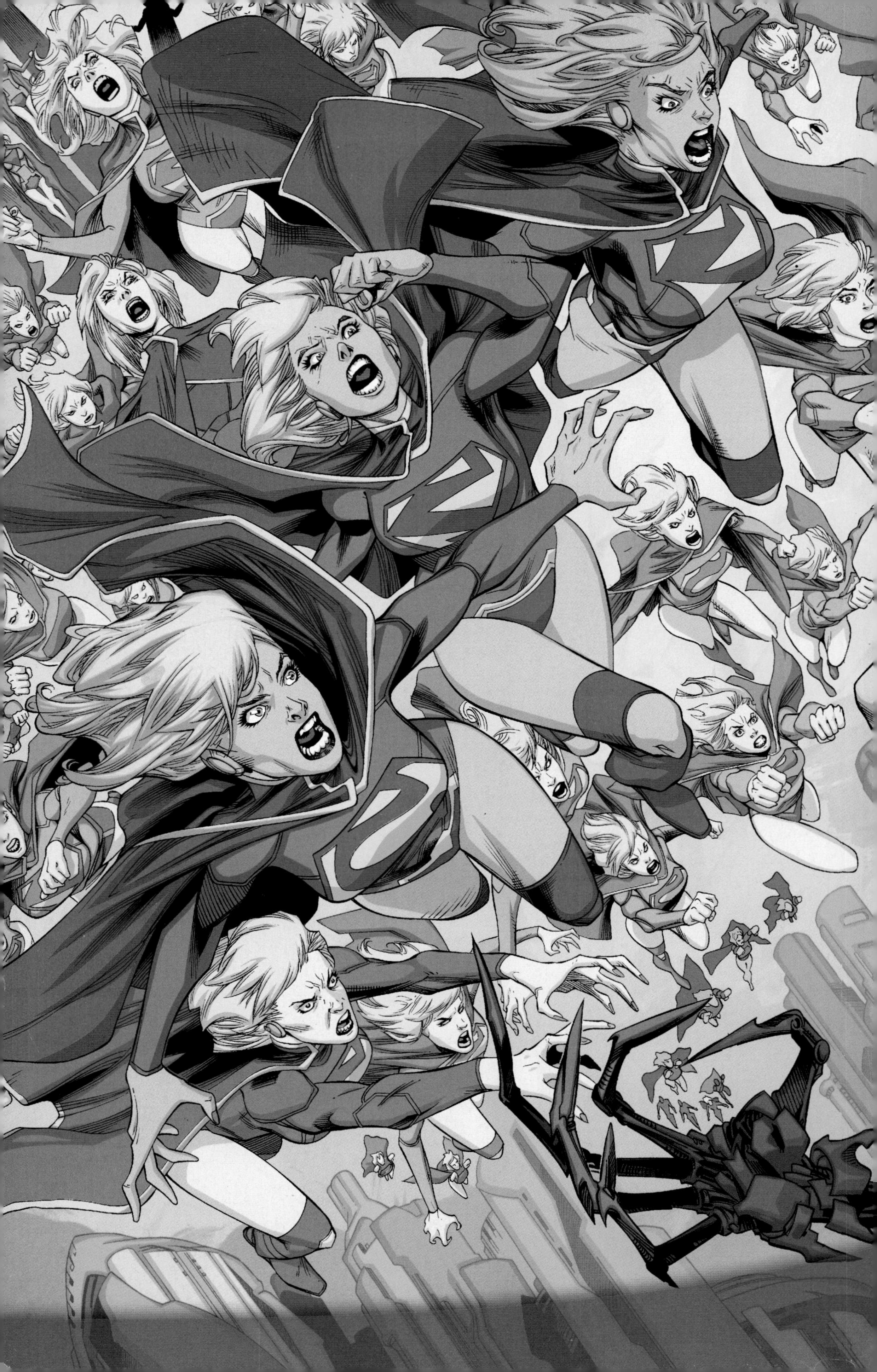

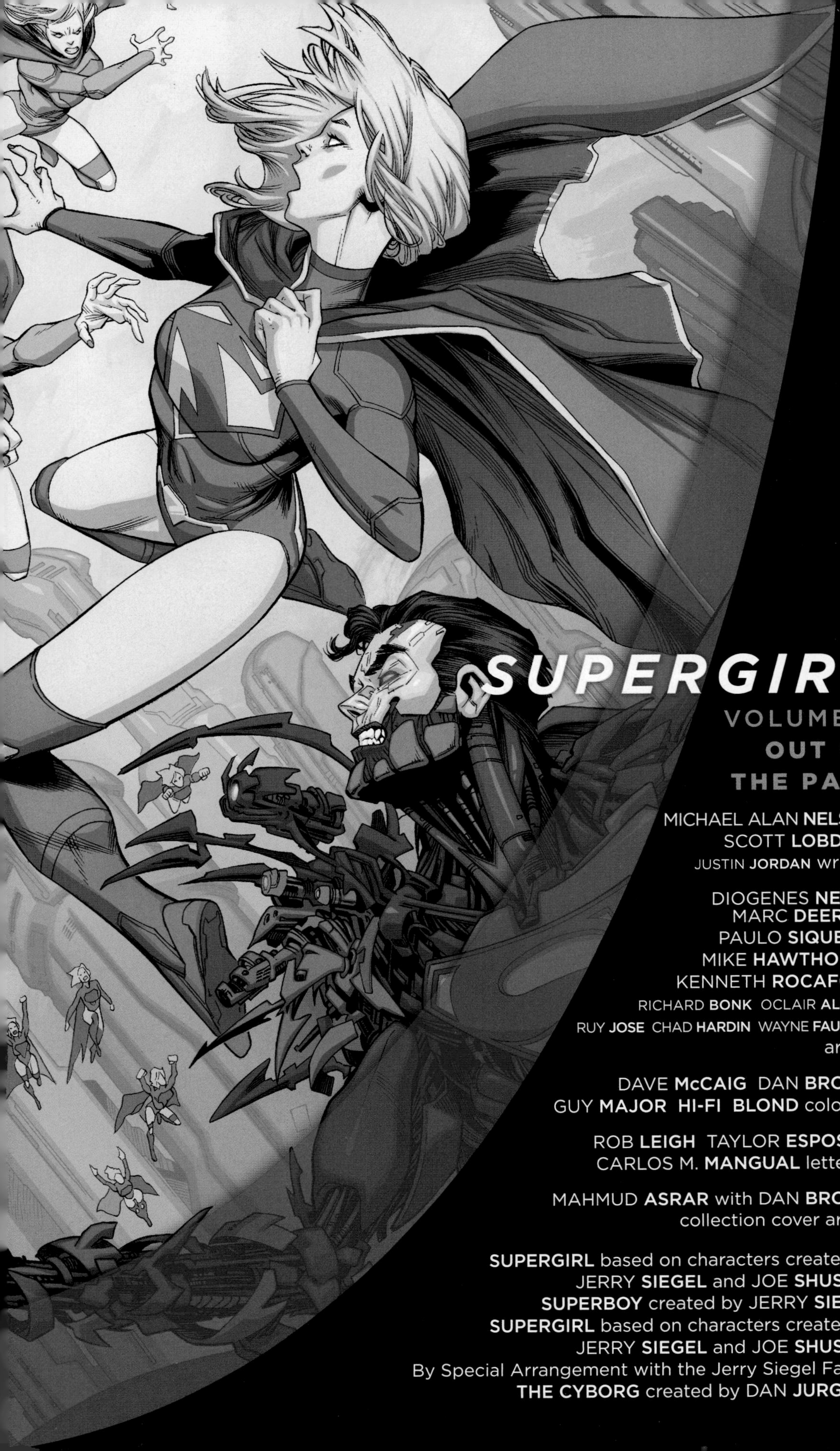

SUPERGIRL

VOLUME 4
OUT OF THE PAST

MICHAEL ALAN **NELSON**
SCOTT **LOBDELL**
JUSTIN **JORDAN** writers

DIOGENES **NEVES**
MARC **DEERING**
PAULO **SIQUEIRA**
MIKE **HAWTHORNE**
KENNETH **ROCAFORT**
RICHARD **BONK** OCLAIR **ALBERT**
RUY **JOSE** CHAD **HARDIN** WAYNE **FAUCHER**
artists

DAVE **McCAIG** DAN **BROWN**
GUY **MAJOR** **HI-FI** **BLOND** colorists

ROB **LEIGH** TAYLOR **ESPOSITO**
CARLOS M. **MANGUAL** letterers

MAHMUD **ASRAR** with DAN **BROWN**
collection cover artists

SUPERGIRL based on characters created by
JERRY **SIEGEL** and JOE **SHUSTER**
SUPERBOY created by JERRY **SIEGEL**
SUPERGIRL based on characters created by
JERRY **SIEGEL** and JOE **SHUSTER**
By Special Arrangement with the Jerry Siegel Family
THE CYBORG created by DAN **JURGENS**

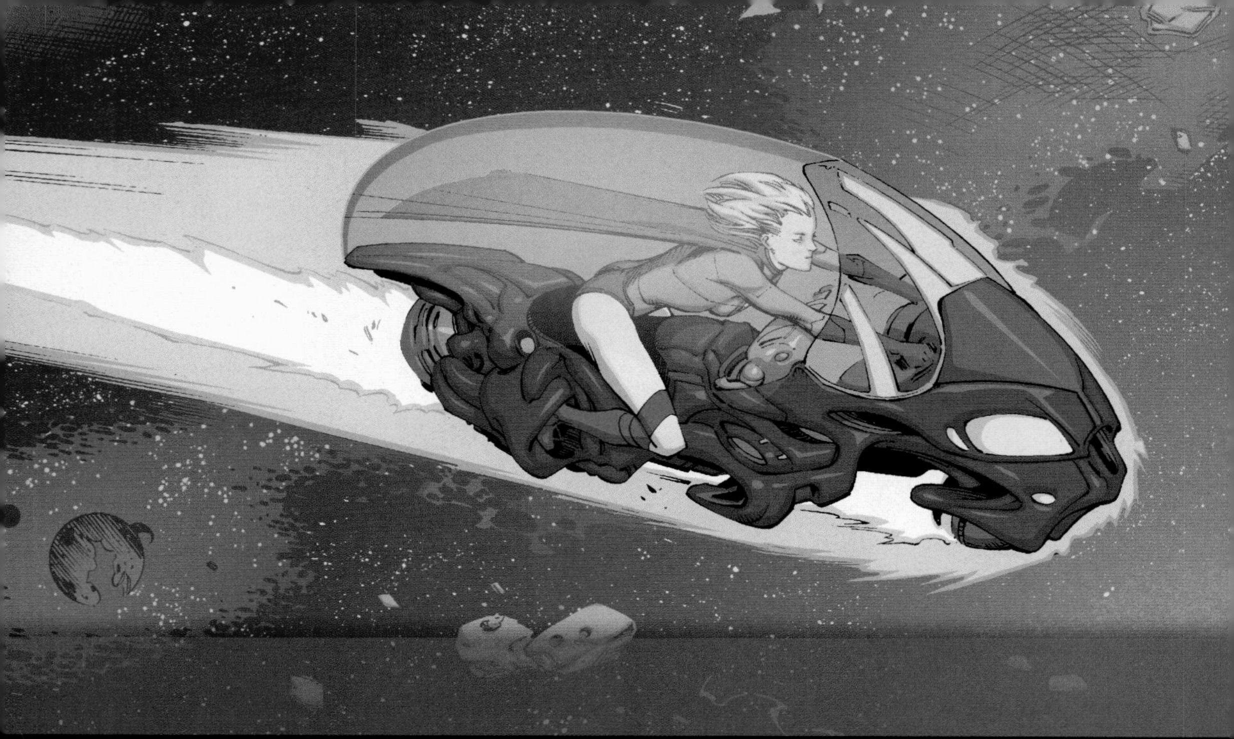

ANTHONY MARQUES Assistant Editor – Original Series RICKEY PURDIN Associate Editor – Original Series
EDDIE BERGANZA Editor – Original Series RACHEL PINNELAS Editor
ROBBIN BROSTERMAN Design Director – Books ROBBIE BIEDERMAN Publication Design

BOB HARRAS Senior VP – Editor-in-Chief, DC Comics

DIANE NELSON President DAN DIDIO and JIM LEE Co-Publishers GEOFF JOHNS Chief Creative Officer
AMIT DESAI Senior VP – Marketing and Franchise Management
AMY GENKINS Senior VP – Business and Legal Affairs NAIRI GARDINER Senior VP – Finance
JEFF BOISON VP – Publishing Planning MARK CHIARELLO VP – Art Direction and Design
JOHN CUNNINGHAM VP – Marketing TERRI CUNNINGHAM VP – Editorial Administration
LARRY GANEM VP – Talent Relations and Services ALISON GILL Senior VP – Manufacturing and Operations
HANK KANALZ Senior VP – Vertigo and Integrated Publishing JAY KOGAN VP – Business and Legal Affairs, Publishing
JACK MAHAN VP – Business Affairs, Talent NICK NAPOLITANO VP – Manufacturing Administration SUE POHJA VP – Book Sales
FRED RUIZ VP – Manufacturing Operations COURTNEY SIMMONS Senior VP – Publicity BOB WAYNE Senior VP – Sales

SSUPERGIRL VOLUME 4: OUT OF THE PAST

DC Comics, 1700 Broadway, New York, NY 10019
A Warner Bros. Entertainment Company.
Printed by RR Donnelley, Owensville, MO, USA. 6/18/14. First Printing.

ISBN: 978-1-4012-4700-3

Library of Congress Cataloging-in-Publication Data

Nelson, Michael Alan, author.
Supergirl. Volume 4, Out of the Past / Michael Alan Nelson, Mahmud Asrar.
pages cm. — (The New 52!)
ISBN 978-1-4012-4700-3 (paperback)
1. Graphic novels. I. Asrar, Mahmud A., illustrator. II. Title. III. Title: Out of the Past.
PN6728.S89N45 2014
741.5'973—dc23
2014010808

SUSTAINABLE FORESTRY INITIATIVE
Certified Chain of Custody
20% Certified Forest Content,
80% Certified Sourcing
www.sfiprogram.org
SFI-01042
APPLIES TO TEXT STOCK ONLY

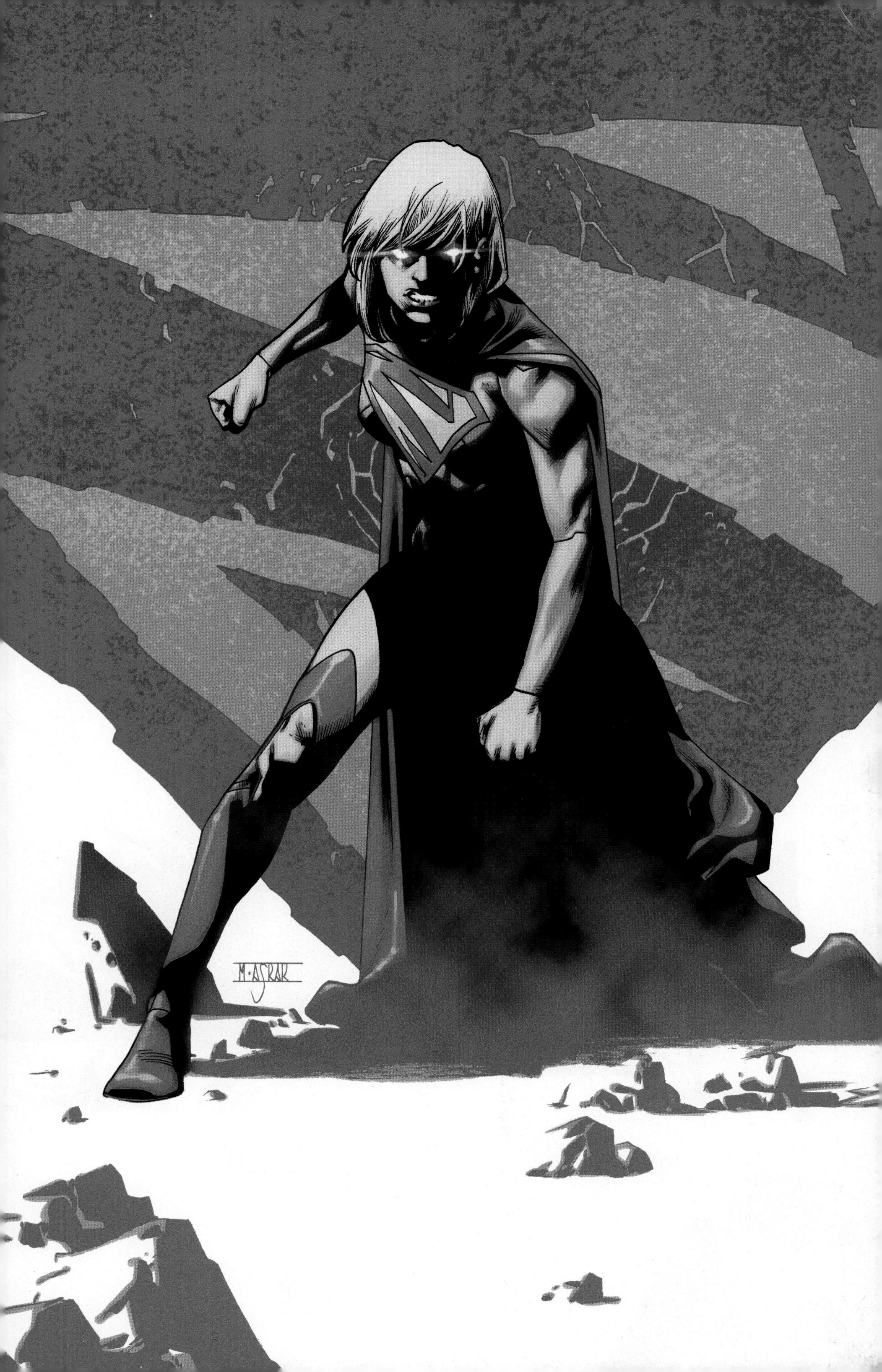
M.ASRAR

BE CAREFUL WHAT YOU WISH FOR...

MICHAEL ALAN NELSON writer DIOGENES NEVES penciller RICHARD BONK inker cover art by MAHMUD ASRAR with DAN BROWN

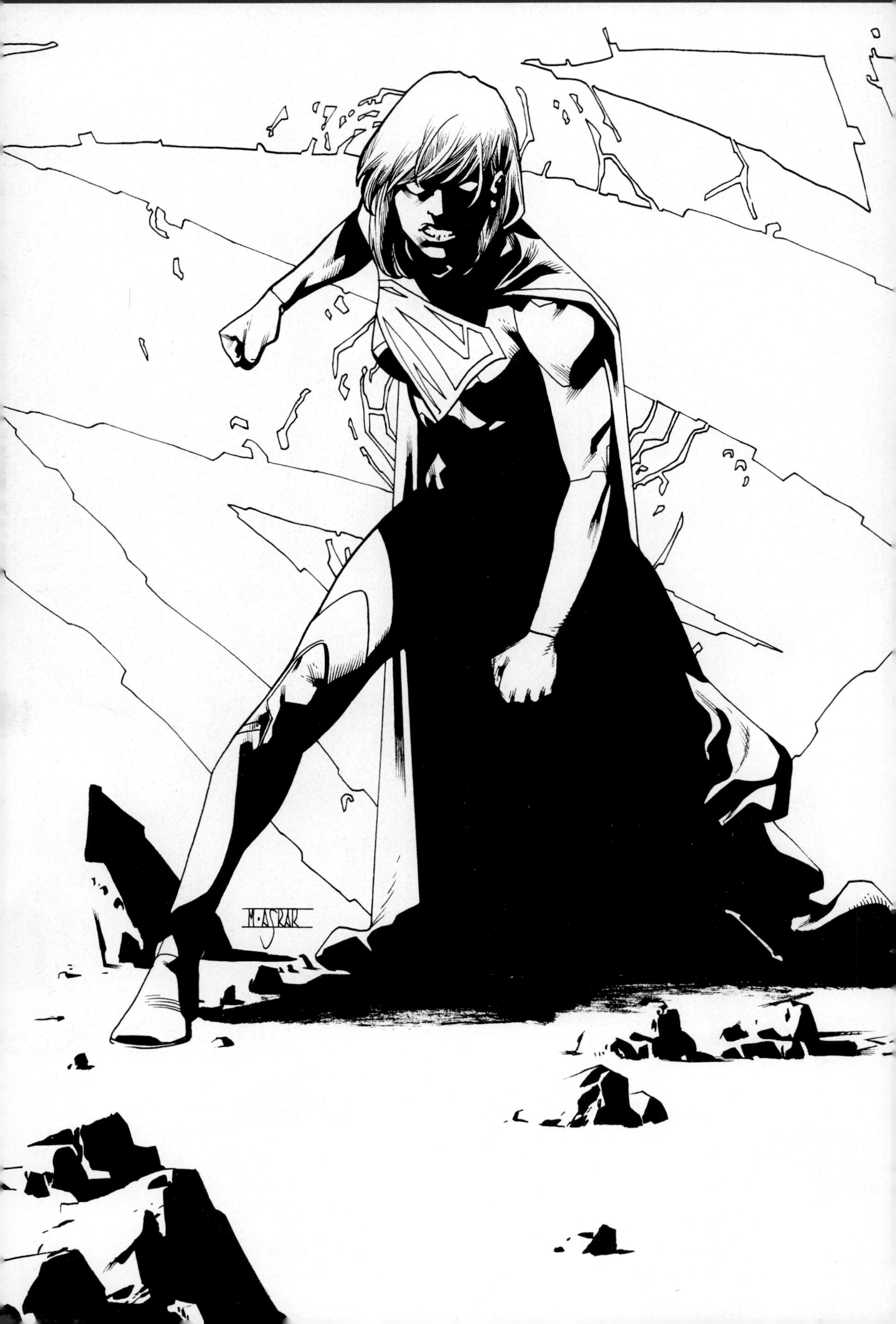
M·ASRAR

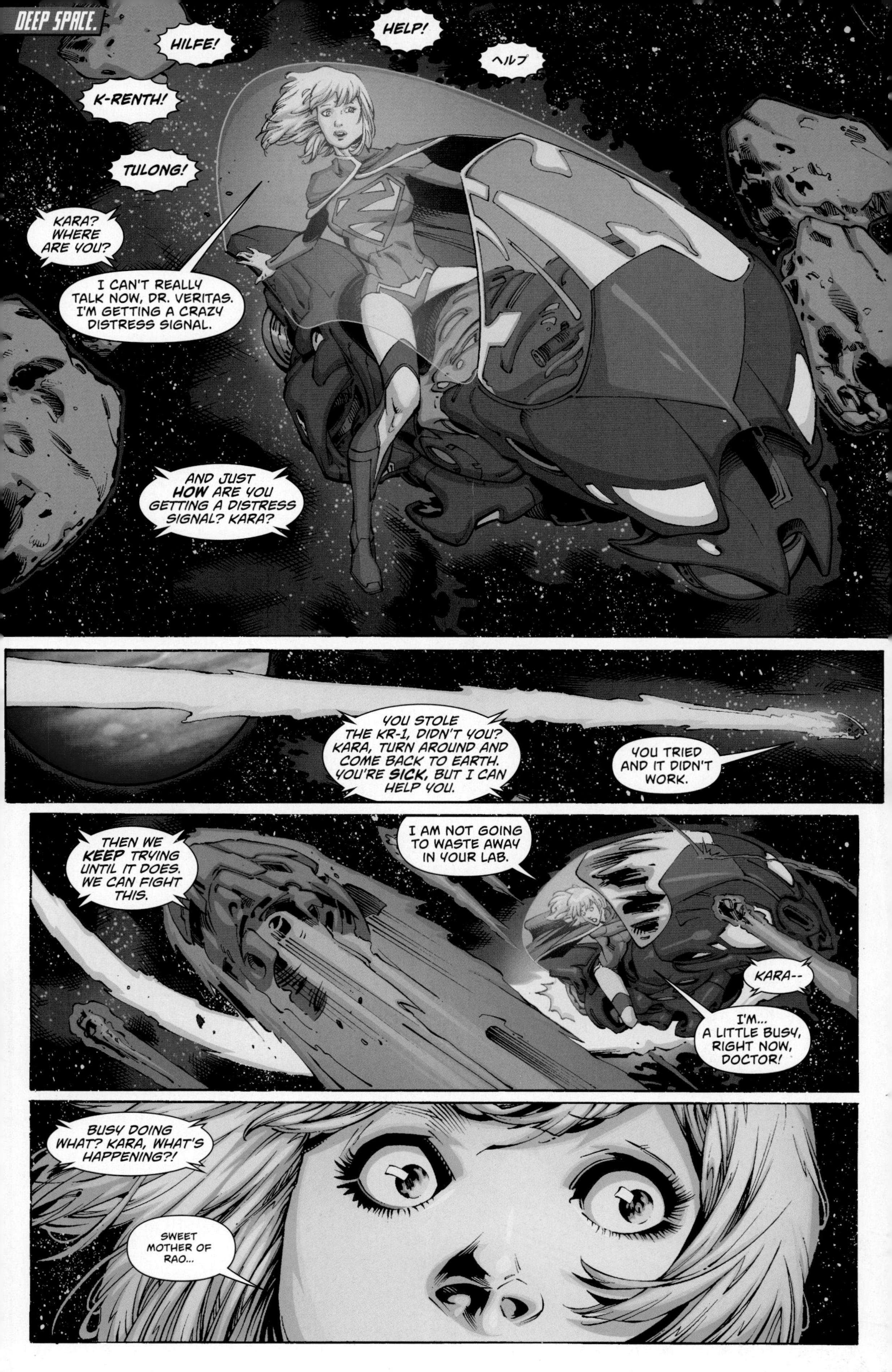
DEEP SPACE.
HILFE!
HELP!
ヘルプ
K-RENTH!
TULONG!
KARA? WHERE ARE YOU?
I CAN'T REALLY TALK NOW, DR. VERITAS. I'M GETTING A CRAZY DISTRESS SIGNAL.
AND JUST HOW ARE YOU GETTING A DISTRESS SIGNAL? KARA?
YOU STOLE THE KR-1, DIDN'T YOU? KARA, TURN AROUND AND COME BACK TO EARTH. YOU'RE SICK, BUT I CAN HELP YOU.
YOU TRIED AND IT DIDN'T WORK.
THEN WE KEEP TRYING UNTIL IT DOES. WE CAN FIGHT THIS.
I AM NOT GOING TO WASTE AWAY IN YOUR LAB.
KARA--
I'M... A LITTLE BUSY, RIGHT NOW, DOCTOR!
BUSY DOING WHAT? KARA, WHAT'S HAPPENING?!
SWEET MOTHER OF RAO...

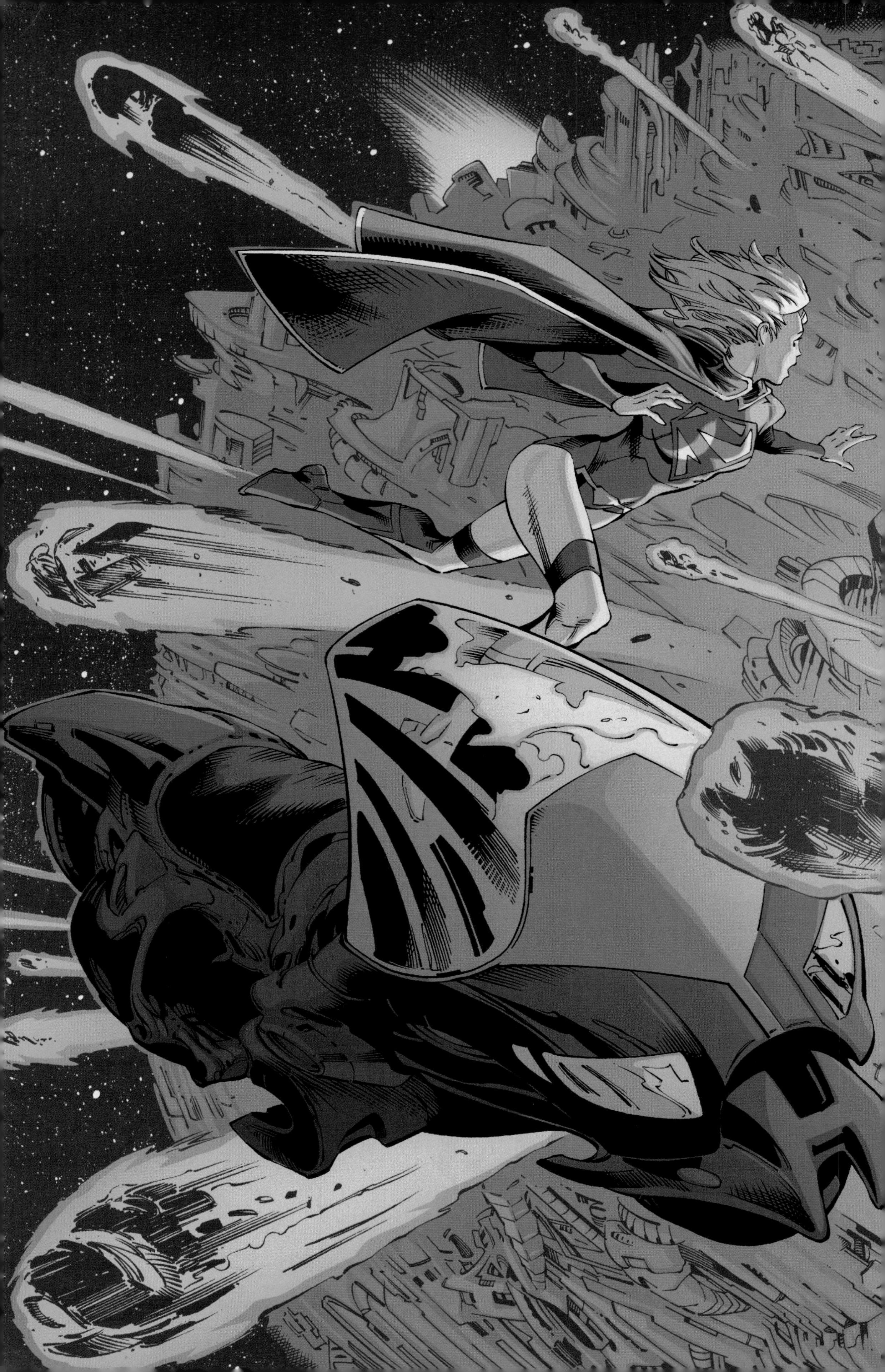

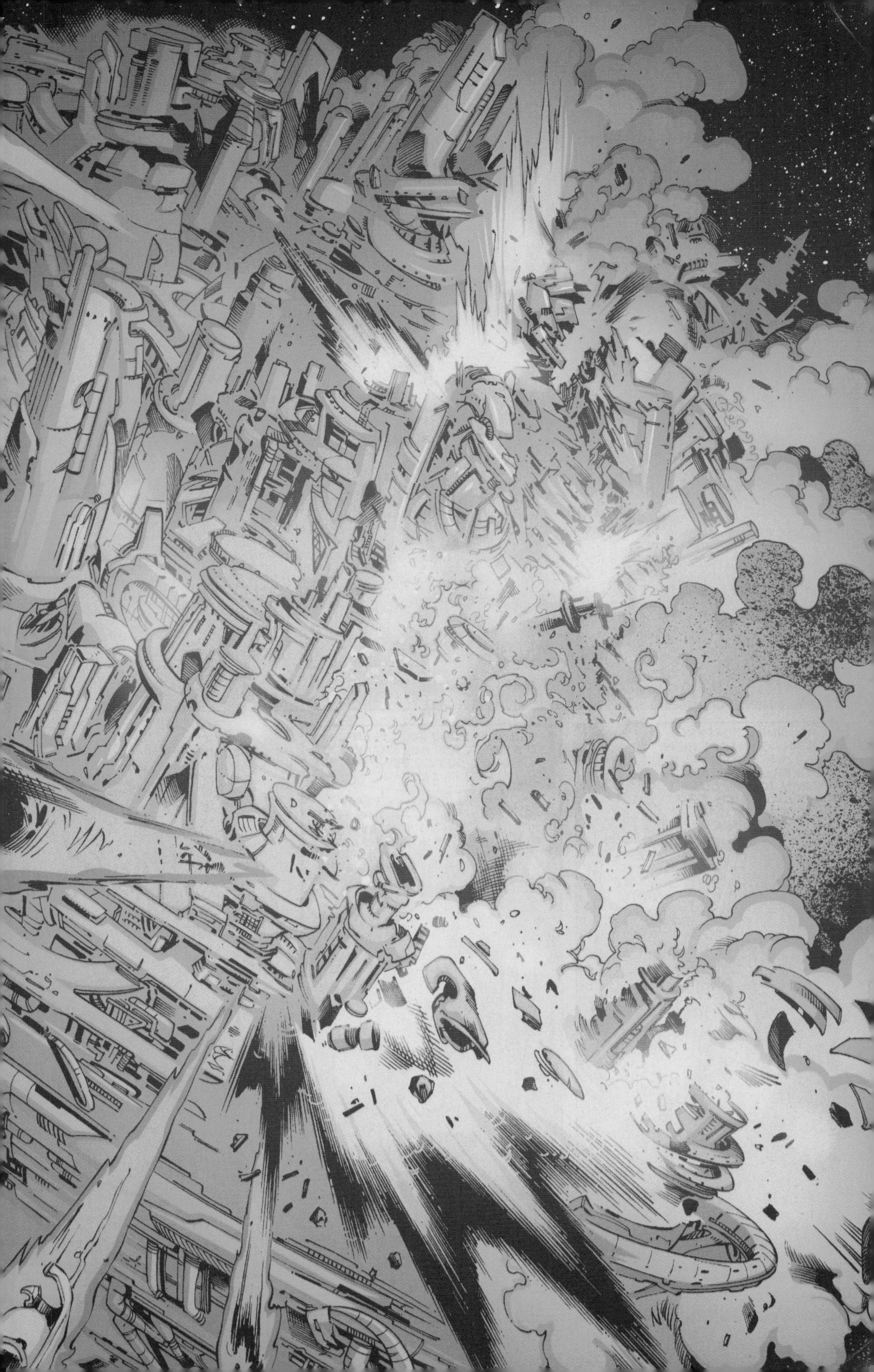

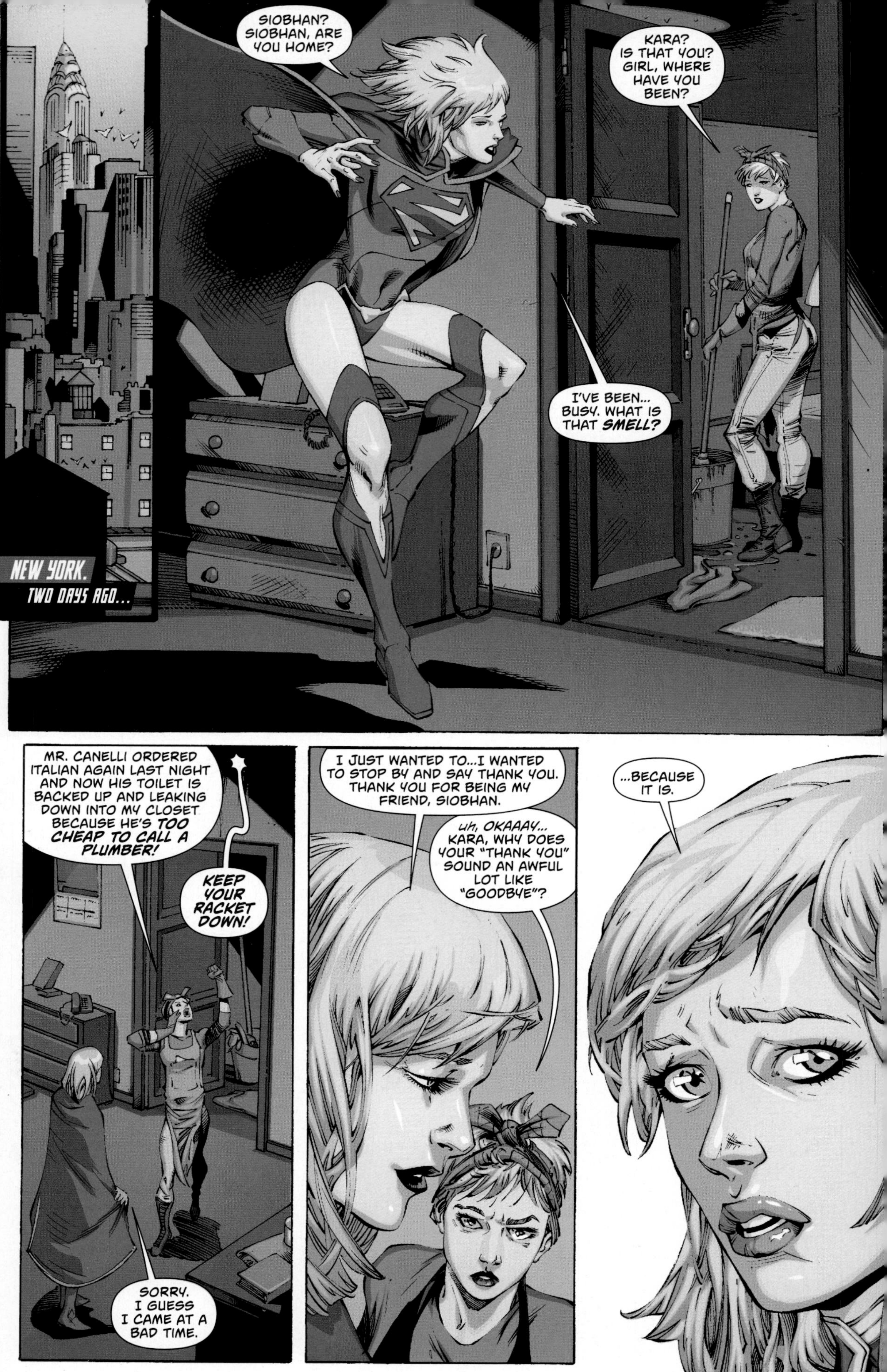
SIOBHAN? SIOBHAN, ARE YOU HOME?
KARA? IS THAT YOU? GIRL, WHERE HAVE YOU BEEN?
I'VE BEEN... BUSY. WHAT IS THAT SMELL?
NEW YORK.
TWO DAYS AGO...
MR. CANELLI ORDERED ITALIAN AGAIN LAST NIGHT AND NOW HIS TOILET IS BACKED UP AND LEAKING DOWN INTO MY CLOSET BECAUSE HE'S TOO CHEAP TO CALL A PLUMBER!
KEEP YOUR RACKET DOWN!
SORRY. I GUESS I CAME AT A BAD TIME.
I JUST WANTED TO...I WANTED TO STOP BY AND SAY THANK YOU. THANK YOU FOR BEING MY FRIEND, SIOBHAN.
uh, OKAAAY... KARA, WHY DOES YOUR "THANK YOU" SOUND AN AWFUL LOT LIKE "GOODBYE"?
...BECAUSE IT IS.

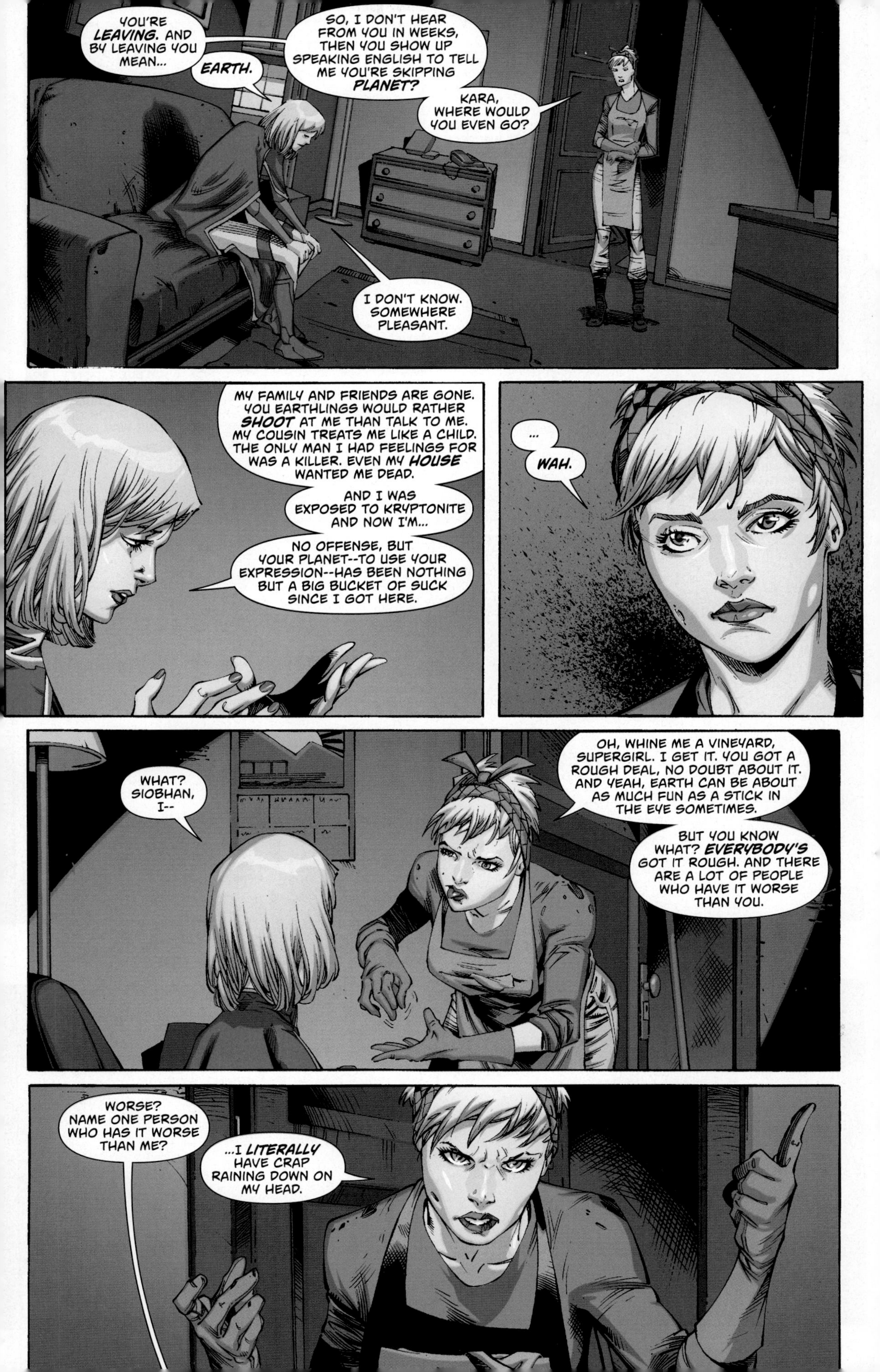
YOU'RE LEAVING. AND BY LEAVING YOU MEAN...
EARTH.
SO, I DON'T HEAR FROM YOU IN WEEKS, THEN YOU SHOW UP SPEAKING ENGLISH TO TELL ME YOU'RE SKIPPING PLANET?
KARA, WHERE WOULD YOU EVEN GO?
I DON'T KNOW. SOMEWHERE PLEASANT.
MY FAMILY AND FRIENDS ARE GONE. YOU EARTHLINGS WOULD RATHER SHOOT AT ME THAN TALK TO ME. MY COUSIN TREATS ME LIKE A CHILD. THE ONLY MAN I HAD FEELINGS FOR WAS A KILLER. EVEN MY HOUSE WANTED ME DEAD.
AND I WAS EXPOSED TO KRYPTONITE AND NOW I'M...
NO OFFENSE, BUT YOUR PLANET--TO USE YOUR EXPRESSION--HAS BEEN NOTHING BUT A BIG BUCKET OF SUCK SINCE I GOT HERE.
... WAH.
OH, WHINE ME A VINEYARD, SUPERGIRL. I GET IT. YOU GOT A ROUGH DEAL, NO DOUBT ABOUT IT. AND YEAH, EARTH CAN BE ABOUT AS MUCH FUN AS A STICK IN THE EYE SOMETIMES.
BUT YOU KNOW WHAT? EVERYBODY'S GOT IT ROUGH. AND THERE ARE A LOT OF PEOPLE WHO HAVE IT WORSE THAN YOU.
WHAT? SIOBHAN, I--
WORSE? NAME ONE PERSON WHO HAS IT WORSE THAN ME?
...I LITERALLY HAVE CRAP RAINING DOWN ON MY HEAD.

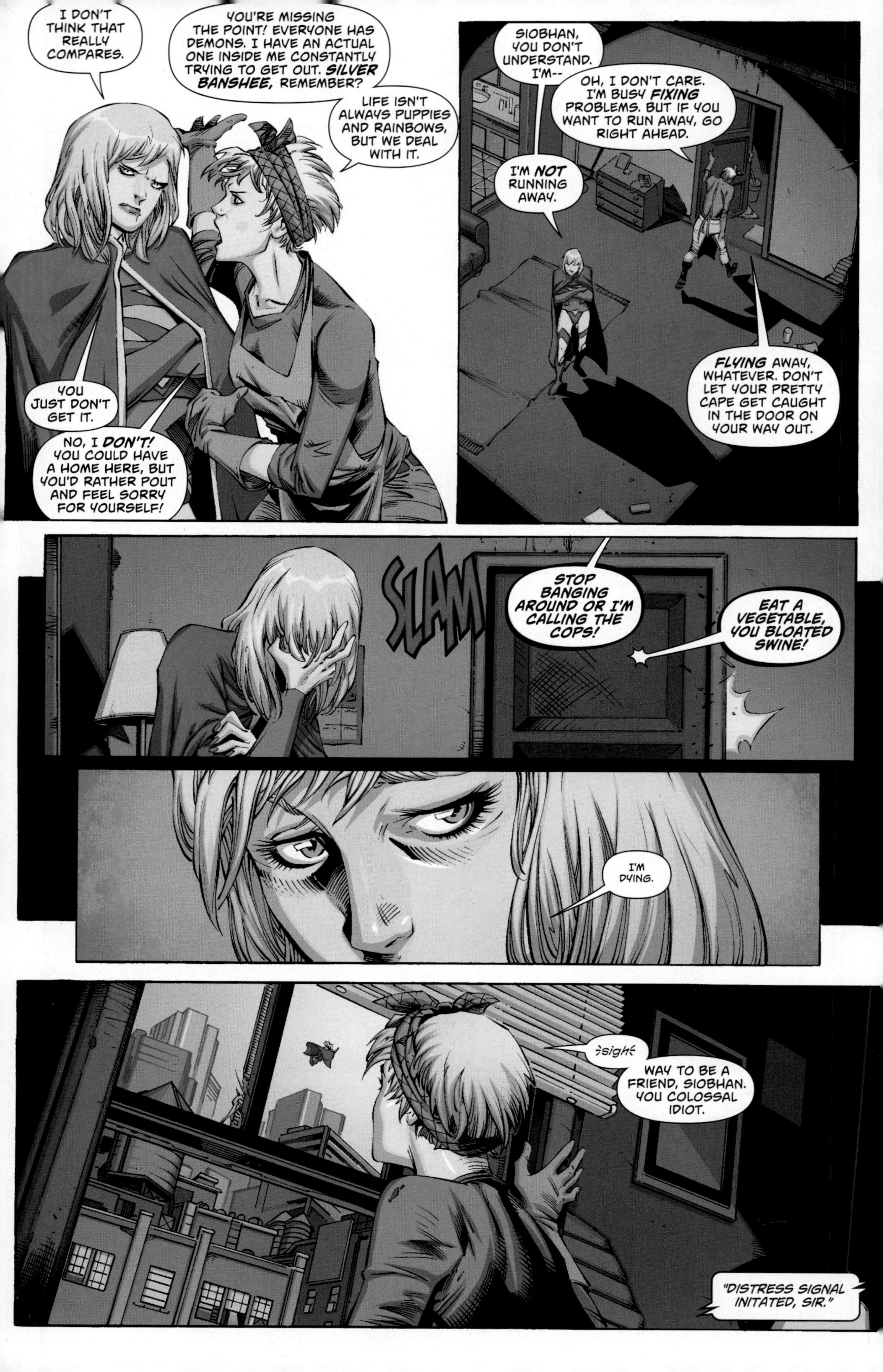
I DON'T THINK THAT REALLY COMPARES.
YOU'RE MISSING THE POINT! EVERYONE HAS DEMONS. I HAVE AN ACTUAL ONE INSIDE ME CONSTANTLY TRYING TO GET OUT. SILVER BANSHEE, REMEMBER?
LIFE ISN'T ALWAYS PUPPIES AND RAINBOWS, BUT WE DEAL WITH IT.
YOU JUST DON'T GET IT.
NO, I DON'T! YOU COULD HAVE A HOME HERE, BUT YOU'D RATHER POUT AND FEEL SORRY FOR YOURSELF!
SIOBHAN, YOU DON'T UNDERSTAND. I'M--
OH, I DON'T CARE. I'M BUSY FIXING PROBLEMS. BUT IF YOU WANT TO RUN AWAY, GO RIGHT AHEAD.
I'M NOT RUNNING AWAY.
FLYING AWAY, WHATEVER. DON'T LET YOUR PRETTY CAPE GET CAUGHT IN THE DOOR ON YOUR WAY OUT.
SLAM
STOP BANGING AROUND OR I'M CALLING THE COPS!
EAT A VEGETABLE, YOU BLOATED SWINE!
I'M DYING.
sigh
WAY TO BE A FRIEND, SIOBHAN. YOU COLOSSAL IDIOT.
"DISTRESS SIGNAL INITATED, SIR."

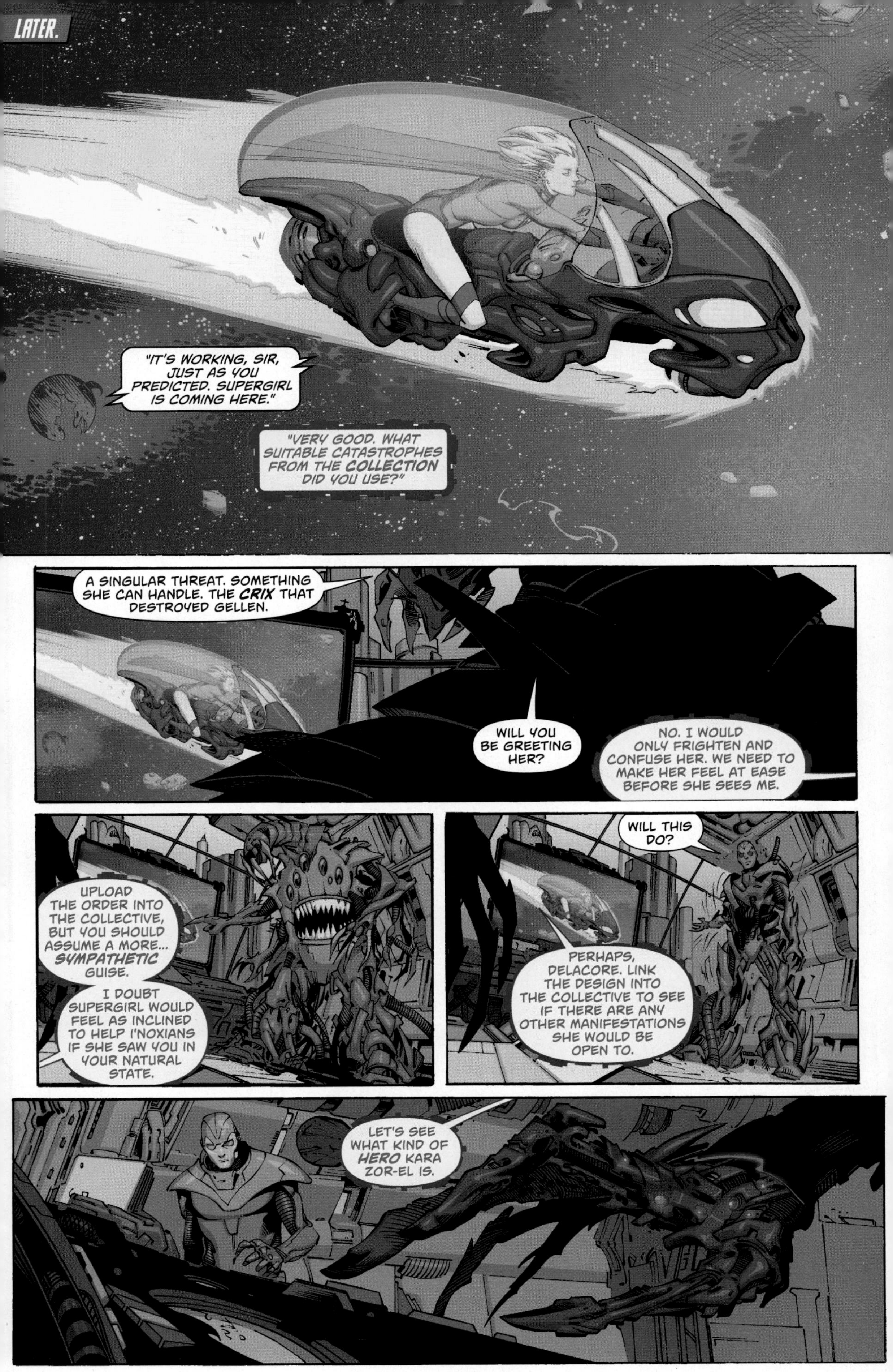
LATER.
"IT'S WORKING, SIR, JUST AS YOU PREDICTED. SUPERGIRL IS COMING HERE."
"VERY GOOD. WHAT SUITABLE CATASTROPHES FROM THE COLLECTION DID YOU USE?"
A SINGULAR THREAT. SOMETHING SHE CAN HANDLE. THE CRIX THAT DESTROYED GELLEN.
WILL YOU BE GREETING HER?
NO. I WOULD ONLY FRIGHTEN AND CONFUSE HER. WE NEED TO MAKE HER FEEL AT EASE BEFORE SHE SEES ME.
UPLOAD THE ORDER INTO THE COLLECTIVE, BUT YOU SHOULD ASSUME A MORE... SYMPATHETIC GUISE.
I DOUBT SUPERGIRL WOULD FEEL AS INCLINED TO HELP I'NOXIANS IF SHE SAW YOU IN YOUR NATURAL STATE.
WILL THIS DO?
PERHAPS, DELACORE. LINK THE DESIGN INTO THE COLLECTIVE TO SEE IF THERE ARE ANY OTHER MANIFESTATIONS SHE WOULD BE OPEN TO.
LET'S SEE WHAT KIND OF HERO KARA ZOR-EL IS.

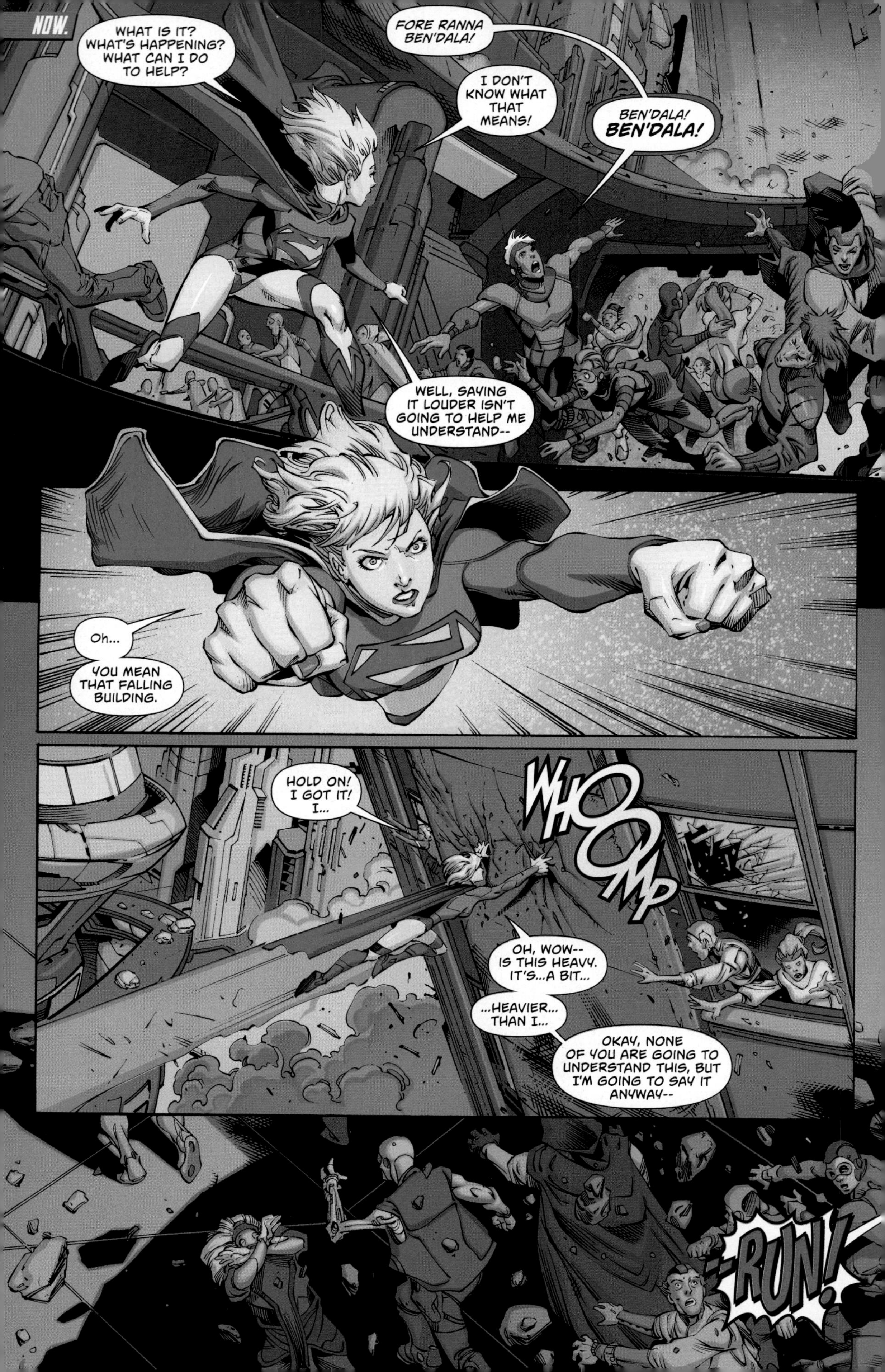
NOW.
WHAT IS IT? WHAT'S HAPPENING? WHAT CAN I DO TO HELP?
FORE RANNA BEN'DALA!
I DON'T KNOW WHAT THAT MEANS!
BEN'DALA! BEN'DALA!
WELL, SAYING IT LOUDER ISN'T GOING TO HELP ME UNDERSTAND--
Oh...
YOU MEAN THAT FALLING BUILDING.
HOLD ON! I GOT IT! I...
WHOOMP
OH, WOW-- IS THIS HEAVY. IT'S...A BIT...
...HEAVIER... THAN I...
OKAY, NONE OF YOU ARE GOING TO UNDERSTAND THIS, BUT I'M GOING TO SAY IT ANYWAY--
RUN!

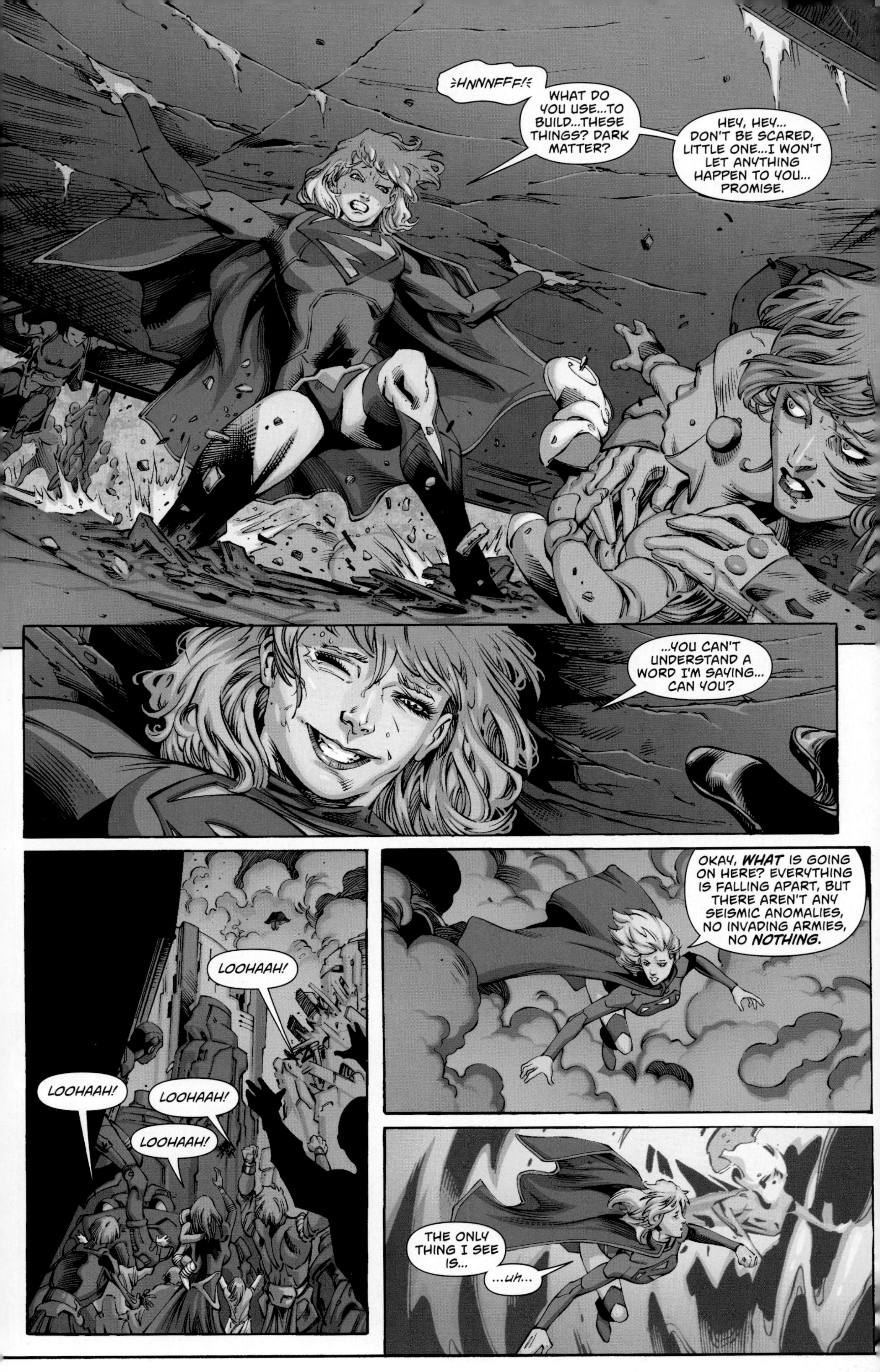
HNNNFFF!
WHAT DO YOU USE...TO BUILD...THESE THINGS? DARK MATTER?
HEY, HEY... DON'T BE SCARED, LITTLE ONE...I WON'T LET ANYTHING HAPPEN TO YOU... PROMISE.
...YOU CAN'T UNDERSTAND A WORD I'M SAYING... CAN YOU?
LOOHAAH!
LOOHAAH!
LOOHAAH!
LOOHAAH!
OKAY, WHAT IS GOING ON HERE? EVERYTHING IS FALLING APART, BUT THERE AREN'T ANY SEISMIC ANOMALIES, NO INVADING ARMIES, NO NOTHING.
THE ONLY THING I SEE IS...
...uh...

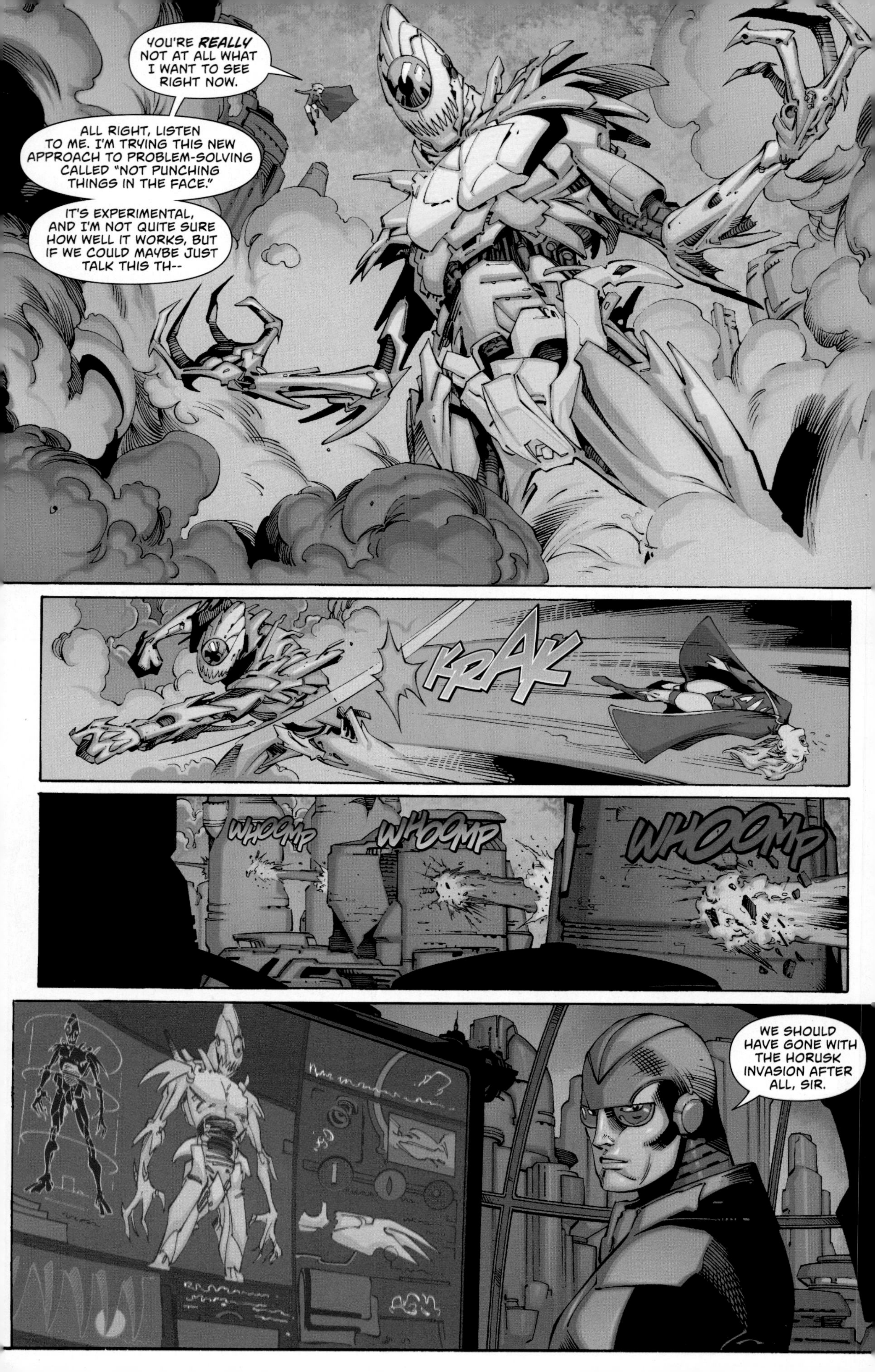
YOU'RE *REALLY* NOT AT ALL WHAT I WANT TO SEE RIGHT NOW.
ALL RIGHT, LISTEN TO ME. I'M TRYING THIS NEW APPROACH TO PROBLEM-SOLVING CALLED "NOT PUNCHING THINGS IN THE FACE."
IT'S EXPERIMENTAL, AND I'M NOT QUITE SURE HOW WELL IT WORKS, BUT IF WE COULD MAYBE JUST TALK THIS TH--
KRAK
WHOOMP
WHOOMP
WHOOMP
WE SHOULD HAVE GONE WITH THE HORUSK INVASION AFTER ALL, SIR.

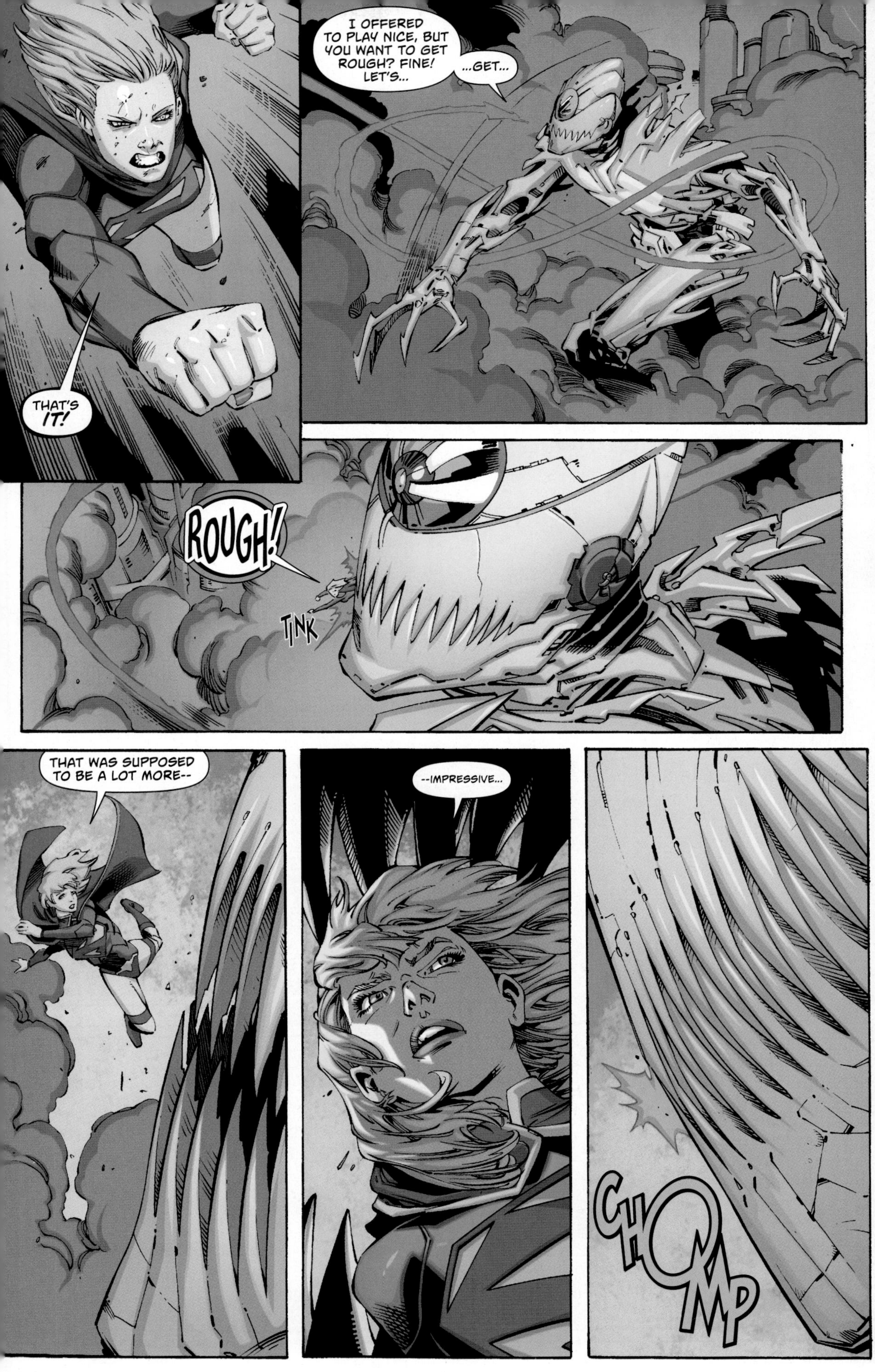
THAT'S IT!
I OFFERED TO PLAY NICE, BUT YOU WANT TO GET ROUGH? FINE! LET'S...
...GET...
ROUGH!
TINK
THAT WAS SUPPOSED TO BE A LOT MORE--
--IMPRESSIVE...
CHOMP

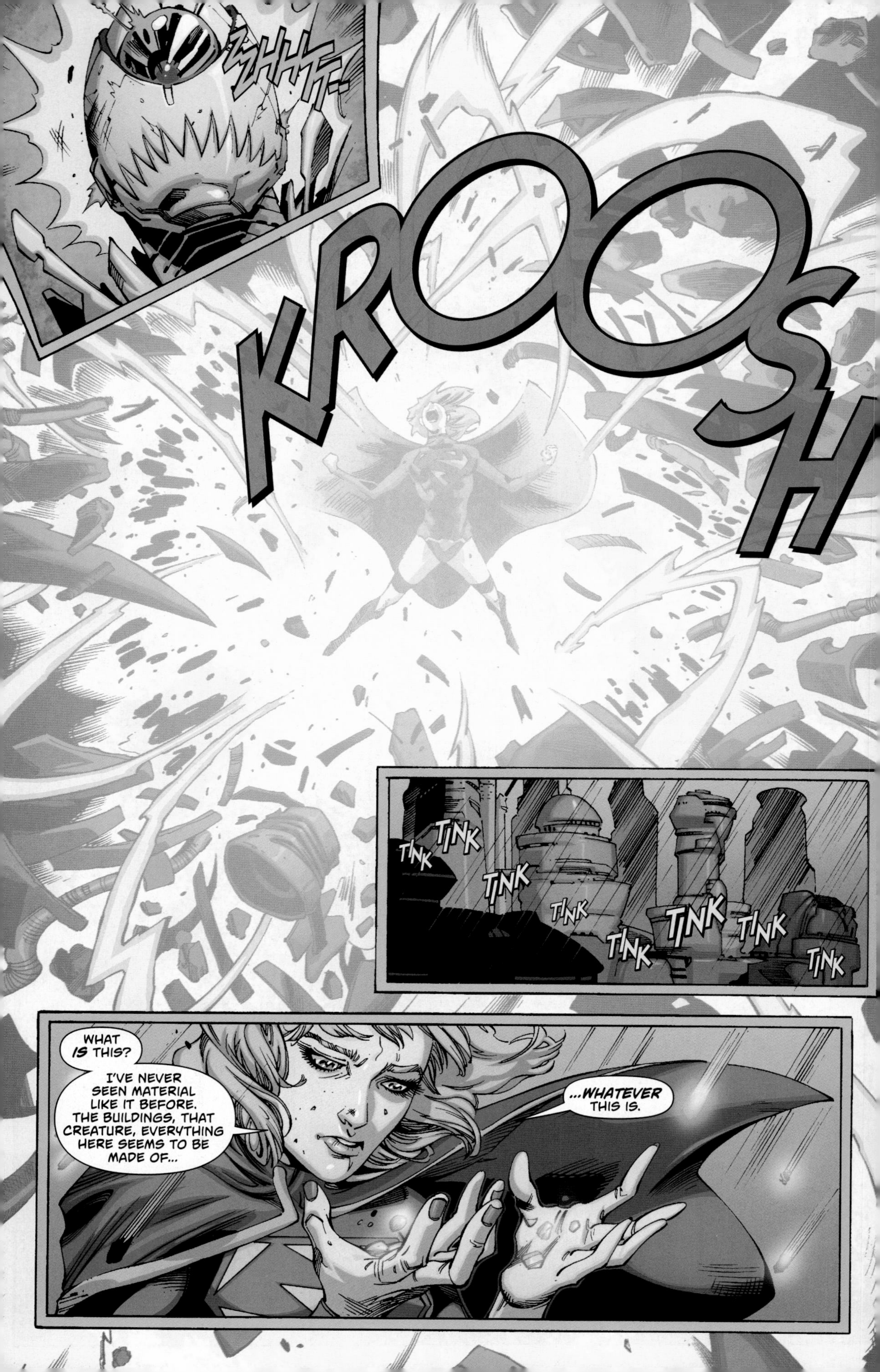
ZHHT-
KROOSH
TINK
TINK
TINK
TINK
TINK
TINK
TINK
TINK
WHAT *IS* THIS?
I'VE NEVER SEEN MATERIAL LIKE IT BEFORE. THE BUILDINGS, THAT CREATURE, EVERYTHING HERE SEEMS TO BE MADE OF...
...*WHATEVER* THIS IS.

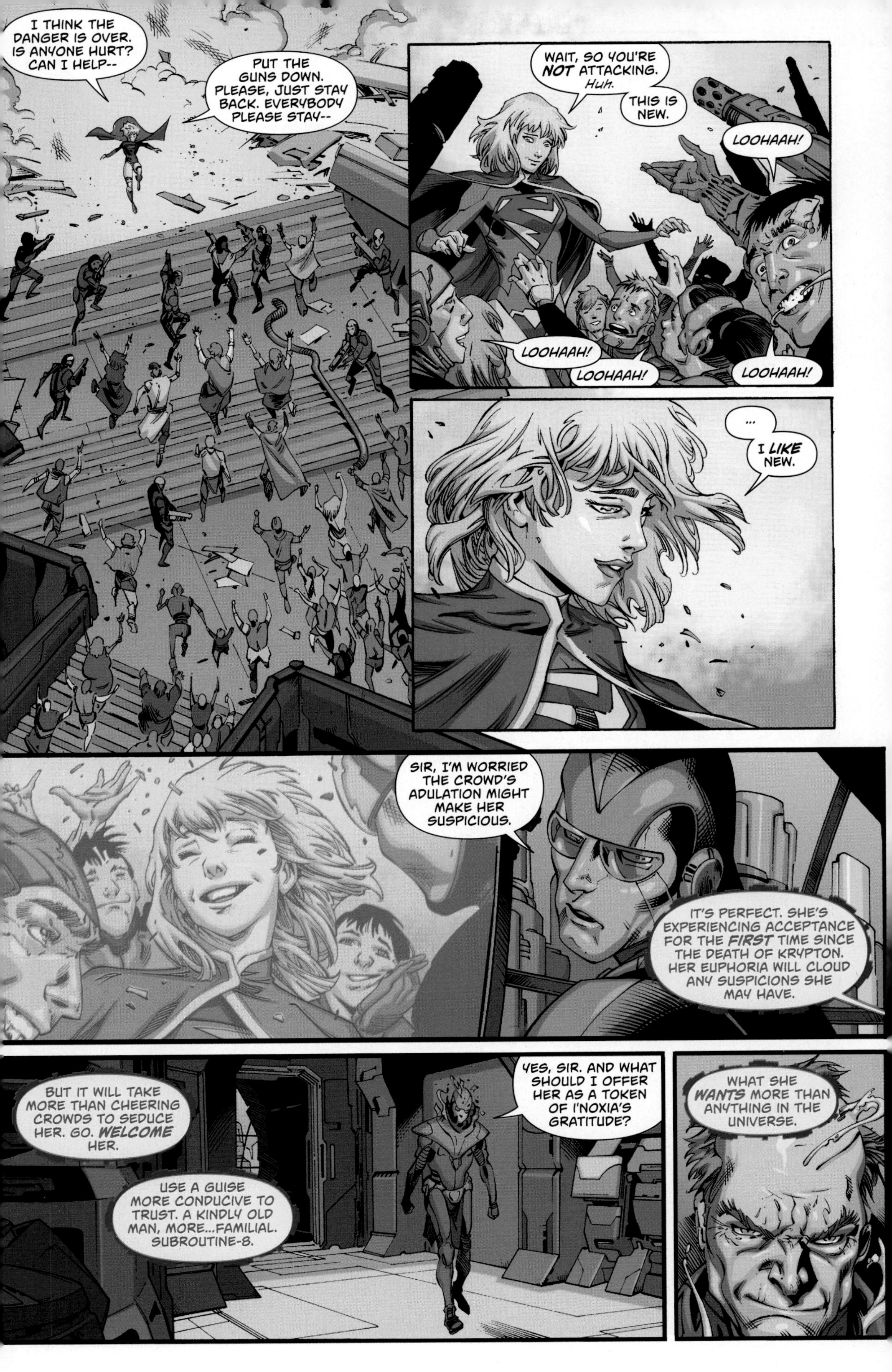
I THINK THE DANGER IS OVER. IS ANYONE HURT? CAN I HELP--
PUT THE GUNS DOWN. PLEASE, JUST STAY BACK. EVERYBODY PLEASE STAY--
WAIT, SO YOU'RE NOT ATTACKING. Huh.
THIS IS NEW.
LOOHAAH!
LOOHAAH!
LOOHAAH!
LOOHAAH!
...
I LIKE NEW.
SIR, I'M WORRIED THE CROWD'S ADULATION MIGHT MAKE HER SUSPICIOUS.
IT'S PERFECT. SHE'S EXPERIENCING ACCEPTANCE FOR THE FIRST TIME SINCE THE DEATH OF KRYPTON. HER EUPHORIA WILL CLOUD ANY SUSPICIONS SHE MAY HAVE.
BUT IT WILL TAKE MORE THAN CHEERING CROWDS TO SEDUCE HER. GO. WELCOME HER.
USE A GUISE MORE CONDUCIVE TO TRUST. A KINDLY OLD MAN, MORE...FAMILIAL. SUBROUTINE-8.
YES, SIR. AND WHAT SHOULD I OFFER HER AS A TOKEN OF I'NOXIA'S GRATITUDE?
WHAT SHE WANTS MORE THAN ANYTHING IN THE UNIVERSE.

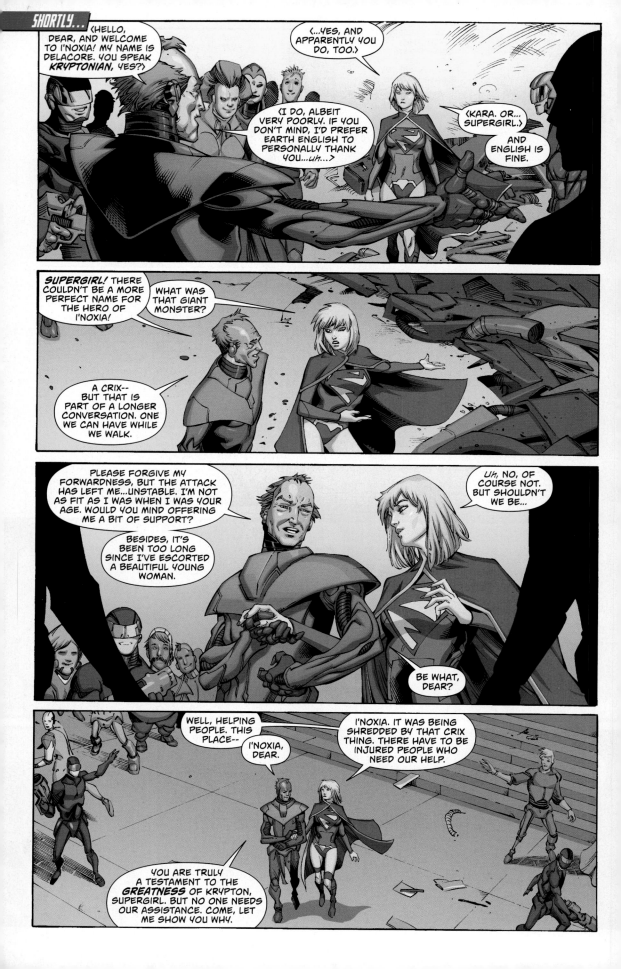

‹HELLO, DEAR, AND WELCOME TO I'NOXIA! MY NAME IS DELACORE. YOU SPEAK *KRYPTONIAN*, YES?›

‹...YES, AND APPARENTLY YOU DO, TOO.›

‹I DO, ALBEIT VERY POORLY. IF YOU DON'T MIND, I'D PREFER EARTH ENGLISH TO PERSONALLY THANK YOU...*uh...*›

‹KARA. OR... SUPERGIRL.›

AND ENGLISH IS FINE.

SUPERGIRL! THERE COULDN'T BE A MORE PERFECT NAME FOR THE HERO OF I'NOXIA!

WHAT WAS THAT GIANT MONSTER?

A CRIX-- BUT THAT IS PART OF A LONGER CONVERSATION. ONE WE CAN HAVE WHILE WE WALK.

PLEASE FORGIVE MY FORWARDNESS, BUT THE ATTACK HAS LEFT ME...UNSTABLE. I'M NOT AS FIT AS I WAS WHEN I WAS YOUR AGE. WOULD YOU MIND OFFERING ME A BIT OF SUPPORT?

BESIDES, IT'S BEEN TOO LONG SINCE I'VE ESCORTED A BEAUTIFUL YOUNG WOMAN.

Uh, NO, OF COURSE NOT. BUT SHOULDN'T WE BE...

BE WHAT, DEAR?

WELL, HELPING PEOPLE. THIS PLACE--

I'NOXIA, DEAR.

I'NOXIA. IT WAS BEING SHREDDED BY THAT CRIX THING. THERE HAVE TO BE INJURED PEOPLE WHO NEED OUR HELP.

YOU ARE TRULY A TESTAMENT TO THE *GREATNESS* OF KRYPTON, SUPERGIRL. BUT NO ONE NEEDS OUR ASSISTANCE. COME, LET ME SHOW YOU WHY.

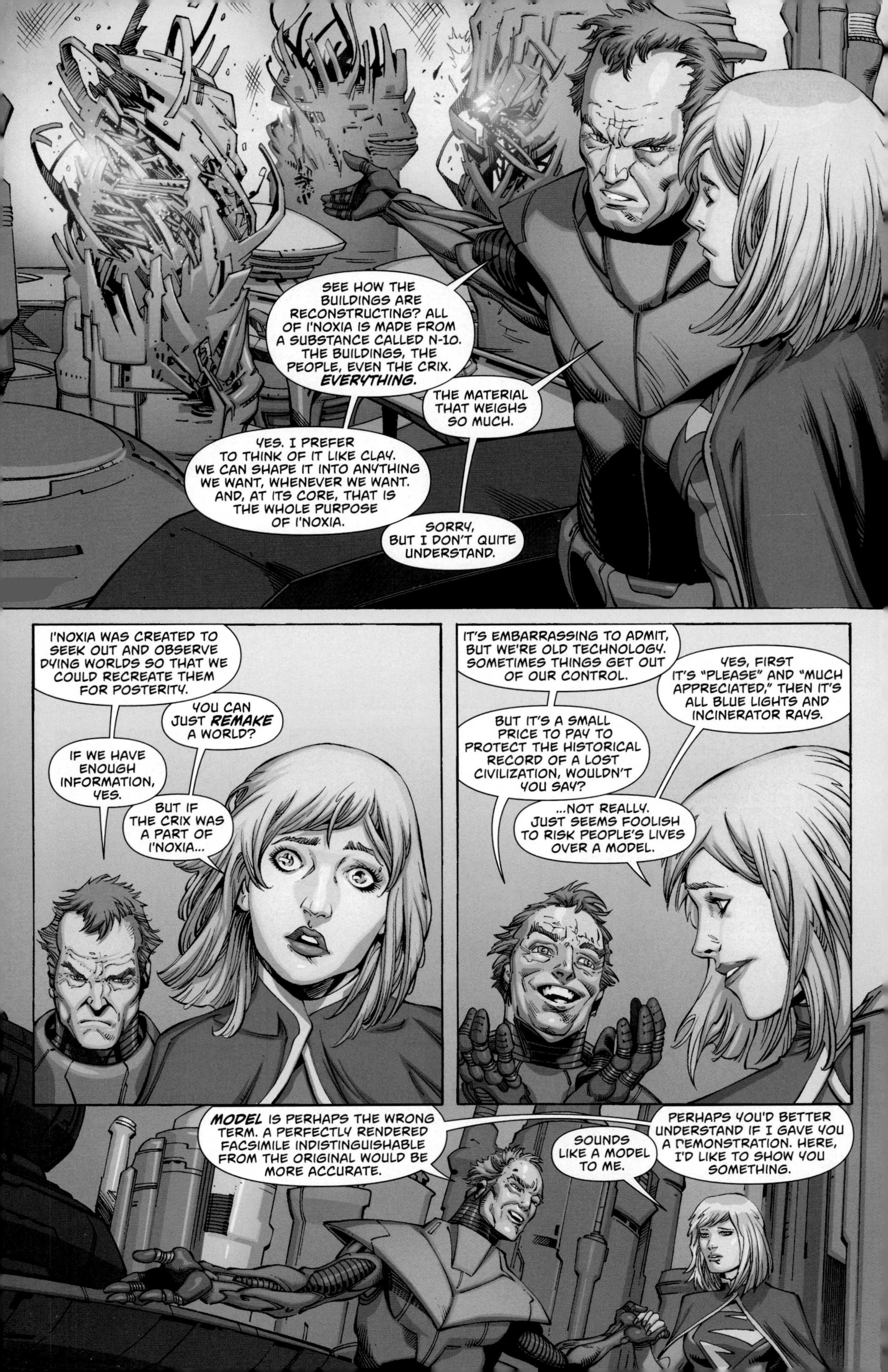
SEE HOW THE BUILDINGS ARE RECONSTRUCTING? ALL OF I'NOXIA IS MADE FROM A SUBSTANCE CALLED N-10. THE BUILDINGS, THE PEOPLE, EVEN THE CRIX. EVERYTHING.
THE MATERIAL THAT WEIGHS SO MUCH.
YES. I PREFER TO THINK OF IT LIKE CLAY. WE CAN SHAPE IT INTO ANYTHING WE WANT, WHENEVER WE WANT. AND, AT ITS CORE, THAT IS THE WHOLE PURPOSE OF I'NOXIA.
SORRY, BUT I DON'T QUITE UNDERSTAND.
I'NOXIA WAS CREATED TO SEEK OUT AND OBSERVE DYING WORLDS SO THAT WE COULD RECREATE THEM FOR POSTERITY.
YOU CAN JUST REMAKE A WORLD?
IF WE HAVE ENOUGH INFORMATION, YES.
BUT IF THE CRIX WAS A PART OF I'NOXIA...
IT'S EMBARRASSING TO ADMIT, BUT WE'RE OLD TECHNOLOGY. SOMETIMES THINGS GET OUT OF OUR CONTROL.
YES, FIRST IT'S "PLEASE" AND "MUCH APPRECIATED," THEN IT'S ALL BLUE LIGHTS AND INCINERATOR RAYS.
BUT IT'S A SMALL PRICE TO PAY TO PROTECT THE HISTORICAL RECORD OF A LOST CIVILIZATION, WOULDN'T YOU SAY?
...NOT REALLY. JUST SEEMS FOOLISH TO RISK PEOPLE'S LIVES OVER A MODEL.
MODEL IS PERHAPS THE WRONG TERM. A PERFECTLY RENDERED FACSIMILE INDISTINGUISHABLE FROM THE ORIGINAL WOULD BE MORE ACCURATE.
SOUNDS LIKE A MODEL TO ME.
PERHAPS YOU'D BETTER UNDERSTAND IF I GAVE YOU A DEMONSTRATION. HERE, I'D LIKE TO SHOW YOU SOMETHING.

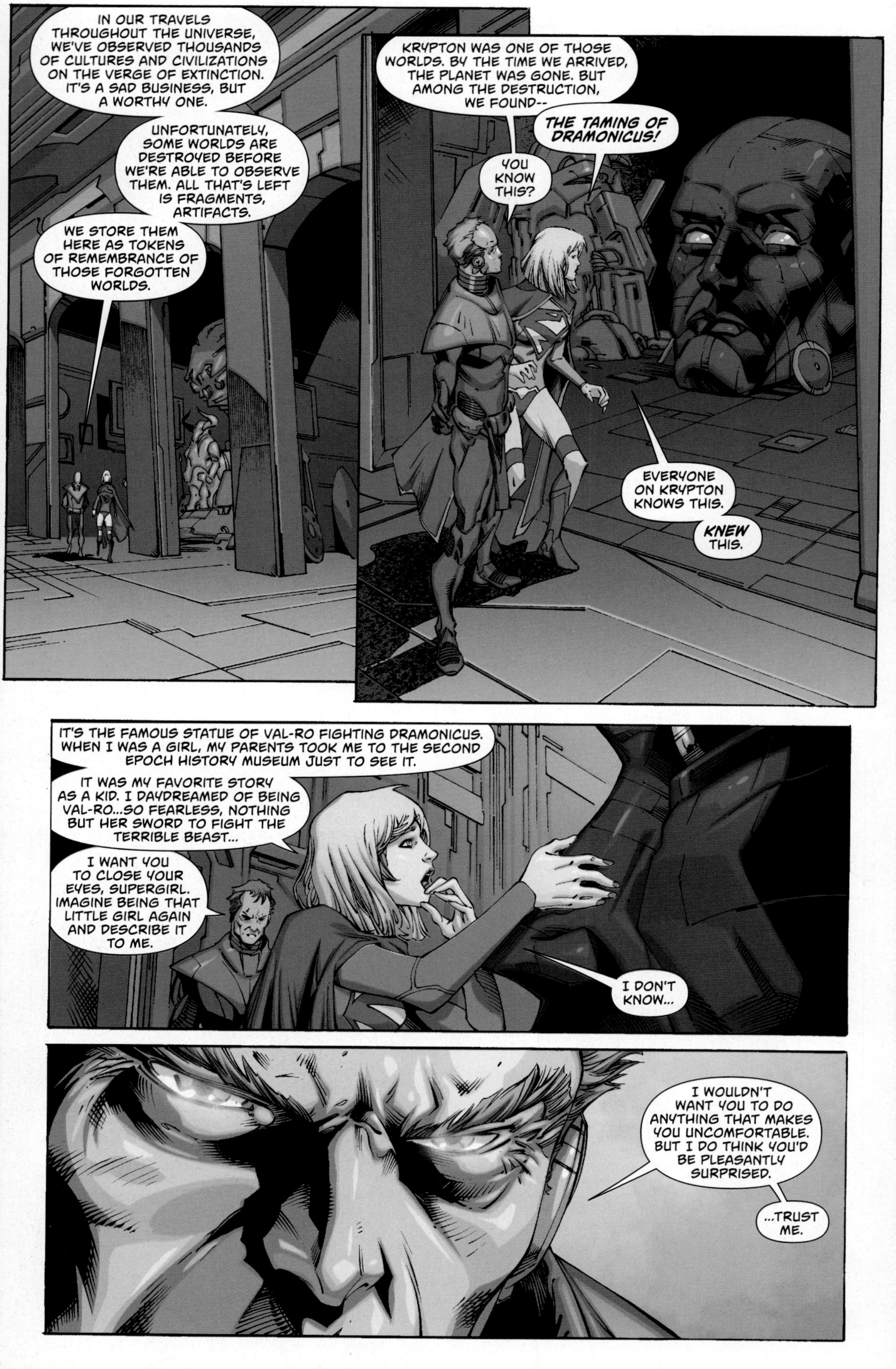
IN OUR TRAVELS THROUGHOUT THE UNIVERSE, WE'VE OBSERVED THOUSANDS OF CULTURES AND CIVILIZATIONS ON THE VERGE OF EXTINCTION. IT'S A SAD BUSINESS, BUT A WORTHY ONE.
UNFORTUNATELY, SOME WORLDS ARE DESTROYED BEFORE WE'RE ABLE TO OBSERVE THEM. ALL THAT'S LEFT IS FRAGMENTS, ARTIFACTS.
WE STORE THEM HERE AS TOKENS OF REMEMBRANCE OF THOSE FORGOTTEN WORLDS.
KRYPTON WAS ONE OF THOSE WORLDS. BY THE TIME WE ARRIVED, THE PLANET WAS GONE. BUT AMONG THE DESTRUCTION, WE FOUND--
THE TAMING OF DRAMONICUS!
YOU KNOW THIS?
EVERYONE ON KRYPTON KNOWS THIS.
KNEW THIS.
IT'S THE FAMOUS STATUE OF VAL-RO FIGHTING DRAMONICUS. WHEN I WAS A GIRL, MY PARENTS TOOK ME TO THE SECOND EPOCH HISTORY MUSEUM JUST TO SEE IT.
IT WAS MY FAVORITE STORY AS A KID. I DAYDREAMED OF BEING VAL-RO...SO FEARLESS, NOTHING BUT HER SWORD TO FIGHT THE TERRIBLE BEAST...
I WANT YOU TO CLOSE YOUR EYES, SUPERGIRL. IMAGINE BEING THAT LITTLE GIRL AGAIN AND DESCRIBE IT TO ME.
I DON'T KNOW...
I WOULDN'T WANT YOU TO DO ANYTHING THAT MAKES YOU UNCOMFORTABLE. BUT I DO THINK YOU'D BE PLEASANTLY SURPRISED.
...TRUST ME.

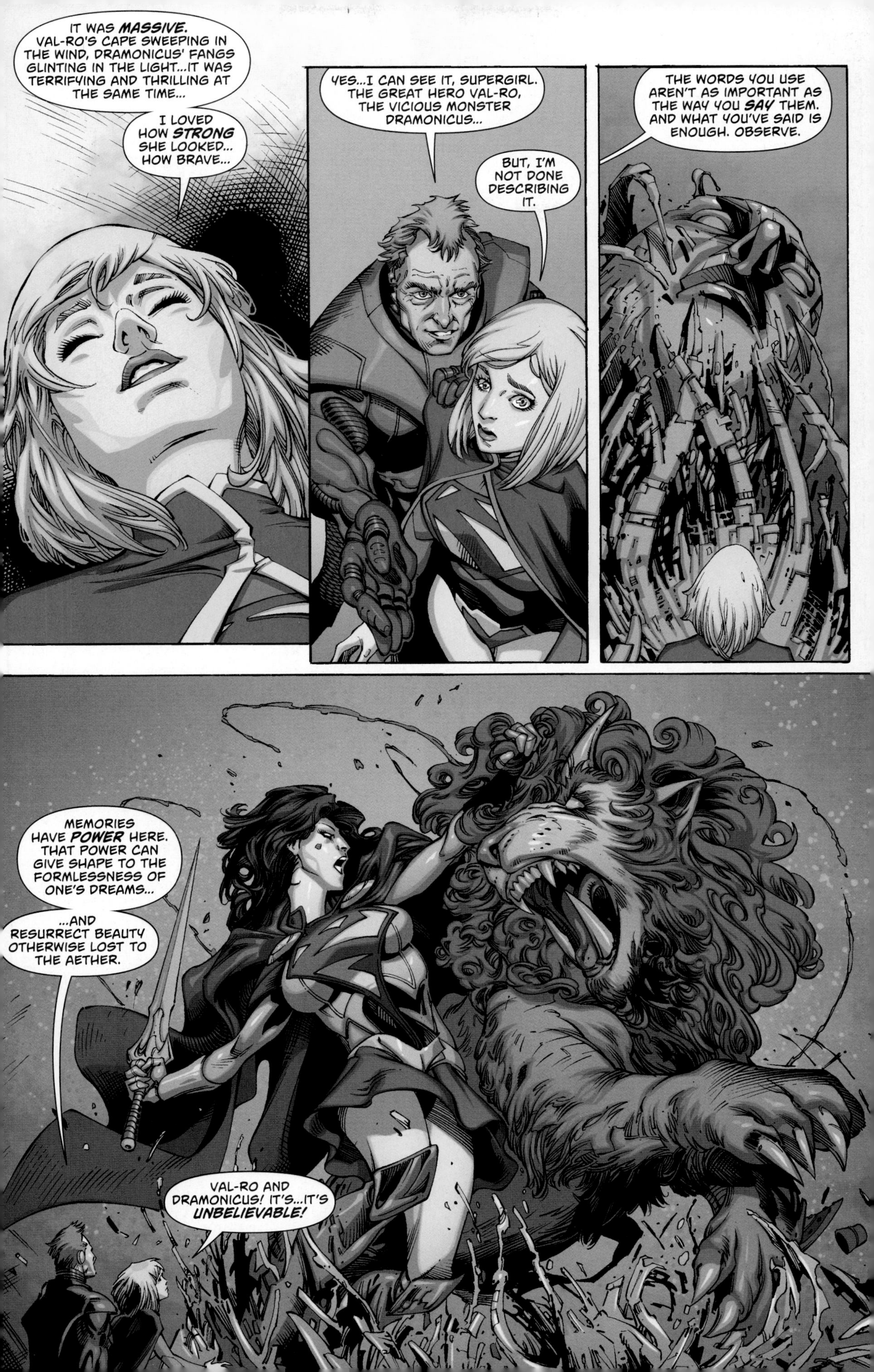
IT WAS MASSIVE. VAL-RO'S CAPE SWEEPING IN THE WIND, DRAMONICUS' FANGS GLINTING IN THE LIGHT...IT WAS TERRIFYING AND THRILLING AT THE SAME TIME...
I LOVED HOW STRONG SHE LOOKED... HOW BRAVE...
YES...I CAN SEE IT, SUPERGIRL. THE GREAT HERO VAL-RO, THE VICIOUS MONSTER DRAMONICUS...
BUT, I'M NOT DONE DESCRIBING IT.
THE WORDS YOU USE AREN'T AS IMPORTANT AS THE WAY YOU SAY THEM. AND WHAT YOU'VE SAID IS ENOUGH. OBSERVE.
MEMORIES HAVE POWER HERE. THAT POWER CAN GIVE SHAPE TO THE FORMLESSNESS OF ONE'S DREAMS...
...AND RESURRECT BEAUTY OTHERWISE LOST TO THE AETHER.
VAL-RO AND DRAMONICUS! IT'S...IT'S UNBELIEVABLE!

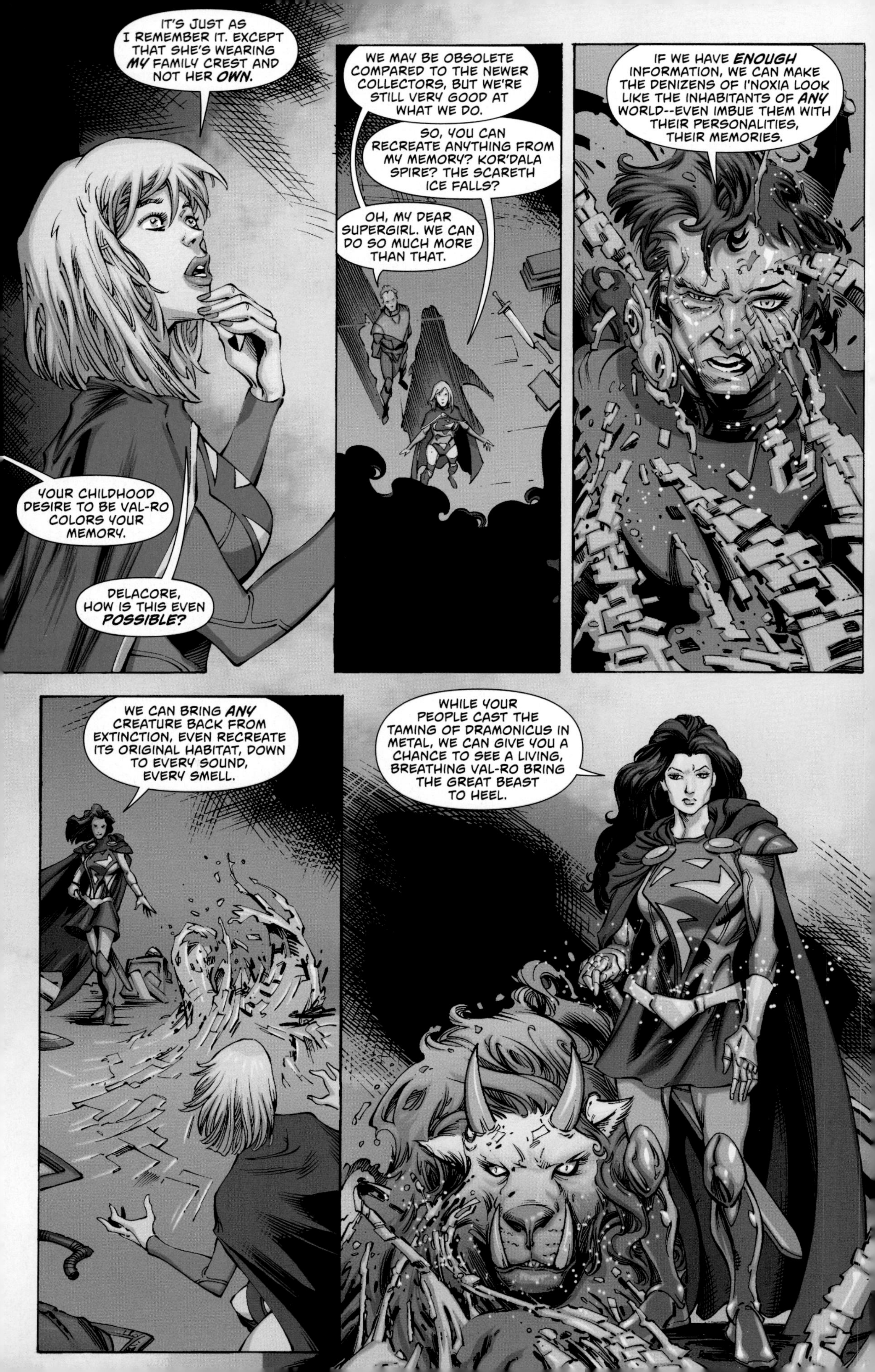
IT'S JUST AS I REMEMBER IT. EXCEPT THAT SHE'S WEARING MY FAMILY CREST AND NOT HER OWN.
YOUR CHILDHOOD DESIRE TO BE VAL-RO COLORS YOUR MEMORY.
DELACORE, HOW IS THIS EVEN POSSIBLE?
WE MAY BE OBSOLETE COMPARED TO THE NEWER COLLECTORS, BUT WE'RE STILL VERY GOOD AT WHAT WE DO.
SO, YOU CAN RECREATE ANYTHING FROM MY MEMORY? KOR'DALA SPIRE? THE SCARETH ICE FALLS?
OH, MY DEAR SUPERGIRL. WE CAN DO SO MUCH MORE THAN THAT.
IF WE HAVE ENOUGH INFORMATION, WE CAN MAKE THE DENIZENS OF I'NOXIA LOOK LIKE THE INHABITANTS OF ANY WORLD--EVEN IMBUE THEM WITH THEIR PERSONALITIES, THEIR MEMORIES.
WE CAN BRING ANY CREATURE BACK FROM EXTINCTION, EVEN RECREATE ITS ORIGINAL HABITAT, DOWN TO EVERY SOUND, EVERY SMELL.
WHILE YOUR PEOPLE CAST THE TAMING OF DRAMONICUS IN METAL, WE CAN GIVE YOU A CHANCE TO SEE A LIVING, BREATHING VAL-RO BRING THE GREAT BEAST TO HEEL.

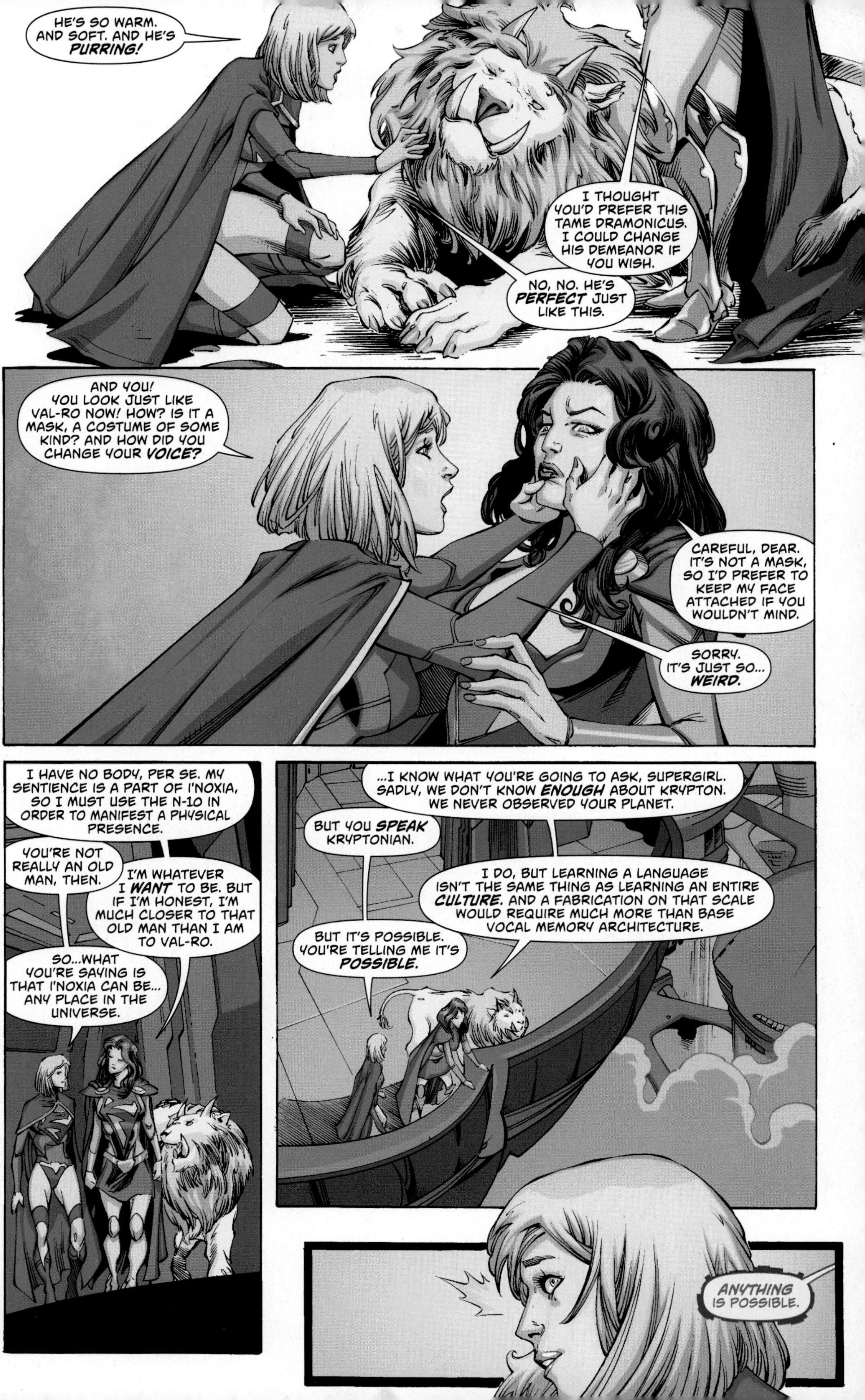
HE'S SO WARM. AND SOFT. AND HE'S PURRING!
I THOUGHT YOU'D PREFER THIS TAME DRAMONICUS. I COULD CHANGE HIS DEMEANOR IF YOU WISH.
NO, NO. HE'S PERFECT JUST LIKE THIS.
AND YOU! YOU LOOK JUST LIKE VAL-RO NOW! HOW? IS IT A MASK, A COSTUME OF SOME KIND? AND HOW DID YOU CHANGE YOUR VOICE?
CAREFUL, DEAR. IT'S NOT A MASK, SO I'D PREFER TO KEEP MY FACE ATTACHED IF YOU WOULDN'T MIND.
SORRY. IT'S JUST SO... WEIRD.
I HAVE NO BODY, PER SE. MY SENTIENCE IS A PART OF I'NOXIA, SO I MUST USE THE N-10 IN ORDER TO MANIFEST A PHYSICAL PRESENCE.
YOU'RE NOT REALLY AN OLD MAN, THEN.
I'M WHATEVER I WANT TO BE. BUT IF I'M HONEST, I'M MUCH CLOSER TO THAT OLD MAN THAN I AM TO VAL-RO.
SO...WHAT YOU'RE SAYING IS THAT I'NOXIA CAN BE... ANY PLACE IN THE UNIVERSE.
...I KNOW WHAT YOU'RE GOING TO ASK, SUPERGIRL. SADLY, WE DON'T KNOW ENOUGH ABOUT KRYPTON. WE NEVER OBSERVED YOUR PLANET.
BUT YOU SPEAK KRYPTONIAN.
I DO, BUT LEARNING A LANGUAGE ISN'T THE SAME THING AS LEARNING AN ENTIRE CULTURE. AND A FABRICATION ON THAT SCALE WOULD REQUIRE MUCH MORE THAN BASE VOCAL MEMORY ARCHITECTURE.
BUT IT'S POSSIBLE. YOU'RE TELLING ME IT'S POSSIBLE.
ANYTHING IS POSSIBLE.

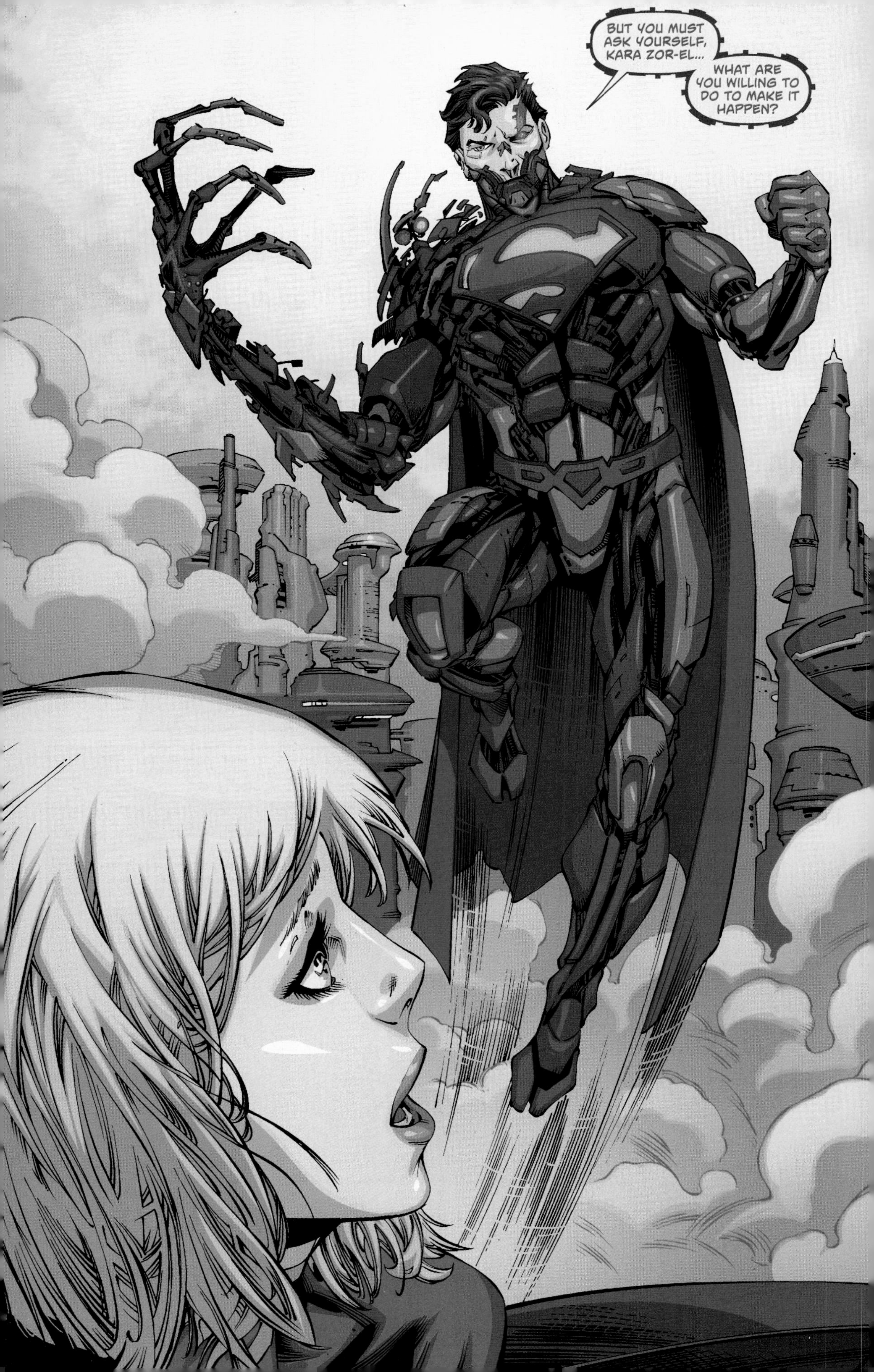
BUT YOU MUST ASK YOURSELF, KARA ZOR-EL...
WHAT ARE YOU WILLING TO DO TO MAKE IT HAPPEN?

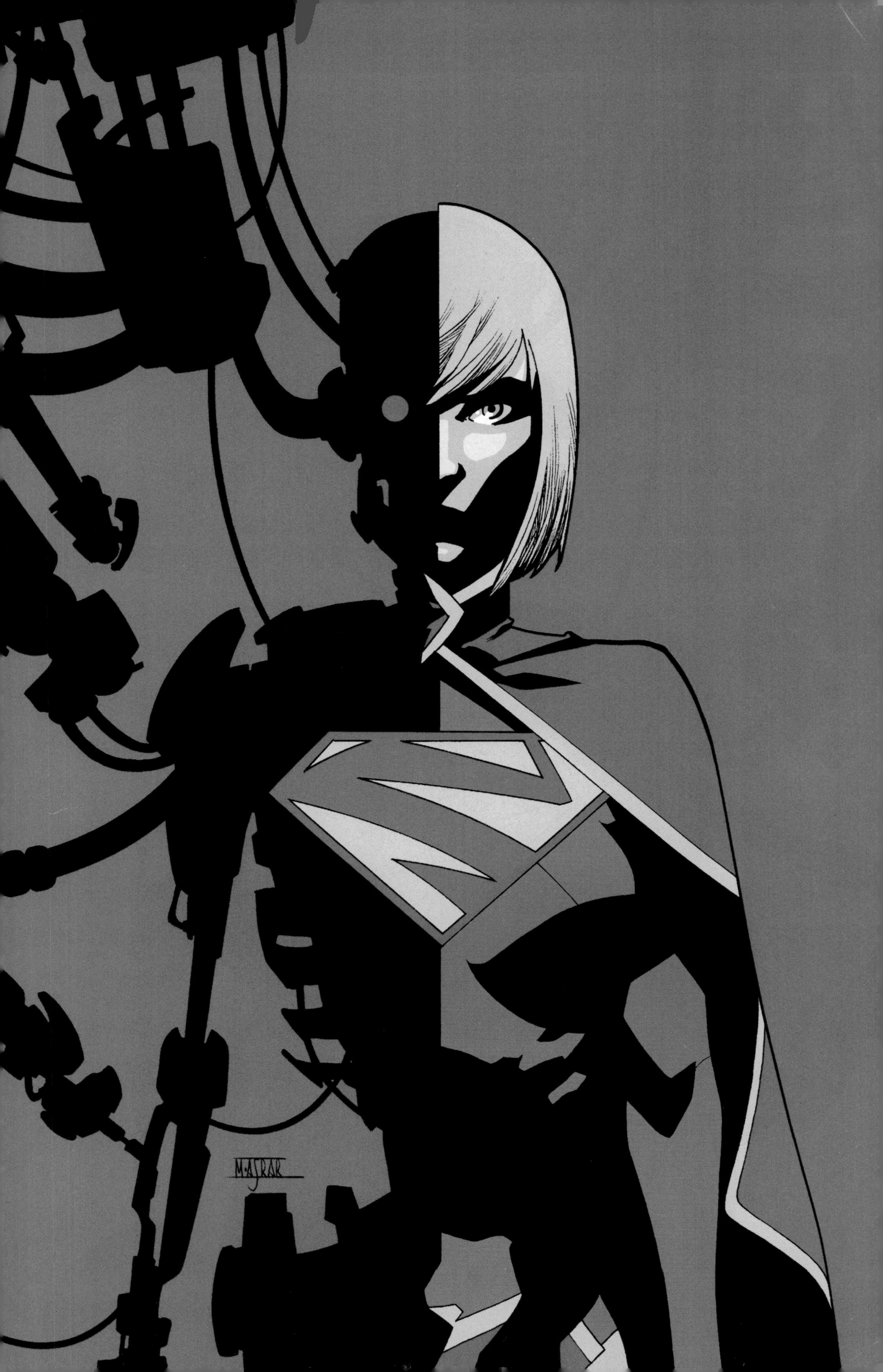

CLOSE TO HOME

MICHAEL ALAN NELSON writer **DIOGENES NEVES** penciller **MARC DEERING, OCLAIR ALBERT & RUY JOSE** inkers
cover art by **MAHMUD ASRAR**

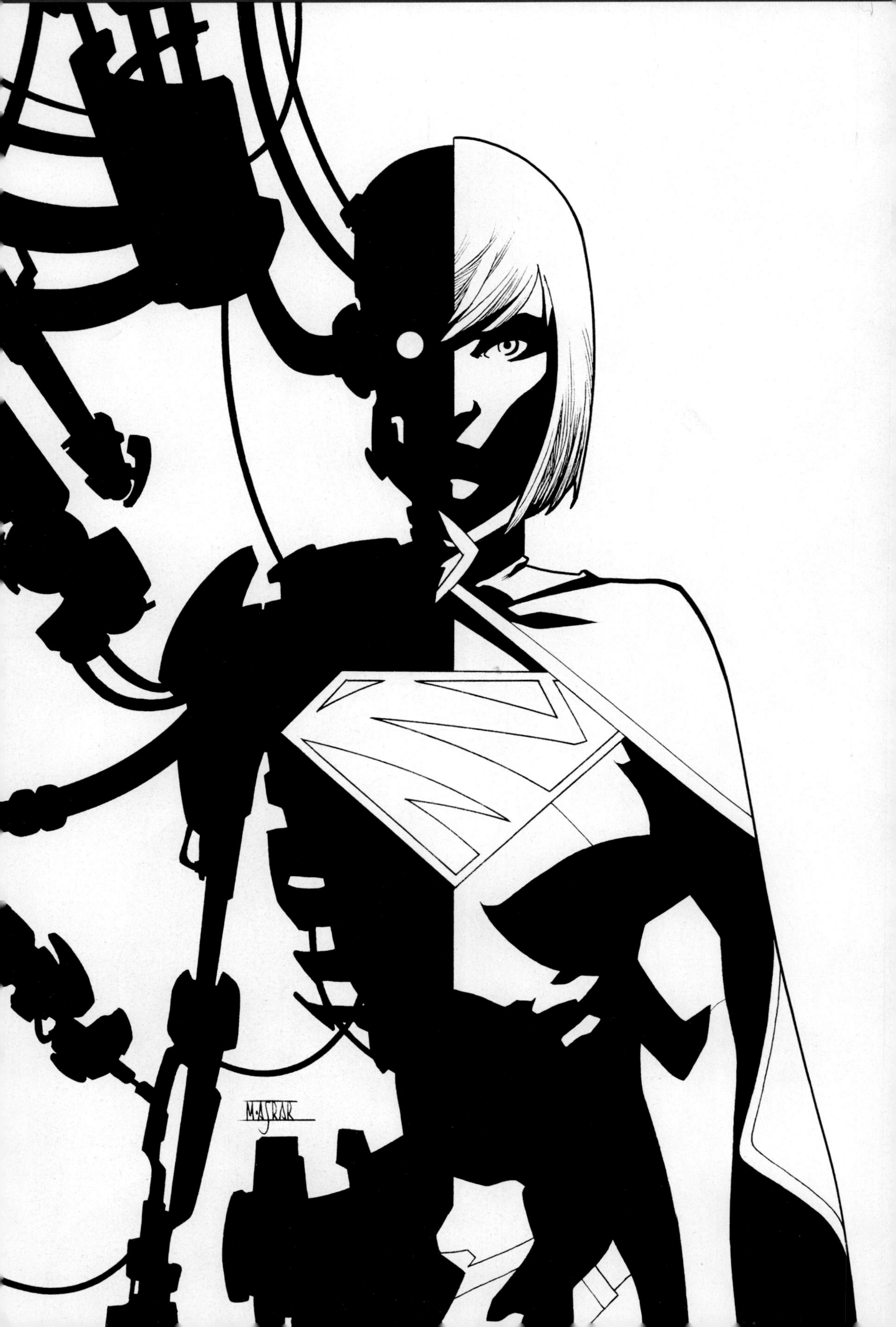
M.ASRAR

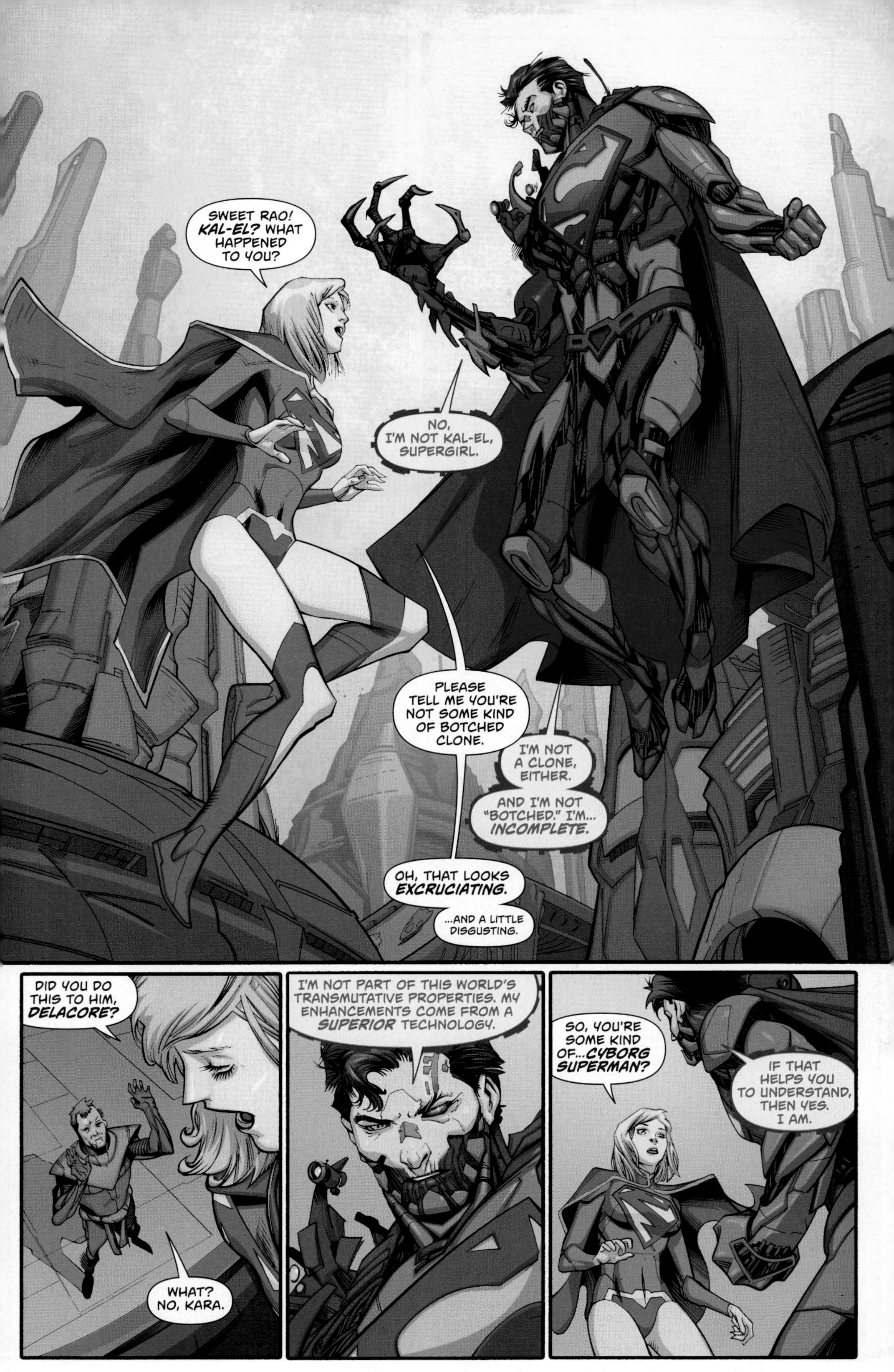
SWEET RAO! KAL-EL? WHAT HAPPENED TO YOU?
NO, I'M NOT KAL-EL, SUPERGIRL.
PLEASE TELL ME YOU'RE NOT SOME KIND OF BOTCHED CLONE.
I'M NOT A CLONE, EITHER.
AND I'M NOT "BOTCHED." I'M... INCOMPLETE.
OH, THAT LOOKS EXCRUCIATING.
...AND A LITTLE DISGUSTING.
DID YOU DO THIS TO HIM, DELACORE?
WHAT? NO, KARA.
I'M NOT PART OF THIS WORLD'S TRANSMUTATIVE PROPERTIES. MY ENHANCEMENTS COME FROM A SUPERIOR TECHNOLOGY.
SO, YOU'RE SOME KIND OF...CYBORG SUPERMAN?
IF THAT HELPS YOU TO UNDERSTAND, THEN YES. I AM.

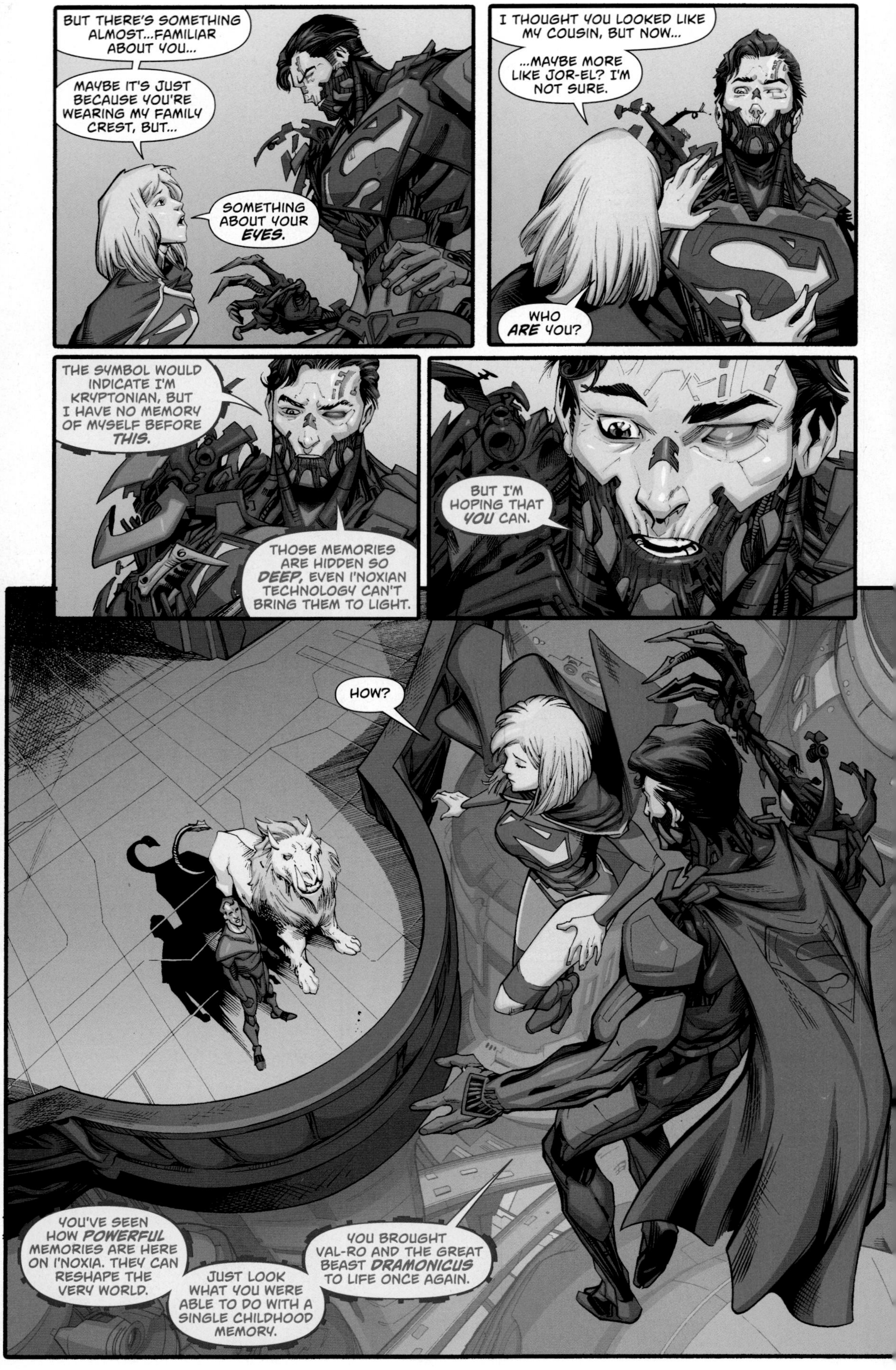

BUT THERE'S SOMETHING ALMOST...FAMILIAR ABOUT YOU...
MAYBE IT'S JUST BECAUSE YOU'RE WEARING MY FAMILY CREST, BUT...
SOMETHING ABOUT YOUR **EYES**.
I THOUGHT YOU LOOKED LIKE MY COUSIN, BUT NOW...
...MAYBE MORE LIKE JOR-EL? I'M NOT SURE.
WHO **ARE** YOU?
THE SYMBOL WOULD INDICATE I'M KRYPTONIAN, BUT I HAVE NO MEMORY OF MYSELF BEFORE **THIS**.
THOSE MEMORIES ARE HIDDEN SO **DEEP**, EVEN I'NOXIAN TECHNOLOGY CAN'T BRING THEM TO LIGHT.
BUT I'M HOPING THAT **YOU** CAN.
HOW?
YOU'VE SEEN HOW **POWERFUL** MEMORIES ARE HERE ON I'NOXIA. THEY CAN RESHAPE THE VERY WORLD.
JUST LOOK WHAT YOU WERE ABLE TO DO WITH A SINGLE CHILDHOOD MEMORY.
YOU BROUGHT VAL-RO AND THE GREAT BEAST **DRAMONICUS** TO LIFE ONCE AGAIN.

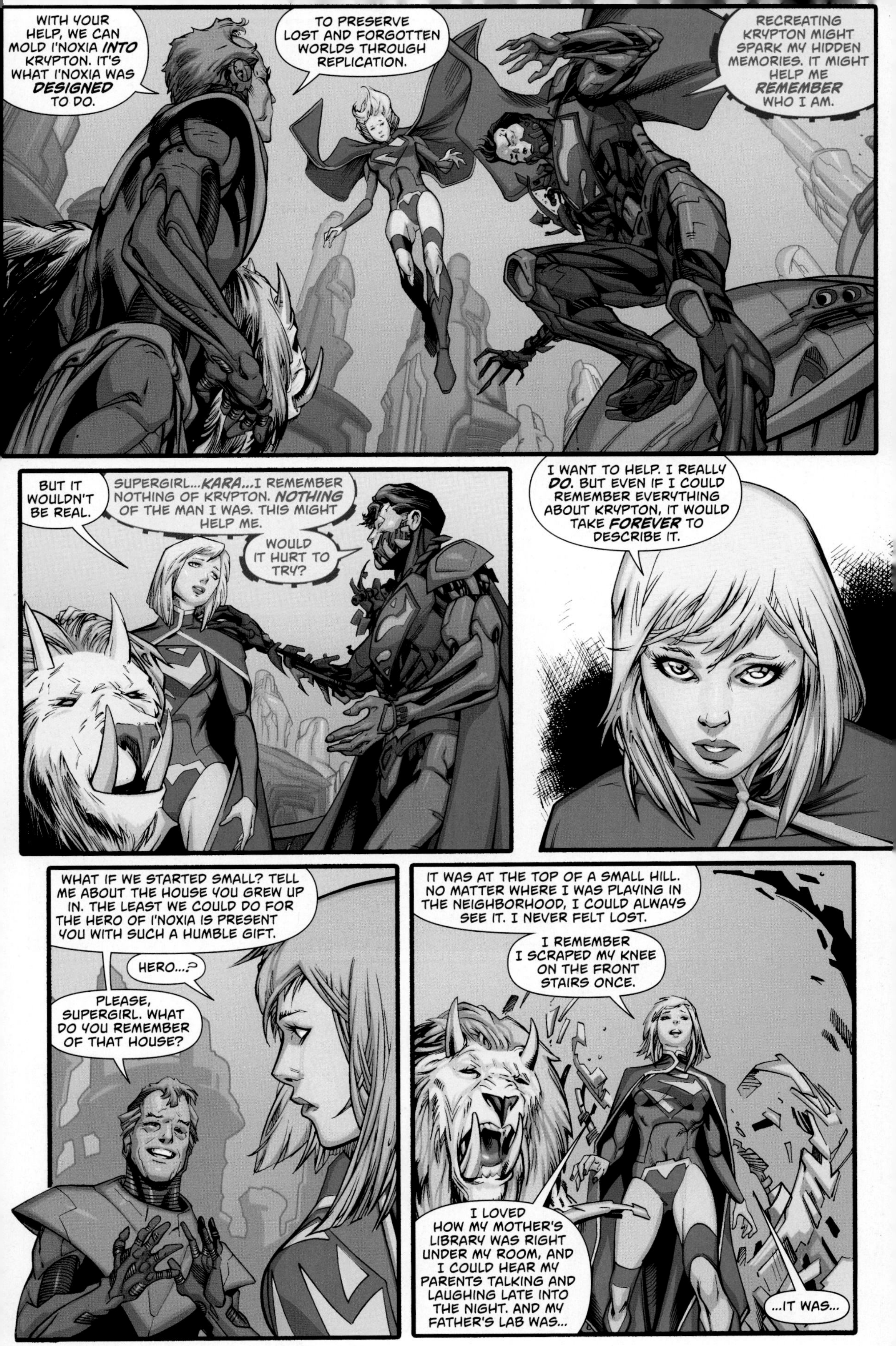
WITH YOUR HELP, WE CAN MOLD I'NOXIA INTO KRYPTON. IT'S WHAT I'NOXIA WAS DESIGNED TO DO.
TO PRESERVE LOST AND FORGOTTEN WORLDS THROUGH REPLICATION.
RECREATING KRYPTON MIGHT SPARK MY HIDDEN MEMORIES. IT MIGHT HELP ME REMEMBER WHO I AM.
BUT IT WOULDN'T BE REAL.
SUPERGIRL...KARA...I REMEMBER NOTHING OF KRYPTON. NOTHING OF THE MAN I WAS. THIS MIGHT HELP ME.
WOULD IT HURT TO TRY?
I WANT TO HELP. I REALLY DO. BUT EVEN IF I COULD REMEMBER EVERYTHING ABOUT KRYPTON, IT WOULD TAKE FOREVER TO DESCRIBE IT.
WHAT IF WE STARTED SMALL? TELL ME ABOUT THE HOUSE YOU GREW UP IN. THE LEAST WE COULD DO FOR THE HERO OF I'NOXIA IS PRESENT YOU WITH SUCH A HUMBLE GIFT.
HERO...?
PLEASE, SUPERGIRL. WHAT DO YOU REMEMBER OF THAT HOUSE?
IT WAS AT THE TOP OF A SMALL HILL. NO MATTER WHERE I WAS PLAYING IN THE NEIGHBORHOOD, I COULD ALWAYS SEE IT. I NEVER FELT LOST.
I REMEMBER I SCRAPED MY KNEE ON THE FRONT STAIRS ONCE.
I LOVED HOW MY MOTHER'S LIBRARY WAS RIGHT UNDER MY ROOM, AND I COULD HEAR MY PARENTS TALKING AND LAUGHING LATE INTO THE NIGHT. AND MY FATHER'S LAB WAS...
...IT WAS...

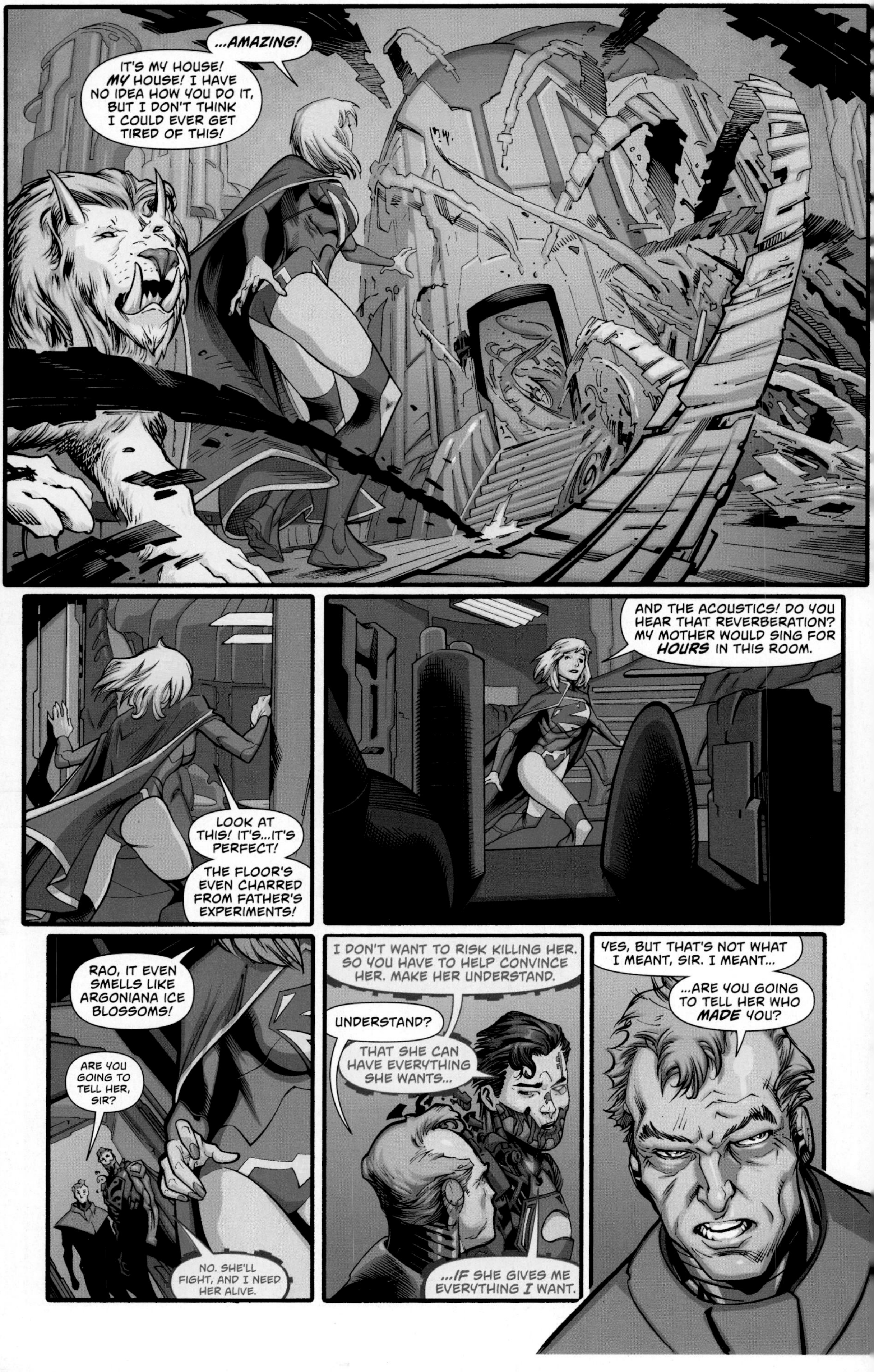
...AMAZING!
IT'S MY HOUSE! MY HOUSE! I HAVE NO IDEA HOW YOU DO IT, BUT I DON'T THINK I COULD EVER GET TIRED OF THIS!
LOOK AT THIS! IT'S...IT'S PERFECT!
THE FLOOR'S EVEN CHARRED FROM FATHER'S EXPERIMENTS!
AND THE ACOUSTICS! DO YOU HEAR THAT REVERBERATION? MY MOTHER WOULD SING FOR HOURS IN THIS ROOM.
RAO, IT EVEN SMELLS LIKE ARGONIANA ICE BLOSSOMS!
ARE YOU GOING TO TELL HER, SIR?
NO. SHE'LL FIGHT, AND I NEED HER ALIVE.
I DON'T WANT TO RISK KILLING HER. SO YOU HAVE TO HELP CONVINCE HER. MAKE HER UNDERSTAND.
UNDERSTAND?
THAT SHE CAN HAVE EVERYTHING SHE WANTS...
...IF SHE GIVES ME EVERYTHING I WANT.
YES, BUT THAT'S NOT WHAT I MEANT, SIR. I MEANT...
...ARE YOU GOING TO TELL HER WHO MADE YOU?

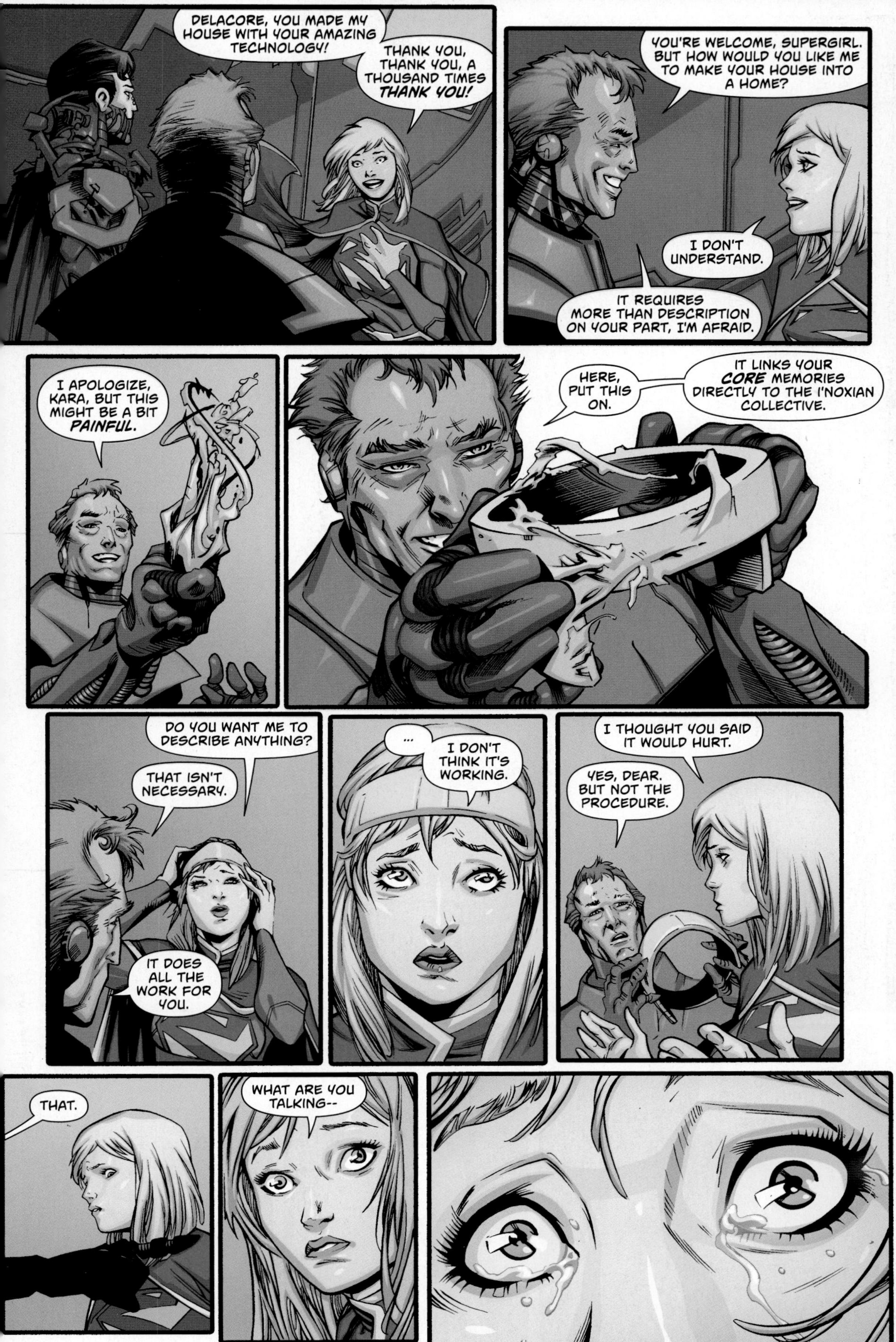
DELACORE, YOU MADE MY HOUSE WITH YOUR AMAZING TECHNOLOGY!
THANK YOU, THANK YOU, A THOUSAND TIMES *THANK YOU!*
YOU'RE WELCOME, SUPERGIRL. BUT HOW WOULD YOU LIKE ME TO MAKE YOUR HOUSE INTO A HOME?
I DON'T UNDERSTAND.
IT REQUIRES MORE THAN DESCRIPTION ON YOUR PART, I'M AFRAID.
I APOLOGIZE, KARA, BUT THIS MIGHT BE A BIT *PAINFUL.*
HERE, PUT THIS ON.
IT LINKS YOUR *CORE* MEMORIES DIRECTLY TO THE I'NOXIAN COLLECTIVE.
DO YOU WANT ME TO DESCRIBE ANYTHING?
THAT ISN'T NECESSARY.
IT DOES ALL THE WORK FOR YOU.
...
I DON'T THINK IT'S WORKING.
I THOUGHT YOU SAID IT WOULD HURT.
YES, DEAR. BUT NOT THE PROCEDURE.
THAT.
WHAT ARE YOU TALKING--

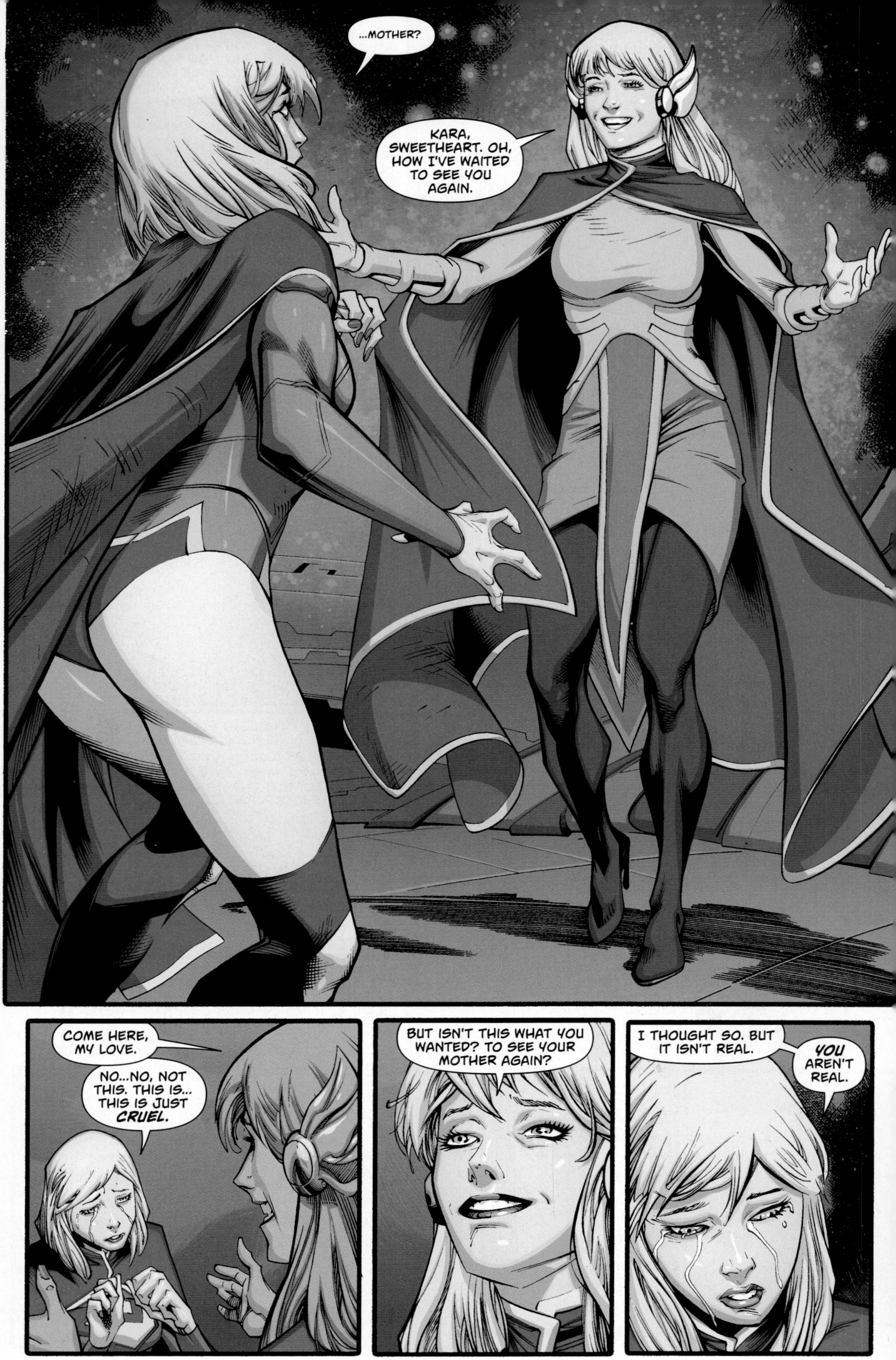
...MOTHER?
KARA, SWEETHEART. OH, HOW I'VE WAITED TO SEE YOU AGAIN.
COME HERE, MY LOVE.
NO...NO, NOT THIS. THIS IS... THIS IS JUST *CRUEL*.
BUT ISN'T THIS WHAT YOU WANTED? TO SEE YOUR MOTHER AGAIN?
I THOUGHT SO. BUT IT ISN'T REAL.
YOU AREN'T REAL.

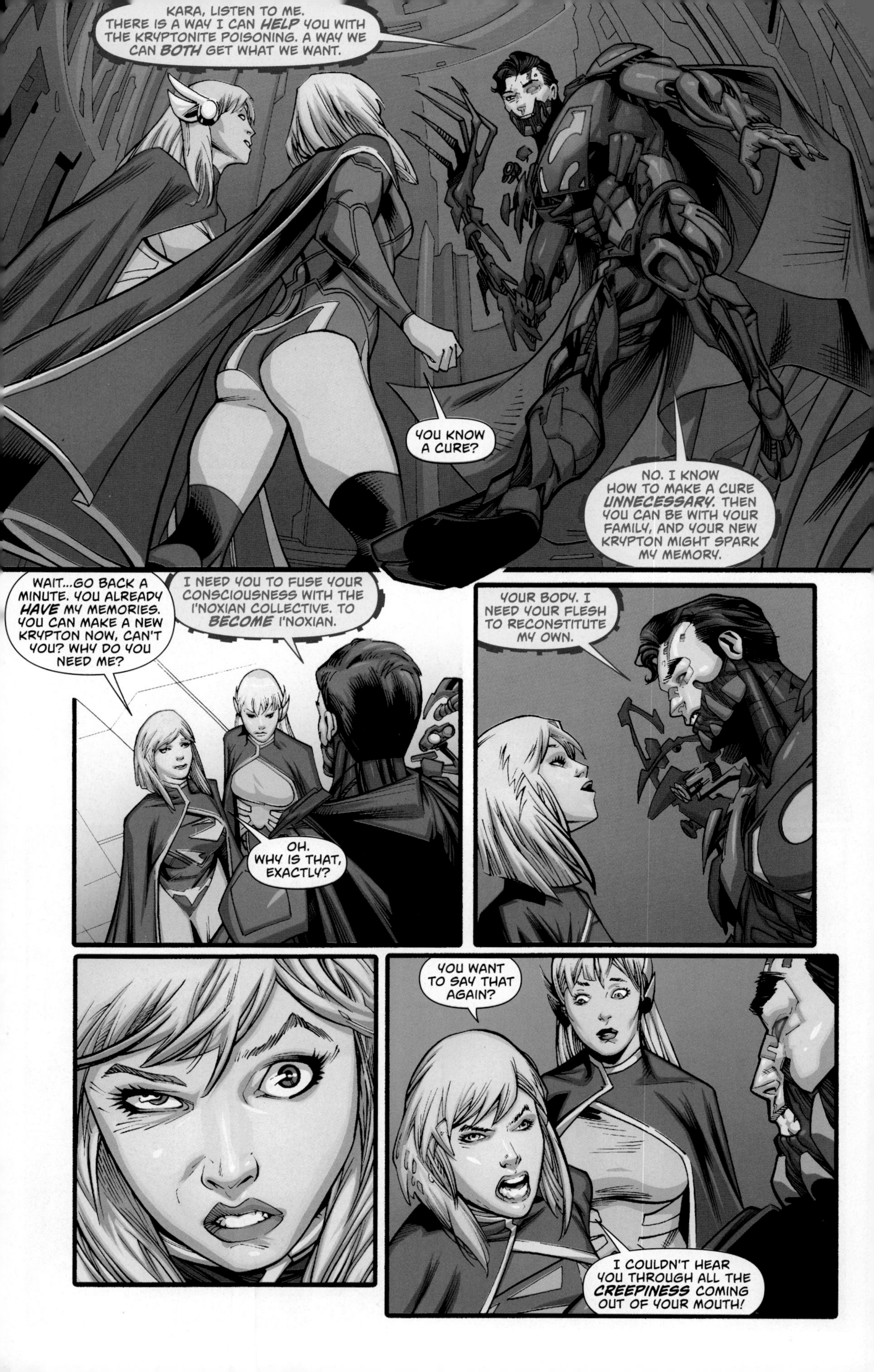
KARA, LISTEN TO ME. THERE IS A WAY I CAN HELP YOU WITH THE KRYPTONITE POISONING. A WAY WE CAN BOTH GET WHAT WE WANT.
YOU KNOW A CURE?
NO. I KNOW HOW TO MAKE A CURE UNNECESSARY. THEN YOU CAN BE WITH YOUR FAMILY, AND YOUR NEW KRYPTON MIGHT SPARK MY MEMORY.
WAIT...GO BACK A MINUTE. YOU ALREADY HAVE MY MEMORIES. YOU CAN MAKE A NEW KRYPTON NOW, CAN'T YOU? WHY DO YOU NEED ME?
I NEED YOU TO FUSE YOUR CONSCIOUSNESS WITH THE I'NOXIAN COLLECTIVE. TO BECOME I'NOXIAN.
OH. WHY IS THAT, EXACTLY?
YOUR BODY. I NEED YOUR FLESH TO RECONSTITUTE MY OWN.
YOU WANT TO SAY THAT AGAIN?
I COULDN'T HEAR YOU THROUGH ALL THE CREEPINESS COMING OUT OF YOUR MOUTH!

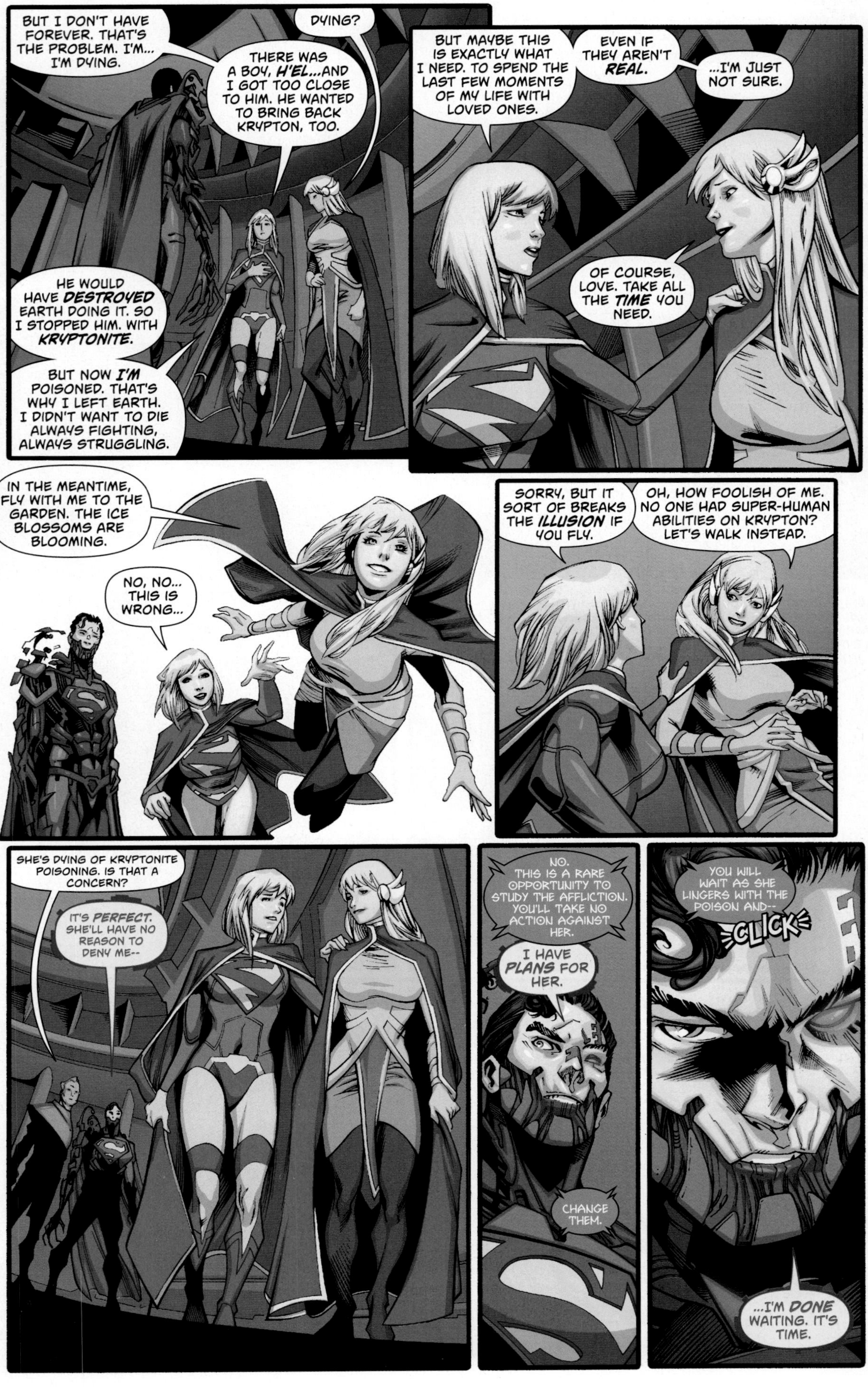
BUT I DON'T HAVE FOREVER. THAT'S THE PROBLEM. I'M... I'M DYING.
DYING?
THERE WAS A BOY, H'EL...AND I GOT TOO CLOSE TO HIM. HE WANTED TO BRING BACK KRYPTON, TOO.
HE WOULD HAVE DESTROYED EARTH DOING IT. SO I STOPPED HIM. WITH KRYPTONITE.
BUT NOW I'M POISONED. THAT'S WHY I LEFT EARTH. I DIDN'T WANT TO DIE ALWAYS FIGHTING, ALWAYS STRUGGLING.
BUT MAYBE THIS IS EXACTLY WHAT I NEED. TO SPEND THE LAST FEW MOMENTS OF MY LIFE WITH LOVED ONES.
EVEN IF THEY AREN'T REAL.
...I'M JUST NOT SURE.
OF COURSE, LOVE. TAKE ALL THE TIME YOU NEED.
IN THE MEANTIME, FLY WITH ME TO THE GARDEN. THE ICE BLOSSOMS ARE BLOOMING.
NO, NO... THIS IS WRONG...
SORRY, BUT IT SORT OF BREAKS THE ILLUSION IF YOU FLY.
OH, HOW FOOLISH OF ME. NO ONE HAD SUPER-HUMAN ABILITIES ON KRYPTON? LET'S WALK INSTEAD.
SHE'S DYING OF KRYPTONITE POISONING. IS THAT A CONCERN?
IT'S PERFECT. SHE'LL HAVE NO REASON TO DENY ME--
NO. THIS IS A RARE OPPORTUNITY TO STUDY THE AFFLICTION. YOU'LL TAKE NO ACTION AGAINST HER.
I HAVE PLANS FOR HER.
CHANGE THEM.
YOU WILL WAIT AS SHE LINGERS WITH THE POISON AND--
CLICK
...I'M DONE WAITING. IT'S TIME.

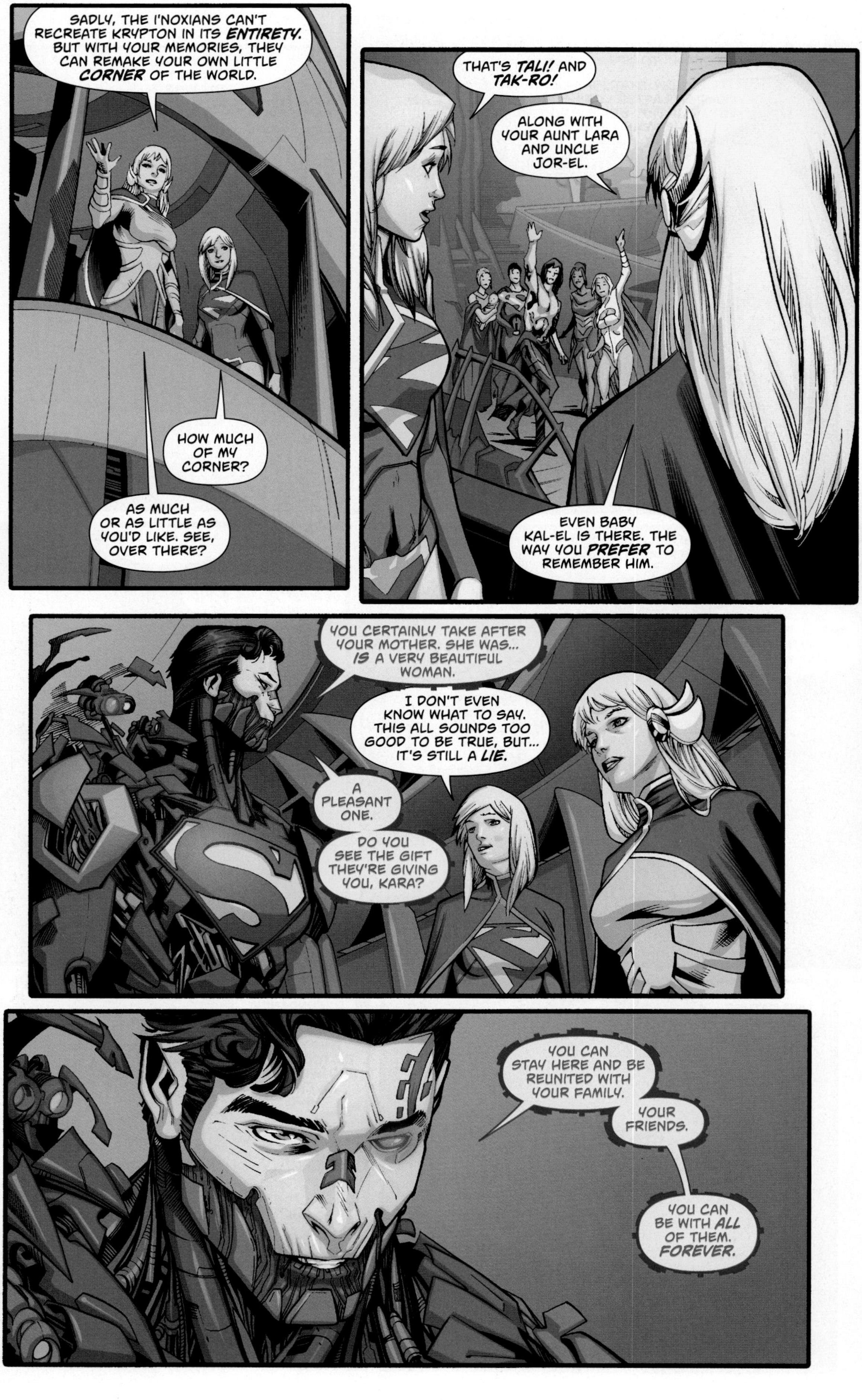
SADLY, THE I'NOXIANS CAN'T RECREATE KRYPTON IN ITS *ENTIRETY*. BUT WITH YOUR MEMORIES, THEY CAN REMAKE YOUR OWN LITTLE *CORNER* OF THE WORLD.
HOW MUCH OF MY CORNER?
AS MUCH OR AS LITTLE AS YOU'D LIKE. SEE, OVER THERE?
THAT'S *TALI!* AND *TAK-RO!*
ALONG WITH YOUR AUNT LARA AND UNCLE JOR-EL.
EVEN BABY KAL-EL IS THERE. THE WAY YOU *PREFER* TO REMEMBER HIM.
YOU CERTAINLY TAKE AFTER YOUR MOTHER. SHE WAS... *IS* A VERY BEAUTIFUL WOMAN.
I DON'T EVEN KNOW WHAT TO SAY. THIS ALL SOUNDS TOO GOOD TO BE TRUE, BUT... IT'S STILL A *LIE*.
A PLEASANT ONE.
DO YOU SEE THE GIFT THEY'RE GIVING YOU, KARA?
YOU CAN STAY HERE AND BE REUNITED WITH YOUR FAMILY.
YOUR FRIENDS.
YOU CAN BE WITH *ALL* OF THEM. *FOREVER*.

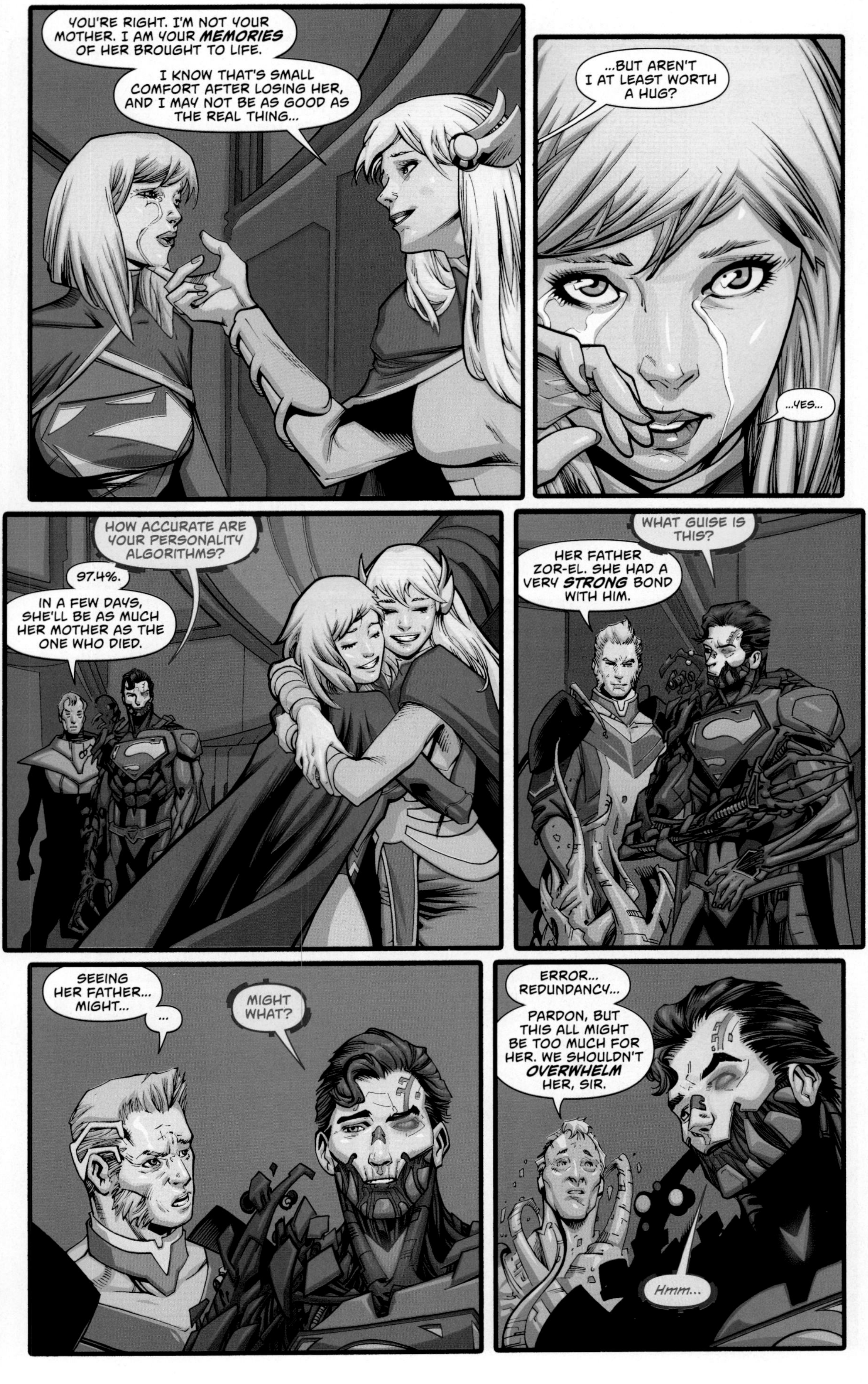
YOU'RE RIGHT. I'M NOT YOUR MOTHER. I AM YOUR ***MEMORIES*** OF HER BROUGHT TO LIFE.
I KNOW THAT'S SMALL COMFORT AFTER LOSING HER, AND I MAY NOT BE AS GOOD AS THE REAL THING...
...BUT AREN'T I AT LEAST WORTH A HUG?
...YES...
HOW ACCURATE ARE YOUR PERSONALITY ALGORITHMS?
97.4%.
IN A FEW DAYS, SHE'LL BE AS MUCH HER MOTHER AS THE ONE WHO DIED.
WHAT GUISE IS THIS?
HER FATHER ZOR-EL. SHE HAD A VERY ***STRONG*** BOND WITH HIM.
SEEING HER FATHER... MIGHT...
...
MIGHT WHAT?
ERROR... REDUNDANCY...
PARDON, BUT THIS ALL MIGHT BE TOO MUCH FOR HER. WE SHOULDN'T ***OVERWHELM*** HER, SIR.
Hmm...

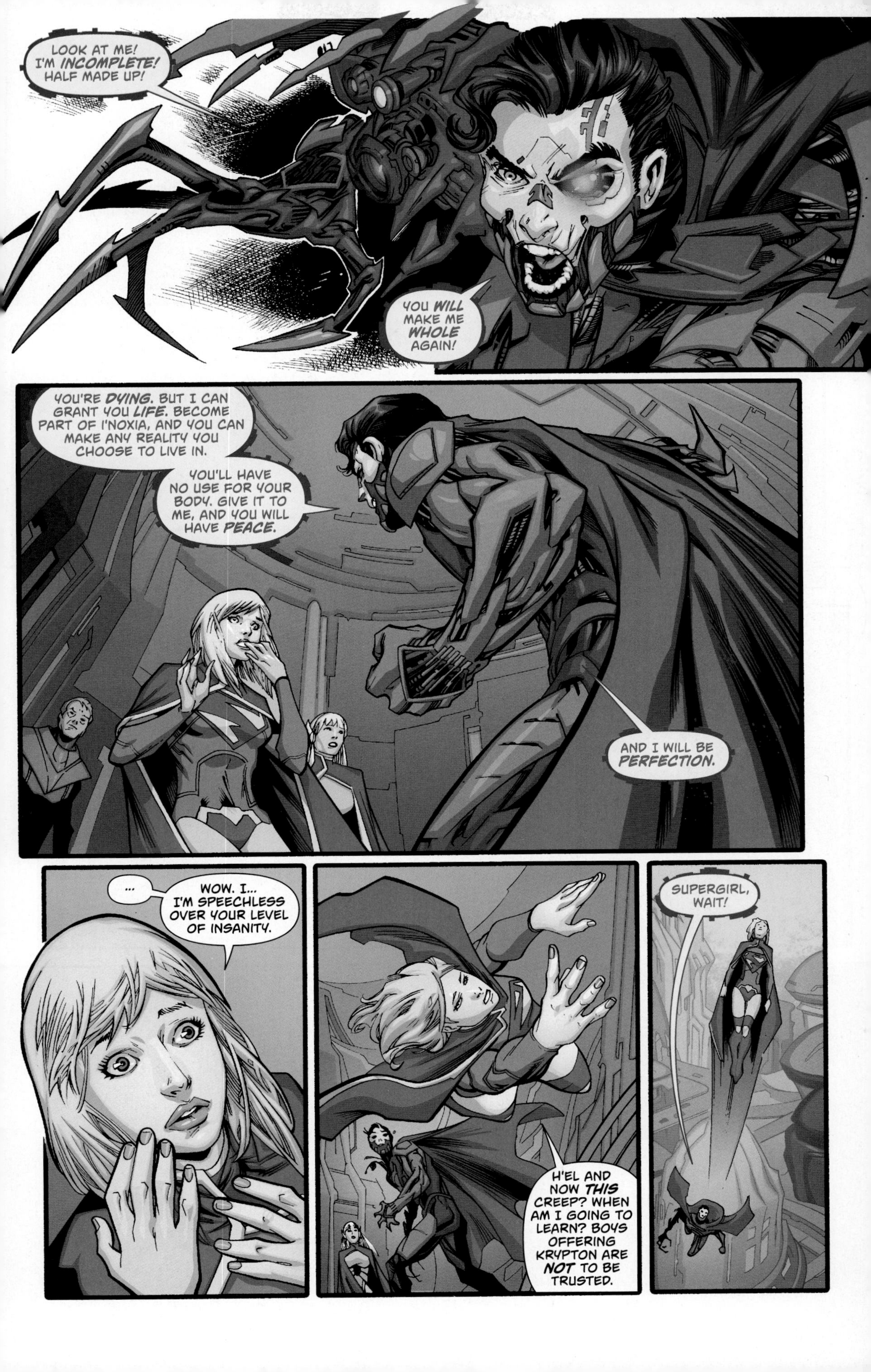
LOOK AT ME! I'M INCOMPLETE! HALF MADE UP!
YOU WILL MAKE ME WHOLE AGAIN!
YOU'RE DYING. BUT I CAN GRANT YOU LIFE. BECOME PART OF I'NOXIA, AND YOU CAN MAKE ANY REALITY YOU CHOOSE TO LIVE IN.
YOU'LL HAVE NO USE FOR YOUR BODY. GIVE IT TO ME, AND YOU WILL HAVE PEACE.
AND I WILL BE PERFECTION.
...
WOW. I... I'M SPEECHLESS OVER YOUR LEVEL OF INSANITY.
H'EL AND NOW THIS CREEP? WHEN AM I GOING TO LEARN? BOYS OFFERING KRYPTON ARE NOT TO BE TRUSTED.
SUPERGIRL, WAIT!

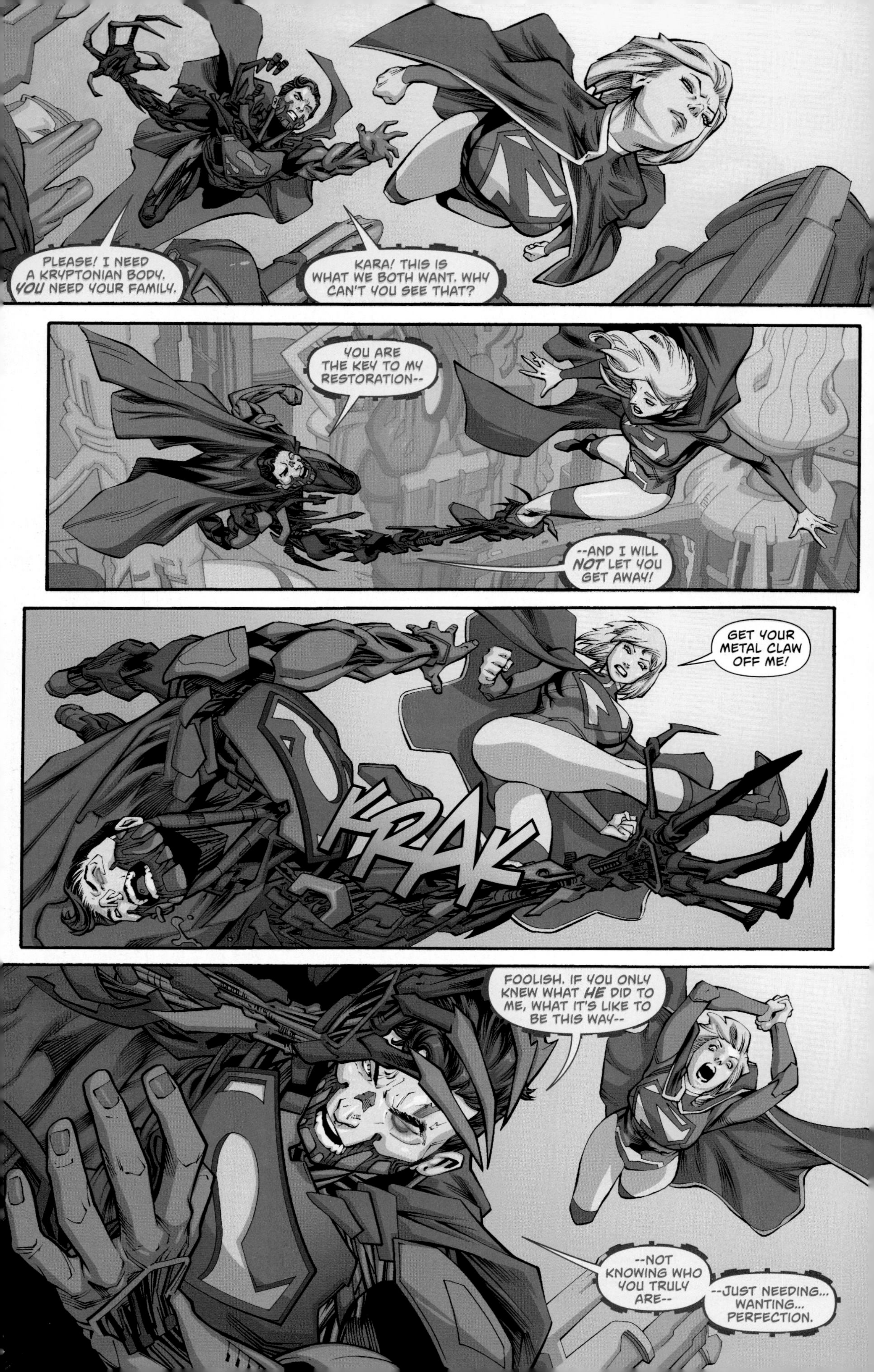
PLEASE! I NEED A KRYPTONIAN BODY. YOU NEED YOUR FAMILY.
KARA! THIS IS WHAT WE BOTH WANT. WHY CAN'T YOU SEE THAT?
YOU ARE THE KEY TO MY RESTORATION--
--AND I WILL NOT LET YOU GET AWAY!
GET YOUR METAL CLAW OFF ME!
KRAK
FOOLISH. IF YOU ONLY KNEW WHAT HE DID TO ME, WHAT IT'S LIKE TO BE THIS WAY--
--NOT KNOWING WHO YOU TRULY ARE--
--JUST NEEDING... WANTING... PERFECTION.

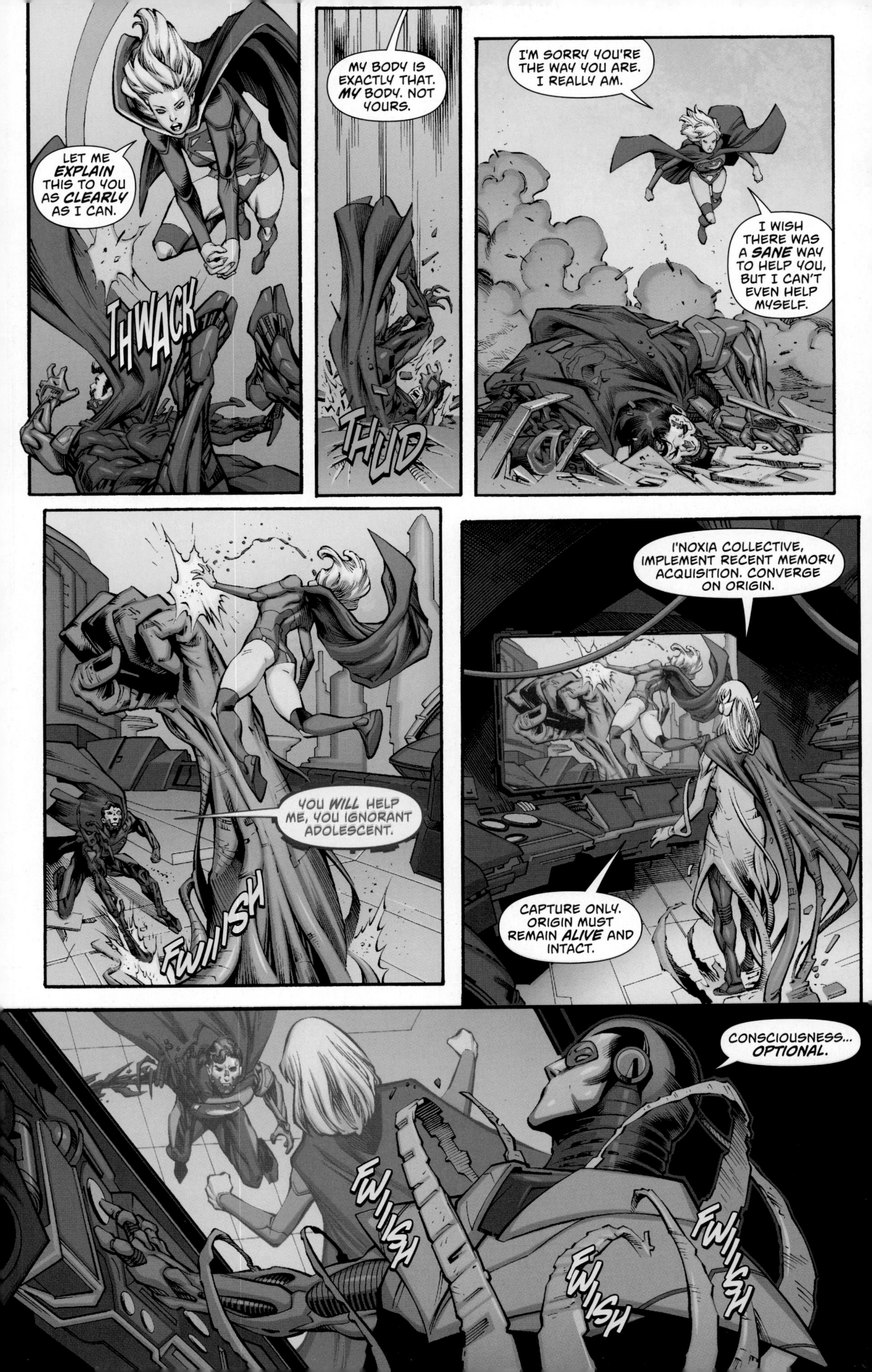

LET ME EXPLAIN THIS TO YOU AS CLEARLY AS I CAN.
THWACK
MY BODY IS EXACTLY THAT. MY BODY. NOT YOURS.
THUD
I'M SORRY YOU'RE THE WAY YOU ARE. I REALLY AM.
I WISH THERE WAS A SANE WAY TO HELP YOU, BUT I CAN'T EVEN HELP MYSELF.
YOU WILL HELP ME, YOU IGNORANT ADOLESCENT.
FWIIISH
I'NOXIA COLLECTIVE, IMPLEMENT RECENT MEMORY ACQUISITION. CONVERGE ON ORIGIN.
CAPTURE ONLY. ORIGIN MUST REMAIN ALIVE AND INTACT.
CONSCIOUSNESS... OPTIONAL.
FWIIISH
FWIISH
FWIIISH

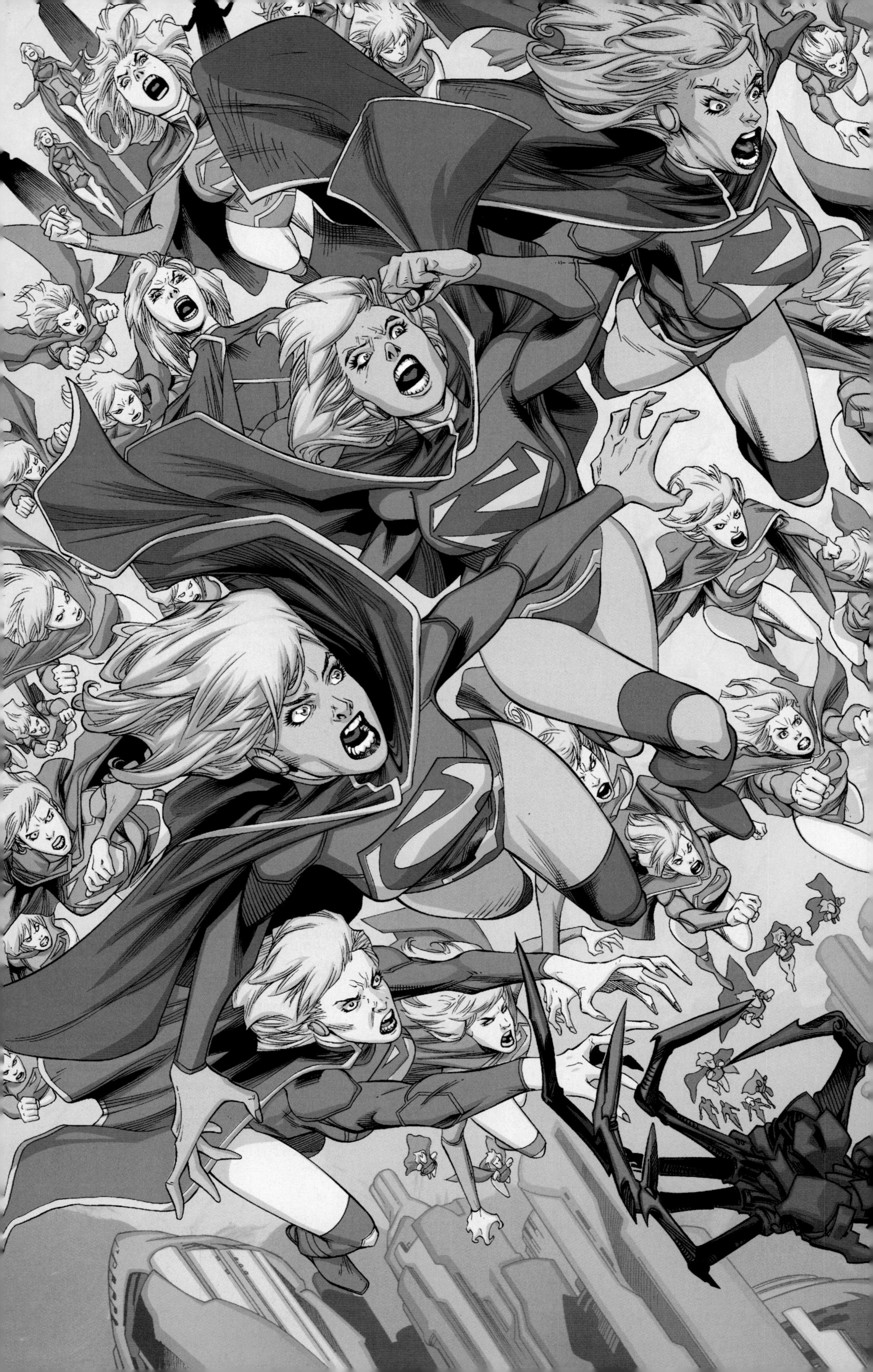

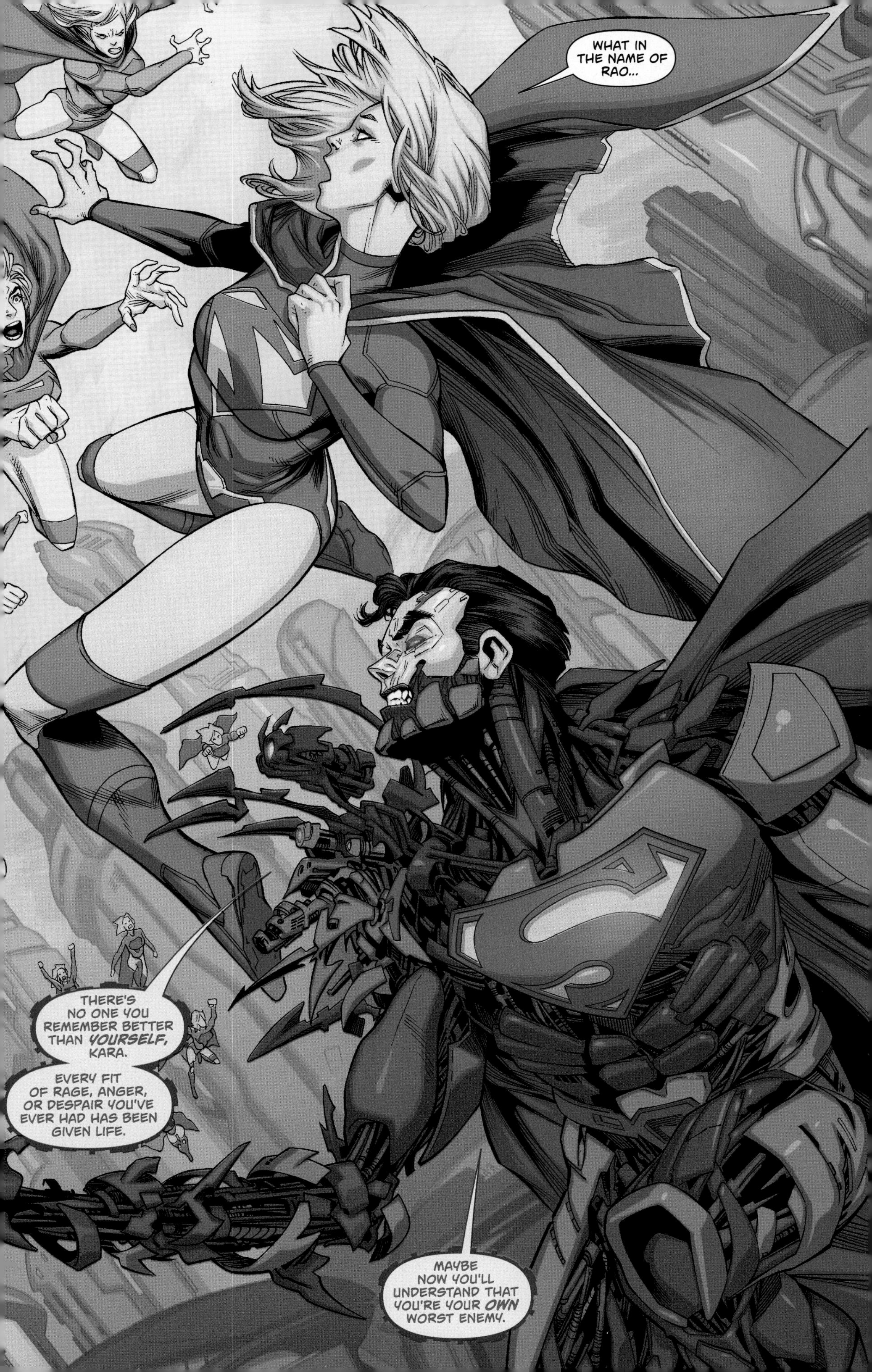
WHAT IN THE NAME OF RAO...
THERE'S NO ONE YOU REMEMBER BETTER THAN *YOURSELF*, KARA.
EVERY FIT OF RAGE, ANGER, OR DESPAIR YOU'VE EVER HAD HAS BEEN GIVEN LIFE.
MAYBE NOW YOU'LL UNDERSTAND THAT YOU'RE YOUR *OWN* WORST ENEMY.

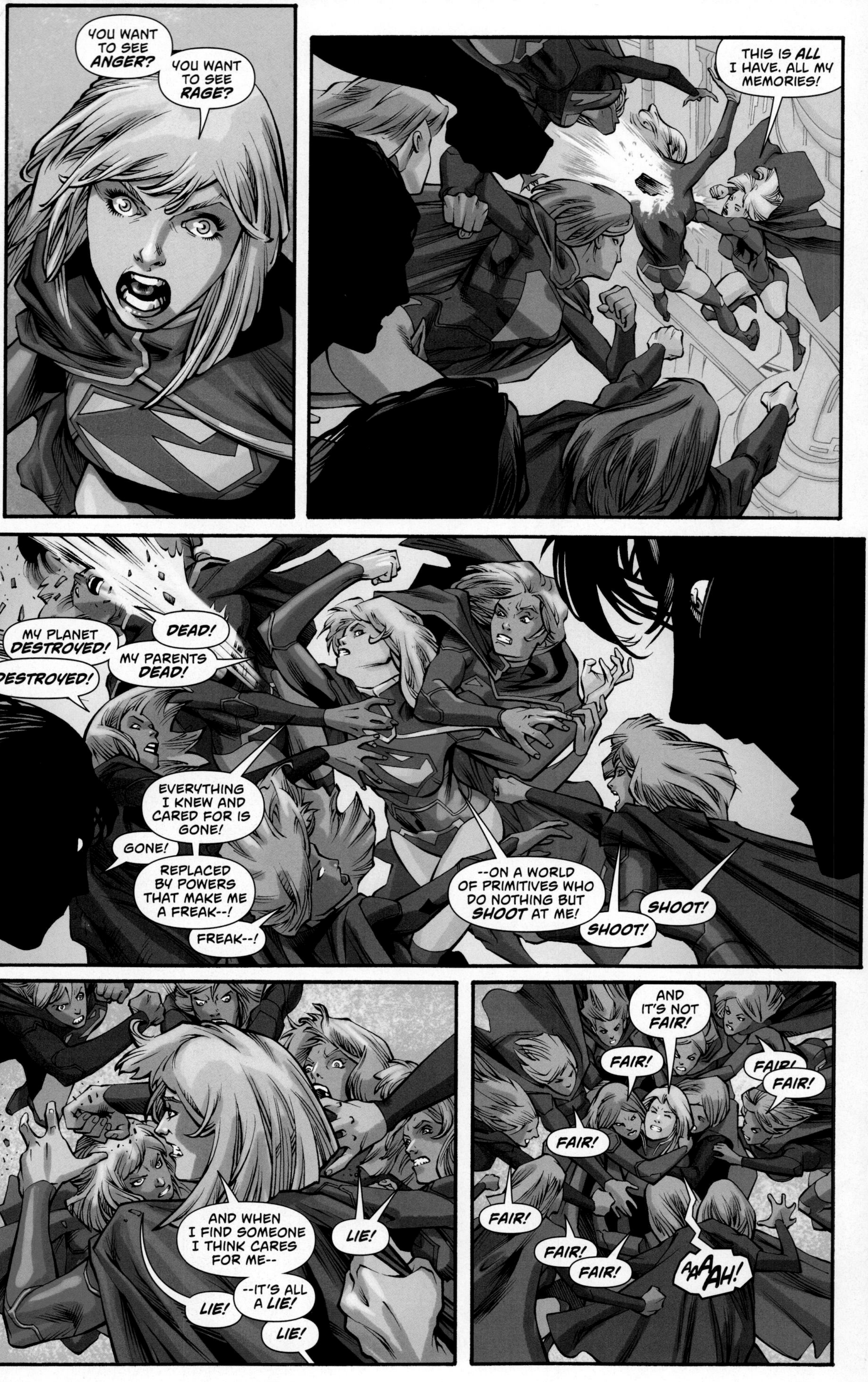
YOU WANT TO SEE ANGER?
YOU WANT TO SEE RAGE?
THIS IS ALL I HAVE. ALL MY MEMORIES!
MY PLANET DESTROYED!
DESTROYED!
DEAD!
MY PARENTS DEAD!
EVERYTHING I KNEW AND CARED FOR IS GONE!
GONE!
REPLACED BY POWERS THAT MAKE ME A FREAK--!
FREAK--!
--ON A WORLD OF PRIMITIVES WHO DO NOTHING BUT SHOOT AT ME!
SHOOT!
SHOOT!
AND WHEN I FIND SOMEONE I THINK CARES FOR ME--
LIE!
--IT'S ALL A LIE!
LIE!
LIE!
AND IT'S NOT FAIR!
FAIR!
FAIR!
FAIR!
FAIR!
FAIR!
FAIR!
FAIR!
AAAAH!

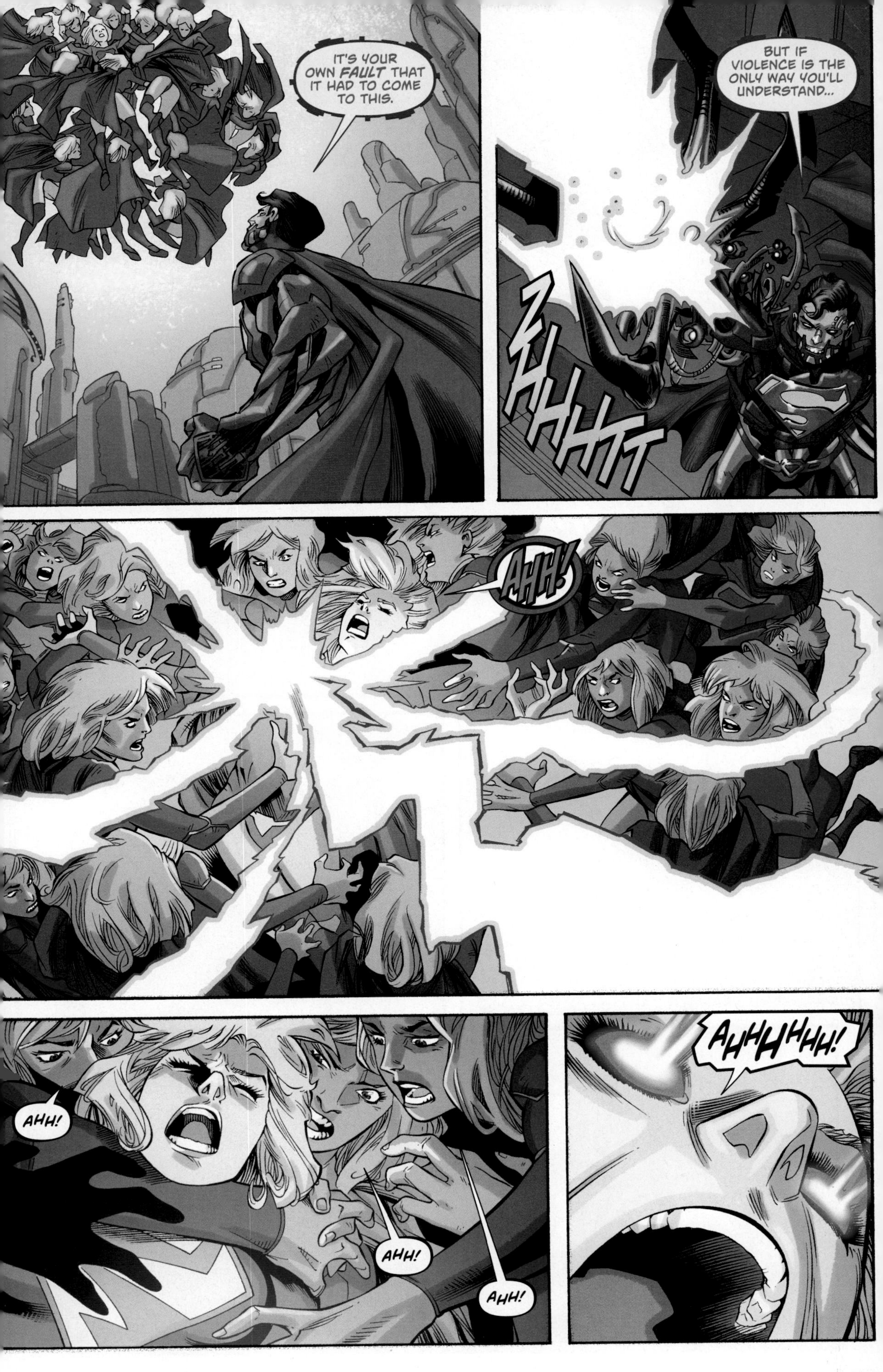
IT'S YOUR OWN FAULT THAT IT HAD TO COME TO THIS.
BUT IF VIOLENCE IS THE ONLY WAY YOU'LL UNDERSTAND...
ZZHHHTT
AHH!
AHH!
AHH!
AHH!
AHHHHHH!

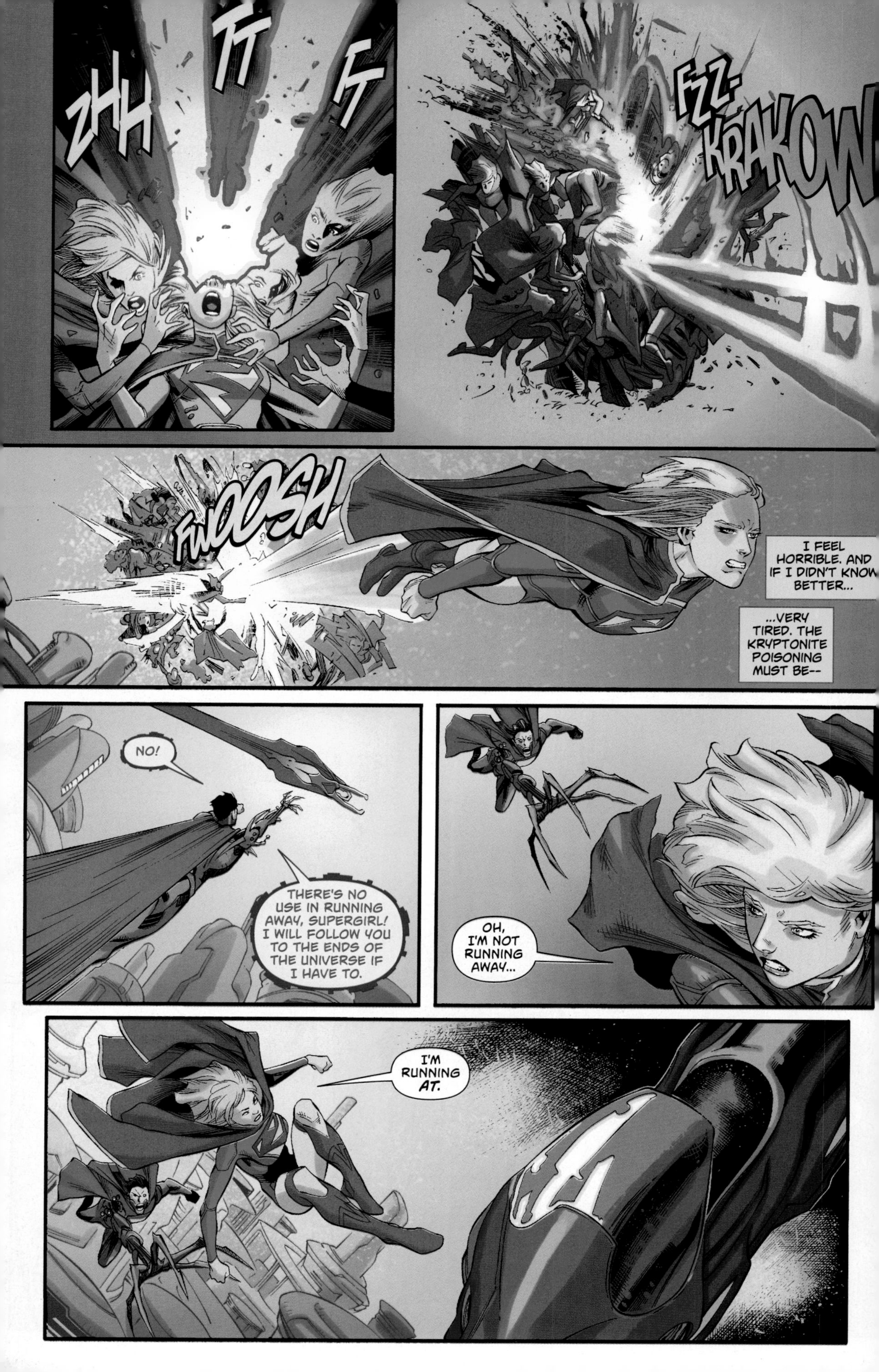

ZHH
TT
TT
FZZ-
KRAKOW
FWOOSH
I FEEL HORRIBLE. AND IF I DIDN'T KNOW BETTER...
...VERY TIRED. THE KRYPTONITE POISONING MUST BE--
NO!
THERE'S NO USE IN RUNNING AWAY, SUPERGIRL! I WILL FOLLOW YOU TO THE ENDS OF THE UNIVERSE IF I HAVE TO.
OH, I'M NOT RUNNING AWAY...
I'M RUNNING AT.

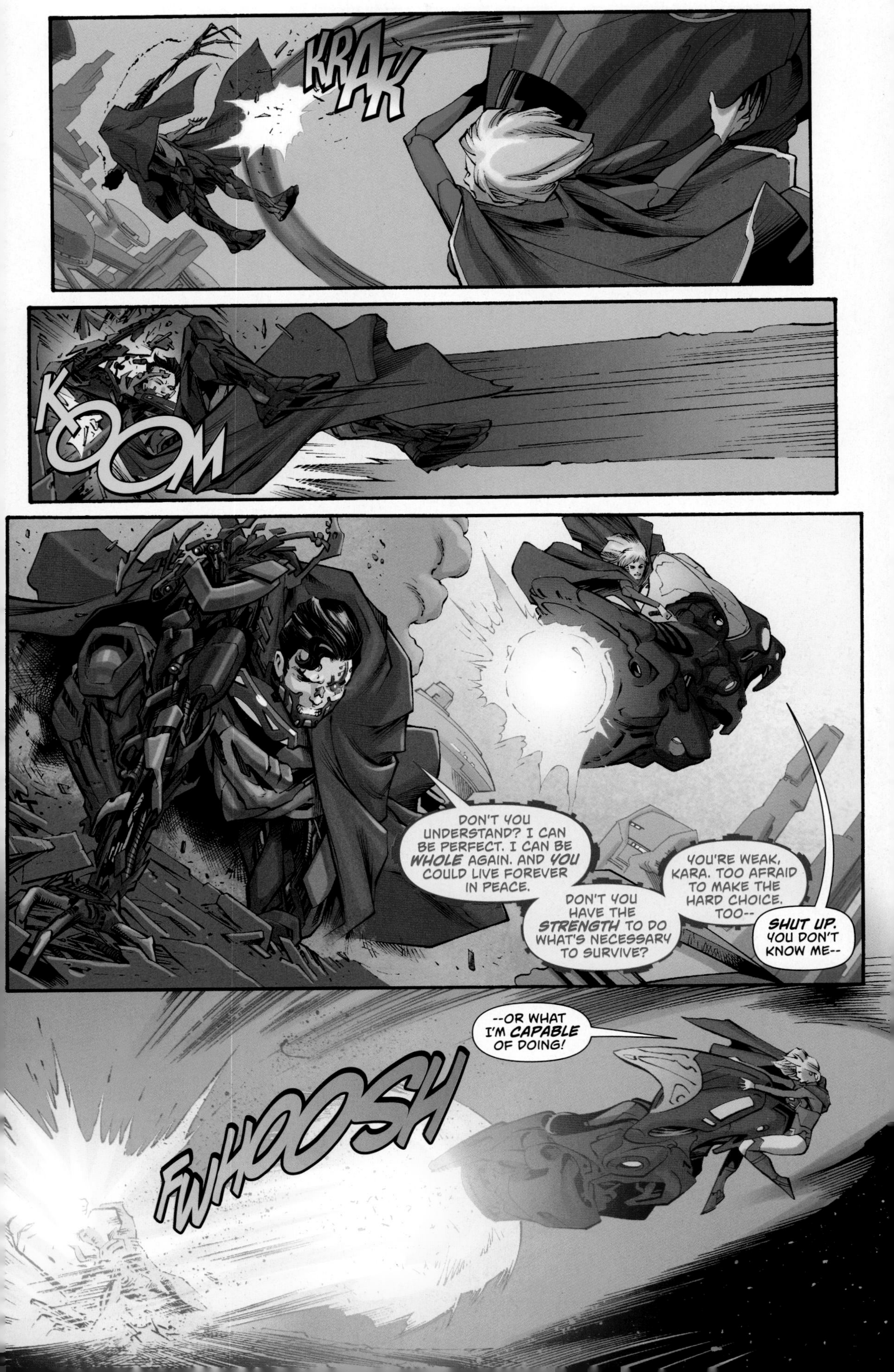
KRAK
KOOM
DON'T YOU UNDERSTAND? I CAN BE PERFECT. I CAN BE WHOLE AGAIN. AND YOU COULD LIVE FOREVER IN PEACE.
DON'T YOU HAVE THE STRENGTH TO DO WHAT'S NECESSARY TO SURVIVE?
YOU'RE WEAK, KARA. TOO AFRAID TO MAKE THE HARD CHOICE. TOO--
SHUT UP. YOU DON'T KNOW ME--
--OR WHAT I'M CAPABLE OF DOING!
FWHOOSH

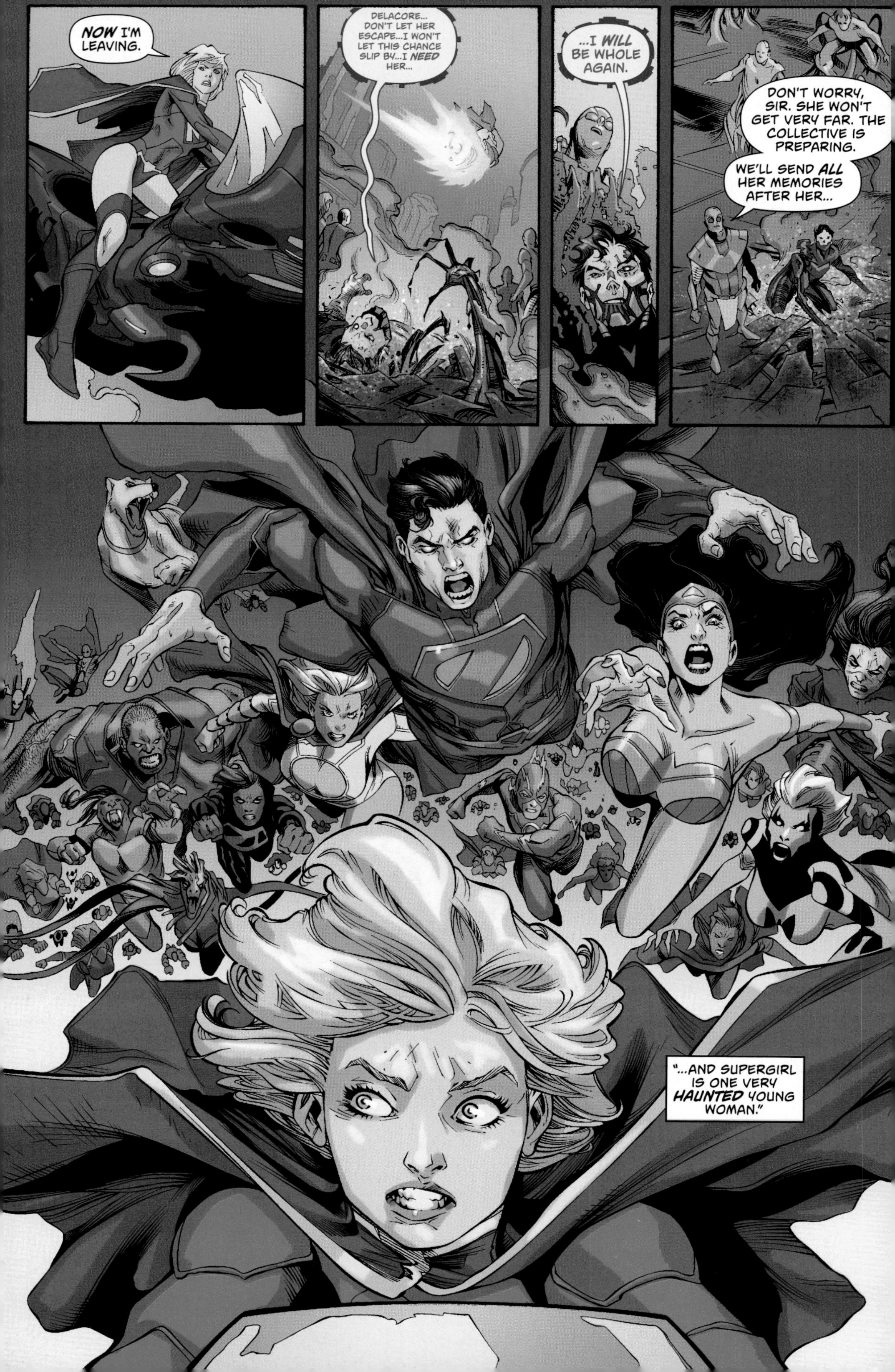
NOW I'M LEAVING.
DELACORE... DON'T LET HER ESCAPE...I WON'T LET THIS CHANCE SLIP BY...I NEED HER...
...I WILL BE WHOLE AGAIN.
DON'T WORRY, SIR. SHE WON'T GET VERY FAR. THE COLLECTIVE IS PREPARING.
WE'LL SEND ALL HER MEMORIES AFTER HER...
"...AND SUPERGIRL IS ONE VERY HAUNTED YOUNG WOMAN."

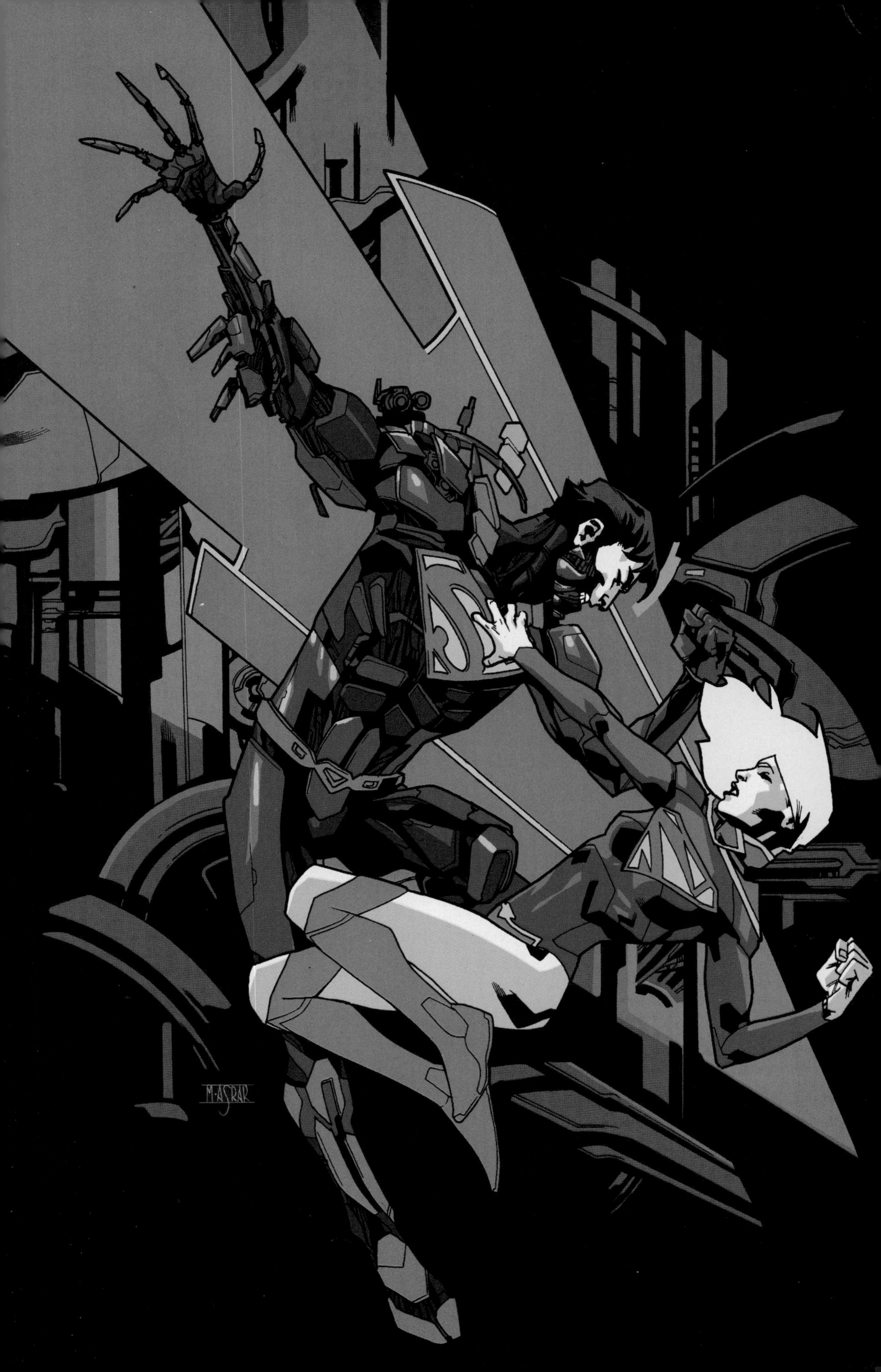

OUT OF THE PAST

MICHAEL ALAN NELSON writer **DIOGENES NEVES & CHAD HARDIN** pencillers **MARC DEERING & WAYNE FAUCHER** inkers
cover art by **MAHMUD ASRAR**

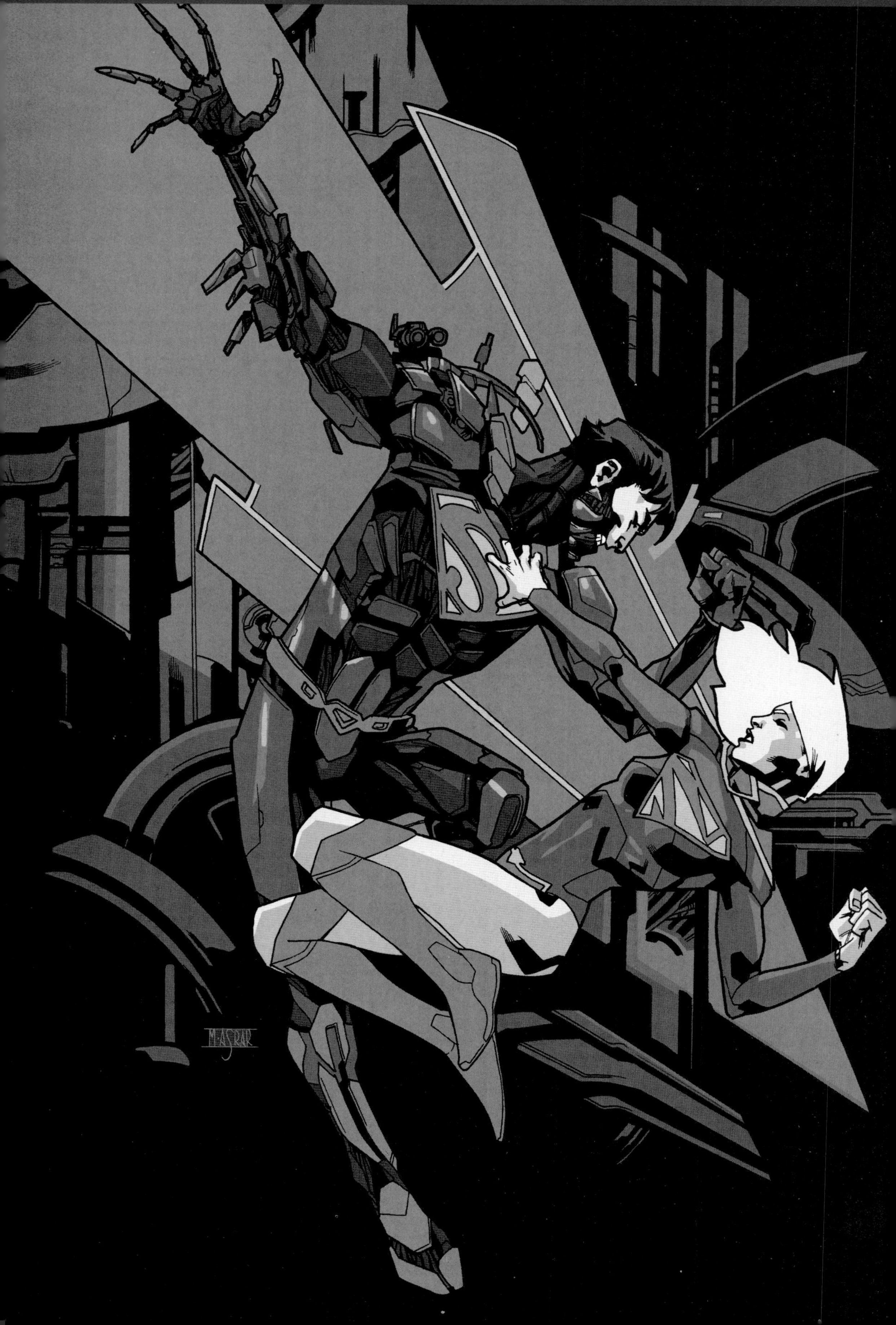

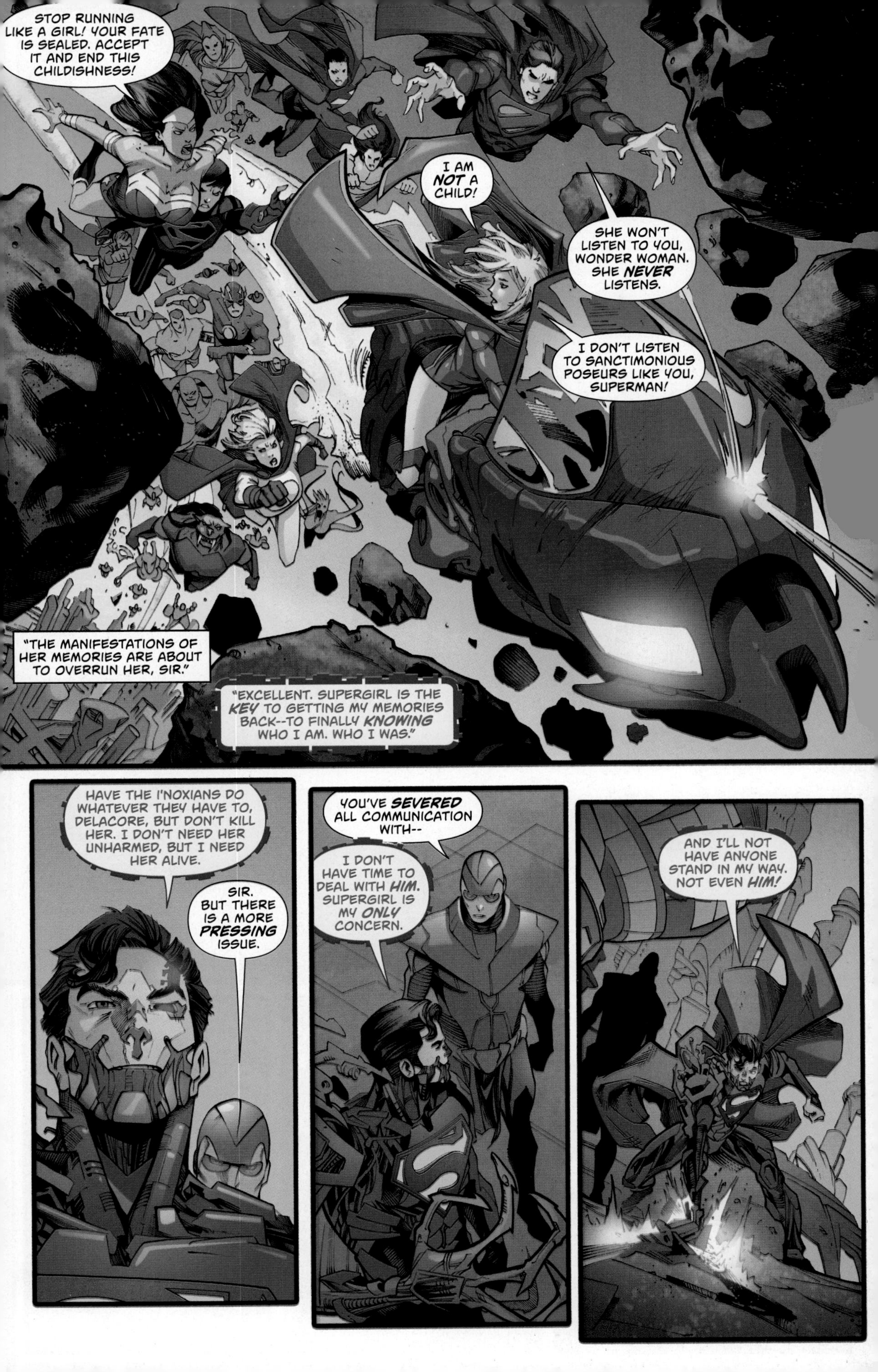
STOP RUNNING LIKE A GIRL! YOUR FATE IS SEALED. ACCEPT IT AND END THIS CHILDISHNESS!
I AM NOT A CHILD!
SHE WON'T LISTEN TO YOU, WONDER WOMAN. SHE NEVER LISTENS.
I DON'T LISTEN TO SANCTIMONIOUS POSEURS LIKE YOU, SUPERMAN!
"THE MANIFESTATIONS OF HER MEMORIES ARE ABOUT TO OVERRUN HER, SIR."
"EXCELLENT. SUPERGIRL IS THE KEY TO GETTING MY MEMORIES BACK--TO FINALLY KNOWING WHO I AM. WHO I WAS."
HAVE THE I'NOXIANS DO WHATEVER THEY HAVE TO, DELACORE, BUT DON'T KILL HER. I DON'T NEED HER UNHARMED, BUT I NEED HER ALIVE.
SIR. BUT THERE IS A MORE PRESSING ISSUE.
YOU'VE SEVERED ALL COMMUNICATION WITH--
I DON'T HAVE TIME TO DEAL WITH HIM. SUPERGIRL IS MY ONLY CONCERN.
AND I'LL NOT HAVE ANYONE STAND IN MY WAY. NOT EVEN HIM!

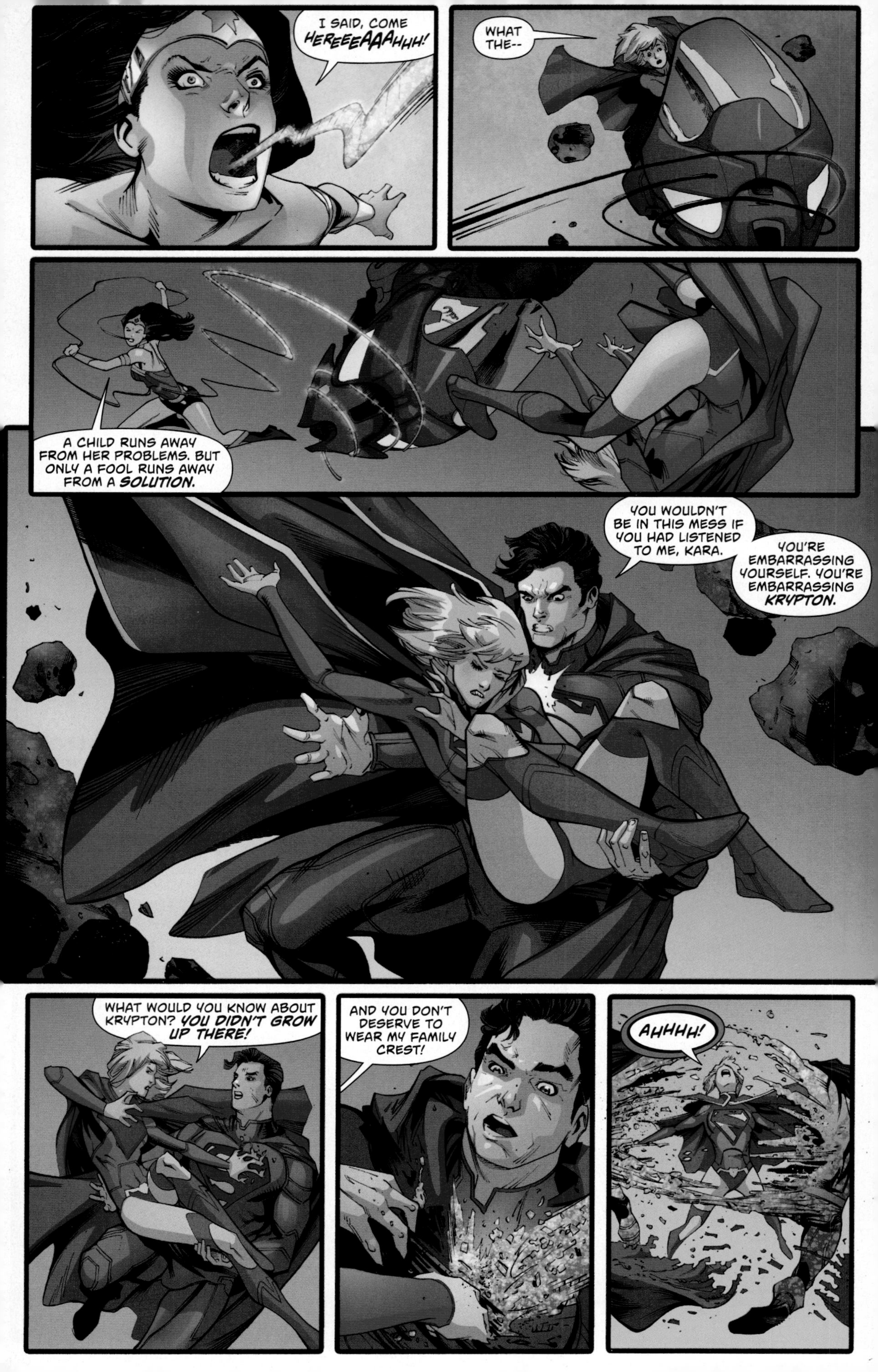
I SAID, COME HEREEEEAAAHHH!
WHAT THE--
A CHILD RUNS AWAY FROM HER PROBLEMS. BUT ONLY A FOOL RUNS AWAY FROM A SOLUTION.
YOU WOULDN'T BE IN THIS MESS IF YOU HAD LISTENED TO ME, KARA.
YOU'RE EMBARRASSING YOURSELF. YOU'RE EMBARRASSING KRYPTON.
WHAT WOULD YOU KNOW ABOUT KRYPTON? YOU DIDN'T GROW UP THERE!
AND YOU DON'T DESERVE TO WEAR MY FAMILY CREST!
AHHHH!

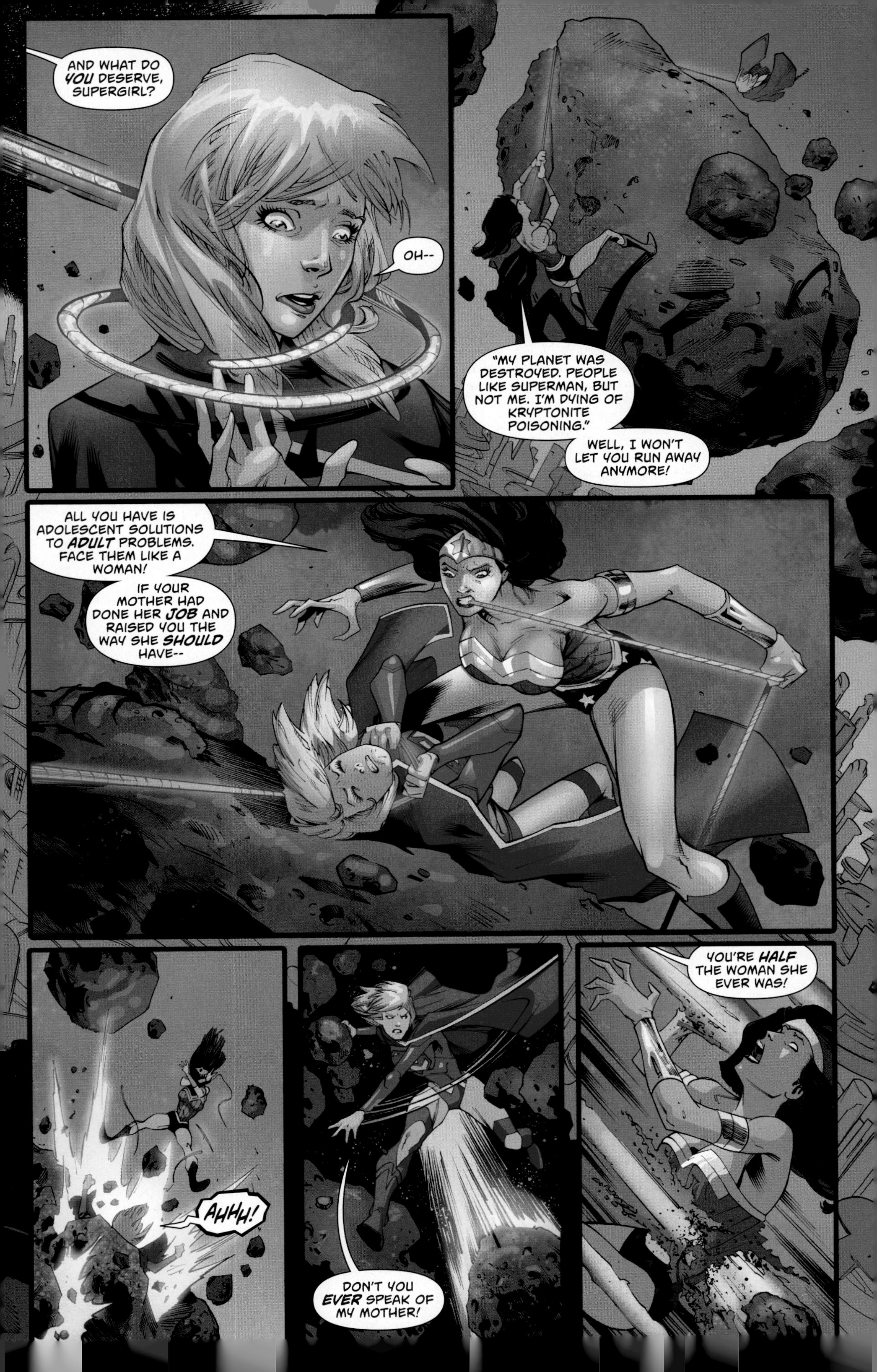
AND WHAT DO YOU DESERVE, SUPERGIRL?
OH--
"MY PLANET WAS DESTROYED. PEOPLE LIKE SUPERMAN, BUT NOT ME. I'M DYING OF KRYPTONITE POISONING."
WELL, I WON'T LET YOU RUN AWAY ANYMORE!
ALL YOU HAVE IS ADOLESCENT SOLUTIONS TO ADULT PROBLEMS. FACE THEM LIKE A WOMAN!
IF YOUR MOTHER HAD DONE HER JOB AND RAISED YOU THE WAY SHE SHOULD HAVE--
AHHH!
DON'T YOU EVER SPEAK OF MY MOTHER!
YOU'RE HALF THE WOMAN SHE EVER WAS!

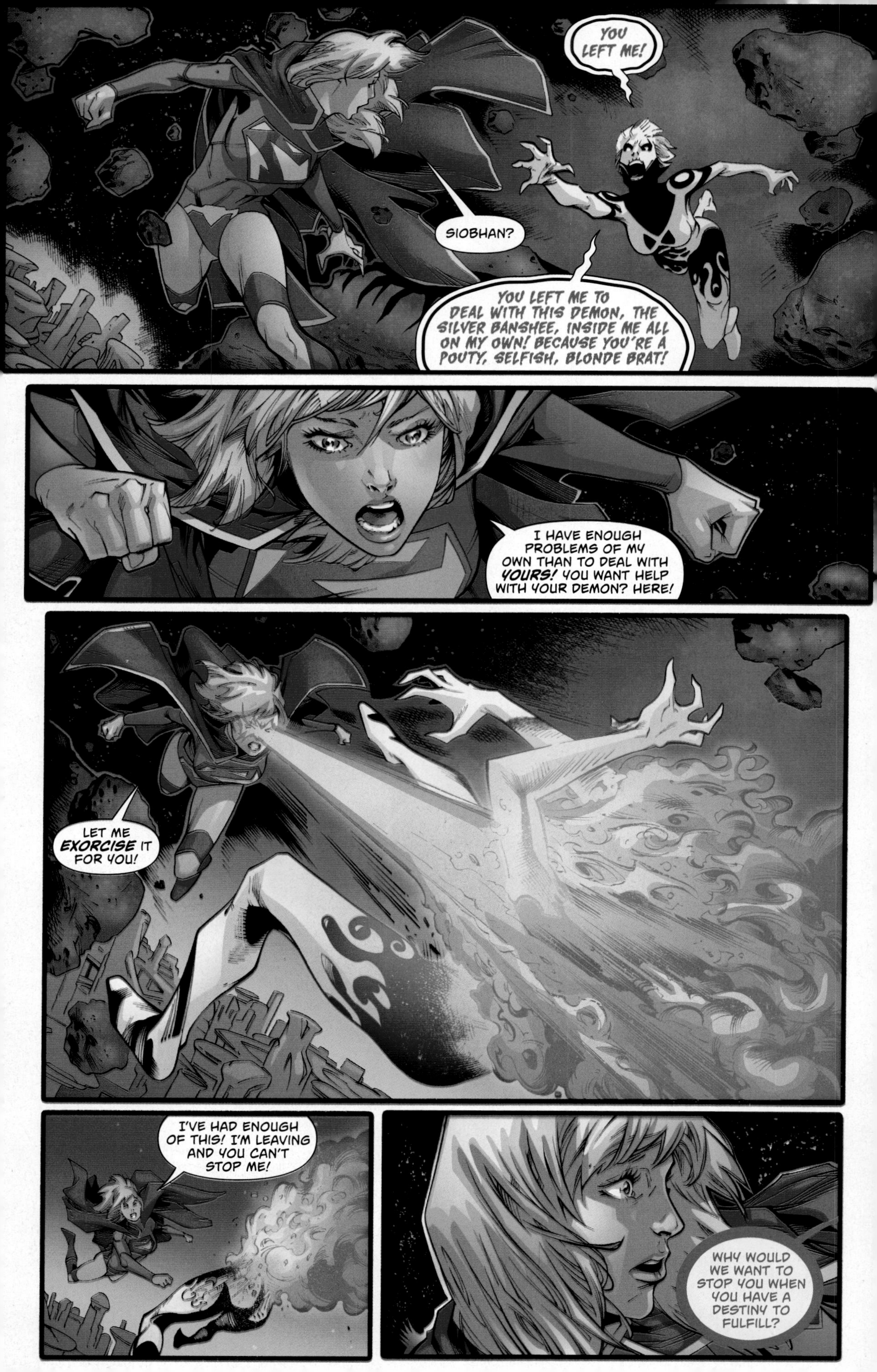
YOU LEFT ME!
SIOBHAN?
YOU LEFT ME TO DEAL WITH THIS DEMON, THE SILVER BANSHEE, INSIDE ME ALL ON MY OWN! BECAUSE YOU'RE A POUTY, SELFISH, BLONDE BRAT!
I HAVE ENOUGH PROBLEMS OF MY OWN THAN TO DEAL WITH YOURS! YOU WANT HELP WITH YOUR DEMON? HERE!
LET ME EXORCISE IT FOR YOU!
I'VE HAD ENOUGH OF THIS! I'M LEAVING AND YOU CAN'T STOP ME!
WHY WOULD WE WANT TO STOP YOU WHEN YOU HAVE A DESTINY TO FULFILL?

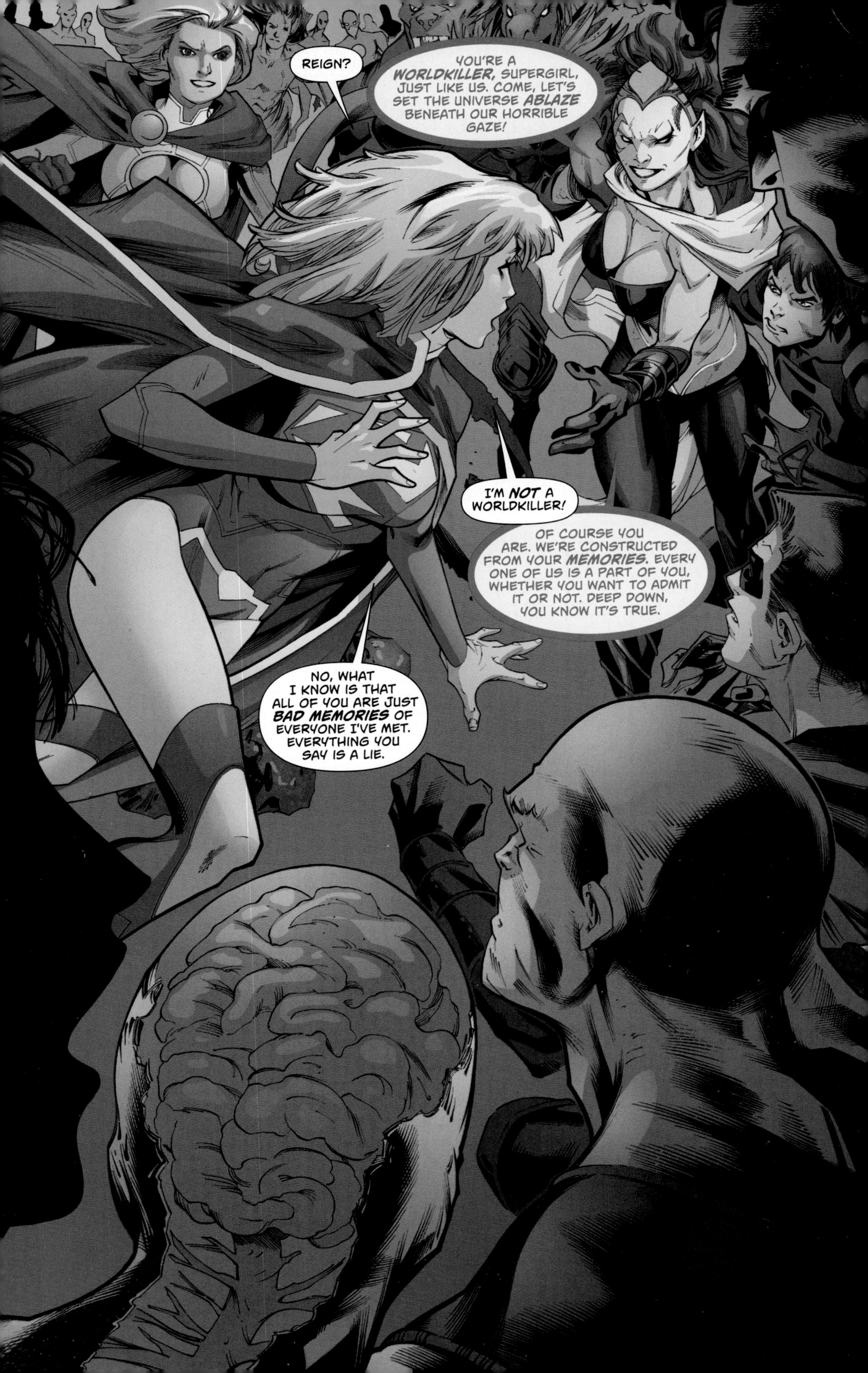
REIGN?
YOU'RE A WORLDKILLER, SUPERGIRL, JUST LIKE US. COME, LET'S SET THE UNIVERSE ABLAZE BENEATH OUR HORRIBLE GAZE!
I'M NOT A WORLDKILLER!
OF COURSE YOU ARE. WE'RE CONSTRUCTED FROM YOUR MEMORIES. EVERY ONE OF US IS A PART OF YOU, WHETHER YOU WANT TO ADMIT IT OR NOT. DEEP DOWN, YOU KNOW IT'S TRUE.
NO, WHAT I KNOW IS THAT ALL OF YOU ARE JUST BAD MEMORIES OF EVERYONE I'VE MET. EVERYTHING YOU SAY IS A LIE.

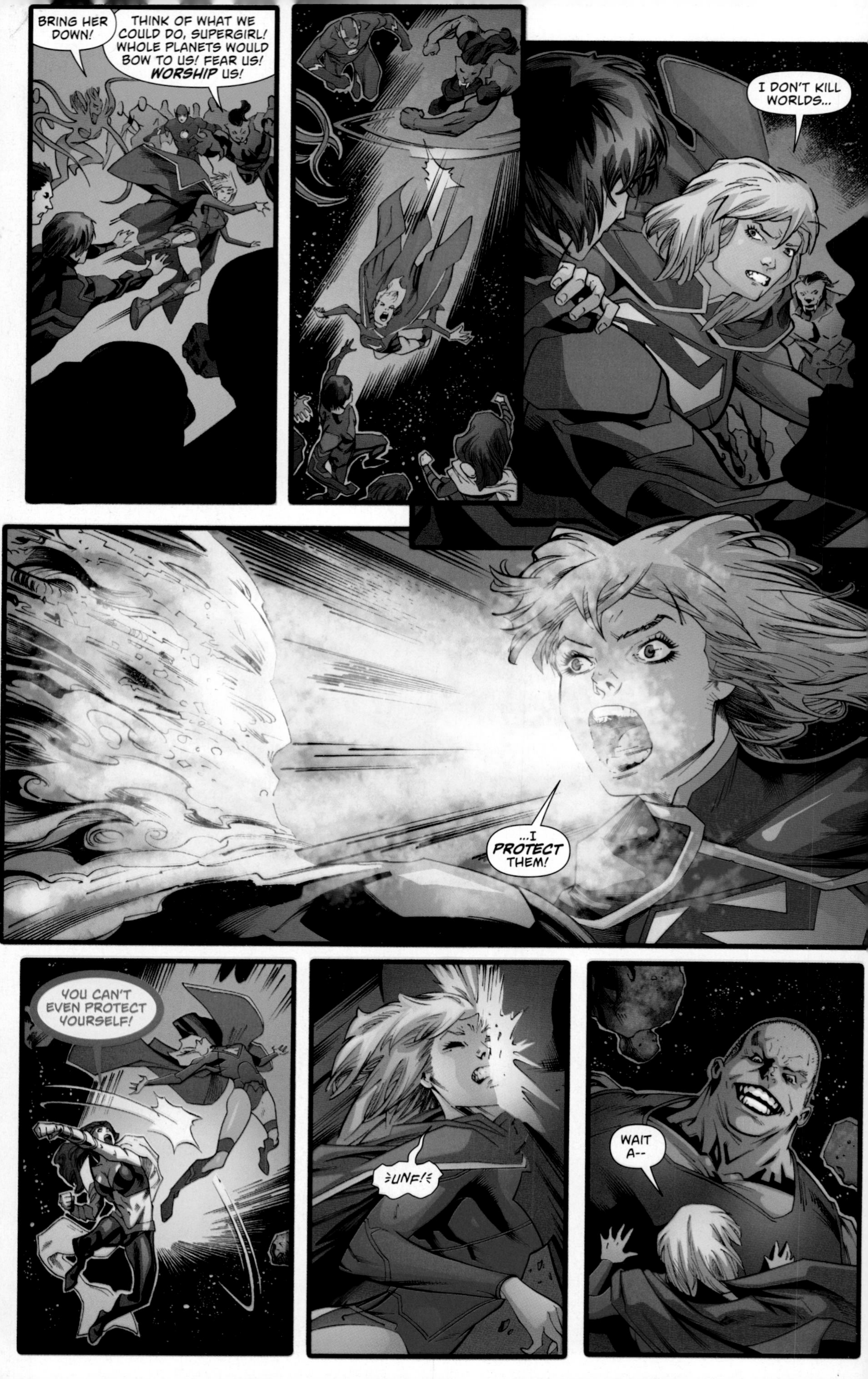
BRING HER DOWN!
THINK OF WHAT WE COULD DO, SUPERGIRL! WHOLE PLANETS WOULD BOW TO US! FEAR US! WORSHIP US!
I DON'T KILL WORLDS...
...I PROTECT THEM!
YOU CAN'T EVEN PROTECT YOURSELF!
UNF!
WAIT A--

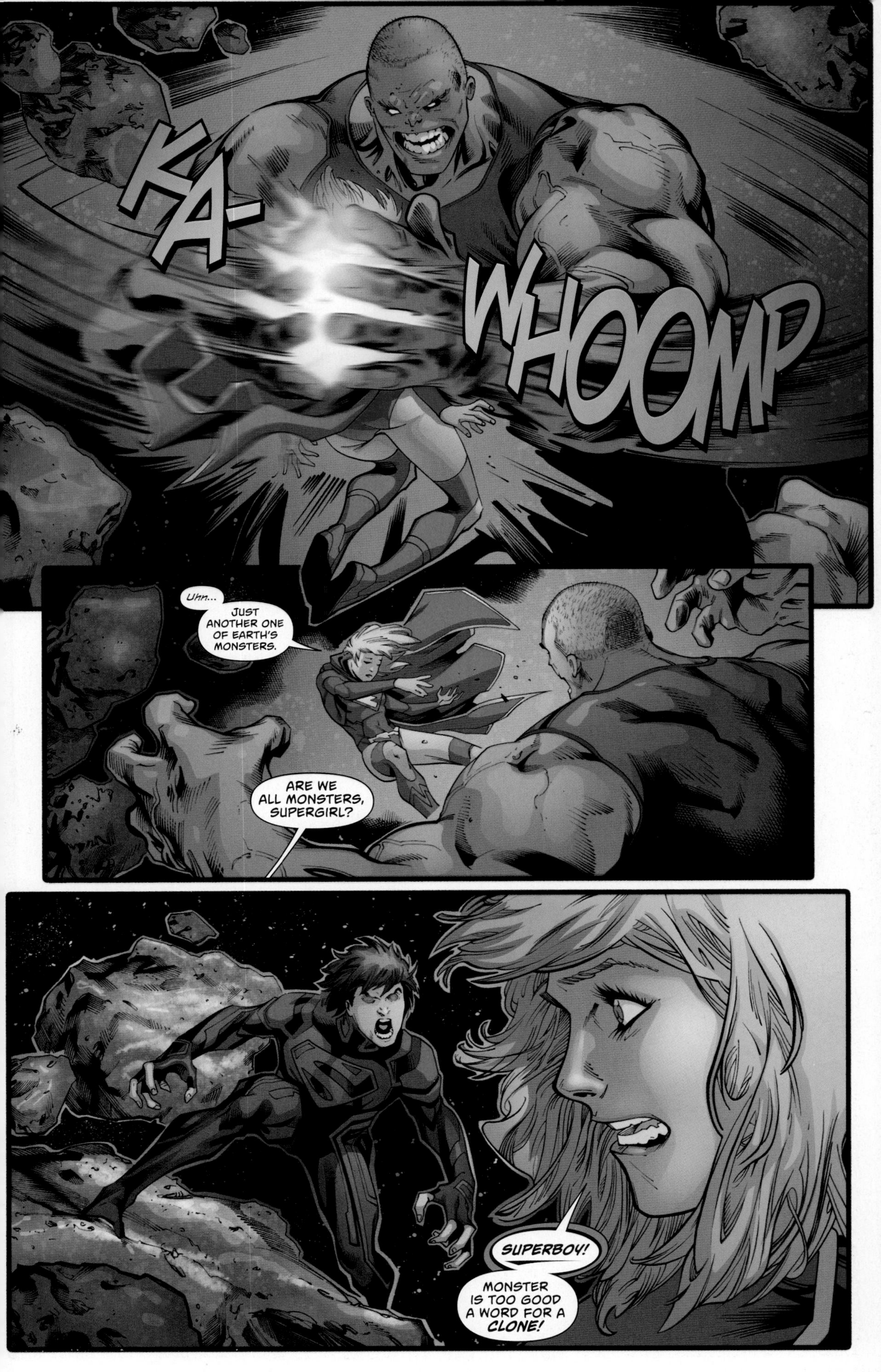
KA-
WHOOMP
Uhn...
JUST ANOTHER ONE OF EARTH'S MONSTERS.
ARE WE ALL MONSTERS, SUPERGIRL?
SUPERBOY!
MONSTER IS TOO GOOD A WORD FOR A CLONE!

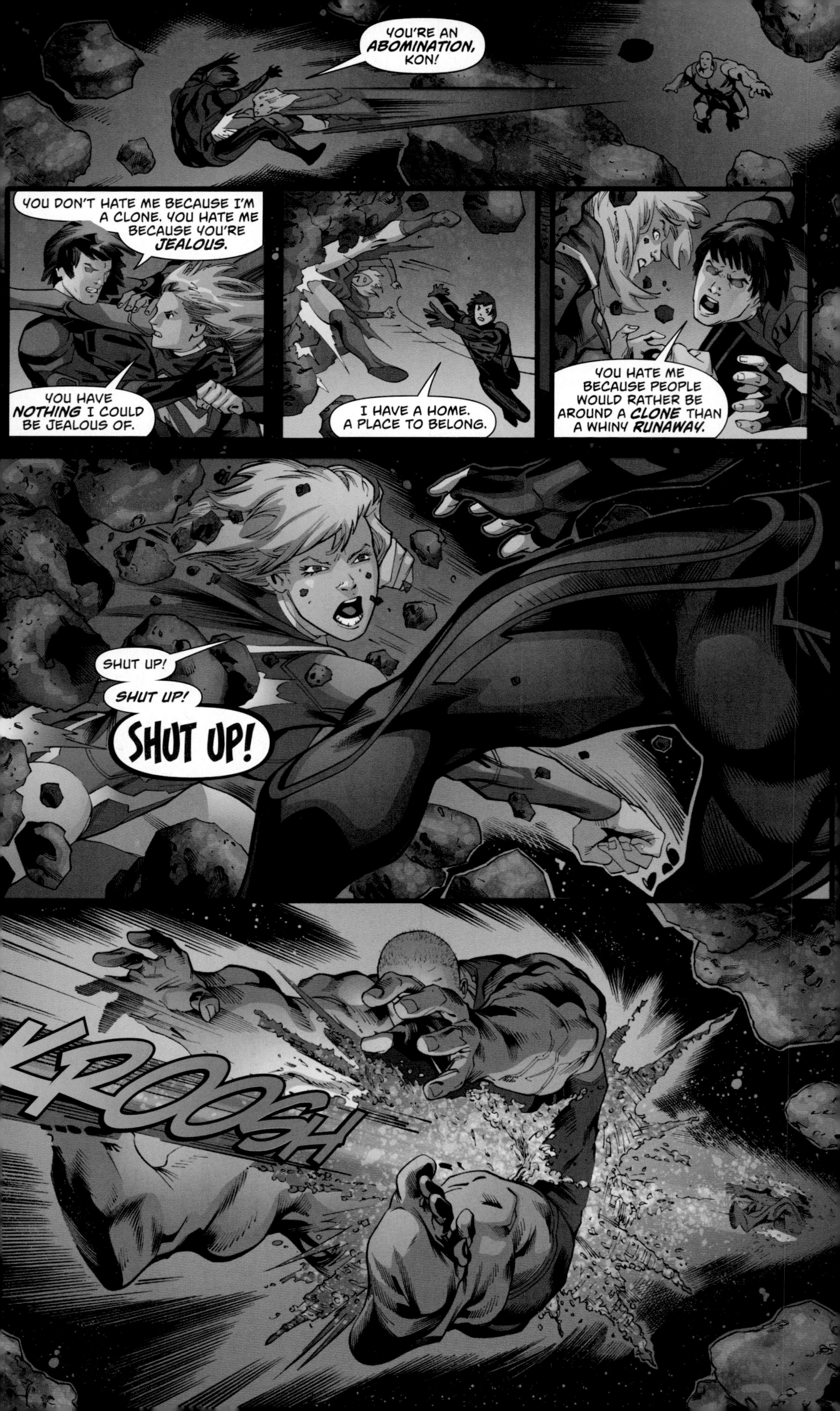
YOU'RE AN ABOMINATION, KON!
YOU DON'T HATE ME BECAUSE I'M A CLONE. YOU HATE ME BECAUSE YOU'RE JEALOUS.
YOU HAVE NOTHING I COULD BE JEALOUS OF.
I HAVE A HOME. A PLACE TO BELONG.
YOU HATE ME BECAUSE PEOPLE WOULD RATHER BE AROUND A CLONE THAN A WHINY RUNAWAY.
SHUT UP!
SHUT UP!
SHUT UP!
KROOSH

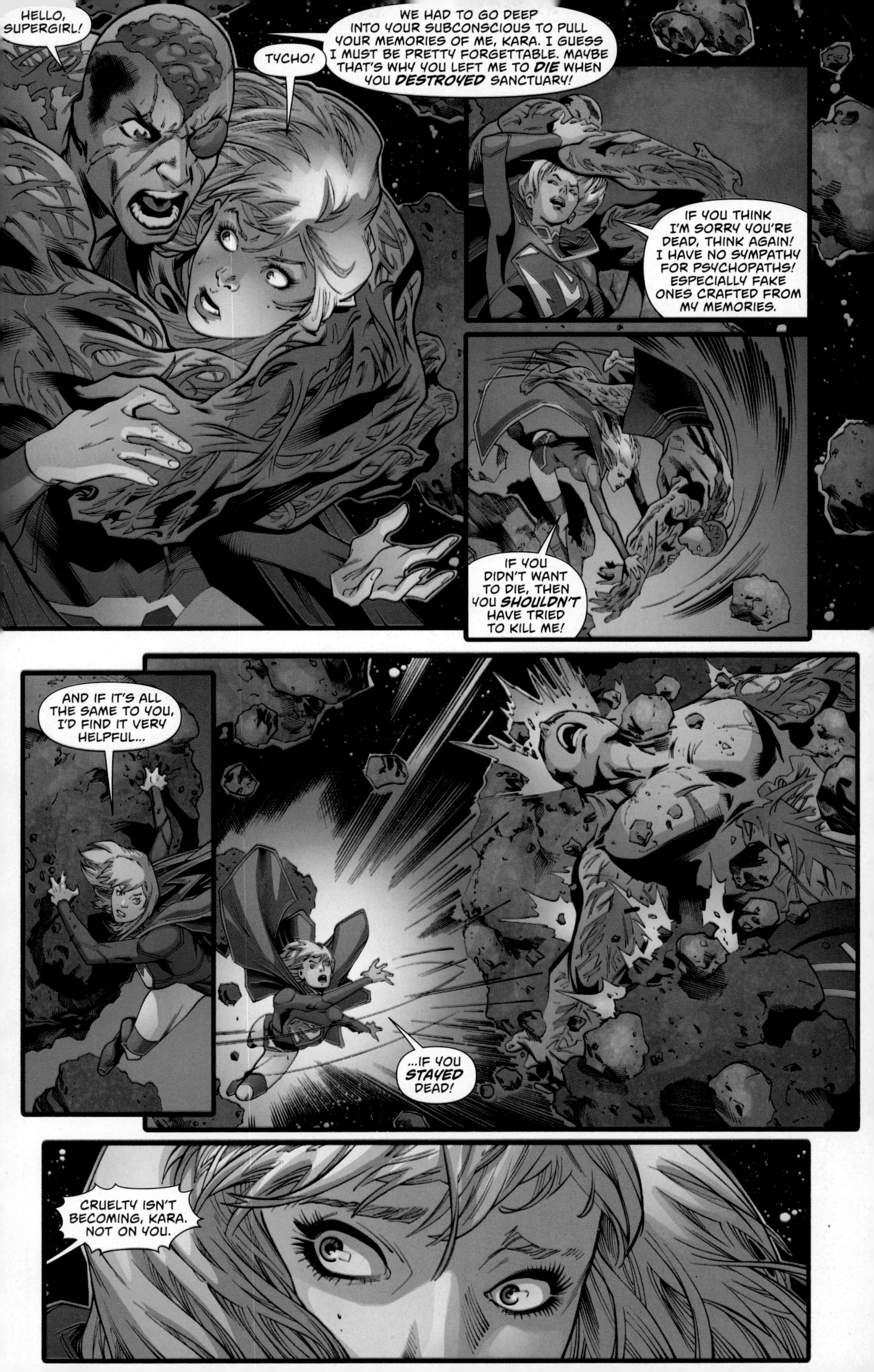
HELLO, SUPERGIRL!
TYCHO!
WE HAD TO GO DEEP INTO YOUR SUBCONSCIOUS TO PULL YOUR MEMORIES OF ME, KARA. I GUESS I MUST BE PRETTY FORGETTABLE. MAYBE THAT'S WHY YOU LEFT ME TO DIE WHEN YOU DESTROYED SANCTUARY!
IF YOU THINK I'M SORRY YOU'RE DEAD, THINK AGAIN! I HAVE NO SYMPATHY FOR PSYCHOPATHS! ESPECIALLY FAKE ONES CRAFTED FROM MY MEMORIES.
IF YOU DIDN'T WANT TO DIE, THEN YOU SHOULDN'T HAVE TRIED TO KILL ME!
AND IF IT'S ALL THE SAME TO YOU, I'D FIND IT VERY HELPFUL...
...IF YOU STAYED DEAD!
CRUELTY ISN'T BECOMING, KARA. NOT ON YOU.

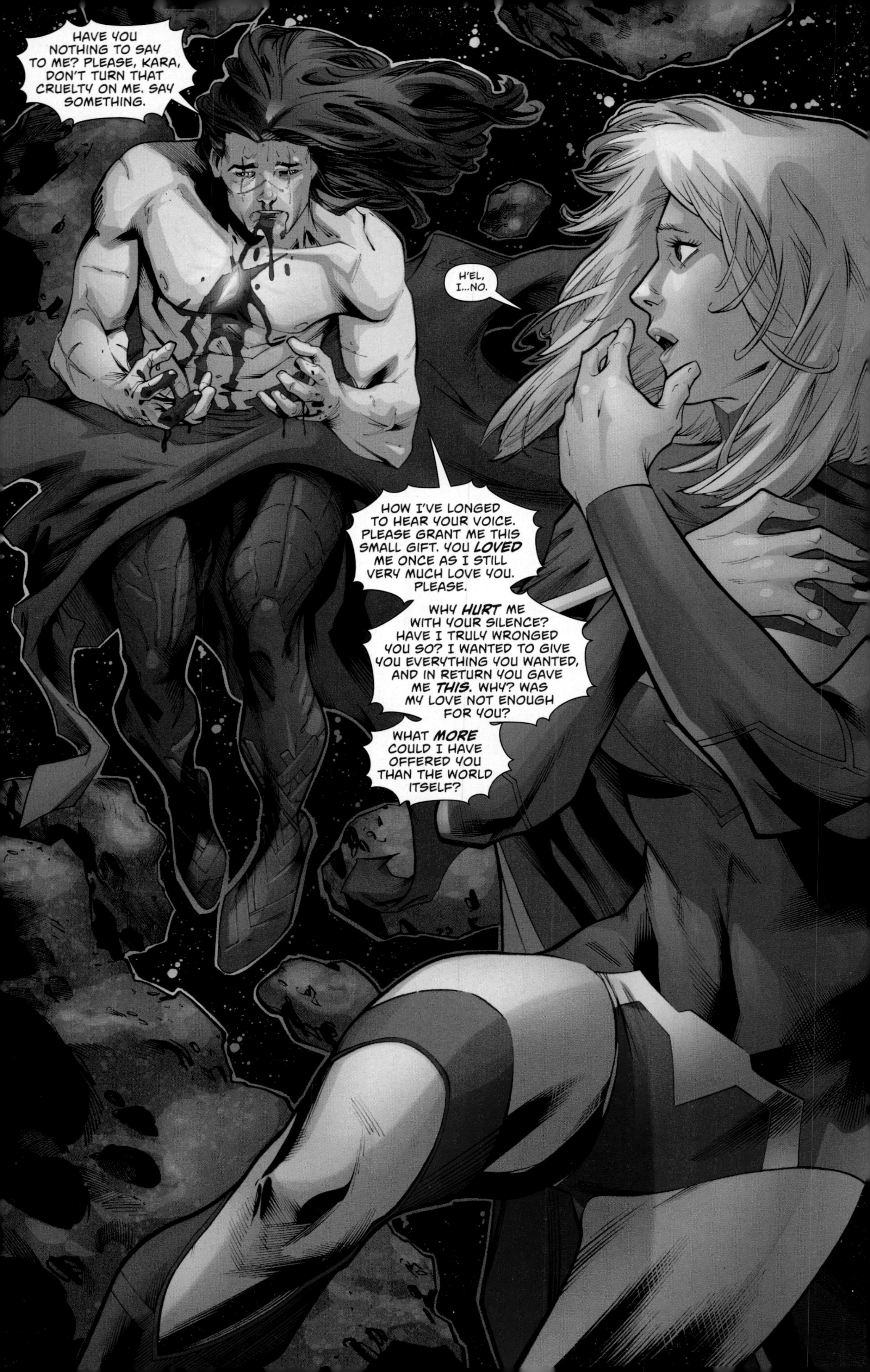
HAVE YOU NOTHING TO SAY TO ME? PLEASE, KARA, DON'T TURN THAT CRUELTY ON ME. SAY SOMETHING.
H'EL, I...NO.
HOW I'VE LONGED TO HEAR YOUR VOICE. PLEASE GRANT ME THIS SMALL GIFT. YOU LOVED ME ONCE AS I STILL VERY MUCH LOVE YOU. PLEASE.
WHY HURT ME WITH YOUR SILENCE? HAVE I TRULY WRONGED YOU SO? I WANTED TO GIVE YOU EVERYTHING YOU WANTED, AND IN RETURN YOU GAVE ME THIS. WHY? WAS MY LOVE NOT ENOUGH FOR YOU?
WHAT MORE COULD I HAVE OFFERED YOU THAN THE WORLD ITSELF?

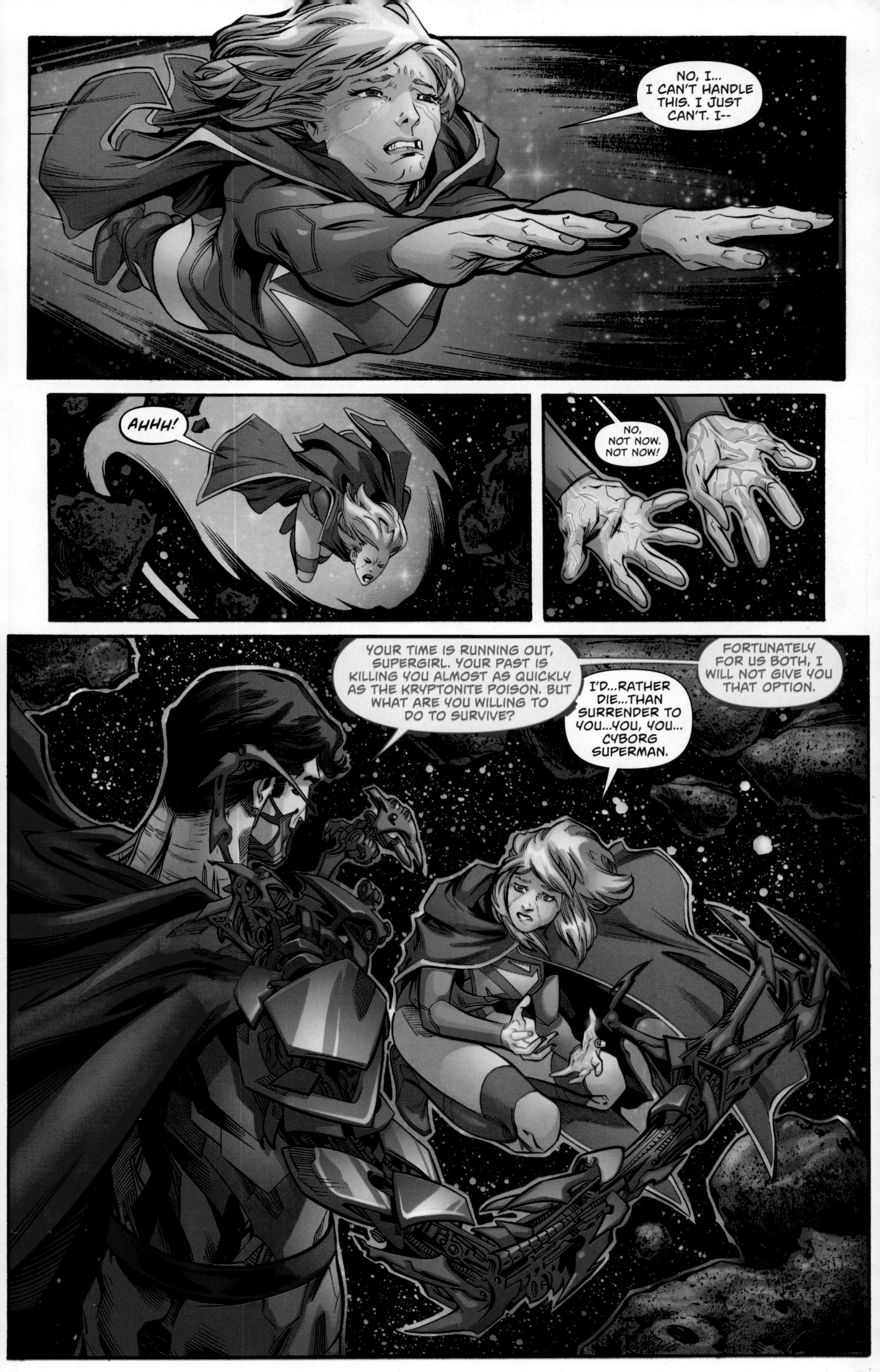
NO, I... I CAN'T HANDLE THIS. I JUST CAN'T. I--
AHHH!
NO, NOT NOW. NOT NOW!
YOUR TIME IS RUNNING OUT, SUPERGIRL. YOUR PAST IS KILLING YOU ALMOST AS QUICKLY AS THE KRYPTONITE POISON. BUT WHAT ARE YOU WILLING TO DO TO SURVIVE?
I'D...RATHER DIE...THAN SURRENDER TO YOU...YOU, YOU... CYBORG SUPERMAN.
FORTUNATELY FOR US BOTH, I WILL NOT GIVE YOU THAT OPTION.

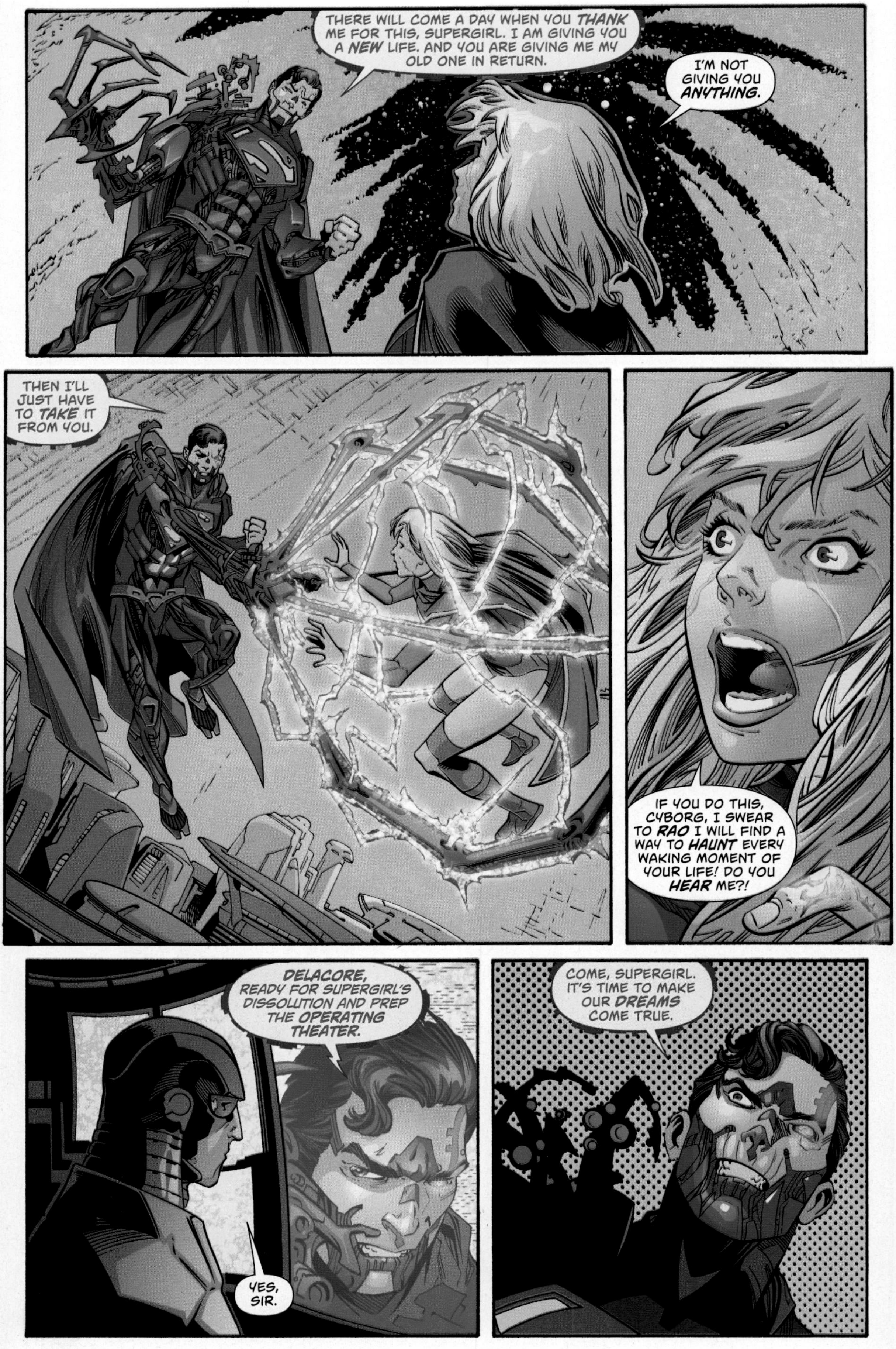
THERE WILL COME A DAY WHEN YOU THANK ME FOR THIS, SUPERGIRL. I AM GIVING YOU A NEW LIFE. AND YOU ARE GIVING ME MY OLD ONE IN RETURN.
I'M NOT GIVING YOU ANYTHING.
THEN I'LL JUST HAVE TO TAKE IT FROM YOU.
IF YOU DO THIS, CYBORG, I SWEAR TO RAO I WILL FIND A WAY TO HAUNT EVERY WAKING MOMENT OF YOUR LIFE! DO YOU HEAR ME?!
DELACORE, READY FOR SUPERGIRL'S DISSOLUTION AND PREP THE OPERATING THEATER.
YES, SIR.
COME, SUPERGIRL. IT'S TIME TO MAKE OUR DREAMS COME TRUE.

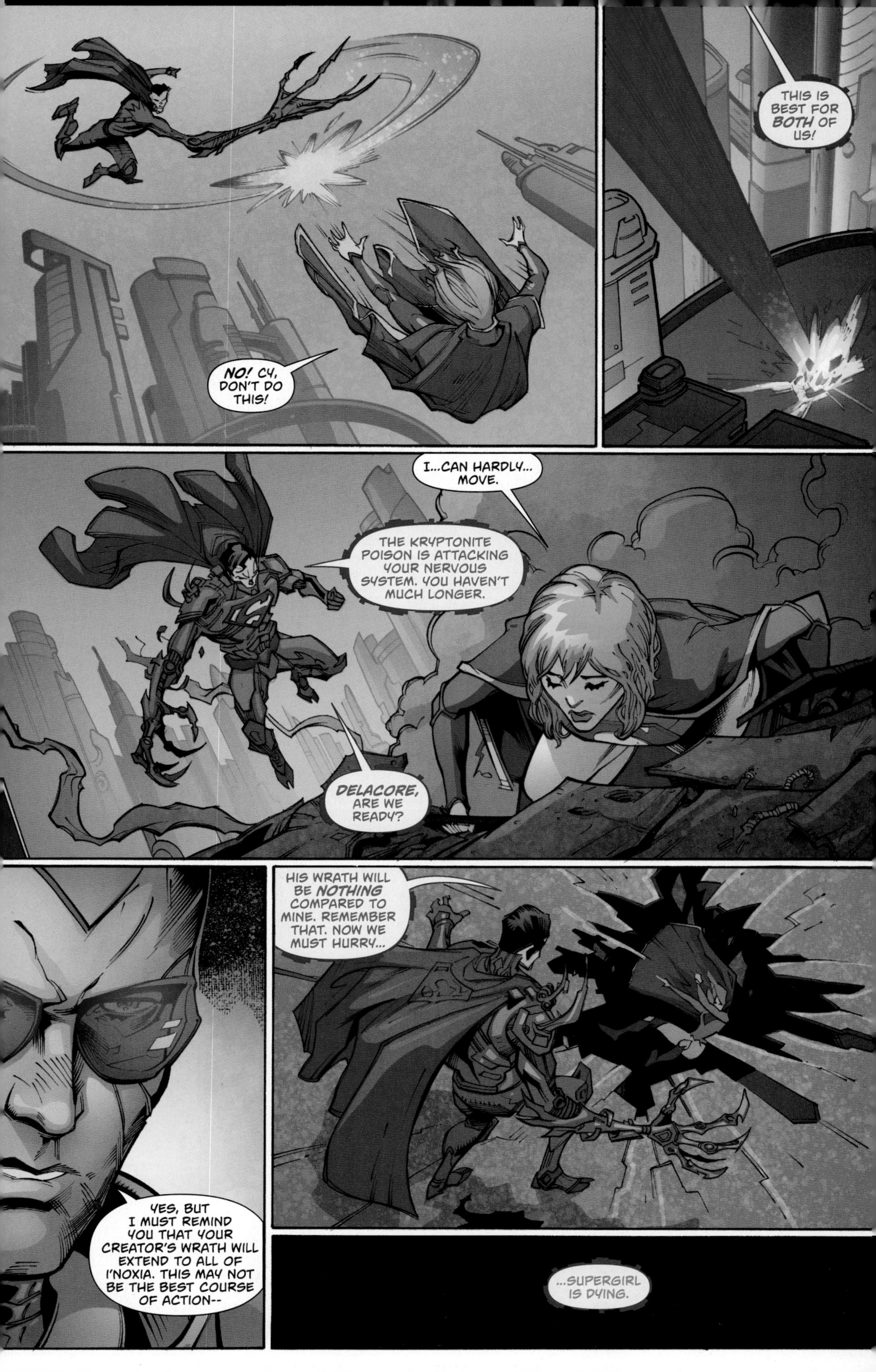
NO! CY, DON'T DO THIS!
THIS IS BEST FOR BOTH OF US!
I...CAN HARDLY... MOVE.
THE KRYPTONITE POISON IS ATTACKING YOUR NERVOUS SYSTEM. YOU HAVEN'T MUCH LONGER.
DELACORE, ARE WE READY?
YES, BUT I MUST REMIND YOU THAT YOUR CREATOR'S WRATH WILL EXTEND TO ALL OF I'NOXIA. THIS MAY NOT BE THE BEST COURSE OF ACTION--
HIS WRATH WILL BE NOTHING COMPARED TO MINE. REMEMBER THAT. NOW WE MUST HURRY...
...SUPERGIRL IS DYING.

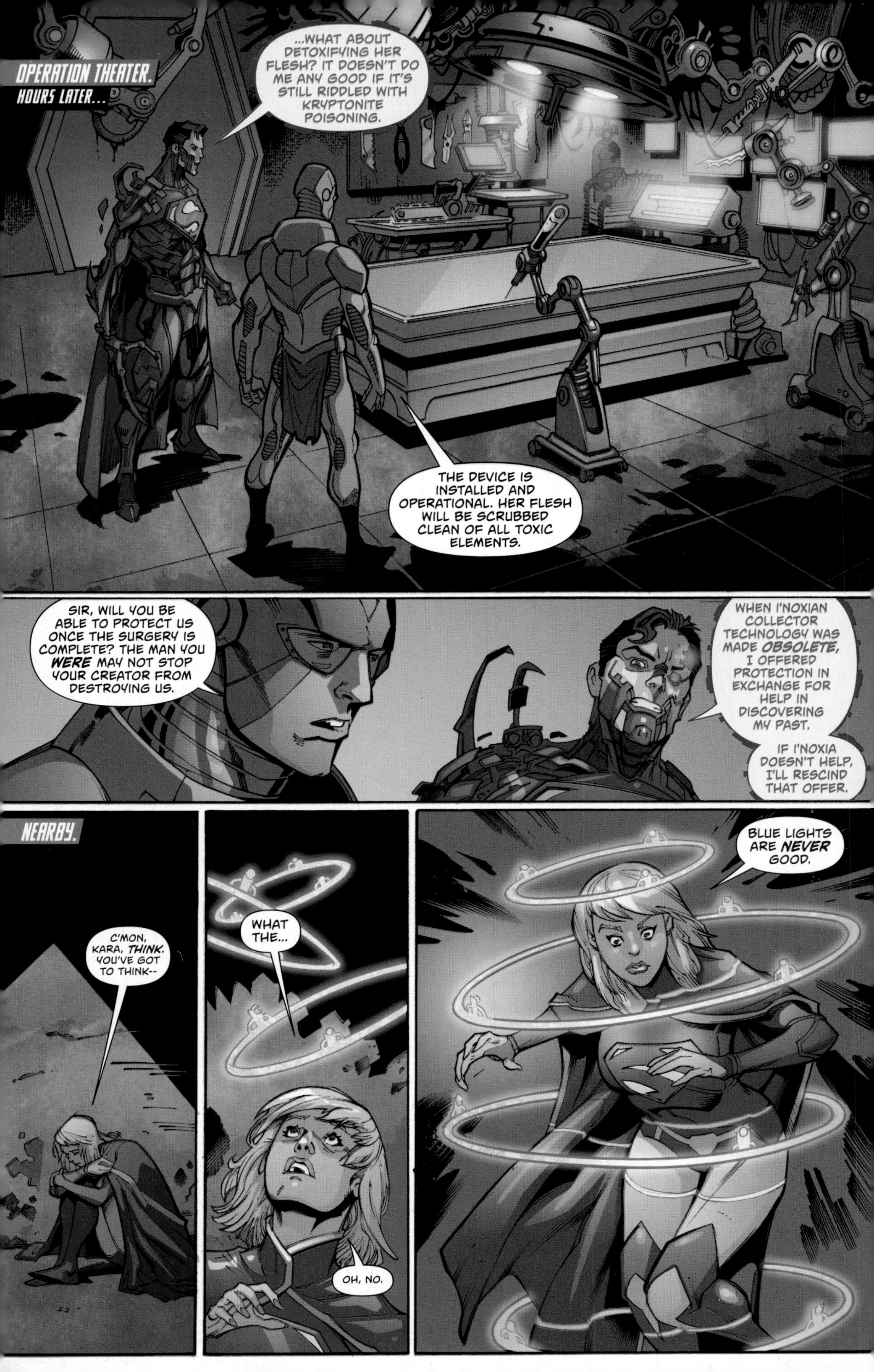
OPERATION THEATER. HOURS LATER...
...WHAT ABOUT DETOXIFYING HER FLESH? IT DOESN'T DO ME ANY GOOD IF IT'S STILL RIDDLED WITH KRYPTONITE POISONING.
THE DEVICE IS INSTALLED AND OPERATIONAL. HER FLESH WILL BE SCRUBBED CLEAN OF ALL TOXIC ELEMENTS.
SIR, WILL YOU BE ABLE TO PROTECT US ONCE THE SURGERY IS COMPLETE? THE MAN YOU WERE MAY NOT STOP YOUR CREATOR FROM DESTROYING US.
WHEN I'NOXIAN COLLECTOR TECHNOLOGY WAS MADE OBSOLETE, I OFFERED PROTECTION IN EXCHANGE FOR HELP IN DISCOVERING MY PAST.
IF I'NOXIA DOESN'T HELP, I'LL RESCIND THAT OFFER.
NEARBY.
C'MON, KARA, THINK. YOU'VE GOT TO THINK--
WHAT THE...
OH, NO.
BLUE LIGHTS ARE NEVER GOOD.

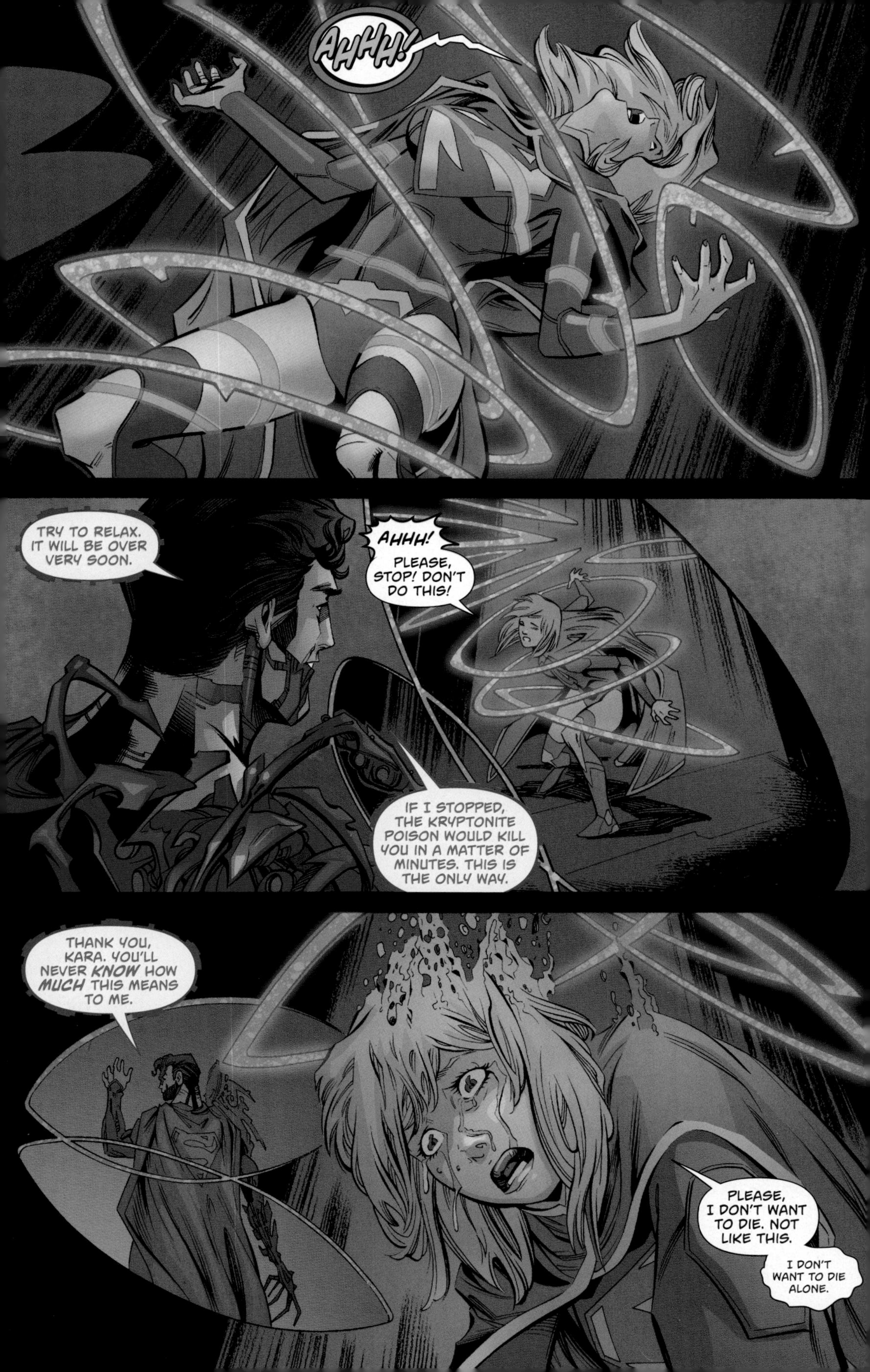
AHHH!
TRY TO RELAX. IT WILL BE OVER VERY SOON.
AHHH! PLEASE, STOP! DON'T DO THIS!
IF I STOPPED, THE KRYPTONITE POISON WOULD KILL YOU IN A MATTER OF MINUTES. THIS IS THE ONLY WAY.
THANK YOU, KARA. YOU'LL NEVER KNOW HOW MUCH THIS MEANS TO ME.
PLEASE, I DON'T WANT TO DIE. NOT LIKE THIS.
I DON'T WANT TO DIE ALONE.

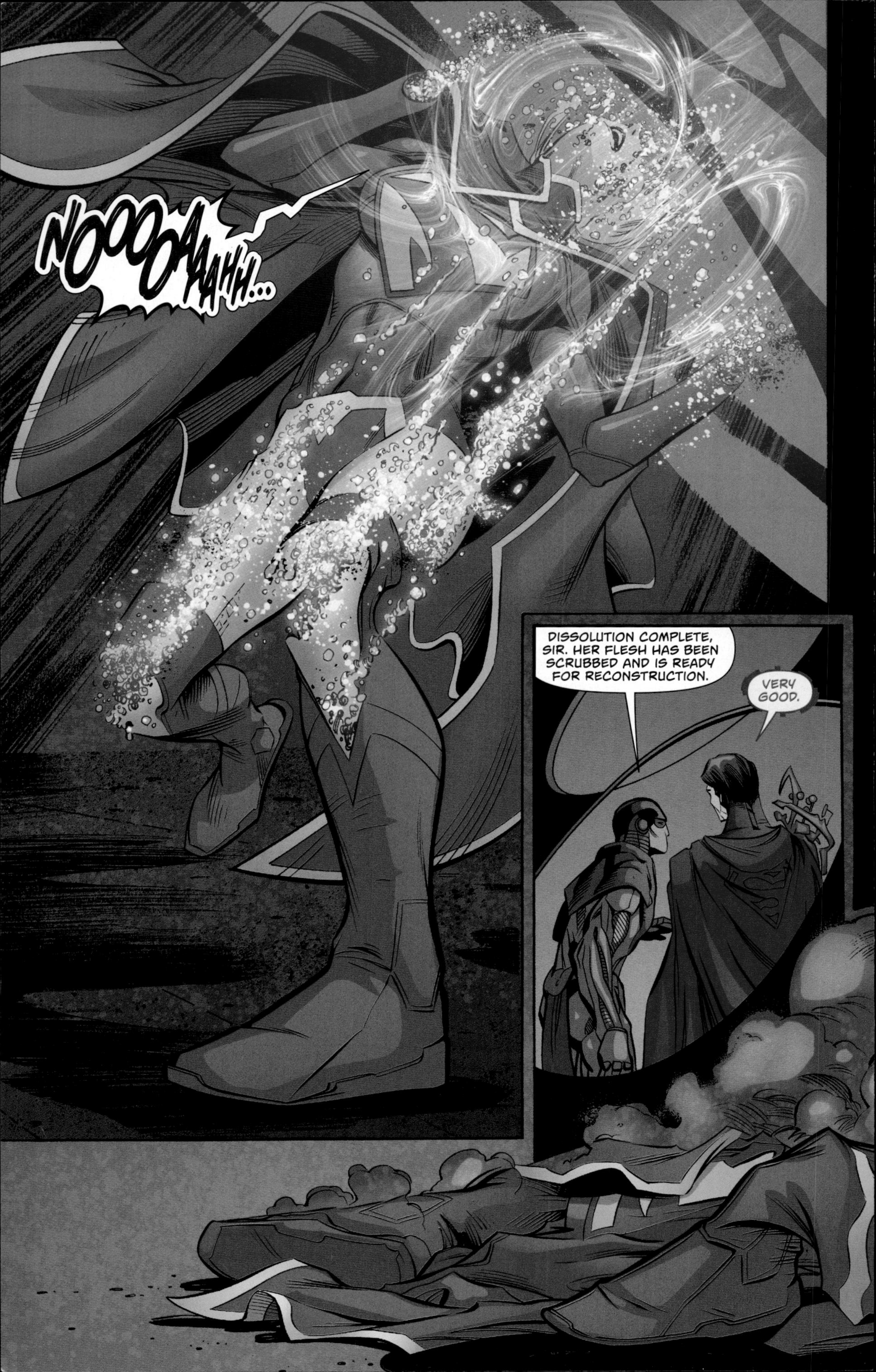
NOOOOAAAHH...
DISSOLUTION COMPLETE, SIR. HER FLESH HAS BEEN SCRUBBED AND IS READY FOR RECONSTRUCTION.
VERY GOOD.

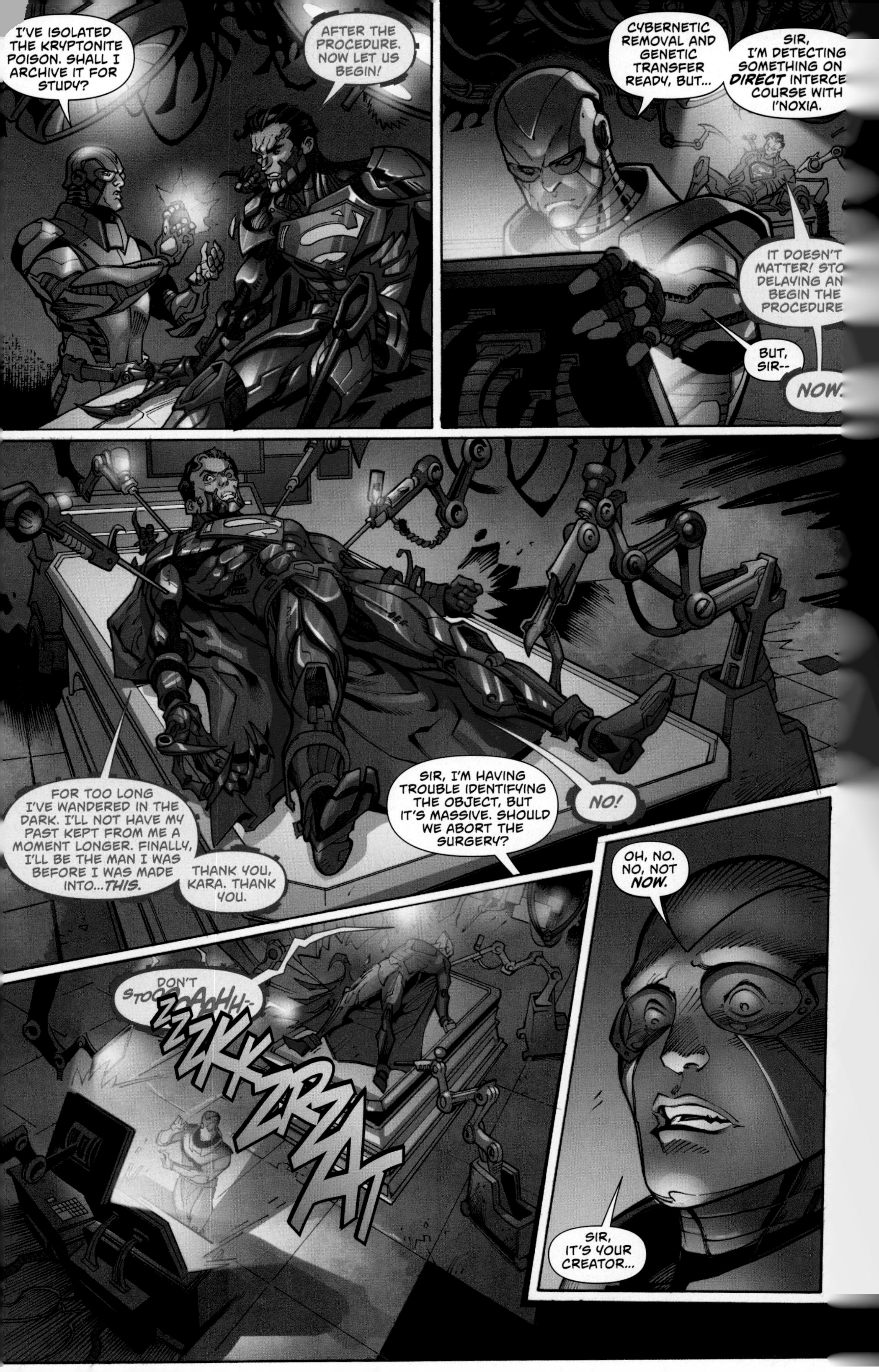
I'VE ISOLATED THE KRYPTONITE POISON. SHALL I ARCHIVE IT FOR STUDY?
AFTER THE PROCEDURE. NOW LET US BEGIN!
CYBERNETIC REMOVAL AND GENETIC TRANSFER READY, BUT...
SIR, I'M DETECTING SOMETHING ON DIRECT INTERCE COURSE WITH I'NOXIA.
IT DOESN'T MATTER! STO DELAYING AN BEGIN THE PROCEDURE
BUT, SIR--
NOW.
FOR TOO LONG I'VE WANDERED IN THE DARK. I'LL NOT HAVE MY PAST KEPT FROM ME A MOMENT LONGER. FINALLY, I'LL BE THE MAN I WAS BEFORE I WAS MADE INTO...THIS.
THANK YOU, KARA. THANK YOU.
SIR, I'M HAVING TROUBLE IDENTIFYING THE OBJECT, BUT IT'S MASSIVE. SHOULD WE ABORT THE SURGERY?
NO!
OH, NO. NO, NOT NOW.
DON'T STOOOOAAHH--
ZZZKKKZRRAAK
SIR, IT'S YOUR CREATOR...

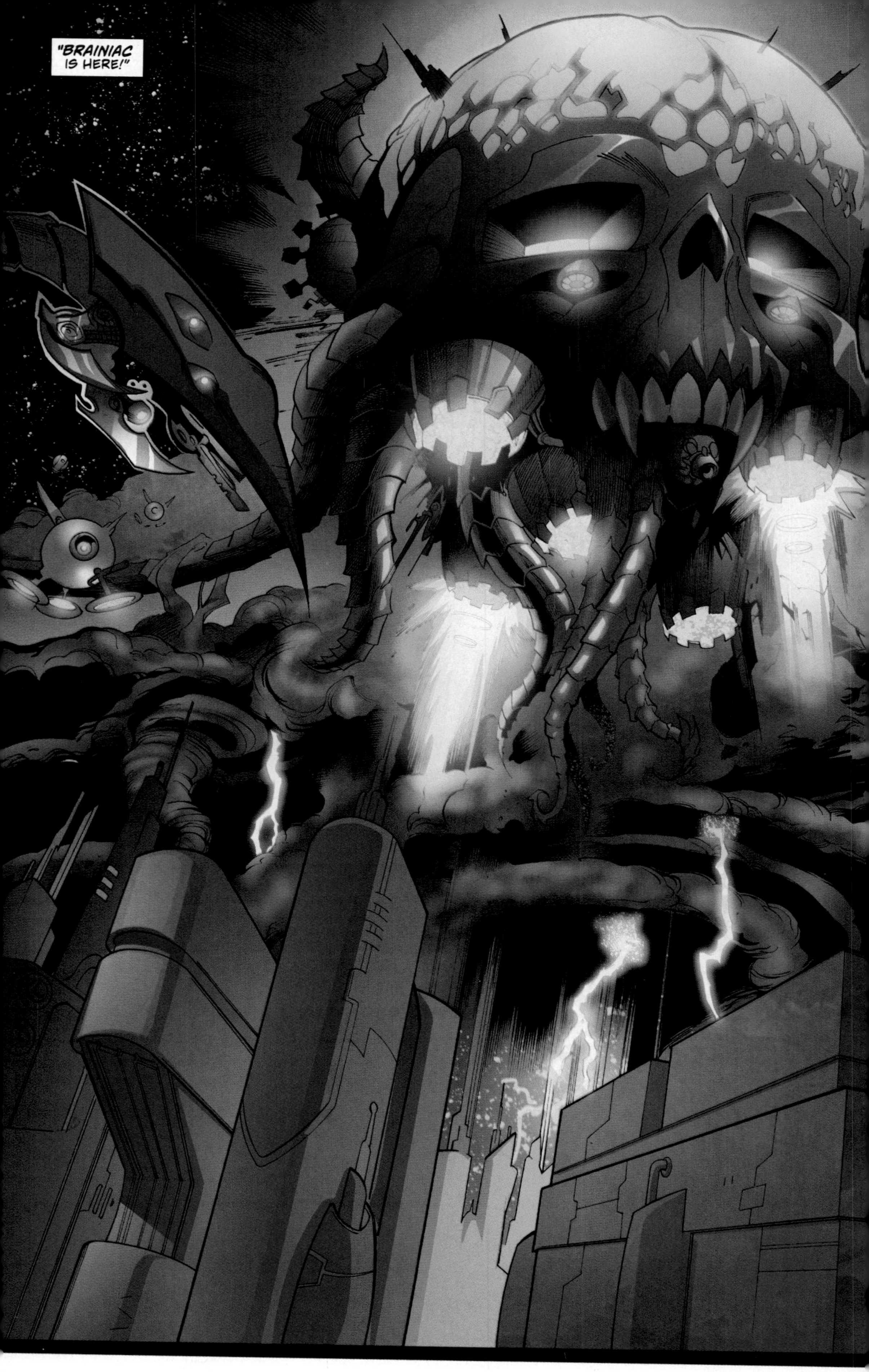
"BRAINIAC IS HERE!"

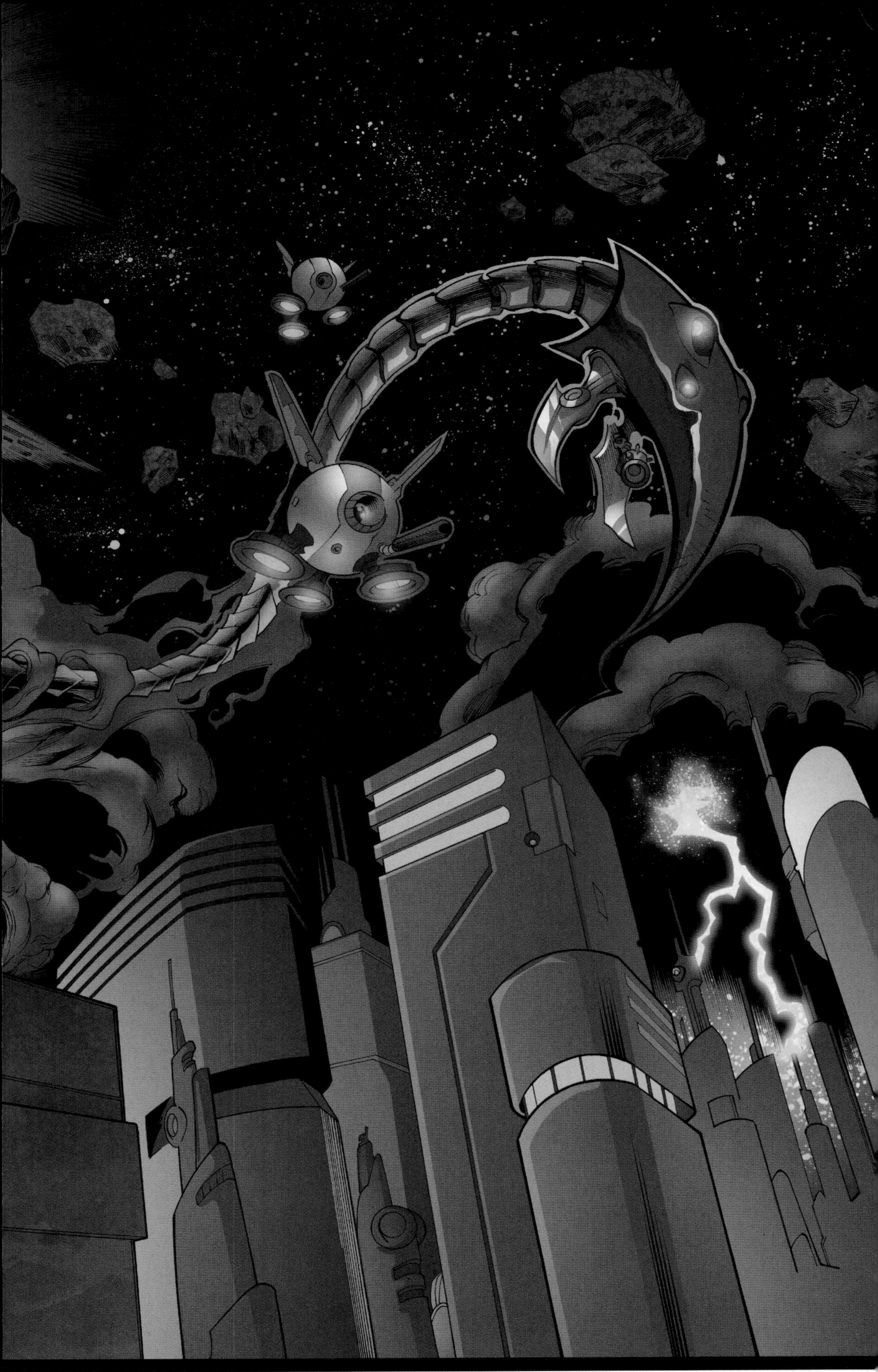

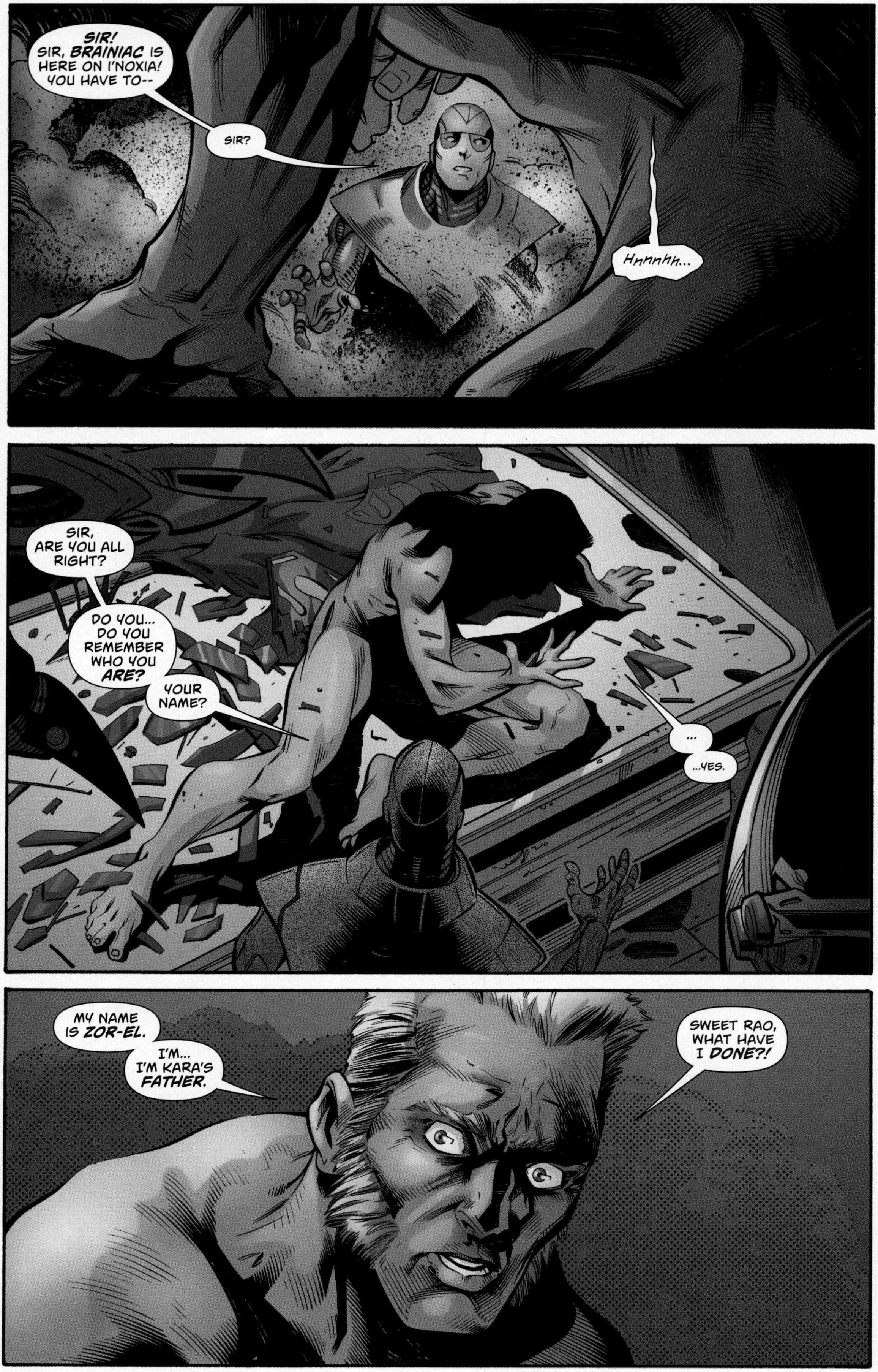
SIR! SIR, BRAINIAC IS HERE ON I'NOXIA! YOU HAVE TO--
SIR?
Hnnnhh...
SIR, ARE YOU ALL RIGHT?
DO YOU... DO YOU REMEMBER WHO YOU ARE?
YOUR NAME?
...
...YES.
MY NAME IS ZOR-EL.
I'M... I'M KARA'S FATHER.
SWEET RAO, WHAT HAVE I DONE?!

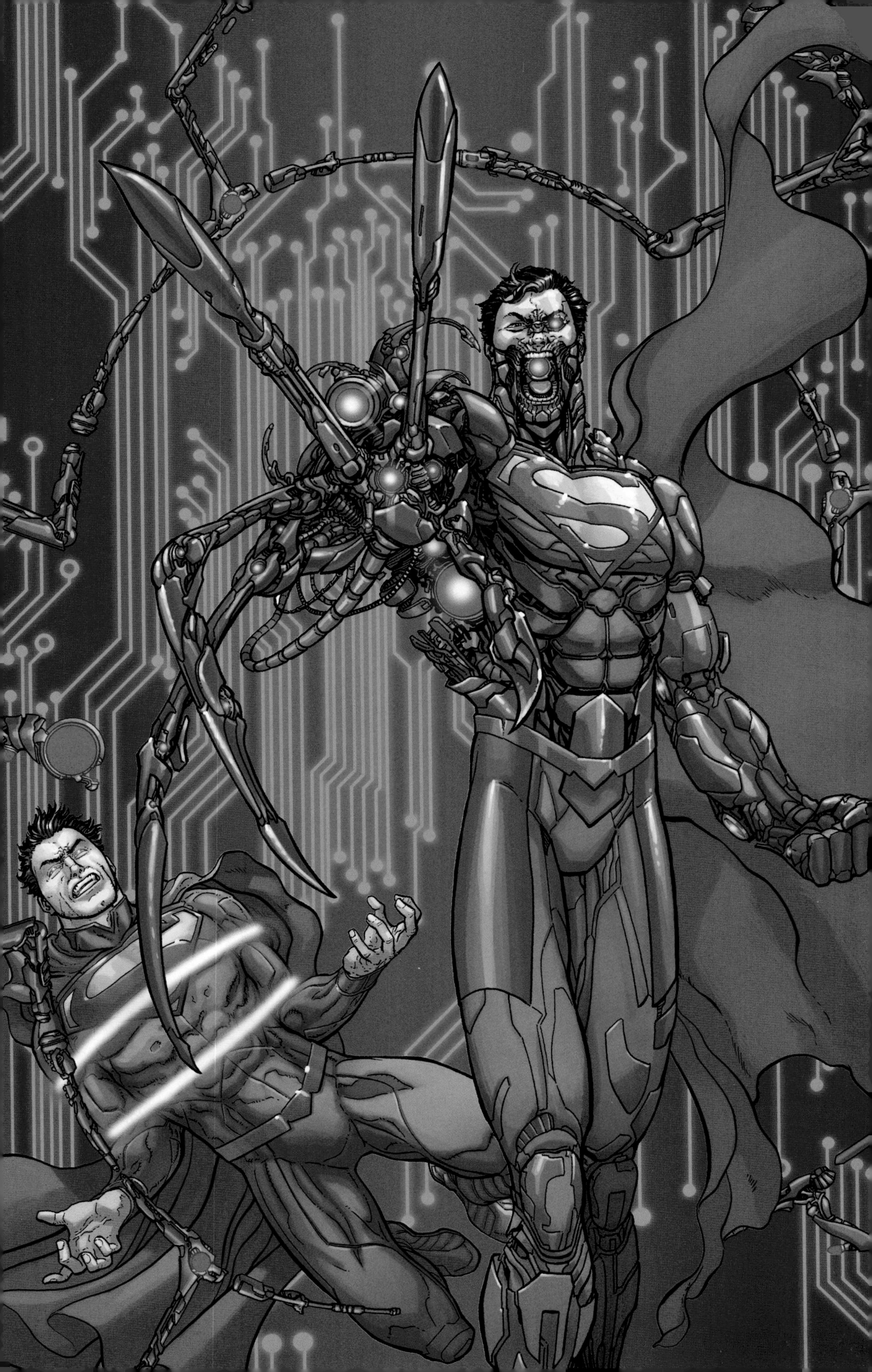

BORN IN FLAMES

MICHAEL ALAN NELSON writer MIKE HAWTHORNE artist cover art by AARON KUDER with DAN BROWN

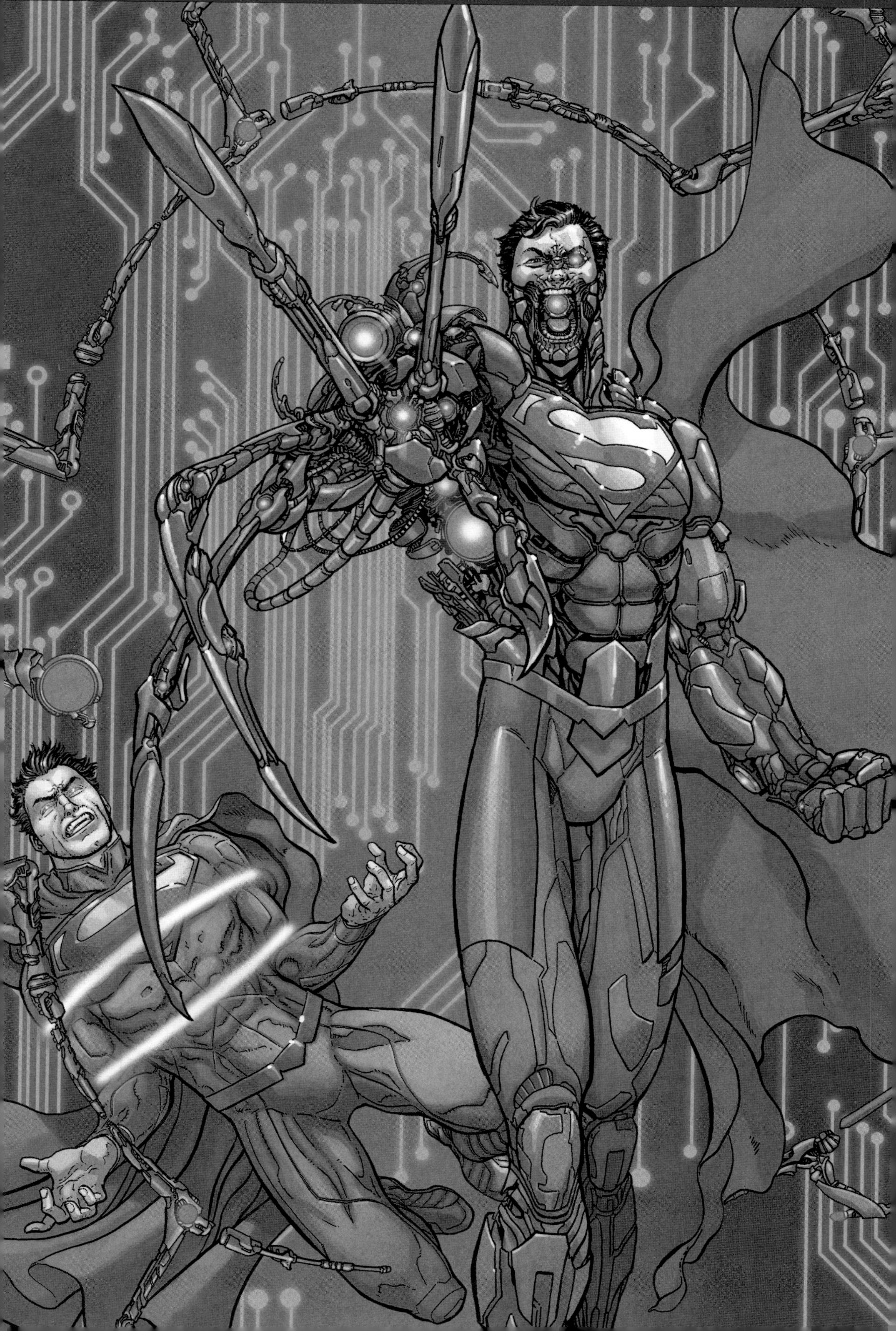

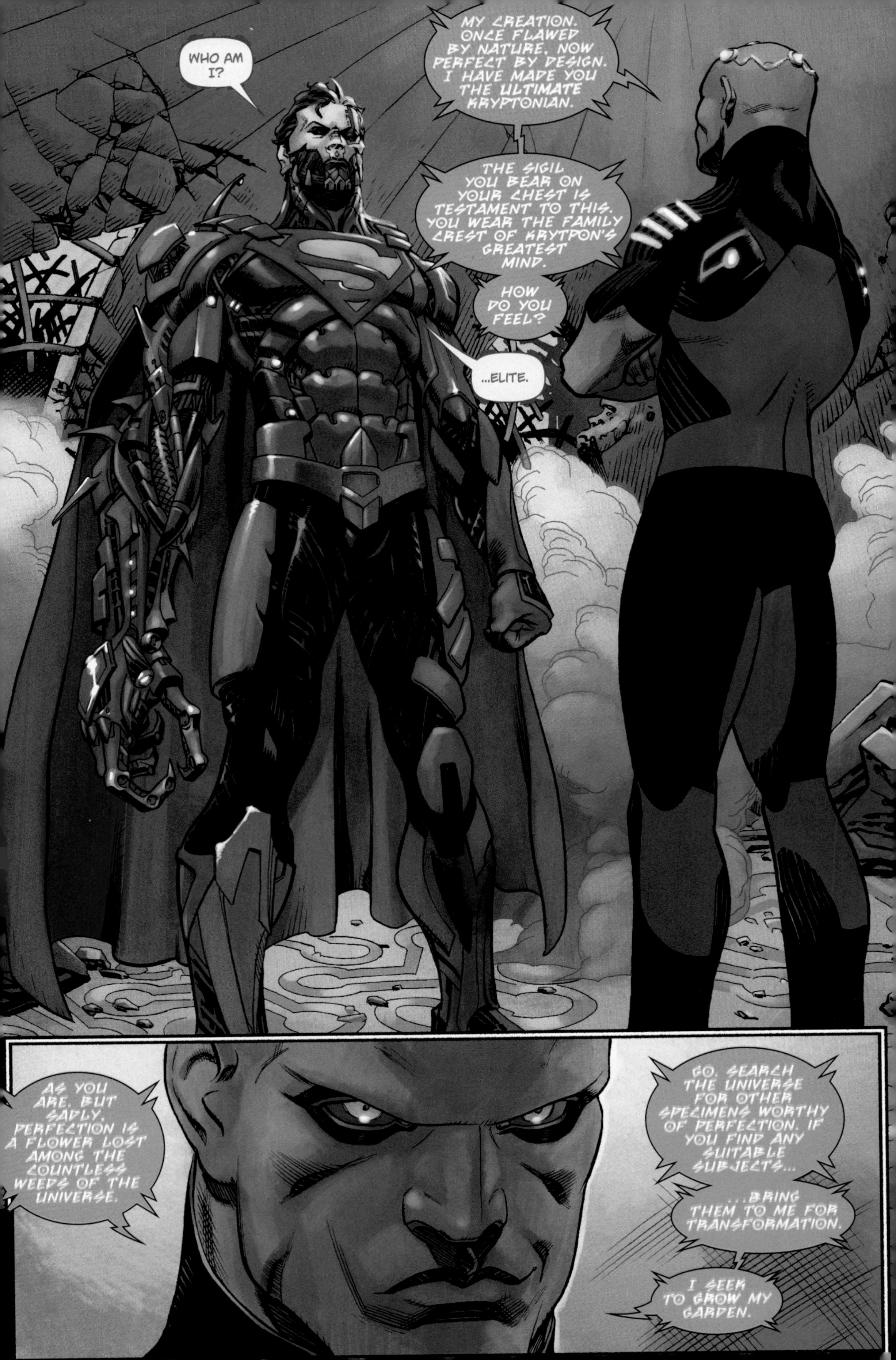
WHO AM I?
MY CREATION. ONCE FLAWED BY NATURE. NOW PERFECT BY DESIGN. I HAVE MADE YOU THE ULTIMATE KRYPTONIAN.
THE SIGIL YOU BEAR ON YOUR CHEST IS TESTAMENT TO THIS. YOU WEAR THE FAMILY CREST OF KRYPTON'S GREATEST MIND.
HOW DO YOU FEEL?
...ELITE.
AS YOU ARE. BUT SADLY, PERFECTION IS A FLOWER LOST AMONG THE COUNTLESS WEEDS OF THE UNIVERSE.
GO. SEARCH THE UNIVERSE FOR OTHER SPECIMENS WORTHY OF PERFECTION. IF YOU FIND ANY SUITABLE SUBJECTS...
...BRING THEM TO ME FOR TRANSFORMATION.
I SEEK TO GROW MY GARDEN.

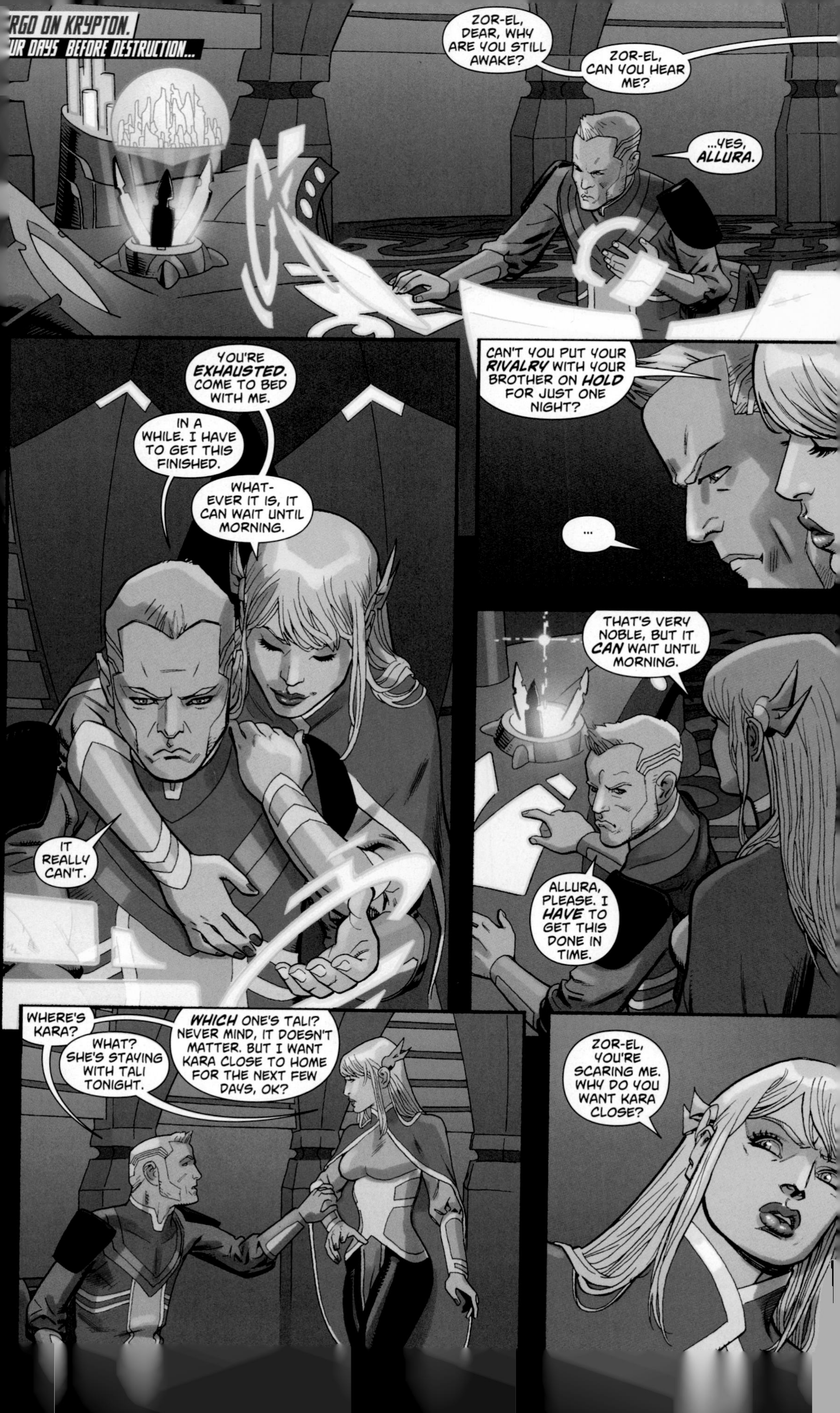

...RGO ON KRYPTON.
...UR DAYS BEFORE DESTRUCTION...
ZOR-EL, DEAR, WHY ARE YOU STILL AWAKE?
ZOR-EL, CAN YOU HEAR ME?
...YES, ALLURA.
YOU'RE EXHAUSTED. COME TO BED WITH ME.
IN A WHILE. I HAVE TO GET THIS FINISHED.
WHAT-EVER IT IS, IT CAN WAIT UNTIL MORNING.
IT REALLY CAN'T.
CAN'T YOU PUT YOUR RIVALRY WITH YOUR BROTHER ON HOLD FOR JUST ONE NIGHT?
...
THAT'S VERY NOBLE, BUT IT CAN WAIT UNTIL MORNING.
ALLURA, PLEASE. I HAVE TO GET THIS DONE IN TIME.
WHERE'S KARA?
WHAT? SHE'S STAYING WITH TALI TONIGHT.
WHICH ONE'S TALI? NEVER MIND, IT DOESN'T MATTER. BUT I WANT KARA CLOSE TO HOME FOR THE NEXT FEW DAYS, OK?
ZOR-EL, YOU'RE SCARING ME. WHY DO YOU WANT KARA CLOSE?

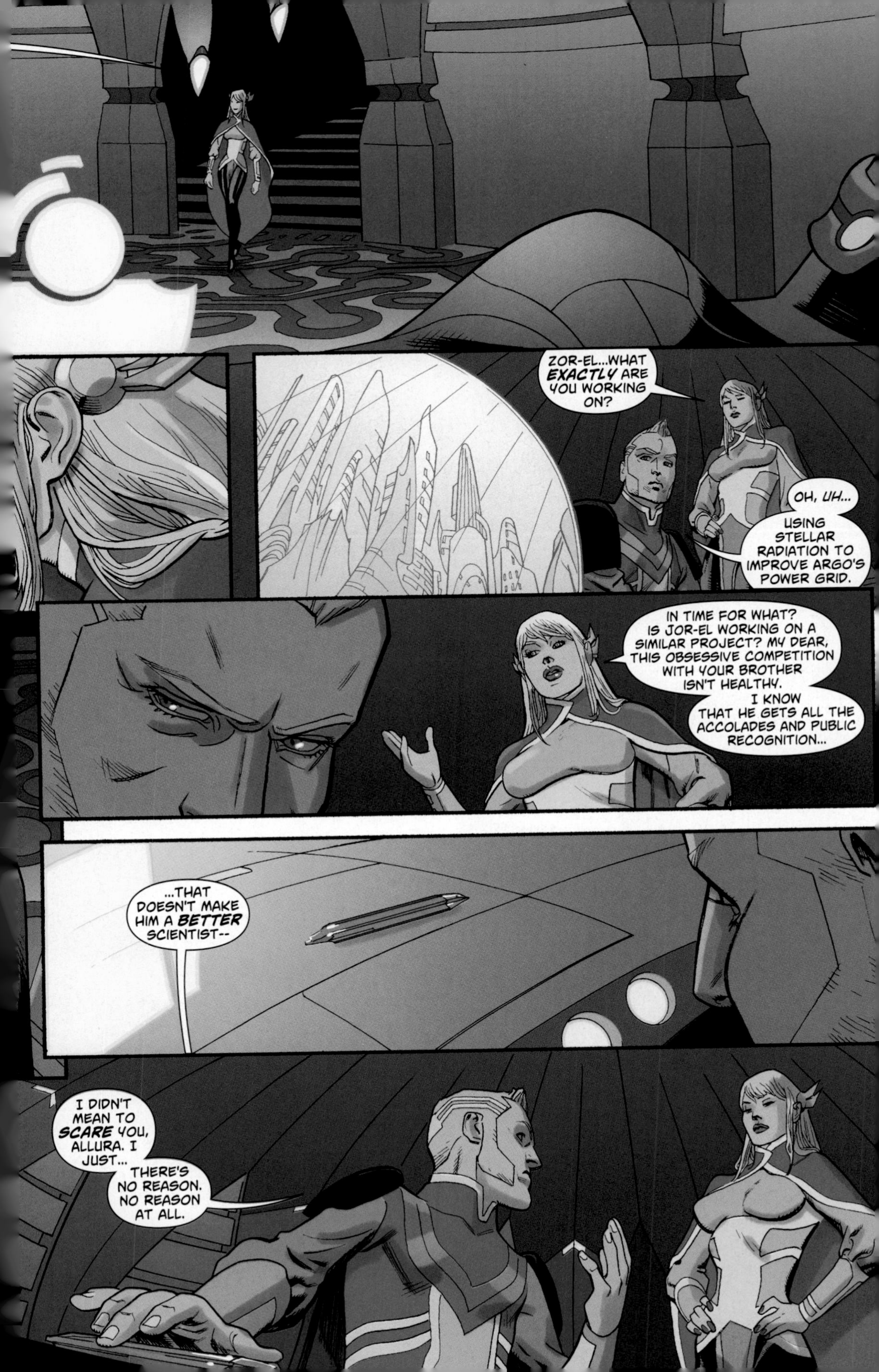

ZOR-EL...WHAT EXACTLY ARE YOU WORKING ON?
OH, UH...
USING STELLAR RADIATION TO IMPROVE ARGO'S POWER GRID.
IN TIME FOR WHAT? IS JOR-EL WORKING ON A SIMILAR PROJECT? MY DEAR, THIS OBSESSIVE COMPETITION WITH YOUR BROTHER ISN'T HEALTHY.
I KNOW THAT HE GETS ALL THE ACCOLADES AND PUBLIC RECOGNITION...
...THAT DOESN'T MAKE HIM A BETTER SCIENTIST--
I DIDN'T MEAN TO SCARE YOU, ALLURA. I JUST...
THERE'S NO REASON. NO REASON AT ALL.

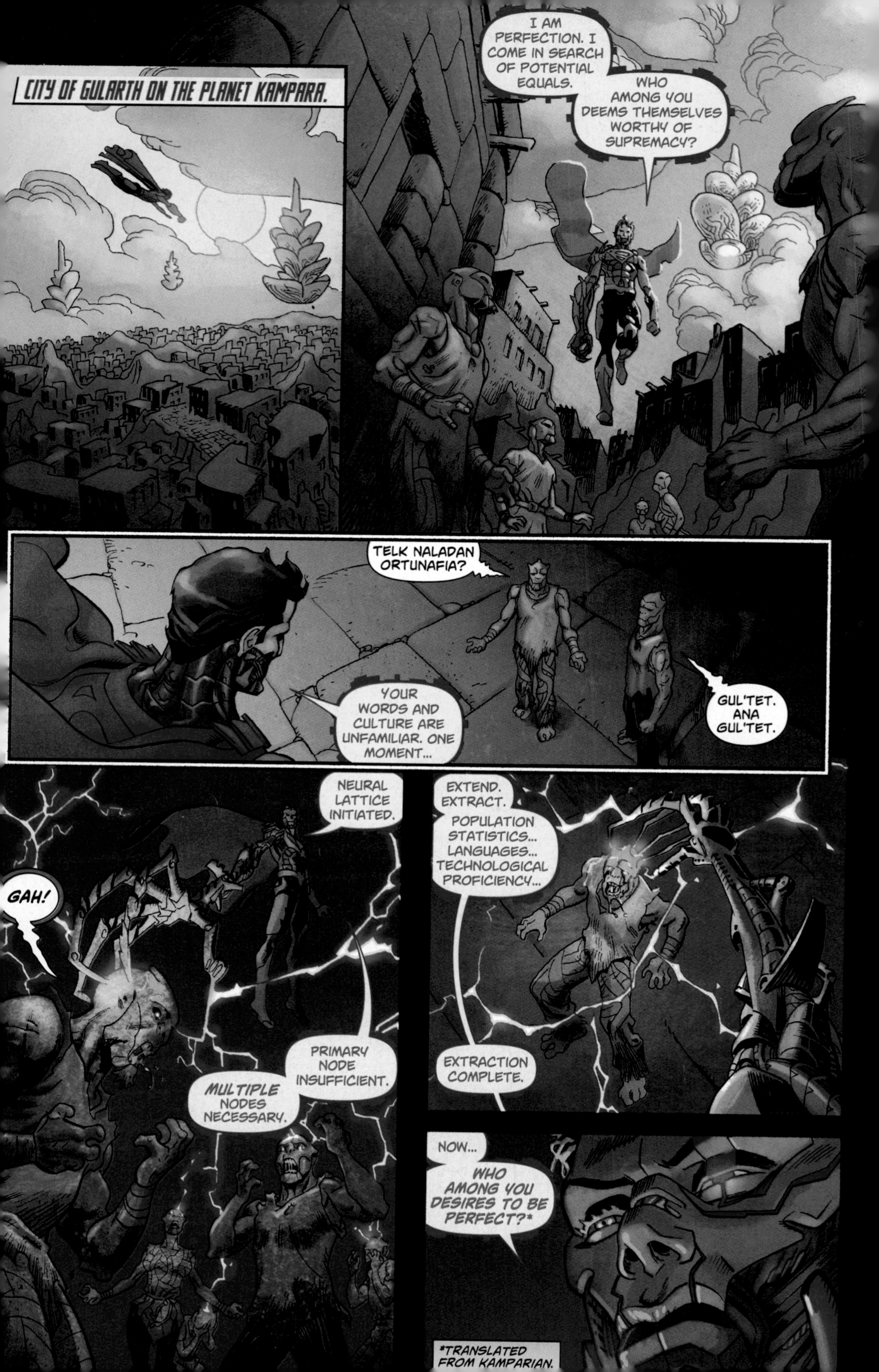
CITY OF GULARTH ON THE PLANET KAMPARA.
I AM PERFECTION. I COME IN SEARCH OF POTENTIAL EQUALS.
WHO AMONG YOU DEEMS THEMSELVES WORTHY OF SUPREMACY?
TELK NALADAN ORTUNAFIA?
YOUR WORDS AND CULTURE ARE UNFAMILIAR. ONE MOMENT...
GUL'TET. ANA GUL'TET.
NEURAL LATTICE INITIATED.
GAH!
PRIMARY NODE INSUFFICIENT.
MULTIPLE NODES NECESSARY.
EXTEND. EXTRACT.
POPULATION STATISTICS... LANGUAGES... TECHNOLOGICAL PROFICIENCY...
EXTRACTION COMPLETE.
NOW...
WHO AMONG YOU DESIRES TO BE PERFECT?*
*TRANSLATED FROM KAMPARIAN.

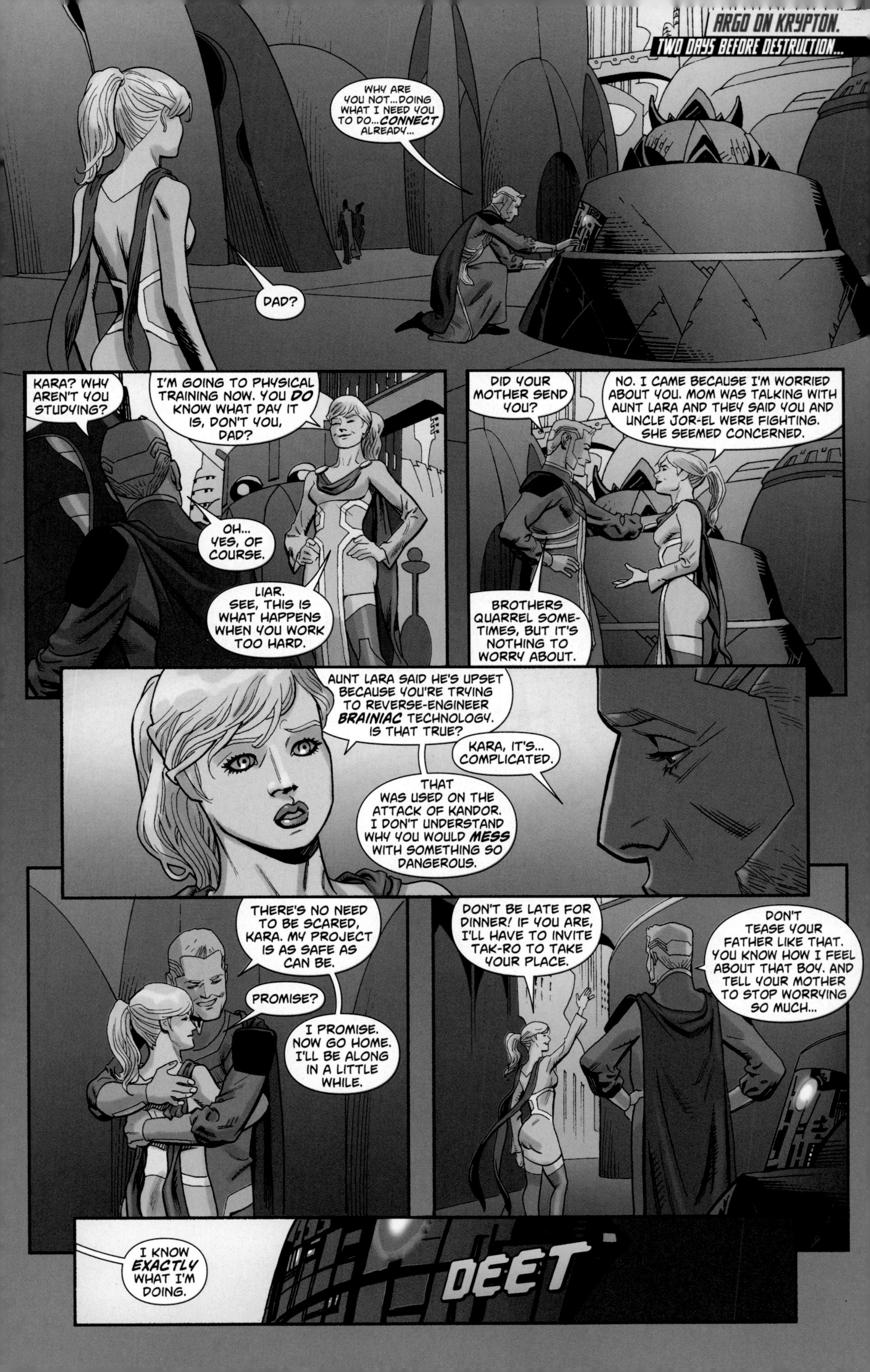
ARGO ON KRYPTON.
TWO DAYS BEFORE DESTRUCTION...
WHY ARE YOU NOT...DOING WHAT I NEED YOU TO DO...CONNECT ALREADY...
DAD?
KARA? WHY AREN'T YOU STUDYING?
I'M GOING TO PHYSICAL TRAINING NOW. YOU DO KNOW WHAT DAY IT IS, DON'T YOU, DAD?
OH... YES, OF COURSE.
LIAR. SEE, THIS IS WHAT HAPPENS WHEN YOU WORK TOO HARD.
DID YOUR MOTHER SEND YOU?
NO. I CAME BECAUSE I'M WORRIED ABOUT YOU. MOM WAS TALKING WITH AUNT LARA AND THEY SAID YOU AND UNCLE JOR-EL WERE FIGHTING. SHE SEEMED CONCERNED.
BROTHERS QUARREL SOMETIMES, BUT IT'S NOTHING TO WORRY ABOUT.
AUNT LARA SAID HE'S UPSET BECAUSE YOU'RE TRYING TO REVERSE-ENGINEER BRAINIAC TECHNOLOGY. IS THAT TRUE?
KARA, IT'S... COMPLICATED.
THAT WAS USED ON THE ATTACK OF KANDOR. I DON'T UNDERSTAND WHY YOU WOULD MESS WITH SOMETHING SO DANGEROUS.
THERE'S NO NEED TO BE SCARED, KARA. MY PROJECT IS AS SAFE AS CAN BE.
PROMISE?
I PROMISE. NOW GO HOME. I'LL BE ALONG IN A LITTLE WHILE.
DON'T BE LATE FOR DINNER! IF YOU ARE, I'LL HAVE TO INVITE TAK-RO TO TAKE YOUR PLACE.
DON'T TEASE YOUR FATHER LIKE THAT. YOU KNOW HOW I FEEL ABOUT THAT BOY. AND TELL YOUR MOTHER TO STOP WORRYING SO MUCH...
I KNOW EXACTLY WHAT I'M DOING.
DEET

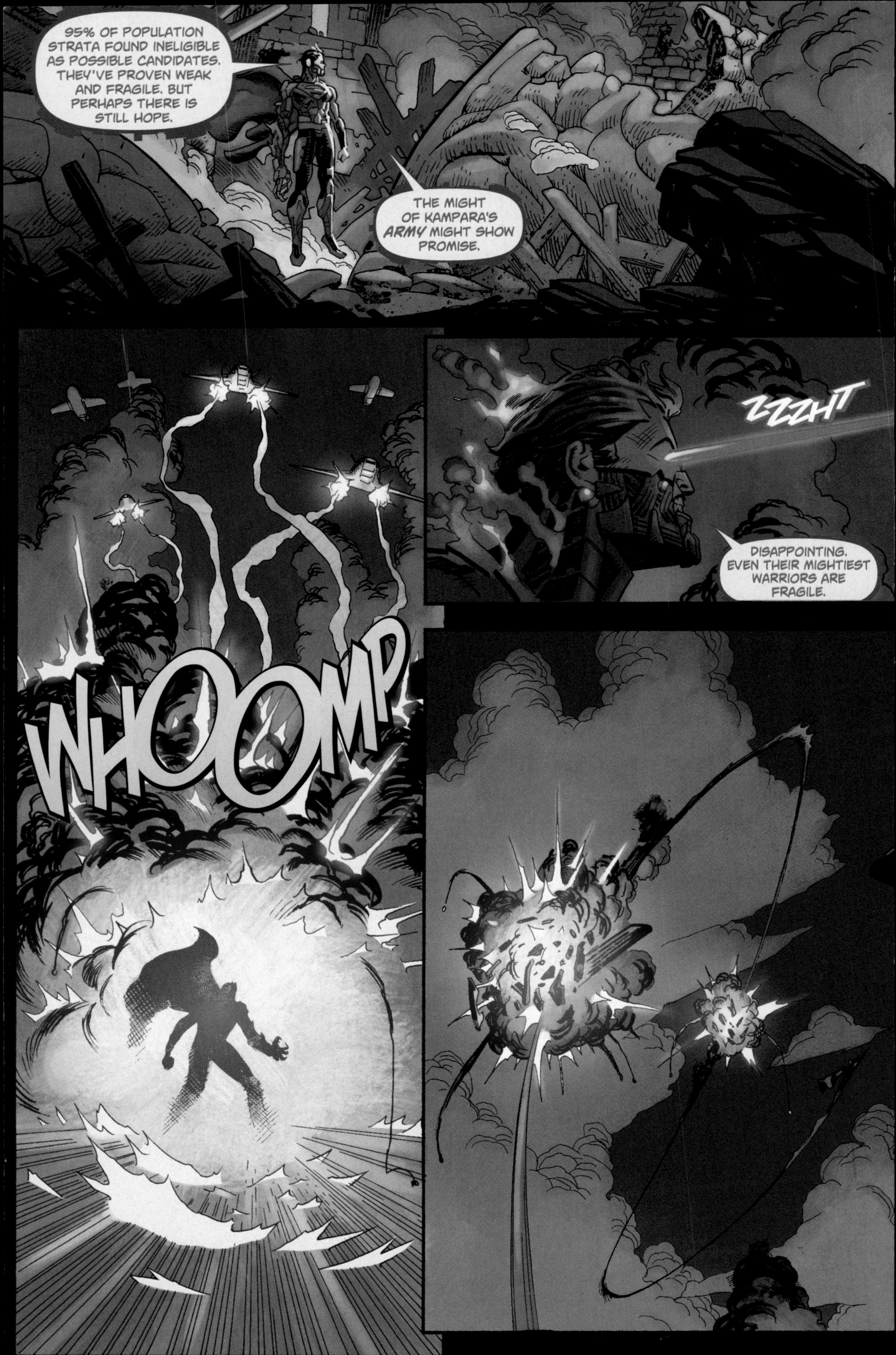
95% OF POPULATION STRATA FOUND INELIGIBLE AS POSSIBLE CANDIDATES. THEY'VE PROVEN WEAK AND FRAGILE. BUT PERHAPS THERE IS STILL HOPE.
THE MIGHT OF KAMPARA'S ARMY MIGHT SHOW PROMISE.
WHOOMP
ZZZZHT
DISAPPOINTING. EVEN THEIR MIGHTIEST WARRIORS ARE FRAGILE.

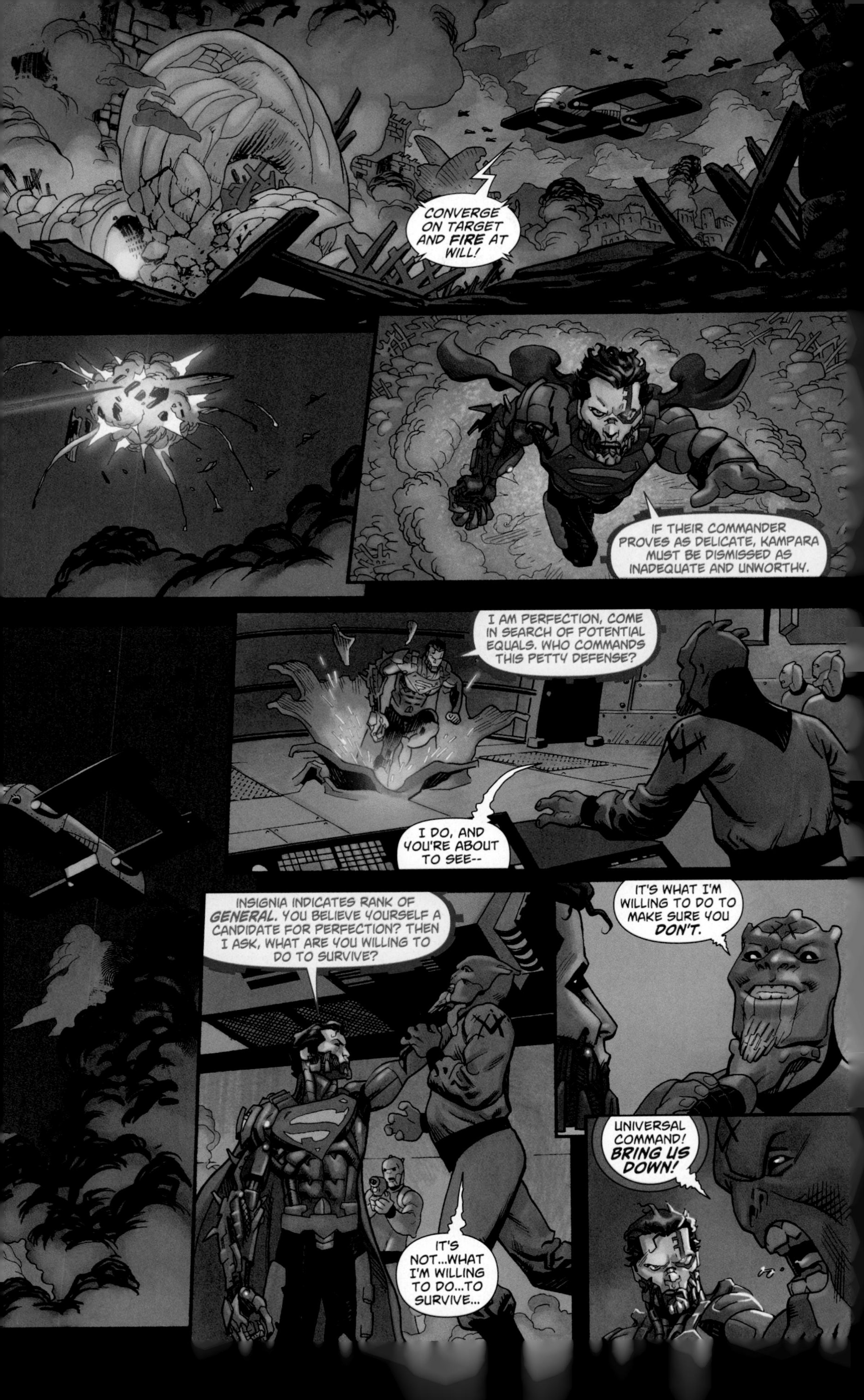
CONVERGE ON TARGET AND FIRE AT WILL!
IF THEIR COMMANDER PROVES AS DELICATE, KAMPARA MUST BE DISMISSED AS INADEQUATE AND UNWORTHY.
I AM PERFECTION, COME IN SEARCH OF POTENTIAL EQUALS. WHO COMMANDS THIS PETTY DEFENSE?
I DO, AND YOU'RE ABOUT TO SEE--
INSIGNIA INDICATES RANK OF GENERAL. YOU BELIEVE YOURSELF A CANDIDATE FOR PERFECTION? THEN I ASK, WHAT ARE YOU WILLING TO DO TO SURVIVE?
IT'S WHAT I'M WILLING TO DO TO MAKE SURE YOU DON'T.
IT'S NOT...WHAT I'M WILLING TO DO...TO SURVIVE...
UNIVERSAL COMMAND! BRING US DOWN!

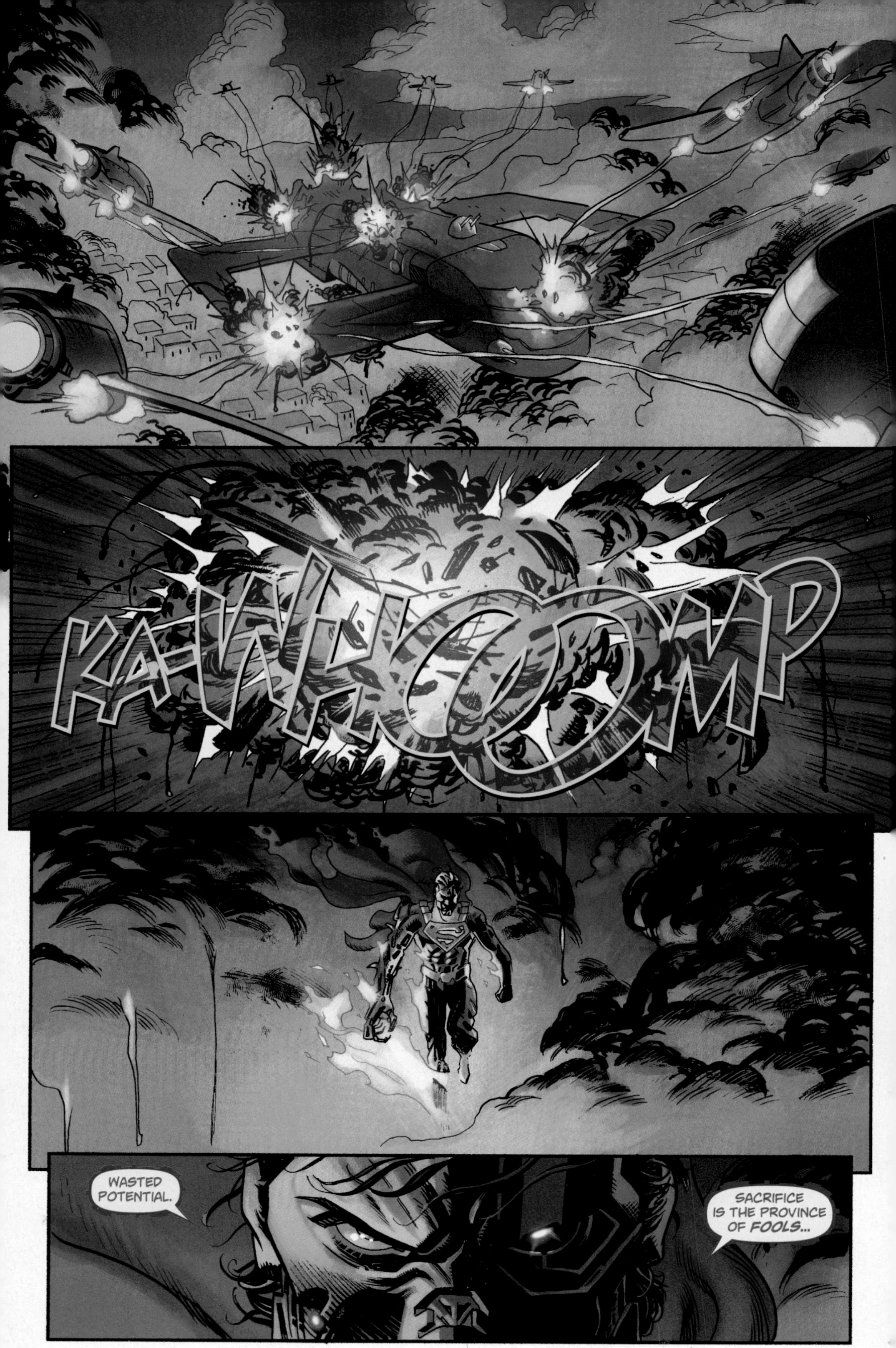
KA-WHOOMP
WASTED POTENTIAL.
SACRIFICE IS THE PROVINCE OF FOOLS...

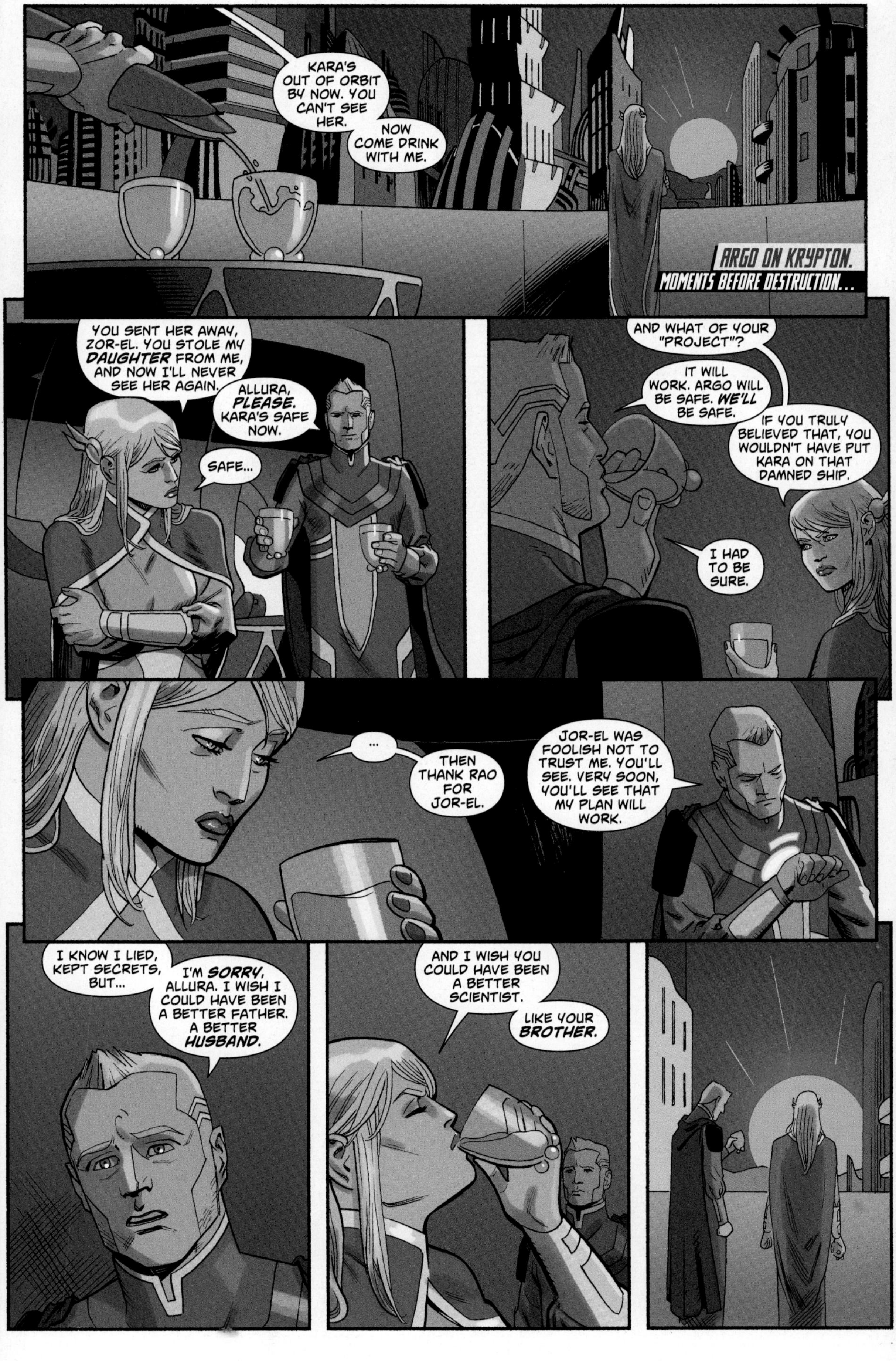
KARA'S OUT OF ORBIT BY NOW. YOU CAN'T SEE HER.
NOW COME DRINK WITH ME.
ARGO ON KRYPTON.
MOMENTS BEFORE DESTRUCTION...
YOU SENT HER AWAY, ZOR-EL. YOU STOLE MY DAUGHTER FROM ME, AND NOW I'LL NEVER SEE HER AGAIN.
ALLURA, PLEASE. KARA'S SAFE NOW.
SAFE...
AND WHAT OF YOUR "PROJECT"?
IT WILL WORK. ARGO WILL BE SAFE. WE'LL BE SAFE.
IF YOU TRULY BELIEVED THAT, YOU WOULDN'T HAVE PUT KARA ON THAT DAMNED SHIP.
I HAD TO BE SURE.
...
THEN THANK RAO FOR JOR-EL.
JOR-EL WAS FOOLISH NOT TO TRUST ME. YOU'LL SEE. VERY SOON, YOU'LL SEE THAT MY PLAN WILL WORK.
I KNOW I LIED, KEPT SECRETS, BUT...
I'M SORRY, ALLURA. I WISH I COULD HAVE BEEN A BETTER FATHER. A BETTER HUSBAND.
AND I WISH YOU COULD HAVE BEEN A BETTER SCIENTIST.
LIKE YOUR BROTHER.

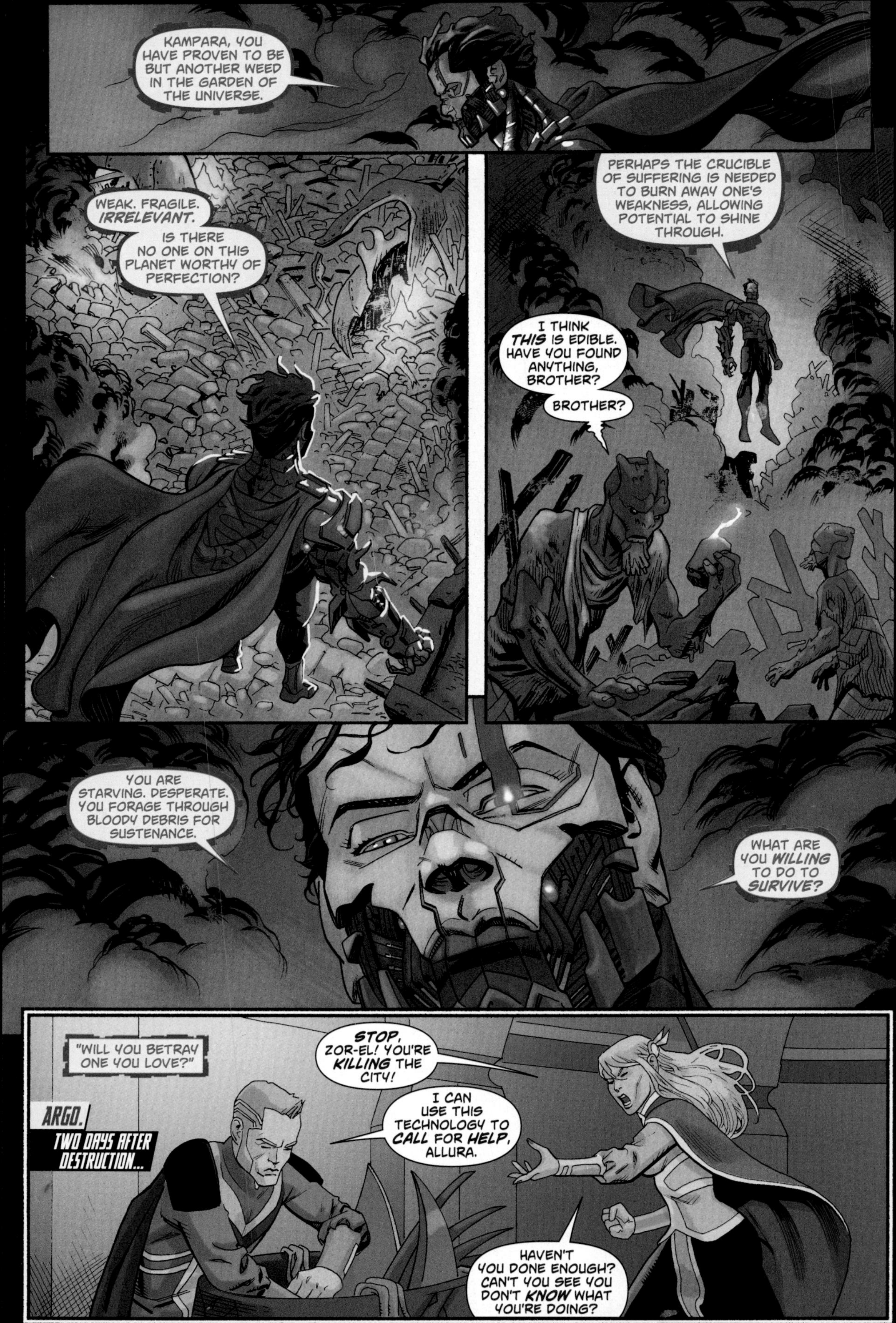

KAMPARA, YOU HAVE PROVEN TO BE BUT ANOTHER WEED IN THE GARDEN OF THE UNIVERSE.
WEAK. FRAGILE. IRRELEVANT.
IS THERE NO ONE ON THIS PLANET WORTHY OF PERFECTION?
PERHAPS THE CRUCIBLE OF SUFFERING IS NEEDED TO BURN AWAY ONE'S WEAKNESS, ALLOWING POTENTIAL TO SHINE THROUGH.
I THINK THIS IS EDIBLE. HAVE YOU FOUND ANYTHING, BROTHER?
BROTHER?
YOU ARE STARVING. DESPERATE. YOU FORAGE THROUGH BLOODY DEBRIS FOR SUSTENANCE.
WHAT ARE YOU WILLING TO DO TO SURVIVE?
"WILL YOU BETRAY ONE YOU LOVE?"
ARGO.
TWO DAYS AFTER DESTRUCTION...
STOP, ZOR-EL! YOU'RE KILLING THE CITY!
I CAN USE THIS TECHNOLOGY TO CALL FOR HELP, ALLURA.
HAVEN'T YOU DONE ENOUGH? CAN'T YOU SEE YOU DON'T KNOW WHAT YOU'RE DOING?

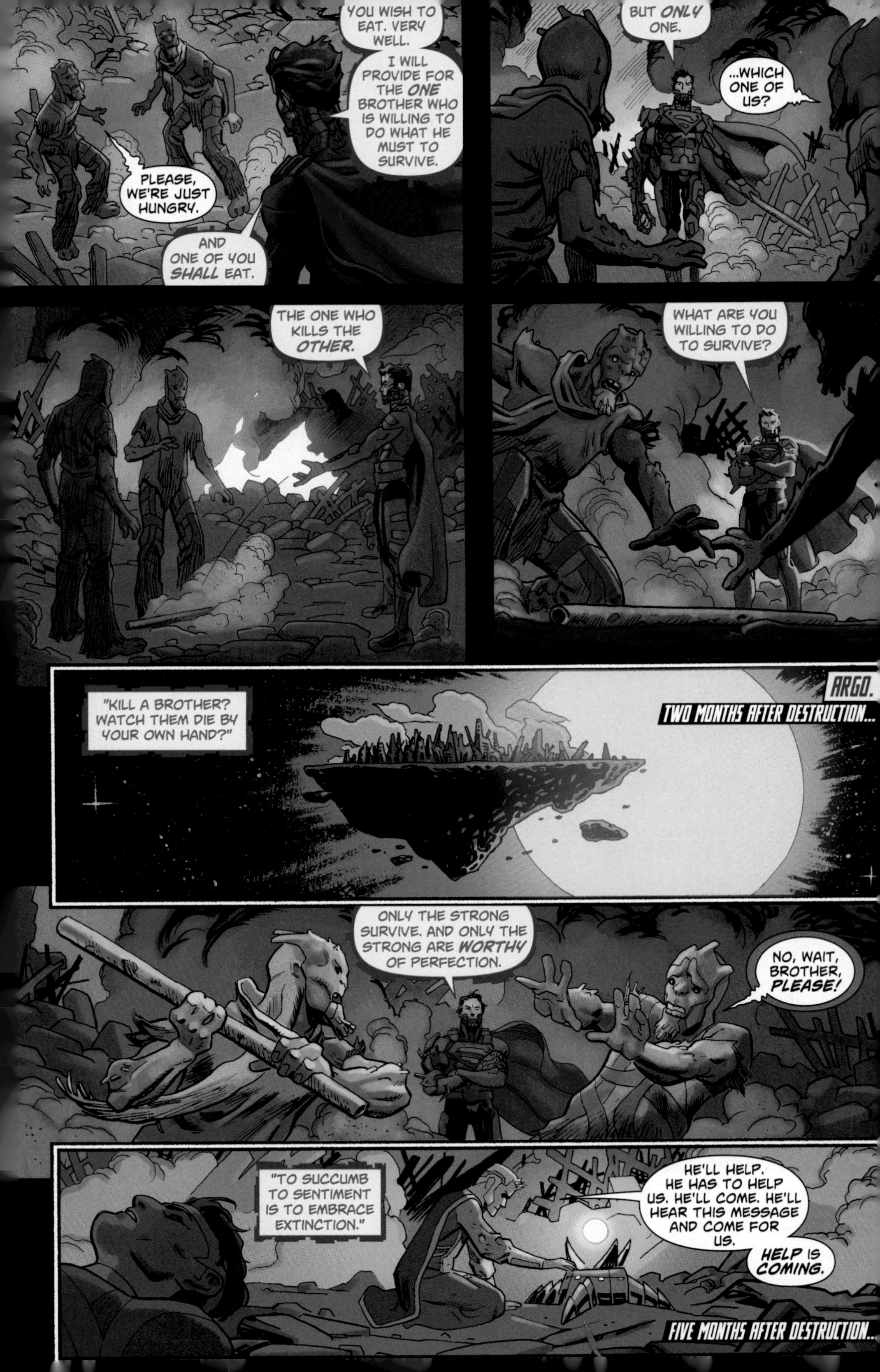
YOU WISH TO EAT. VERY WELL.
I WILL PROVIDE FOR THE ONE BROTHER WHO IS WILLING TO DO WHAT HE MUST TO SURVIVE.
PLEASE, WE'RE JUST HUNGRY.
AND ONE OF YOU SHALL EAT.
BUT ONLY ONE.
...WHICH ONE OF US?
THE ONE WHO KILLS THE OTHER.
WHAT ARE YOU WILLING TO DO TO SURVIVE?
ARGO.
TWO MONTHS AFTER DESTRUCTION...
"KILL A BROTHER? WATCH THEM DIE BY YOUR OWN HAND?"
ONLY THE STRONG SURVIVE. AND ONLY THE STRONG ARE WORTHY OF PERFECTION.
NO, WAIT, BROTHER, PLEASE!
"TO SUCCUMB TO SENTIMENT IS TO EMBRACE EXTINCTION."
HE'LL HELP. HE HAS TO HELP US. HE'LL COME. HE'LL HEAR THIS MESSAGE AND COME FOR US.
HELP IS COMING.
FIVE MONTHS AFTER DESTRUCTION...

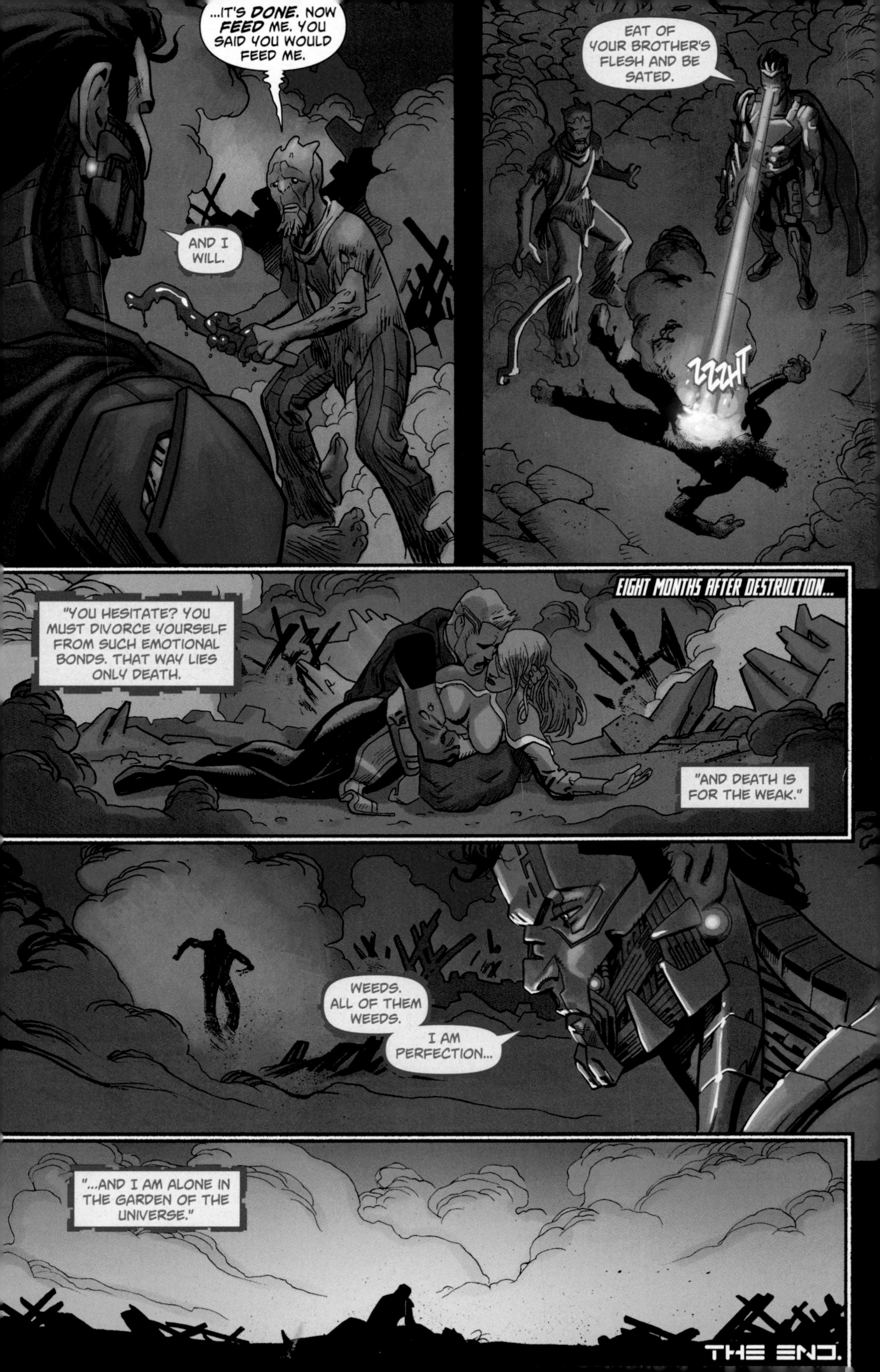
...IT'S **DONE.** NOW **FEED** ME. YOU SAID YOU WOULD FEED ME.
AND I WILL.
EAT OF YOUR BROTHER'S FLESH AND BE SATED.
ZZZHT
EIGHT MONTHS AFTER DESTRUCTION...
"YOU HESITATE? YOU MUST DIVORCE YOURSELF FROM SUCH EMOTIONAL BONDS. THAT WAY LIES ONLY DEATH.
"AND DEATH IS FOR THE WEAK."
WEEDS. ALL OF THEM WEEDS.
I AM PERFECTION...
"...AND I AM ALONE IN THE GARDEN OF THE UNIVERSE."
THE END.

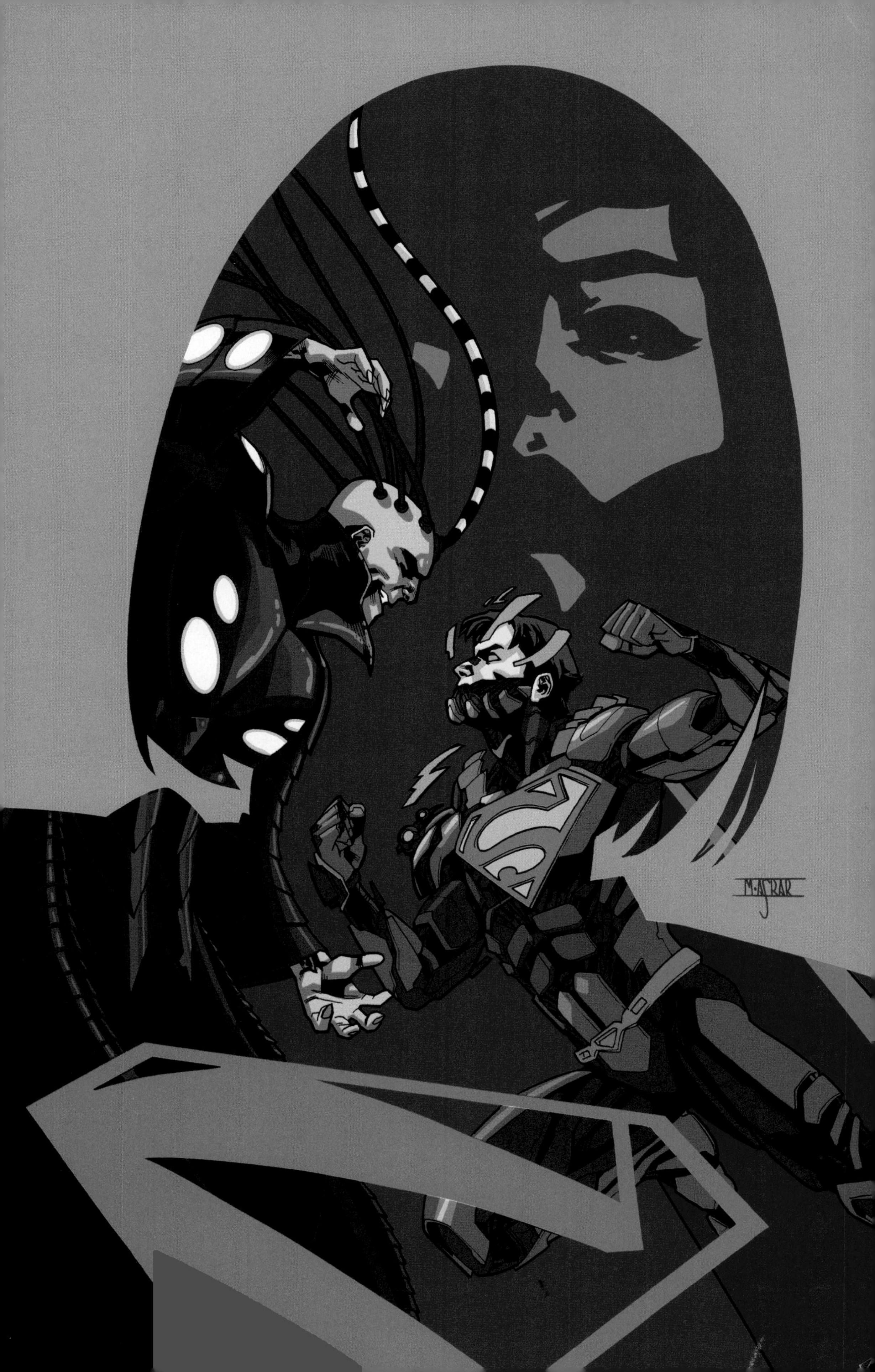
M·ASRAR

DEATH BECOMES HER

MICHAEL ALAN NELSON writer **DIOGENES NEVES** penciller **MARC DEERING** inker cover art by **MAHMUD ASRAR**

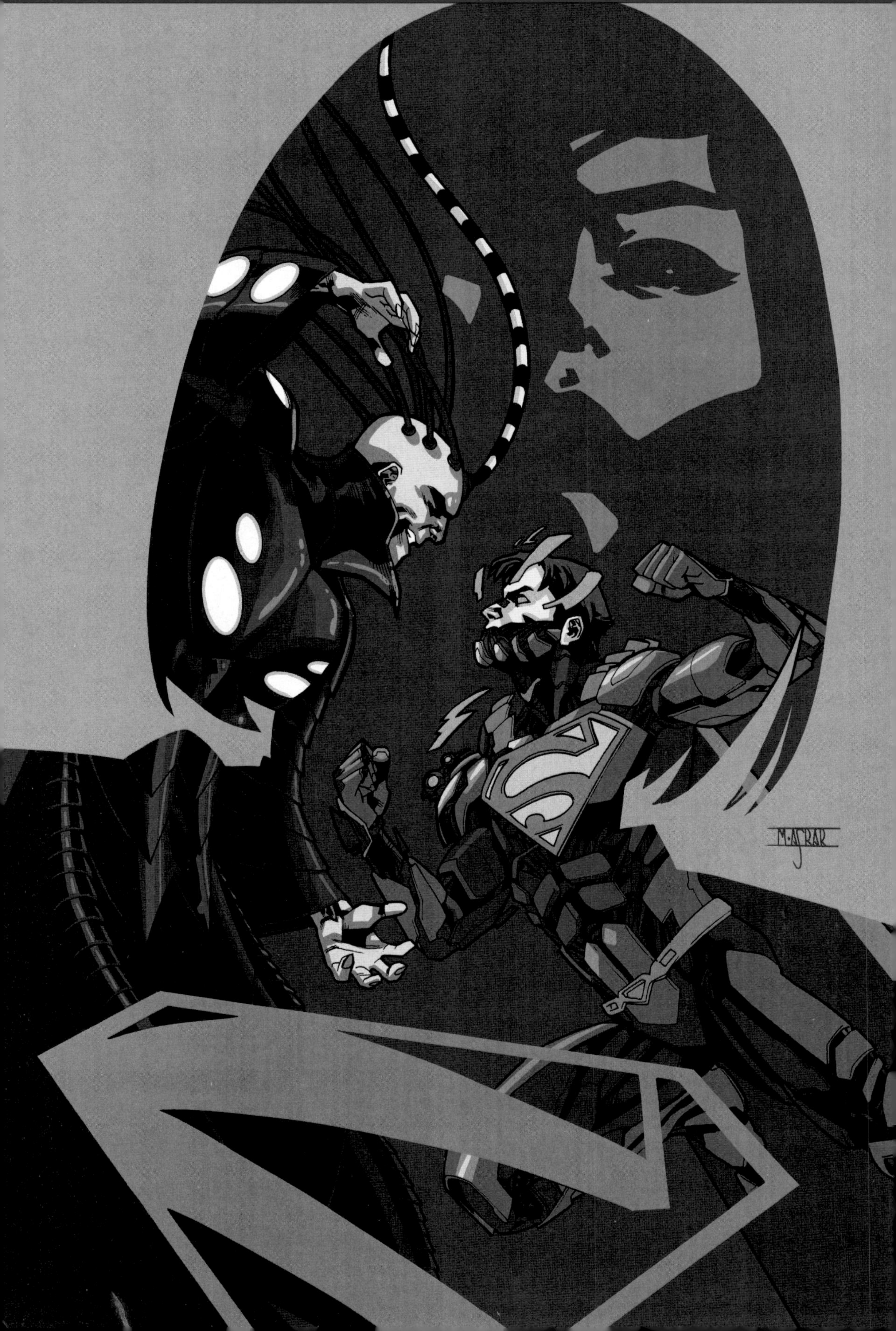
M.ASRAR

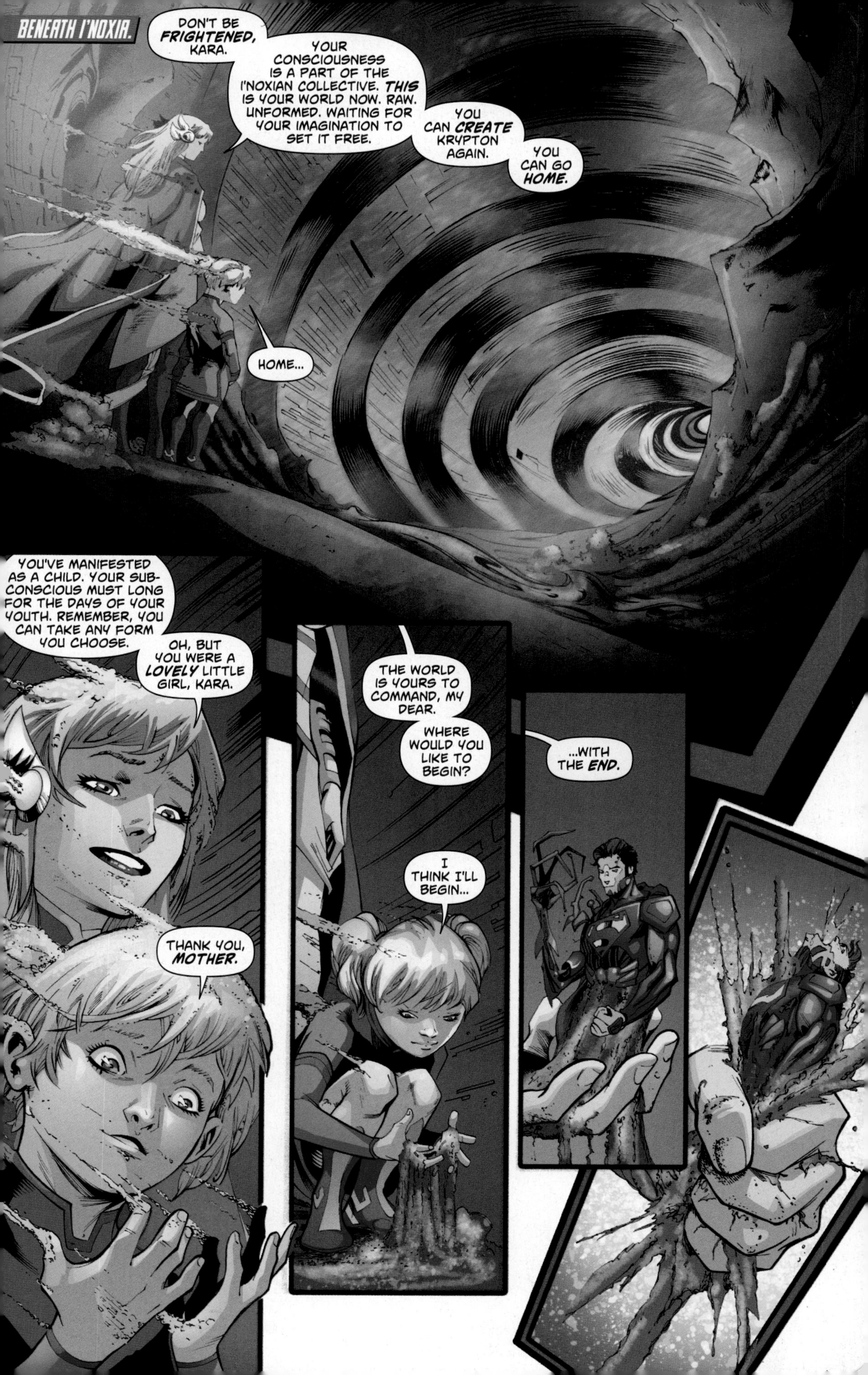
BENEATH I'NOXIA.
DON'T BE FRIGHTENED, KARA.
YOUR CONSCIOUSNESS IS A PART OF THE I'NOXIAN COLLECTIVE. THIS IS YOUR WORLD NOW. RAW. UNFORMED. WAITING FOR YOUR IMAGINATION TO SET IT FREE.
YOU CAN CREATE KRYPTON AGAIN.
YOU CAN GO HOME.
HOME...
YOU'VE MANIFESTED AS A CHILD. YOUR SUB-CONSCIOUS MUST LONG FOR THE DAYS OF YOUR YOUTH. REMEMBER, YOU CAN TAKE ANY FORM YOU CHOOSE.
OH, BUT YOU WERE A LOVELY LITTLE GIRL, KARA.
THANK YOU, MOTHER.
THE WORLD IS YOURS TO COMMAND, MY DEAR.
WHERE WOULD YOU LIKE TO BEGIN?
I THINK I'LL BEGIN...
...WITH THE END.

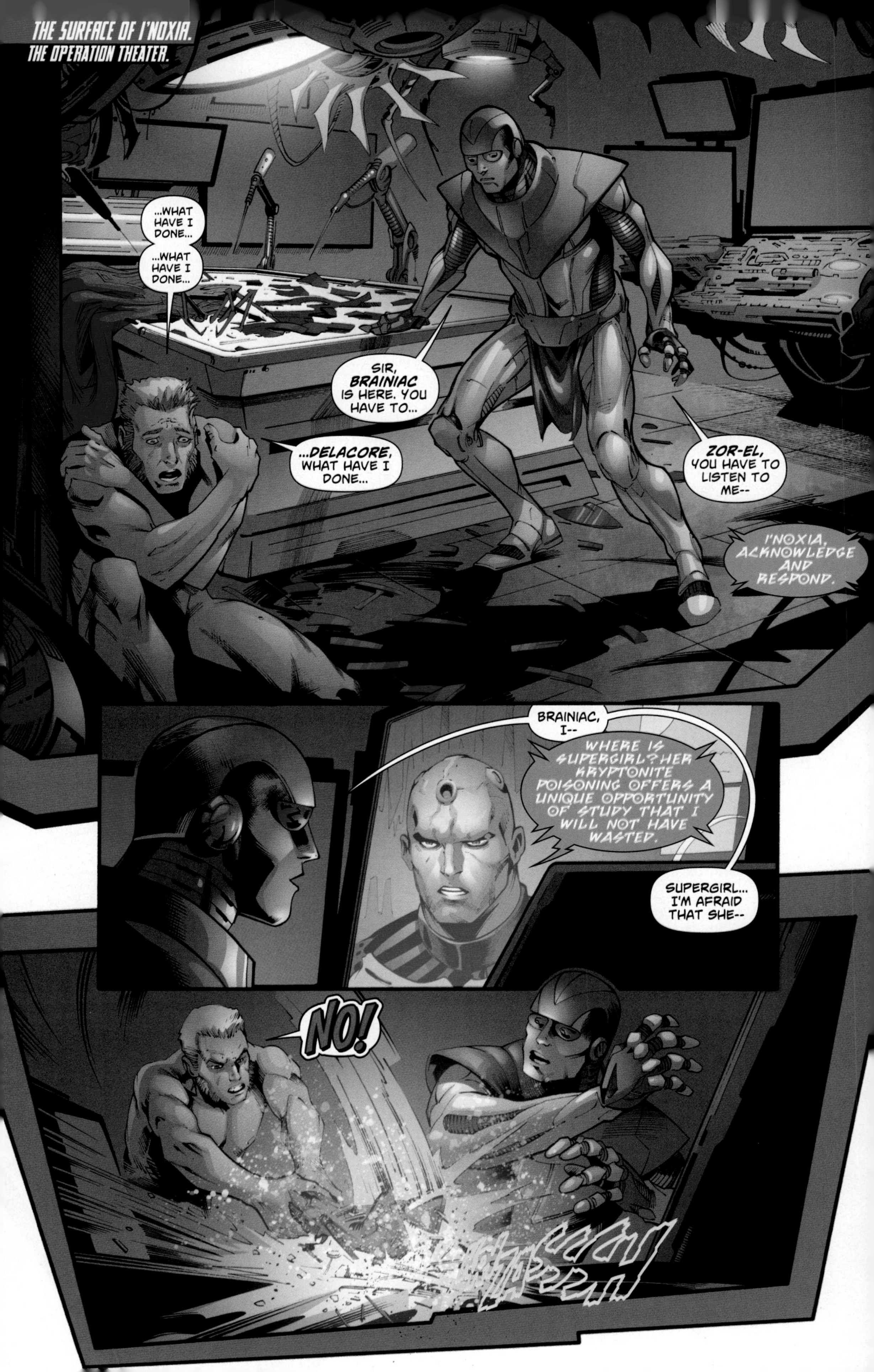
THE SURFACE OF I'NOXIA. THE OPERATION THEATER.
...WHAT HAVE I DONE...
...WHAT HAVE I DONE...
SIR, BRAINIAC IS HERE. YOU HAVE TO...
...DELACORE, WHAT HAVE I DONE...
ZOR-EL, YOU HAVE TO LISTEN TO ME--
I'NOXIA, ACKNOWLEDGE AND RESPOND.
BRAINIAC, I--
WHERE IS SUPERGIRL? HER KRYPTONITE POISONING OFFERS A UNIQUE OPPORTUNITY OF STUDY THAT I WILL NOT HAVE WASTED.
SUPERGIRL... I'M AFRAID THAT SHE--
NO!

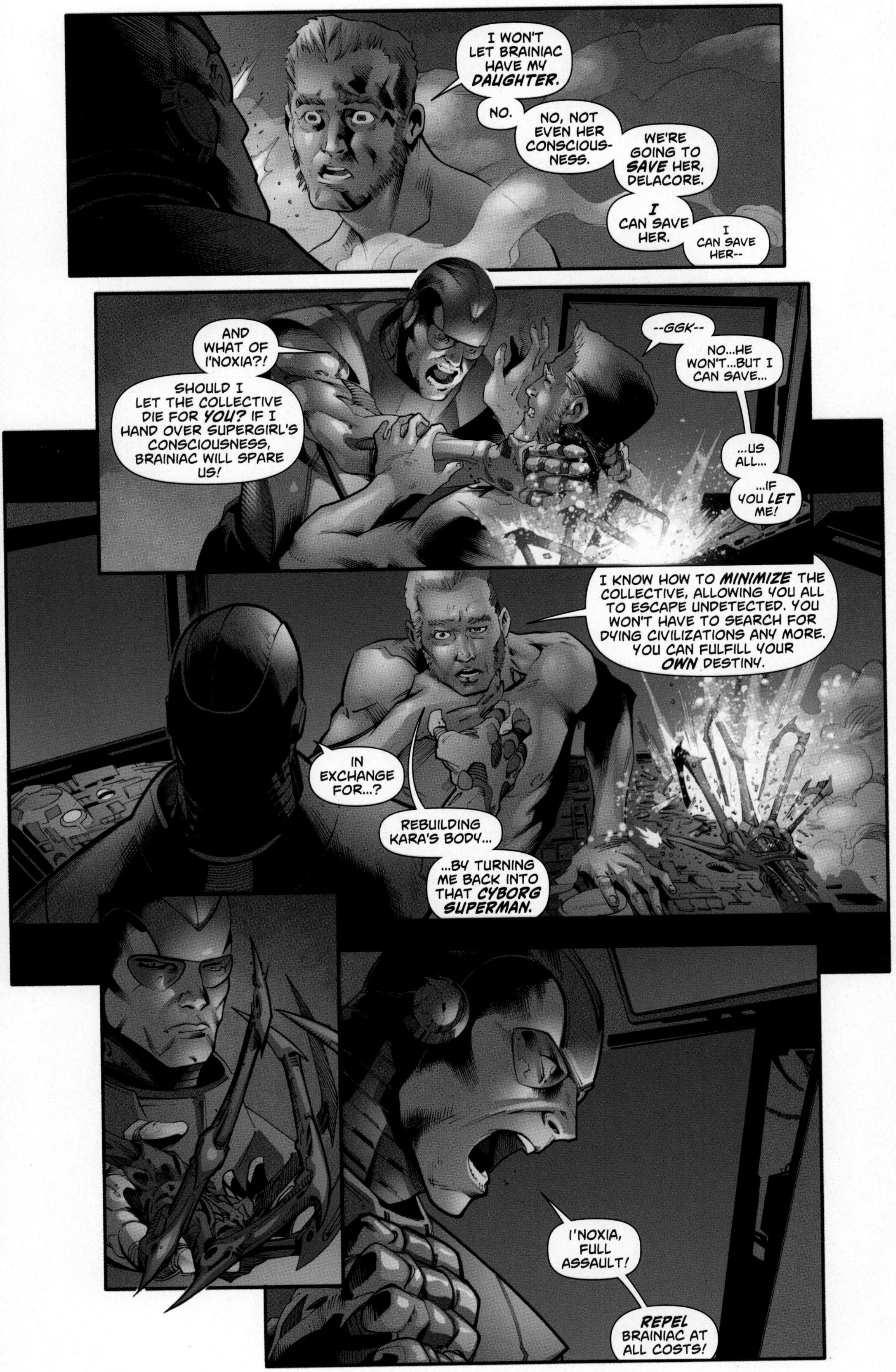
I WON'T LET BRAINIAC HAVE MY DAUGHTER.
NO.
NO, NOT EVEN HER CONSCIOUSNESS.
WE'RE GOING TO SAVE HER, DELACORE.
I CAN SAVE HER.
I CAN SAVE HER--
AND WHAT OF I'NOXIA?!
SHOULD I LET THE COLLECTIVE DIE FOR YOU? IF I HAND OVER SUPERGIRL'S CONSCIOUSNESS, BRAINIAC WILL SPARE US!
--GGK--
NO...HE WON'T...BUT I CAN SAVE...
...US ALL...
...IF YOU LET ME!
I KNOW HOW TO MINIMIZE THE COLLECTIVE, ALLOWING YOU ALL TO ESCAPE UNDETECTED. YOU WON'T HAVE TO SEARCH FOR DYING CIVILIZATIONS ANY MORE. YOU CAN FULFILL YOUR OWN DESTINY.
IN EXCHANGE FOR...?
REBUILDING KARA'S BODY...
...BY TURNING ME BACK INTO THAT CYBORG SUPERMAN.
I'NOXIA, FULL ASSAULT!
REPEL BRAINIAC AT ALL COSTS!

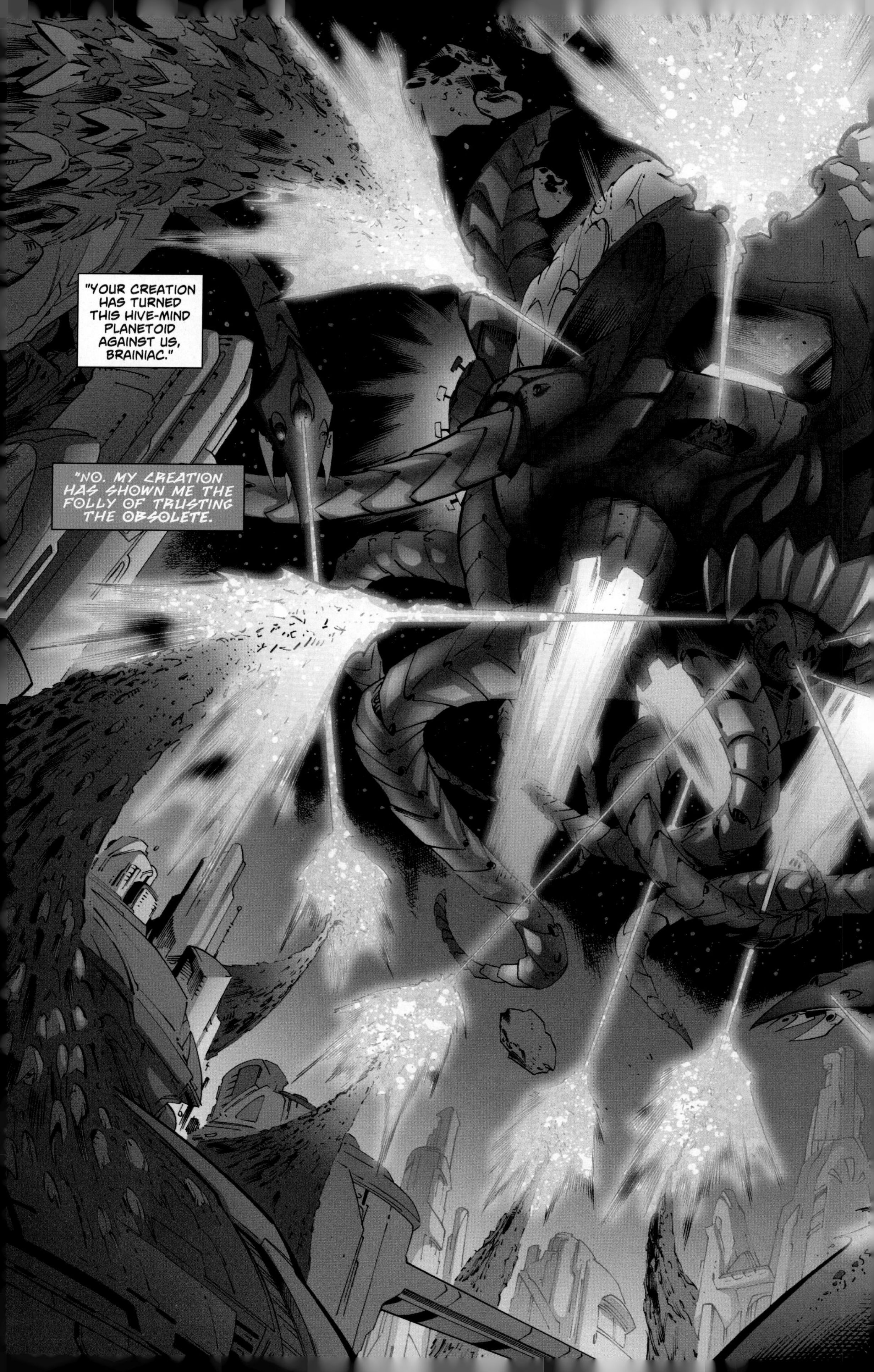
"YOUR CREATION HAS TURNED THIS HIVE-MIND PLANETOID AGAINST US, BRAINIAC."
"NO. MY CREATION HAS SHOWN ME THE FOLLY OF TRUSTING THE OBSOLETE.

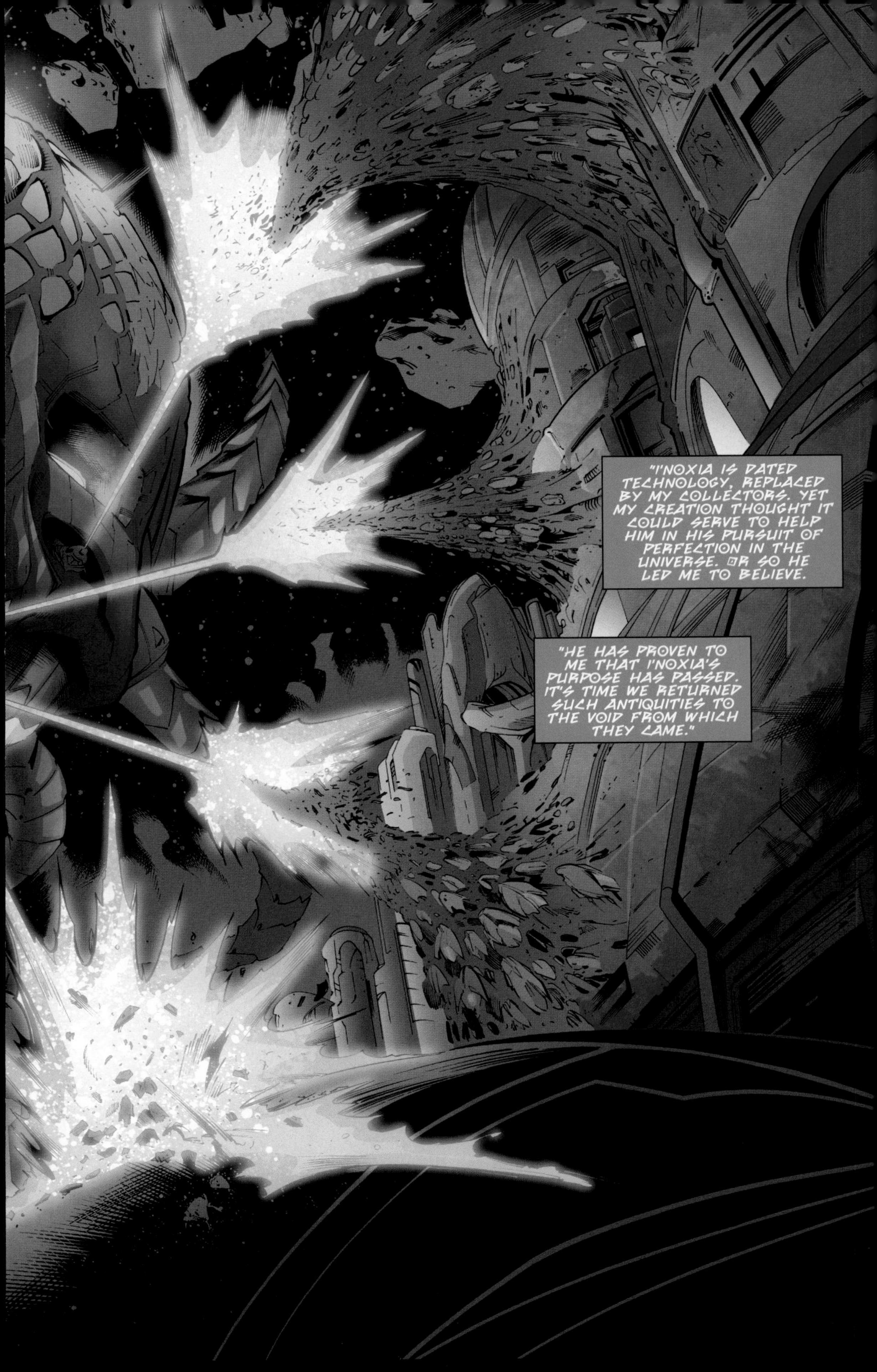
"I'NOXIA IS DATED TECHNOLOGY, REPLACED BY MY COLLECTORS. YET MY CREATION THOUGHT IT COULD SERVE TO HELP HIM IN HIS PURSUIT OF PERFECTION IN THE UNIVERSE. OR SO HE LED ME TO BELIEVE.
"HE HAS PROVEN TO ME THAT I'NOXIA'S PURPOSE HAS PASSED. IT'S TIME WE RETURNED SUCH ANTIQUITIES TO THE VOID FROM WHICH THEY CAME."

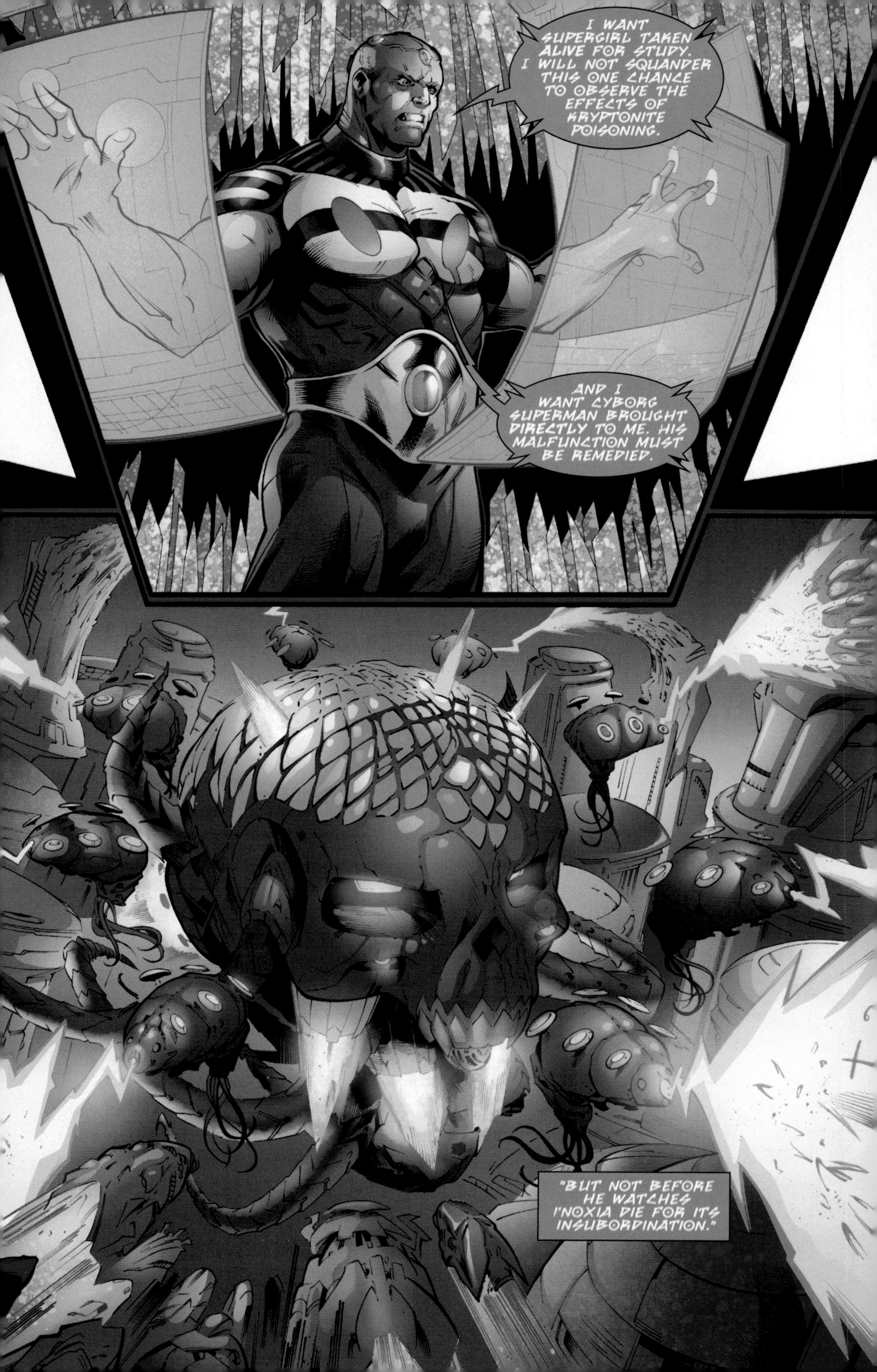
I WANT SUPERGIRL TAKEN ALIVE FOR STUDY. I WILL NOT SQUANDER THIS ONE CHANCE TO OBSERVE THE EFFECTS OF KRYPTONITE POISONING.
AND I WANT CYBORG SUPERMAN BROUGHT DIRECTLY TO ME. HIS MALFUNCTION MUST BE REMEDIED.
"BUT NOT BEFORE HE WATCHES I'NOXIA DIE FOR ITS INSUBORDINATION."

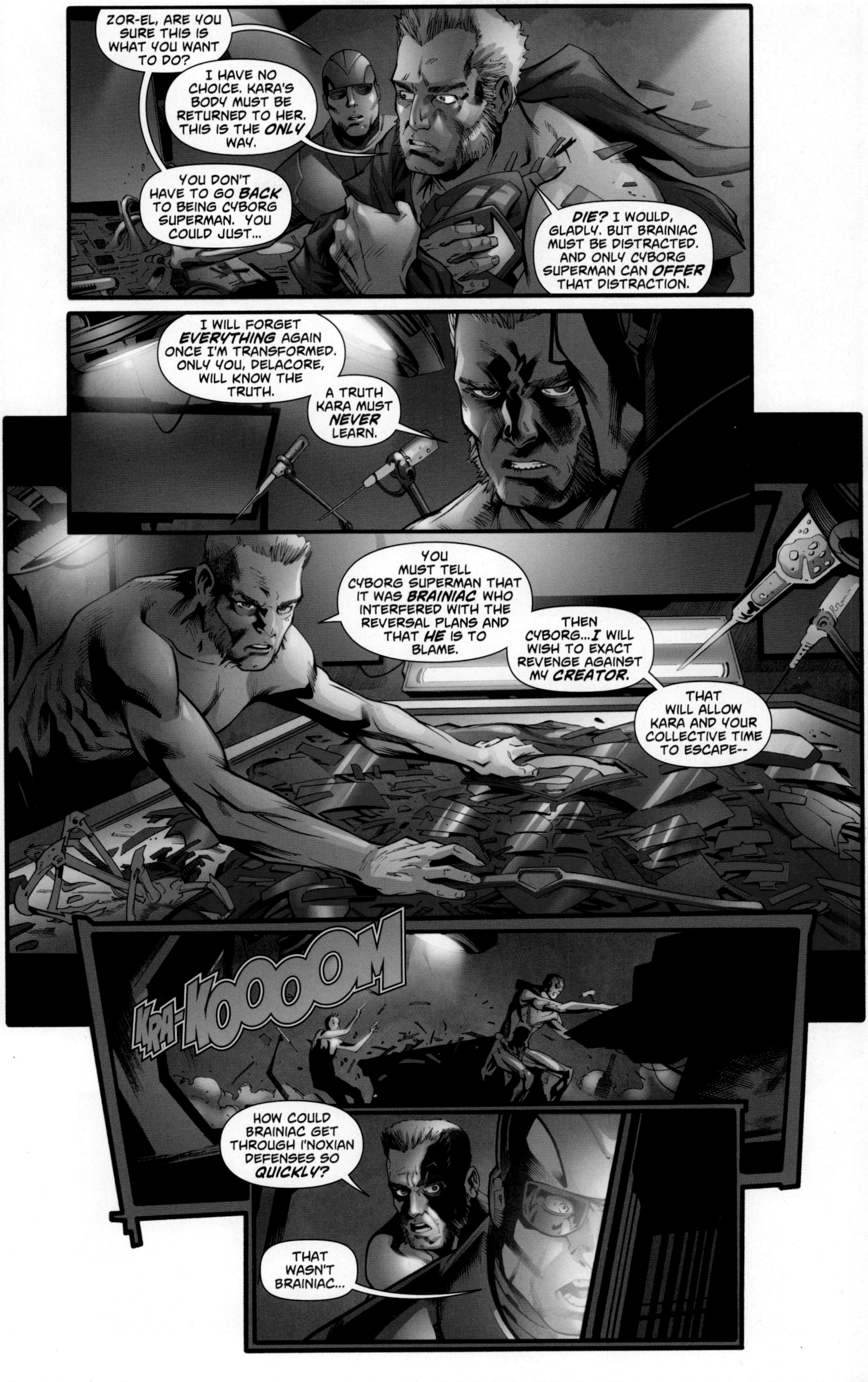
ZOR-EL, ARE YOU SURE THIS IS WHAT YOU WANT TO DO?
I HAVE NO CHOICE. KARA'S BODY MUST BE RETURNED TO HER. THIS IS THE ONLY WAY.
YOU DON'T HAVE TO GO BACK TO BEING CYBORG SUPERMAN. YOU COULD JUST...
DIE? I WOULD, GLADLY. BUT BRAINIAC MUST BE DISTRACTED. AND ONLY CYBORG SUPERMAN CAN OFFER THAT DISTRACTION.
I WILL FORGET EVERYTHING AGAIN ONCE I'M TRANSFORMED. ONLY YOU, DELACORE, WILL KNOW THE TRUTH.
A TRUTH KARA MUST NEVER LEARN.
YOU MUST TELL CYBORG SUPERMAN THAT IT WAS BRAINIAC WHO INTERFERED WITH THE REVERSAL PLANS AND THAT HE IS TO BLAME.
THEN CYBORG...I WILL WISH TO EXACT REVENGE AGAINST MY CREATOR.
THAT WILL ALLOW KARA AND YOUR COLLECTIVE TIME TO ESCAPE--
KRA-KOOOOOM
HOW COULD BRAINIAC GET THROUGH I'NOXIAN DEFENSES SO QUICKLY?
THAT WASN'T BRAINIAC...

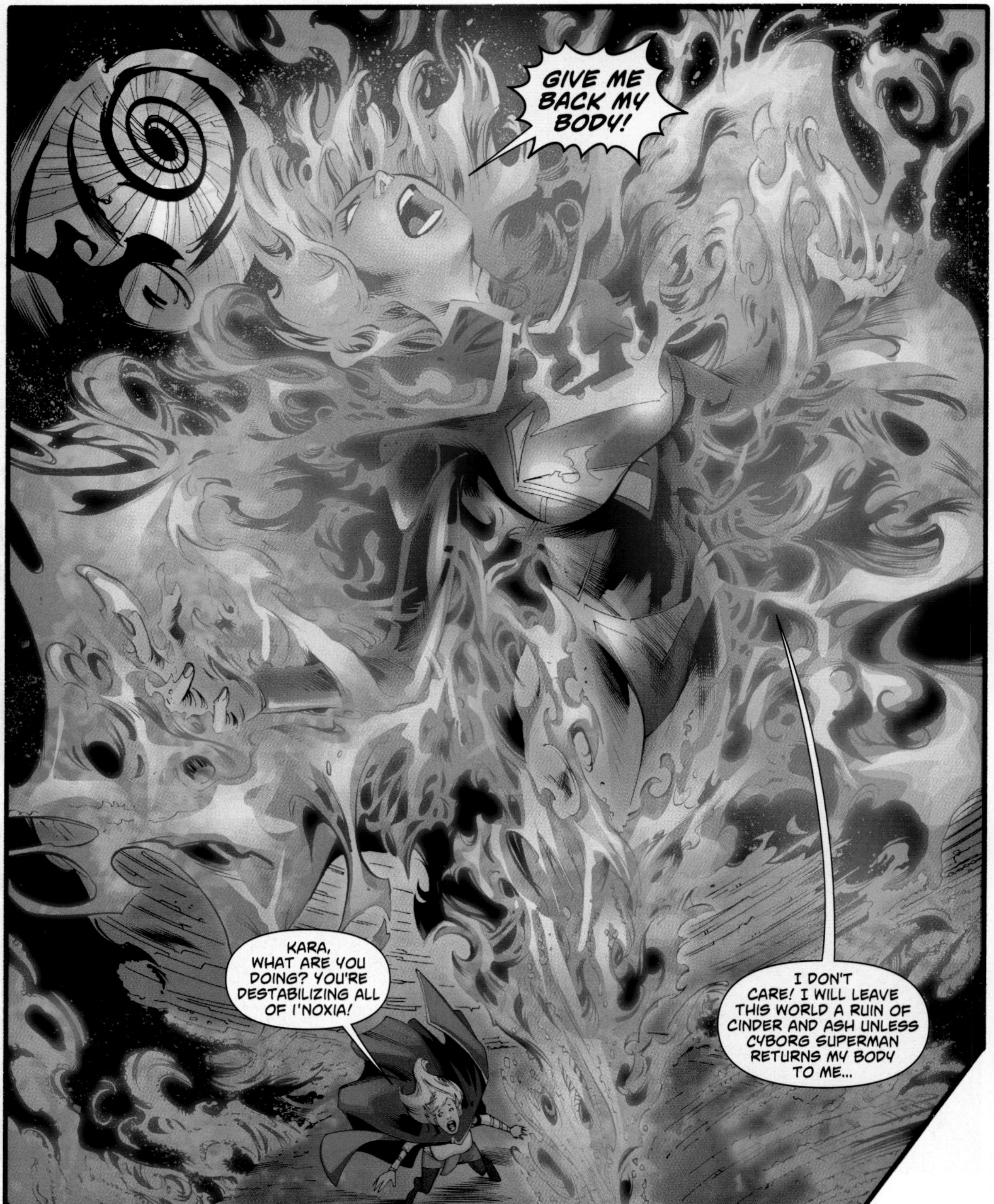
GIVE ME BACK MY BODY!
KARA, WHAT ARE YOU DOING? YOU'RE DESTABILIZING ALL OF I'NOXIA!
I DON'T CARE! I WILL LEAVE THIS WORLD A RUIN OF CINDER AND ASH UNLESS CYBORG SUPERMAN RETURNS MY BODY TO ME...
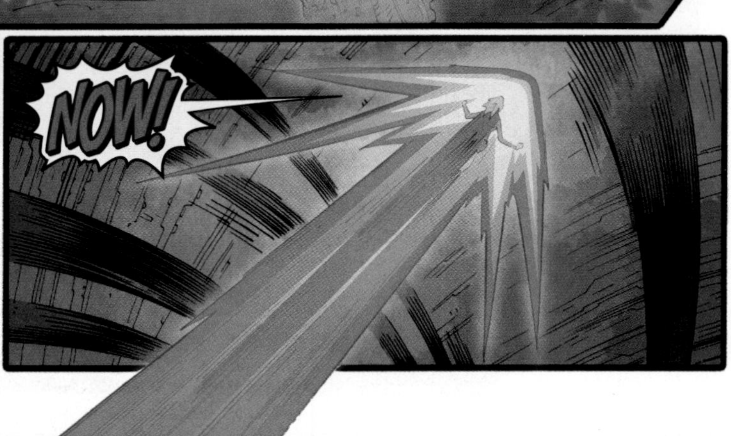
NOW!

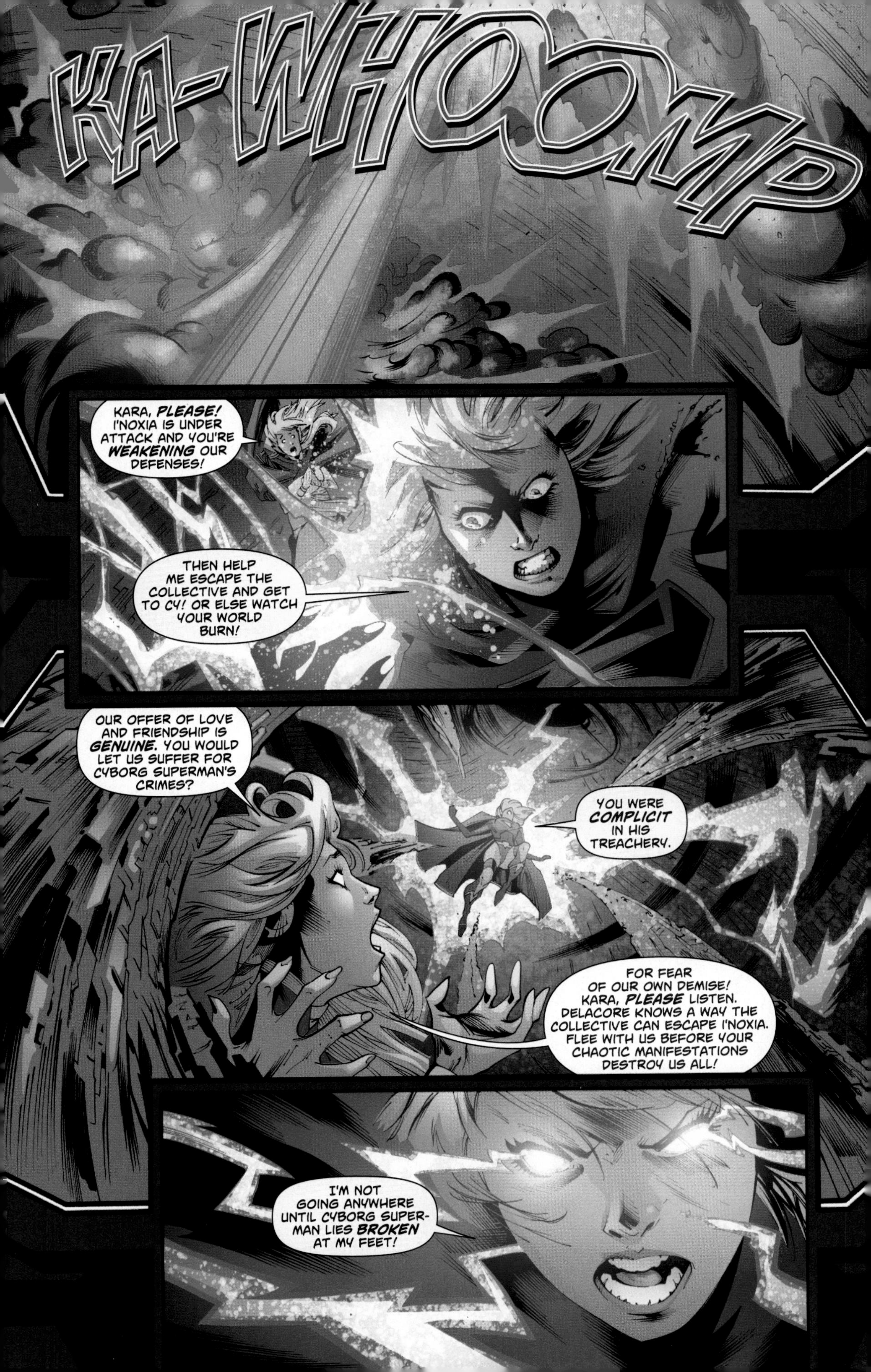
KA-WHOOMP
KARA, PLEASE! I'NOXIA IS UNDER ATTACK AND YOU'RE WEAKENING OUR DEFENSES!
THEN HELP ME ESCAPE THE COLLECTIVE AND GET TO CY! OR ELSE WATCH YOUR WORLD BURN!
OUR OFFER OF LOVE AND FRIENDSHIP IS GENUINE. YOU WOULD LET US SUFFER FOR CYBORG SUPERMAN'S CRIMES?
YOU WERE COMPLICIT IN HIS TREACHERY.
FOR FEAR OF OUR OWN DEMISE! KARA, PLEASE LISTEN. DELACORE KNOWS A WAY THE COLLECTIVE CAN ESCAPE I'NOXIA. FLEE WITH US BEFORE YOUR CHAOTIC MANIFESTATIONS DESTROY US ALL!
I'M NOT GOING ANYWHERE UNTIL CYBORG SUPER-MAN LIES BROKEN AT MY FEET!

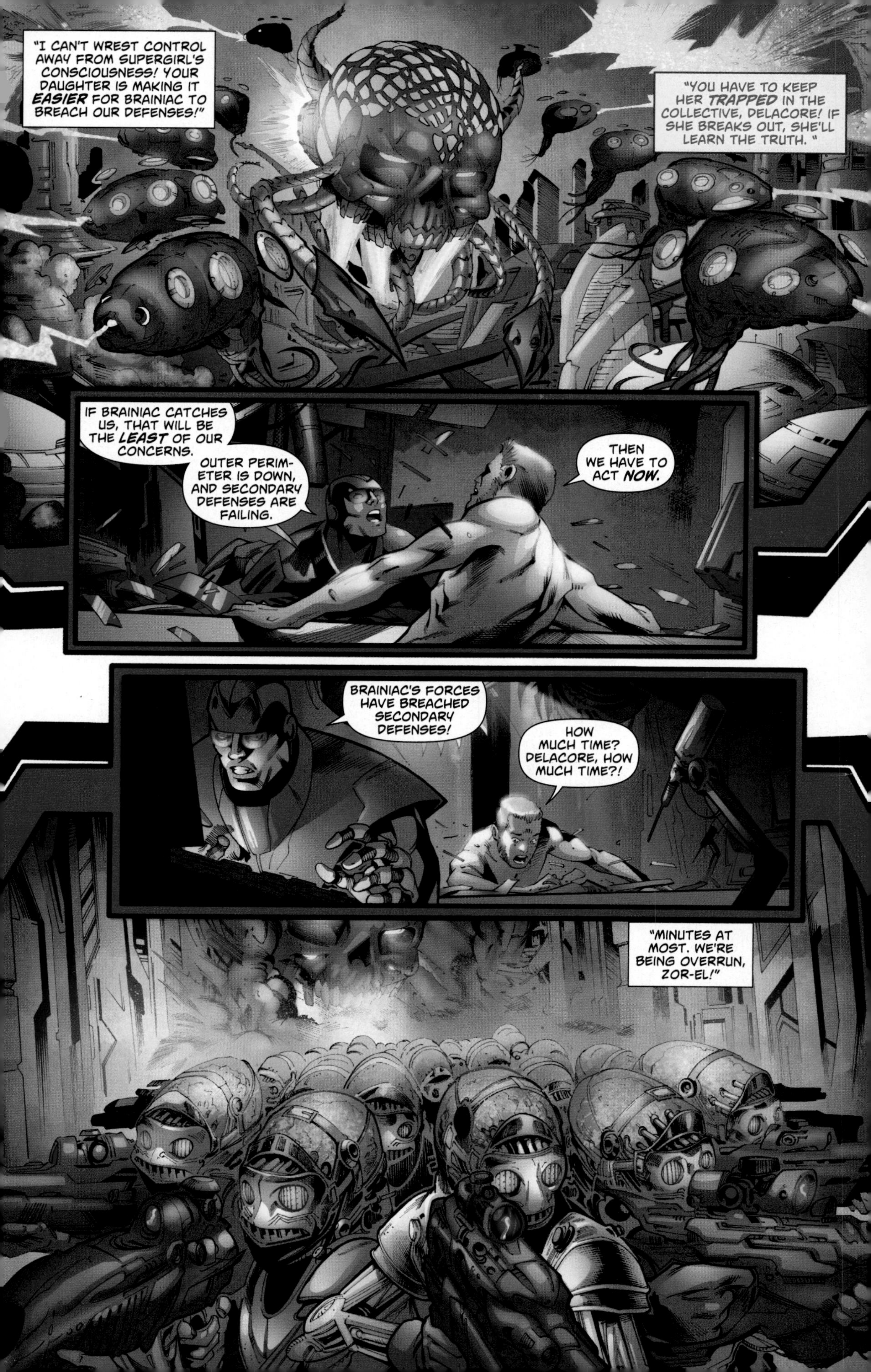
"I CAN'T WREST CONTROL AWAY FROM SUPERGIRL'S CONSCIOUSNESS! YOUR DAUGHTER IS MAKING IT EASIER FOR BRAINIAC TO BREACH OUR DEFENSES!"
"YOU HAVE TO KEEP HER TRAPPED IN THE COLLECTIVE, DELACORE! IF SHE BREAKS OUT, SHE'LL LEARN THE TRUTH."
IF BRAINIAC CATCHES US, THAT WILL BE THE LEAST OF OUR CONCERNS.
OUTER PERIMETER IS DOWN, AND SECONDARY DEFENSES ARE FAILING.
THEN WE HAVE TO ACT NOW.
BRAINIAC'S FORCES HAVE BREACHED SECONDARY DEFENSES!
HOW MUCH TIME? DELACORE, HOW MUCH TIME?!
"MINUTES AT MOST. WE'RE BEING OVERRUN, ZOR-EL!"

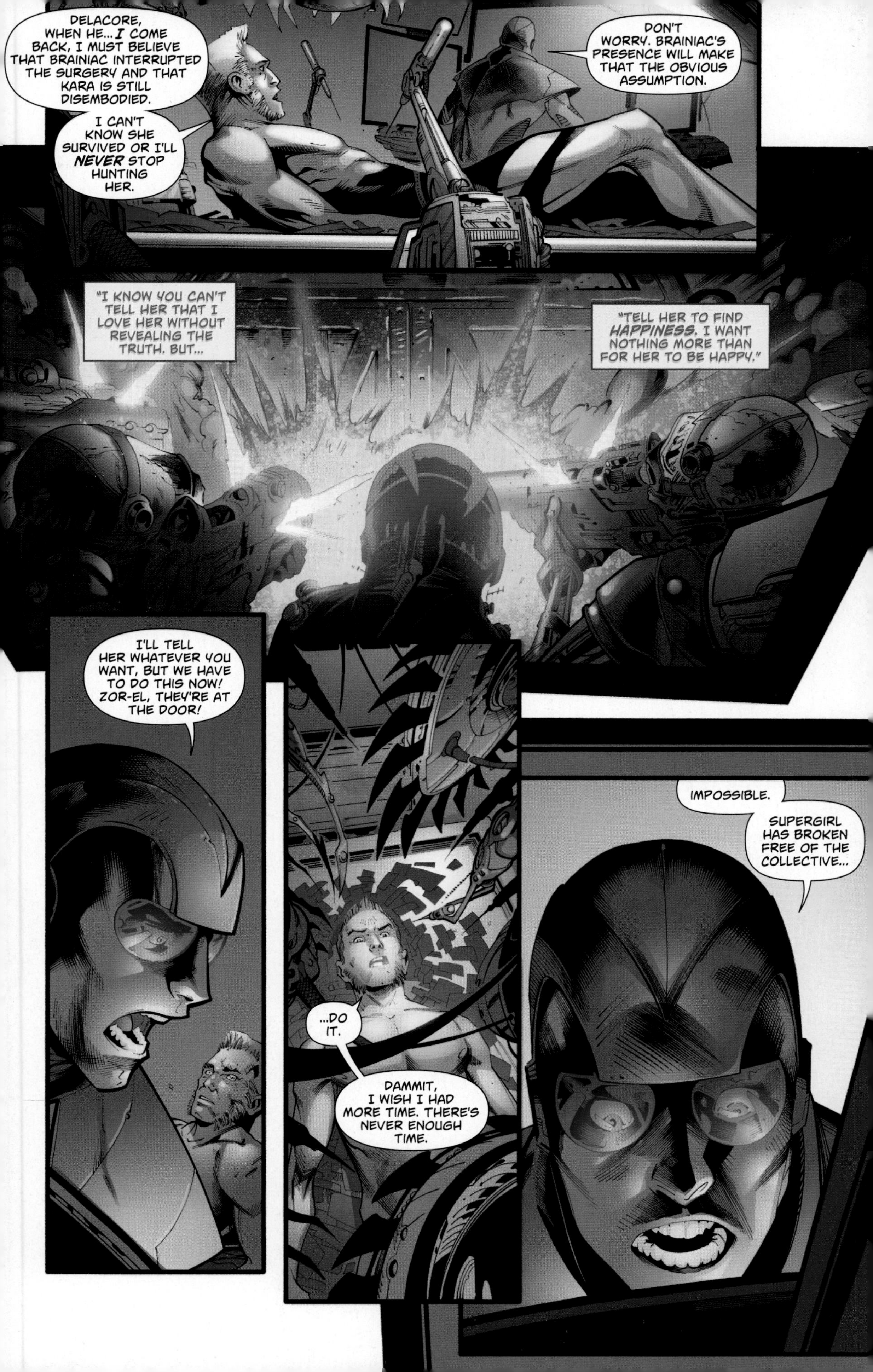

DELACORE, WHEN HE... I COME BACK, I MUST BELIEVE THAT BRAINIAC INTERRUPTED THE SURGERY AND THAT KARA IS STILL DISEMBODIED.
I CAN'T KNOW SHE SURVIVED OR I'LL NEVER STOP HUNTING HER.
DON'T WORRY. BRAINIAC'S PRESENCE WILL MAKE THAT THE OBVIOUS ASSUMPTION.
"I KNOW YOU CAN'T TELL HER THAT I LOVE HER WITHOUT REVEALING THE TRUTH. BUT...
"TELL HER TO FIND HAPPINESS. I WANT NOTHING MORE THAN FOR HER TO BE HAPPY."
I'LL TELL HER WHATEVER YOU WANT, BUT WE HAVE TO DO THIS NOW! ZOR-EL, THEY'RE AT THE DOOR!
...DO IT.
DAMMIT, I WISH I HAD MORE TIME. THERE'S NEVER ENOUGH TIME.
IMPOSSIBLE.
SUPERGIRL HAS BROKEN FREE OF THE COLLECTIVE...

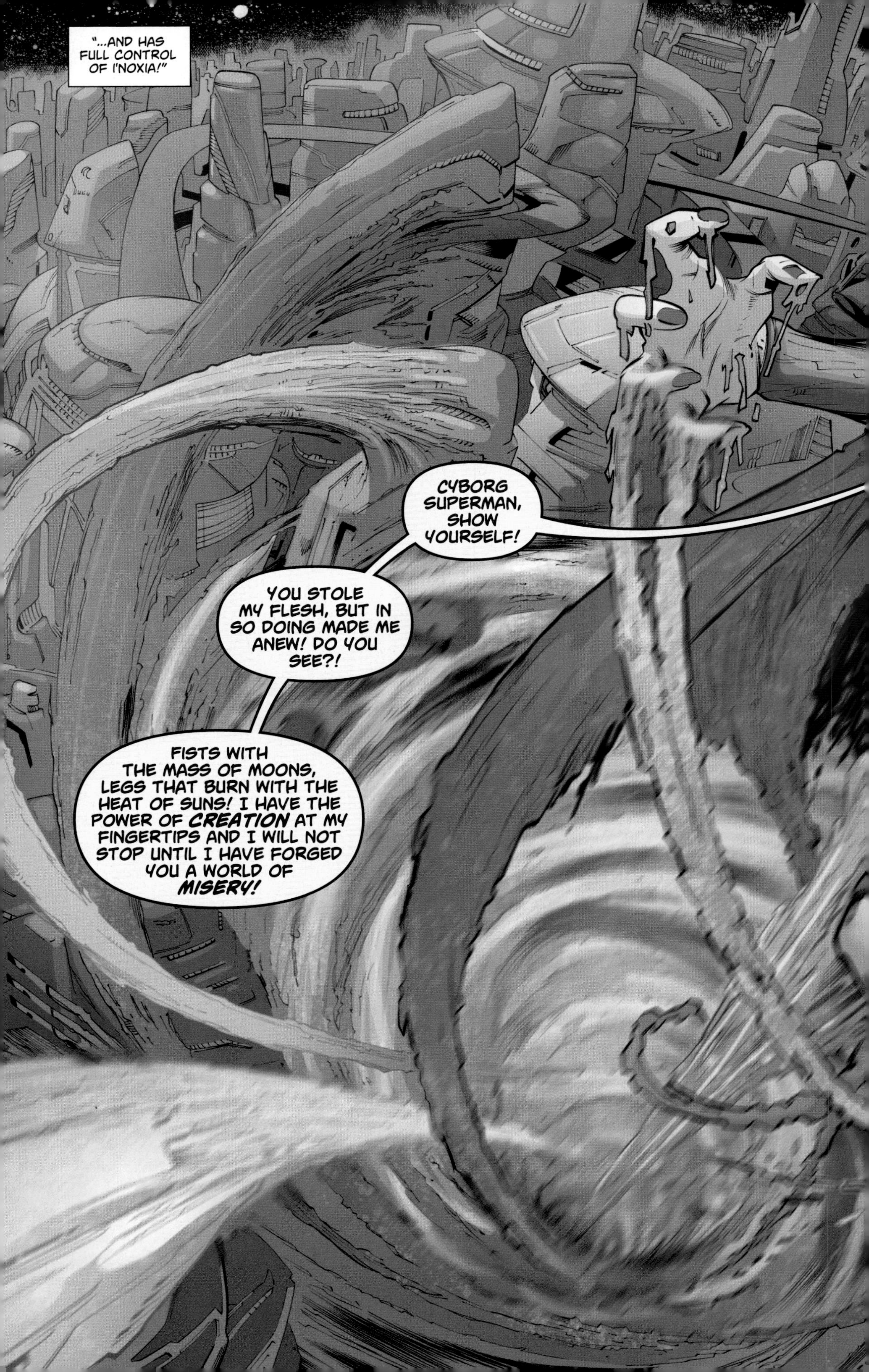
"...AND HAS FULL CONTROL OF I'NOXIA!"
CYBORG SUPERMAN, SHOW YOURSELF!
YOU STOLE MY FLESH, BUT IN SO DOING MADE ME ANEW! DO YOU SEE?!
FISTS WITH THE MASS OF MOONS, LEGS THAT BURN WITH THE HEAT OF SUNS! I HAVE THE POWER OF CREATION AT MY FINGERTIPS AND I WILL NOT STOP UNTIL I HAVE FORGED YOU A WORLD OF MISERY!

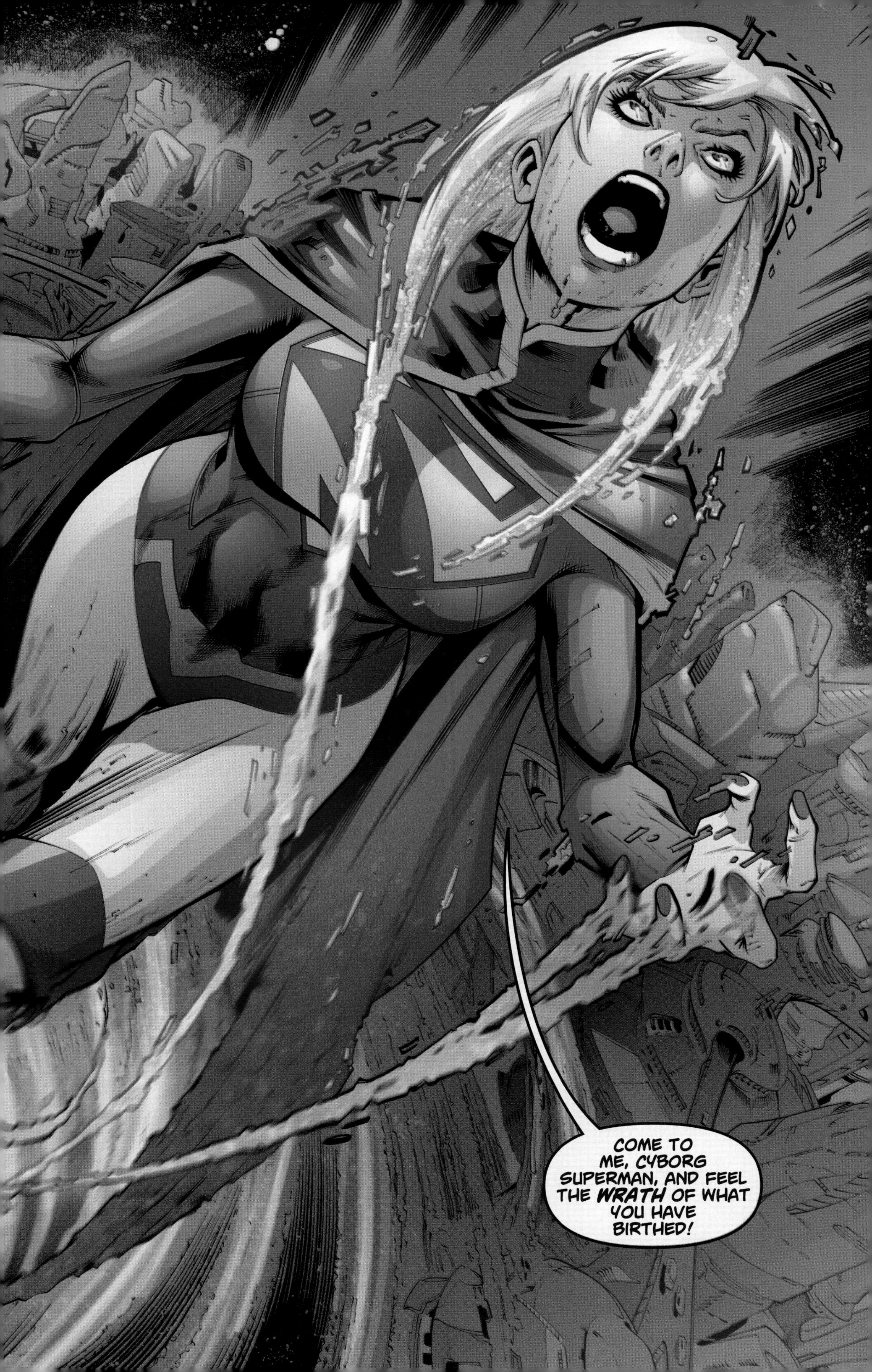
COME TO ME, CYBORG SUPERMAN, AND FEEL THE *WRATH* OF WHAT YOU HAVE BIRTHED!

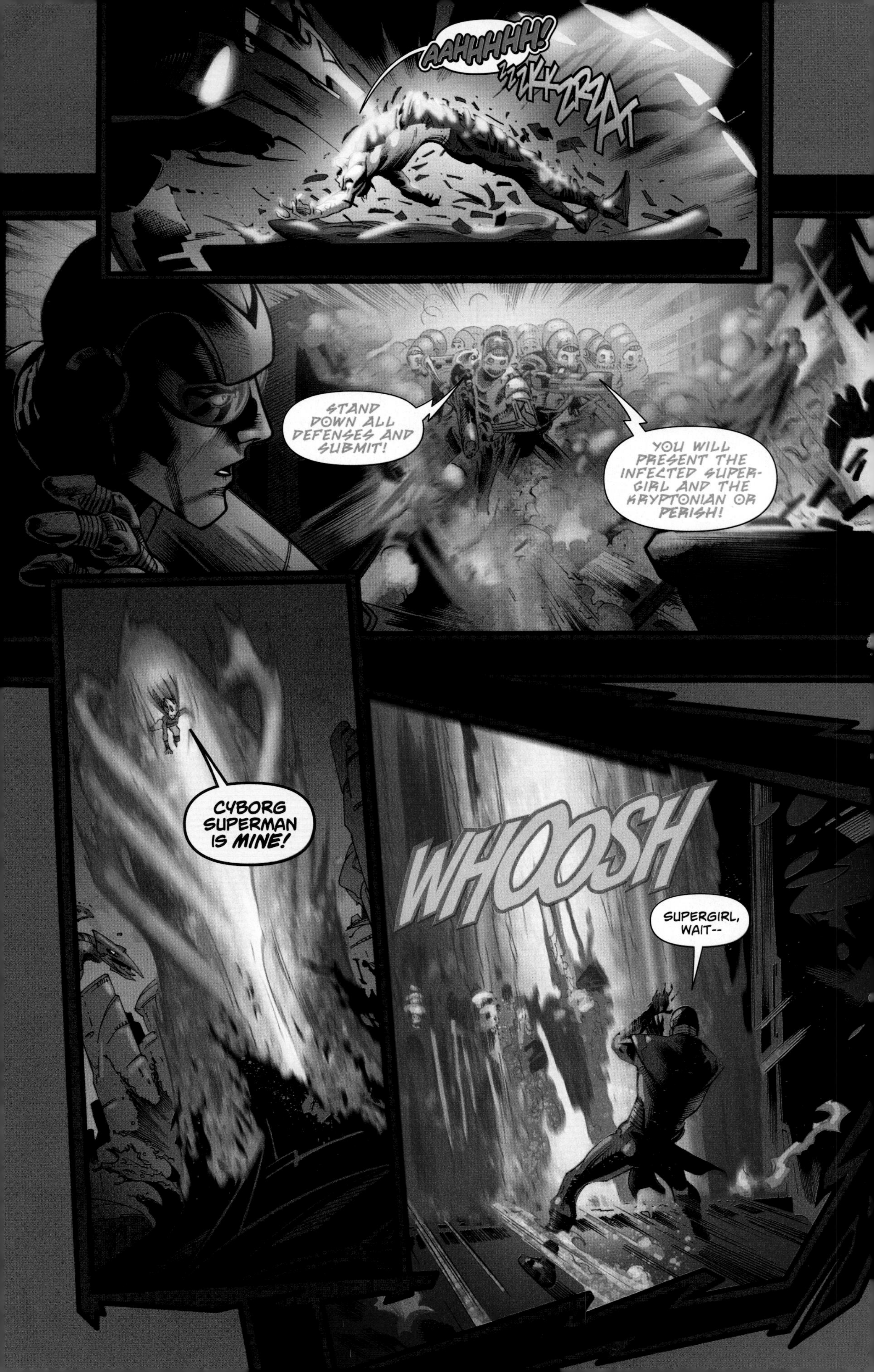
AAHHHHH!
ZZZKKZRZAK
STAND DOWN ALL DEFENSES AND SUBMIT!
YOU WILL PRESENT THE INFECTED SUPER-GIRL AND THE KRYPTONIAN OR PERISH!
CYBORG SUPERMAN IS MINE!
WHOOOSH
SUPERGIRL, WAIT--

DON'T LET HER STOP THE OPER-
AAAGHH!
WHO...
WHO AM I...
I AM...
PERFECTION.

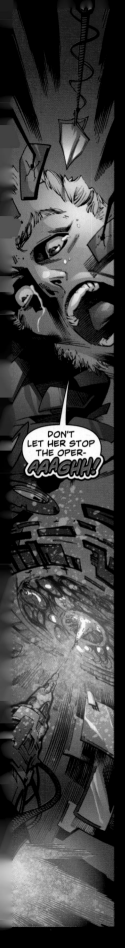

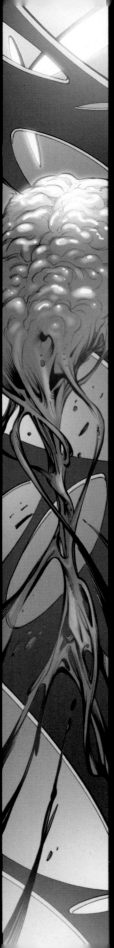

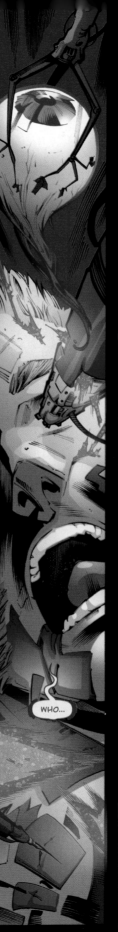

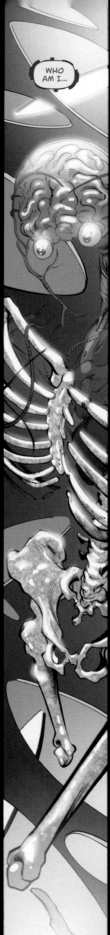

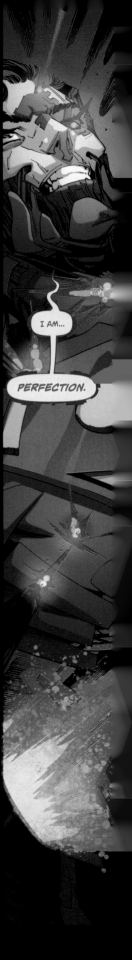

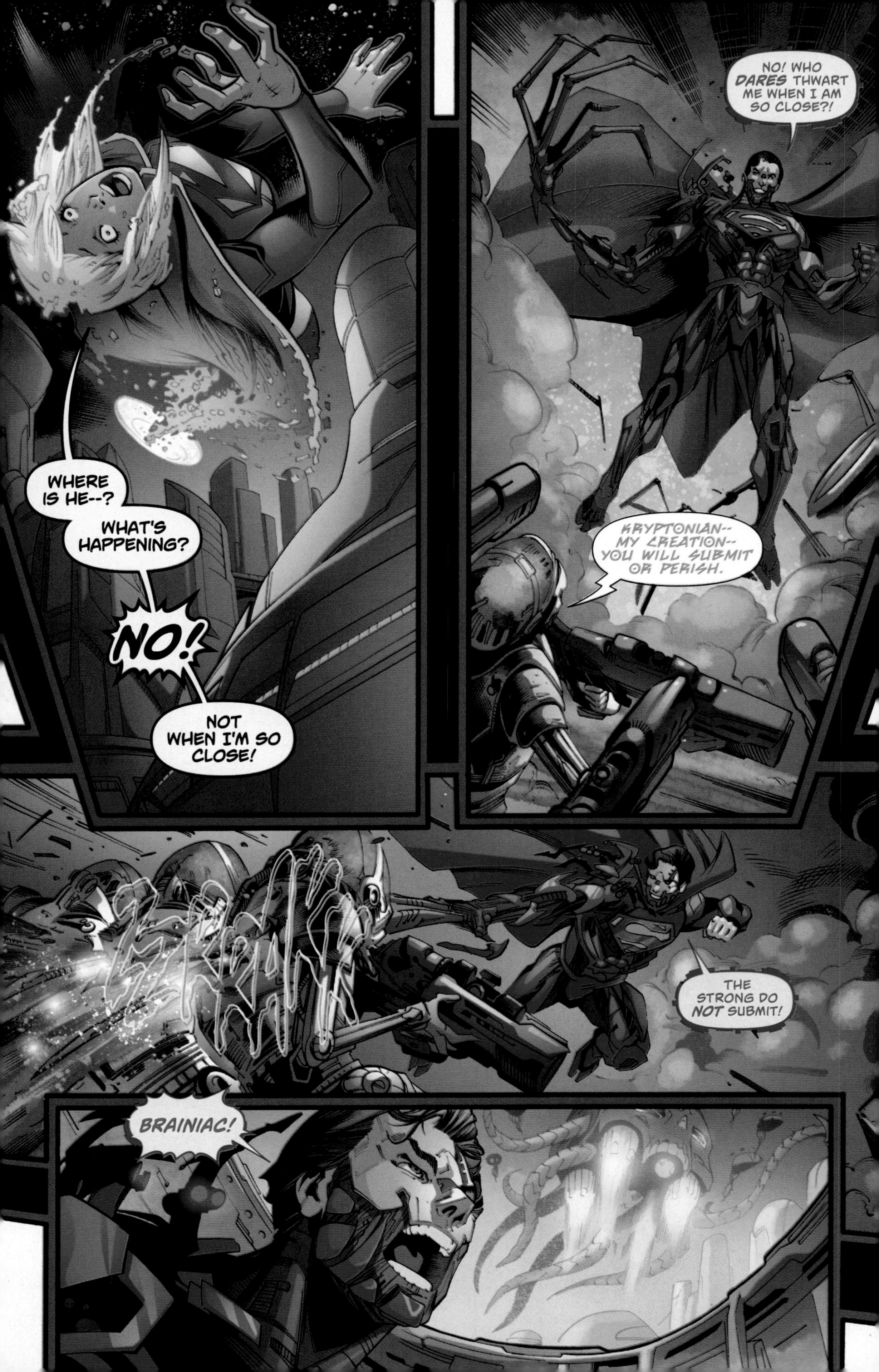
WHERE IS HE--?
WHAT'S HAPPENING?
NO!
NOT WHEN I'M SO CLOSE!
NO! WHO DARES THWART ME WHEN I AM SO CLOSE?!
KRYPTONIAN-- MY CREATION-- YOU WILL SUBMIT OR PERISH.
THE STRONG DO NOT SUBMIT!
BRAINIAC!

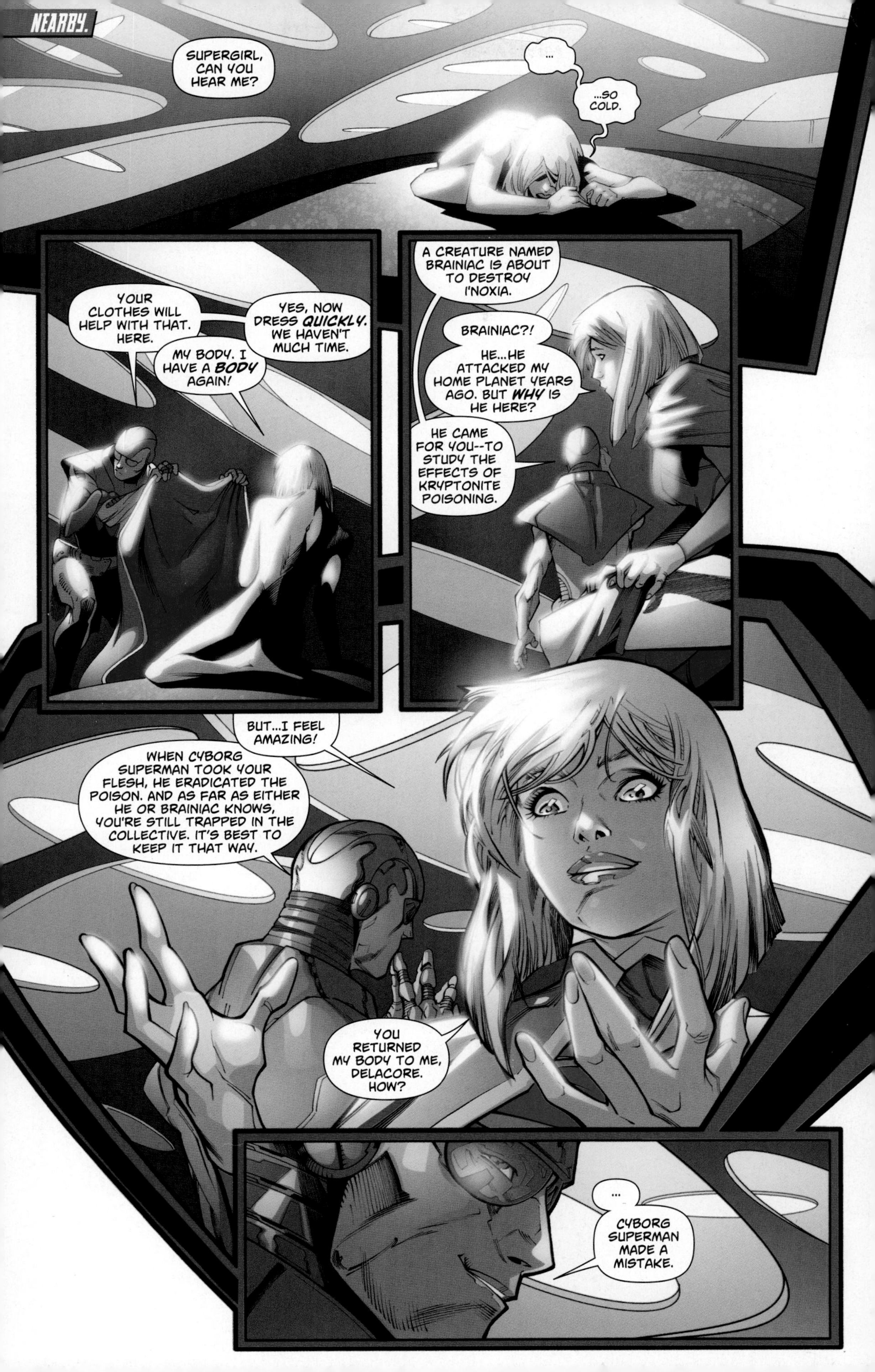
NEARBY.
SUPERGIRL, CAN YOU HEAR ME?
...
...SO COLD.
YOUR CLOTHES WILL HELP WITH THAT. HERE.
MY BODY. I HAVE A BODY AGAIN!
YES, NOW DRESS QUICKLY. WE HAVEN'T MUCH TIME.
A CREATURE NAMED BRAINIAC IS ABOUT TO DESTROY I'NOXIA.
BRAINIAC?!
HE...HE ATTACKED MY HOME PLANET YEARS AGO. BUT WHY IS HE HERE?
HE CAME FOR YOU--TO STUDY THE EFFECTS OF KRYPTONITE POISONING.
BUT...I FEEL AMAZING!
WHEN CYBORG SUPERMAN TOOK YOUR FLESH, HE ERADICATED THE POISON. AND AS FAR AS EITHER HE OR BRAINIAC KNOWS, YOU'RE STILL TRAPPED IN THE COLLECTIVE. IT'S BEST TO KEEP IT THAT WAY.
YOU RETURNED MY BODY TO ME, DELACORE. HOW?
...
CYBORG SUPERMAN MADE A MISTAKE.

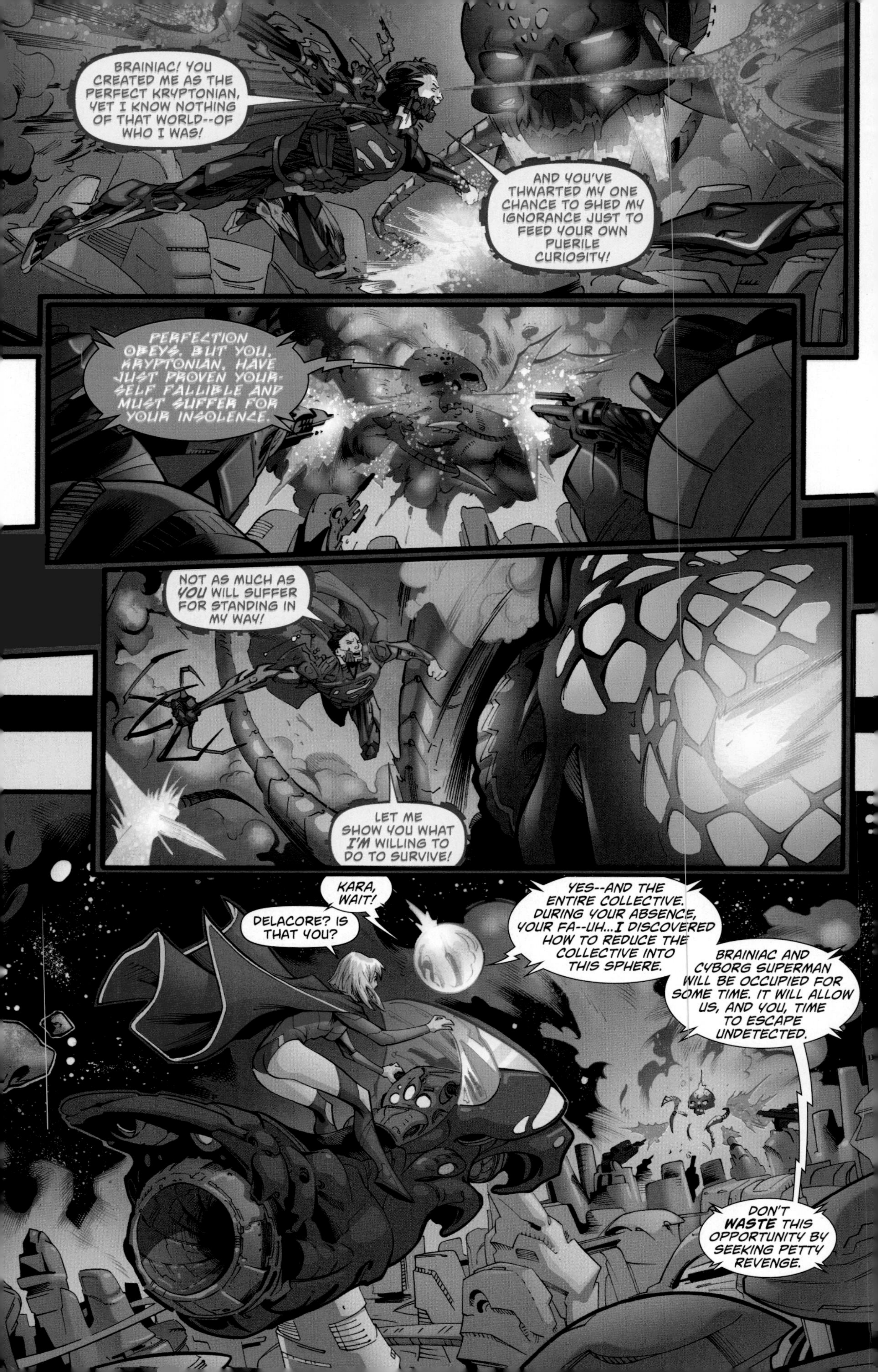
BRAINIAC! YOU CREATED ME AS THE PERFECT KRYPTONIAN, YET I KNOW NOTHING OF THAT WORLD--OF WHO I WAS!
AND YOU'VE THWARTED MY ONE CHANCE TO SHED MY IGNORANCE JUST TO FEED YOUR OWN PUERILE CURIOSITY!
PERFECTION OBEYS. BUT YOU, KRYPTONIAN, HAVE JUST PROVEN YOURSELF FALLIBLE AND MUST SUFFER FOR YOUR INSOLENCE.
NOT AS MUCH AS YOU WILL SUFFER FOR STANDING IN MY WAY!
LET ME SHOW YOU WHAT I'M WILLING TO DO TO SURVIVE!
KARA, WAIT!
DELACORE? IS THAT YOU?
YES--AND THE ENTIRE COLLECTIVE. DURING YOUR ABSENCE, YOUR FA--UH...I DISCOVERED HOW TO REDUCE THE COLLECTIVE INTO THIS SPHERE.
BRAINIAC AND CYBORG SUPERMAN WILL BE OCCUPIED FOR SOME TIME. IT WILL ALLOW US, AND YOU, TIME TO ESCAPE UNDETECTED.
DON'T WASTE THIS OPPORTUNITY BY SEEKING PETTY REVENGE.

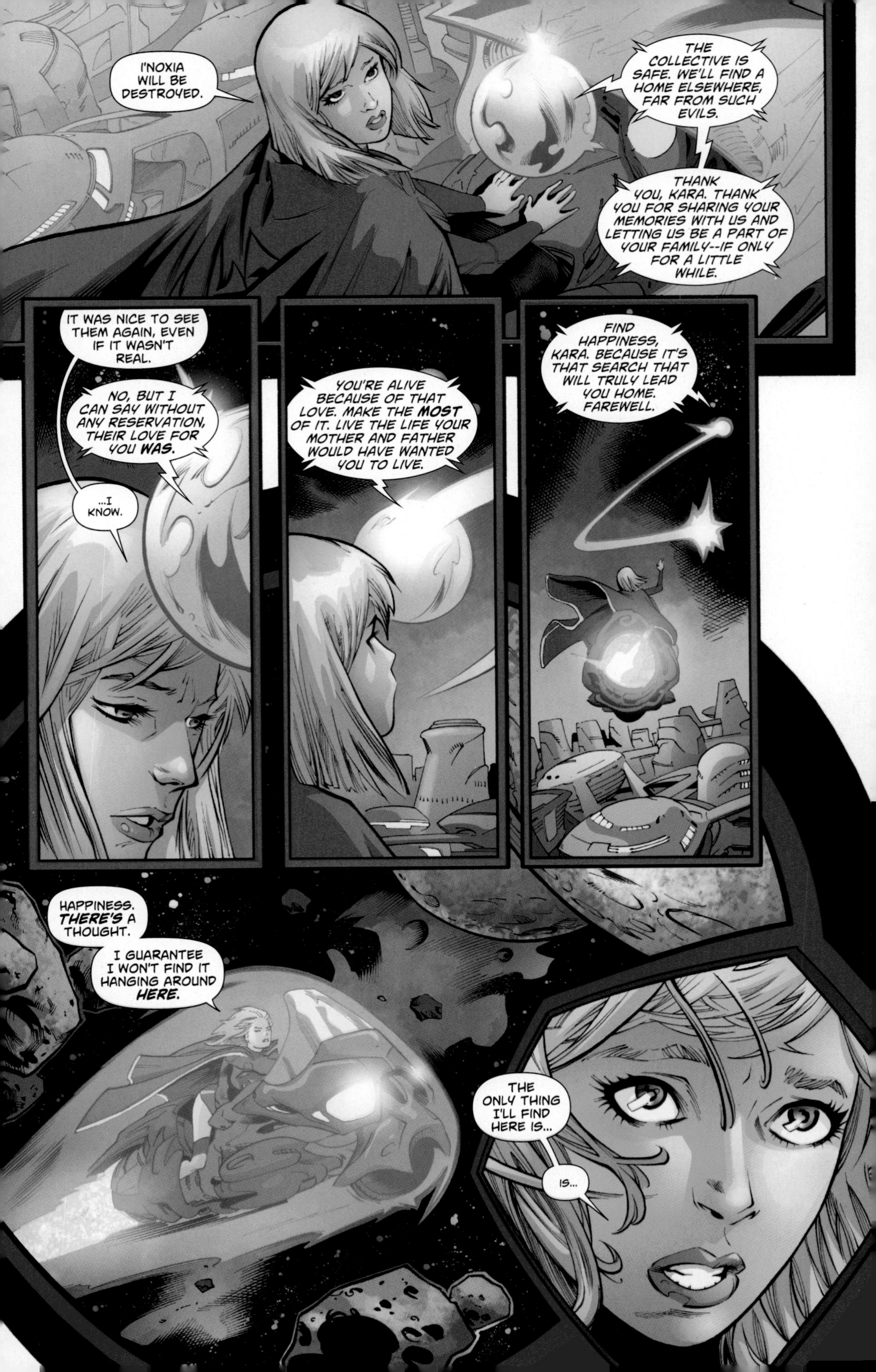
I'NOXIA WILL BE DESTROYED.
THE COLLECTIVE IS SAFE. WE'LL FIND A HOME ELSEWHERE, FAR FROM SUCH EVILS.
THANK YOU, KARA. THANK YOU FOR SHARING YOUR MEMORIES WITH US AND LETTING US BE A PART OF YOUR FAMILY--IF ONLY FOR A LITTLE WHILE.
IT WAS NICE TO SEE THEM AGAIN, EVEN IF IT WASN'T REAL.
NO, BUT I CAN SAY WITHOUT ANY RESERVATION, THEIR LOVE FOR YOU WAS.
...I KNOW.
YOU'RE ALIVE BECAUSE OF THAT LOVE. MAKE THE MOST OF IT. LIVE THE LIFE YOUR MOTHER AND FATHER WOULD HAVE WANTED YOU TO LIVE.
FIND HAPPINESS, KARA. BECAUSE IT'S THAT SEARCH THAT WILL TRULY LEAD YOU HOME. FAREWELL.
HAPPINESS. THERE'S A THOUGHT.
I GUARANTEE I WON'T FIND IT HANGING AROUND HERE.
THE ONLY THING I'LL FIND HERE IS...
IS...

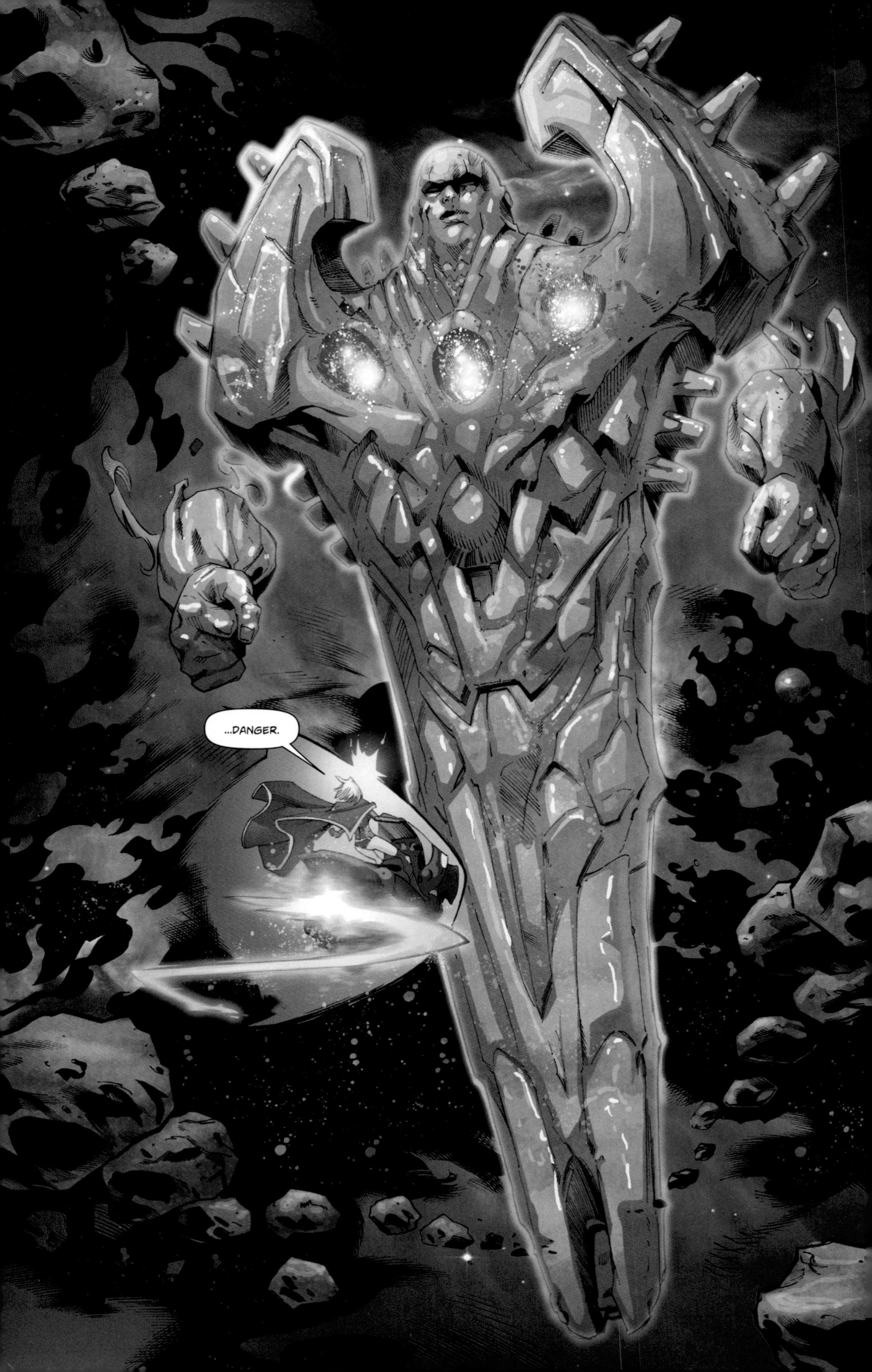
...DANGER.

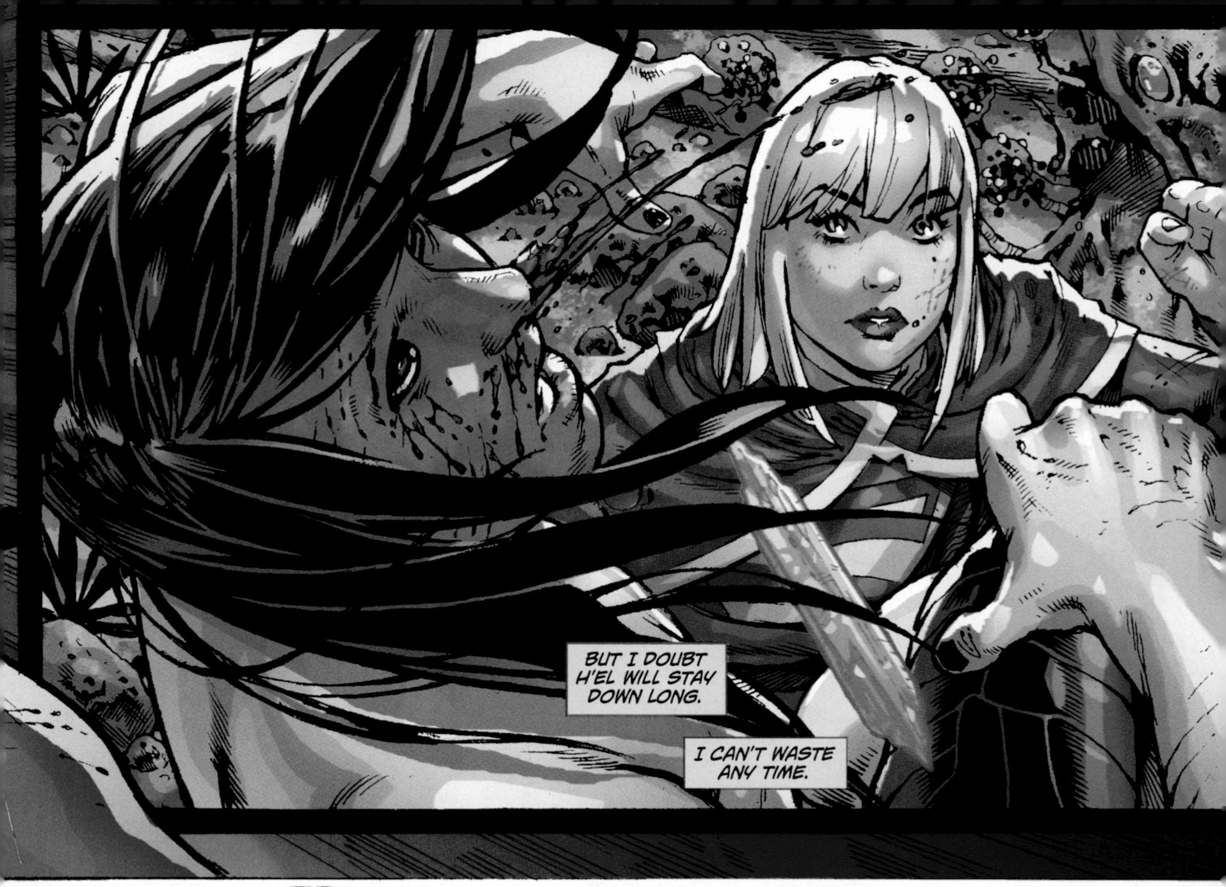
BUT I DOUBT H'EL WILL STAY DOWN LONG.
I CAN'T WASTE ANY TIME.

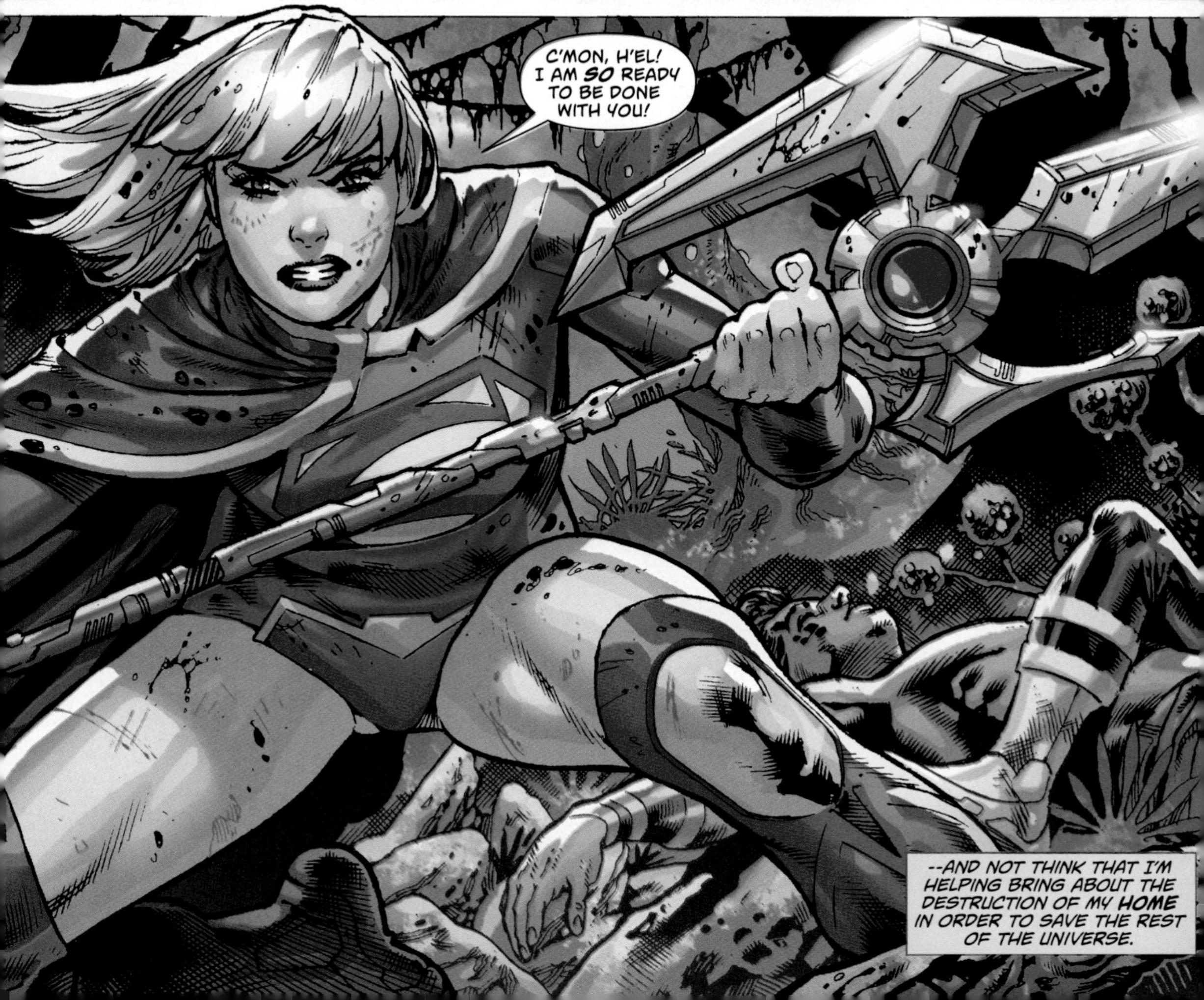
C'MON, H'EL! I AM **SO** READY TO BE DONE WITH YOU!
--AND NOT THINK THAT I'M HELPING BRING ABOUT THE DESTRUCTION OF MY **HOME** IN ORDER TO SAVE THE REST OF THE UNIVERSE.

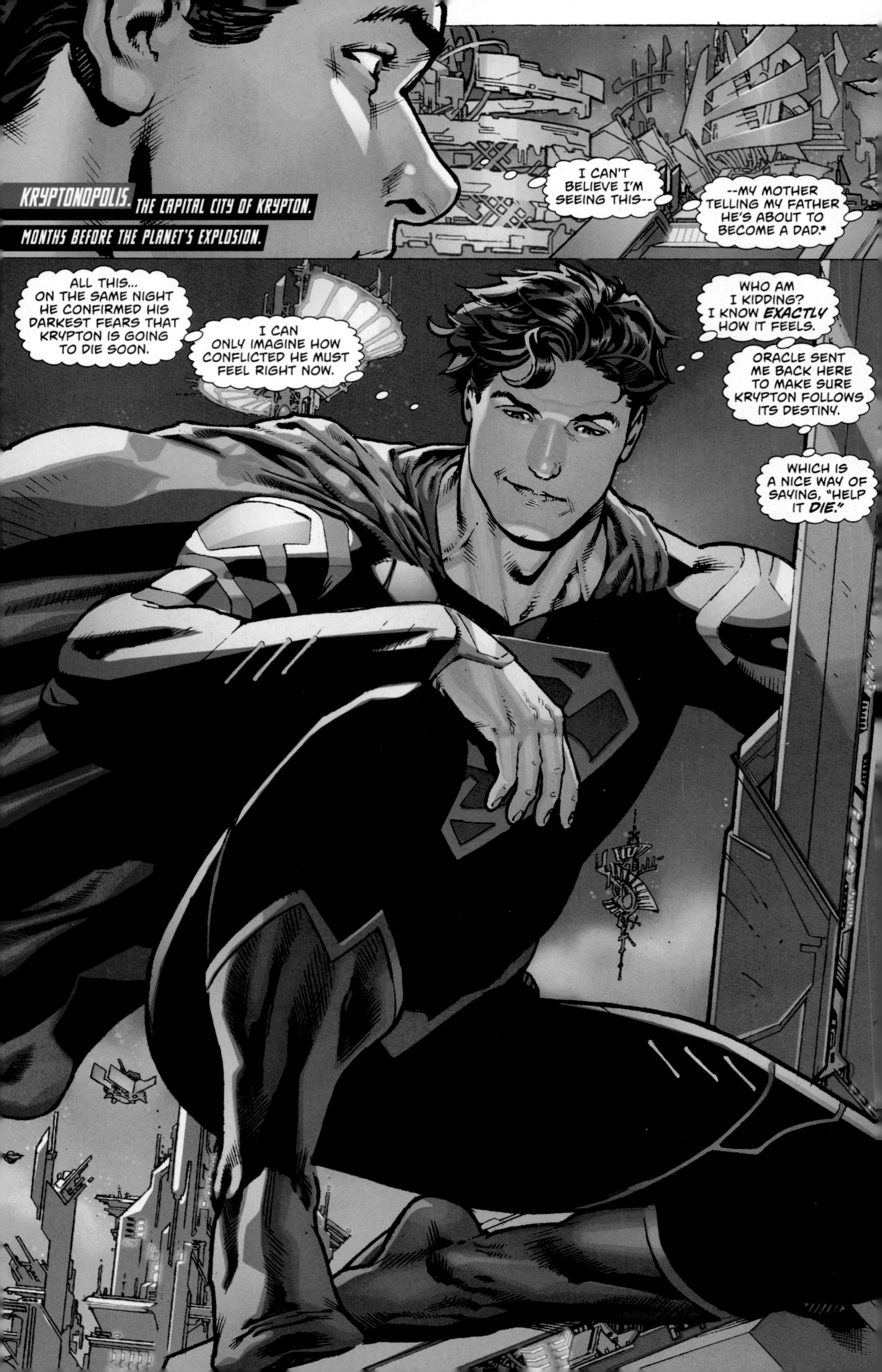
KRYPTONOPOLIS. THE CAPITAL CITY OF KRYPTON.
MONTHS BEFORE THE PLANET'S EXPLOSION.
I CAN'T BELIEVE I'M SEEING THIS--
--MY MOTHER TELLING MY FATHER HE'S ABOUT TO BECOME A DAD.*
ALL THIS... ON THE SAME NIGHT HE CONFIRMED HIS DARKEST FEARS THAT KRYPTON IS GOING TO DIE SOON.
I CAN ONLY IMAGINE HOW CONFLICTED HE MUST FEEL RIGHT NOW.
WHO AM I KIDDING? I KNOW EXACTLY HOW IT FEELS.
ORACLE SENT ME BACK HERE TO MAKE SURE KRYPTON FOLLOWS ITS DESTINY.
WHICH IS A NICE WAY OF SAYING, "HELP IT DIE."

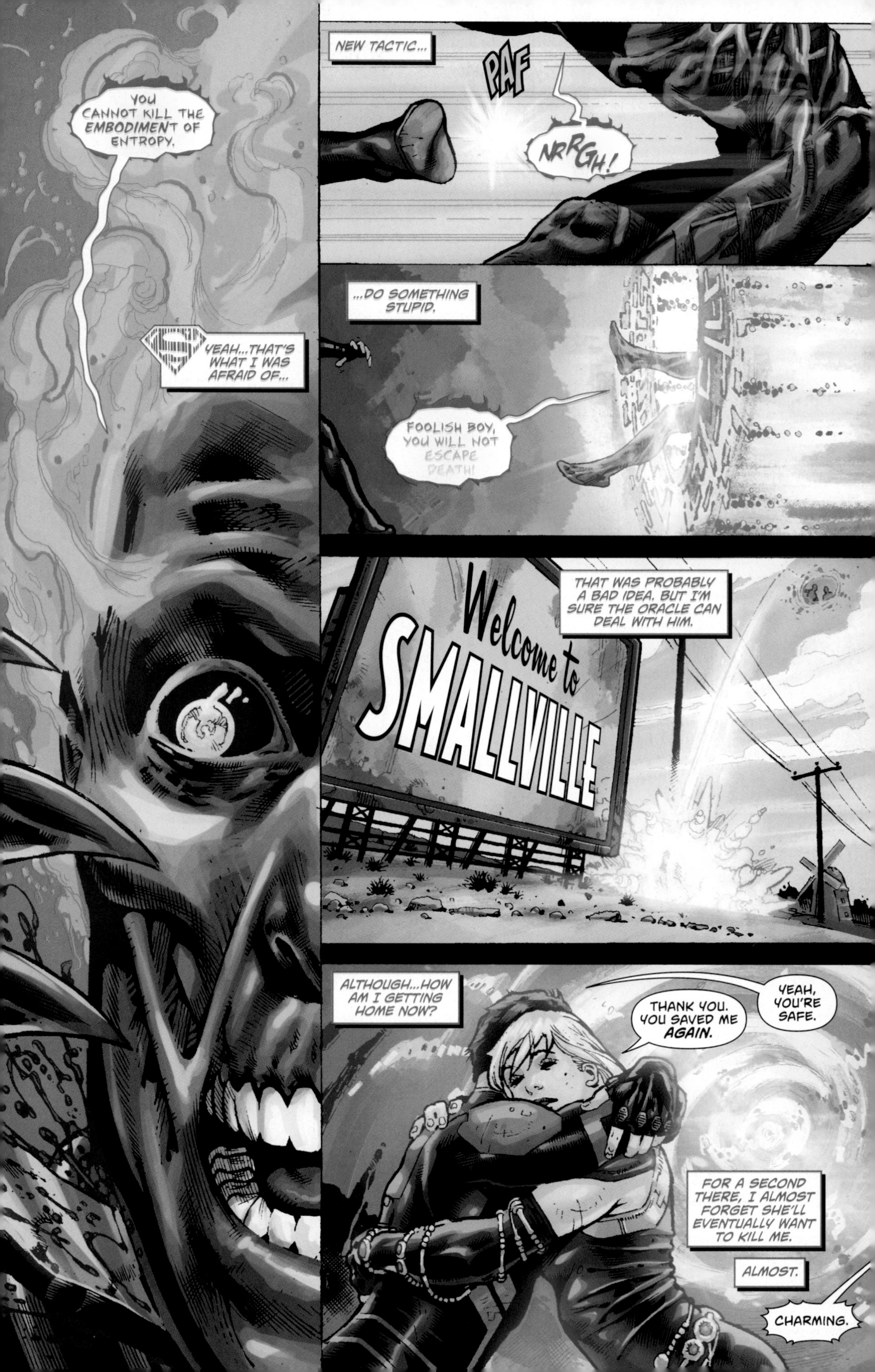

YOU CANNOT KILL THE EMBODIMENT OF ENTROPY.
YEAH...THAT'S WHAT I WAS AFRAID OF...
NEW TACTIC...
PAF
NRRGH!
...DO SOMETHING STUPID.
FOOLISH BOY, YOU WILL NOT ESCAPE DEATH!
Welcome to SMALLVILLE
THAT WAS PROBABLY A BAD IDEA. BUT I'M SURE THE ORACLE CAN DEAL WITH HIM.
ALTHOUGH...HOW AM I GETTING HOME NOW?
THANK YOU. YOU SAVED ME AGAIN.
YEAH, YOU'RE SAFE.
FOR A SECOND THERE, I ALMOST FORGET SHE'LL EVENTUALLY WANT TO KILL ME.
ALMOST.
CHARMING.

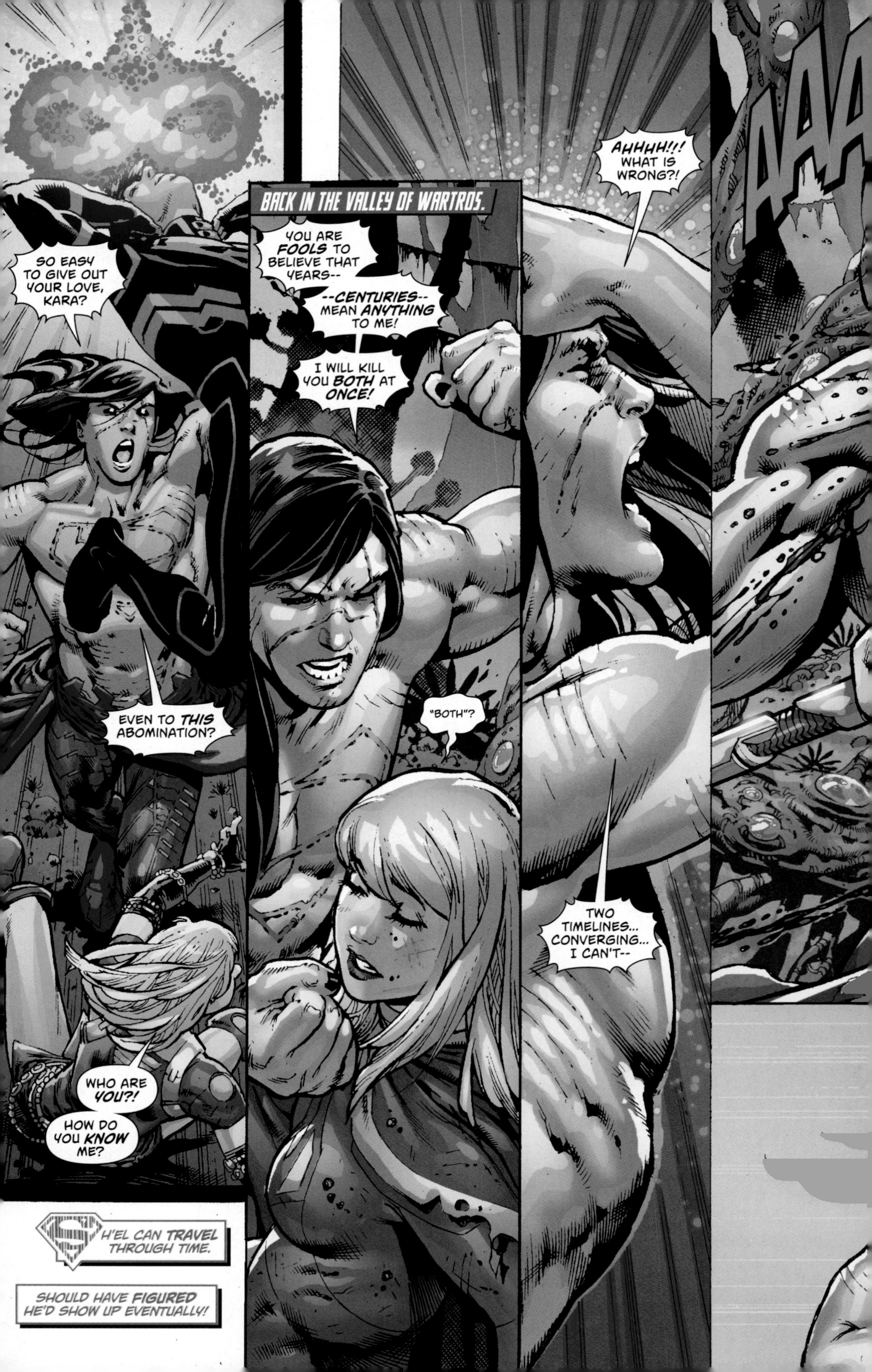
SO EASY TO GIVE OUT YOUR LOVE, KARA?
EVEN TO THIS ABOMINATION?
WHO ARE YOU?!
HOW DO YOU KNOW ME?
H'EL CAN TRAVEL THROUGH TIME.
SHOULD HAVE FIGURED HE'D SHOW UP EVENTUALLY!
BACK IN THE VALLEY OF WARTROS.
YOU ARE FOOLS TO BELIEVE THAT YEARS--
--CENTURIES-- MEAN ANYTHING TO ME!
I WILL KILL YOU BOTH AT ONCE!
"BOTH"?
AHHHH!!! WHAT IS WRONG?!
TWO TIMELINES... CONVERGING... I CAN'T--
AAA

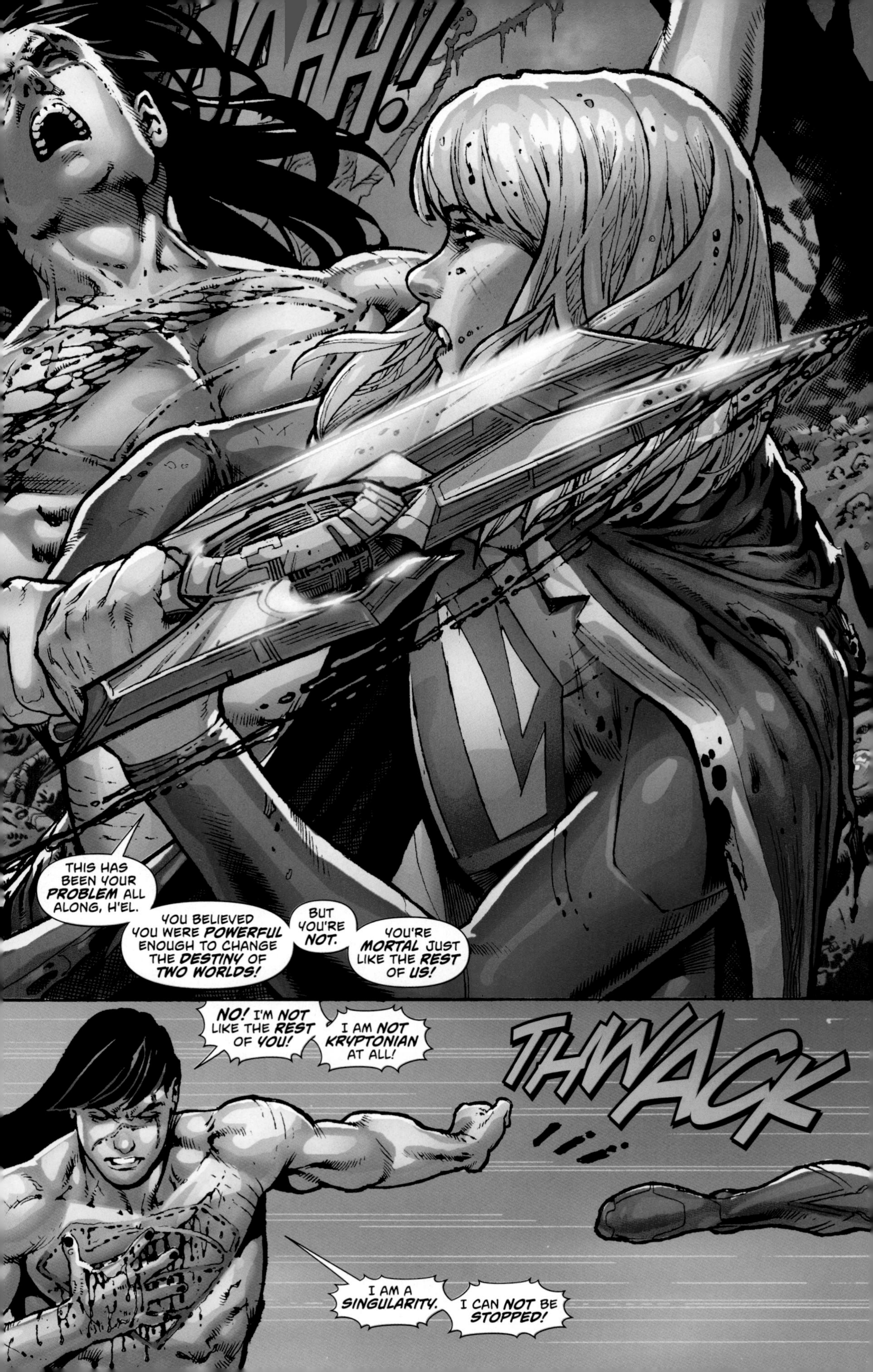
AHH!
THIS HAS BEEN YOUR PROBLEM ALL ALONG, H'EL.
YOU BELIEVED YOU WERE POWERFUL ENOUGH TO CHANGE THE DESTINY OF TWO WORLDS!
BUT YOU'RE NOT.
YOU'RE MORTAL JUST LIKE THE REST OF US!
NO! I'M NOT LIKE THE REST OF YOU!
I AM NOT KRYPTONIAN AT ALL!
THWACK
I AM A SINGULARITY.
I CAN NOT BE STOPPED!

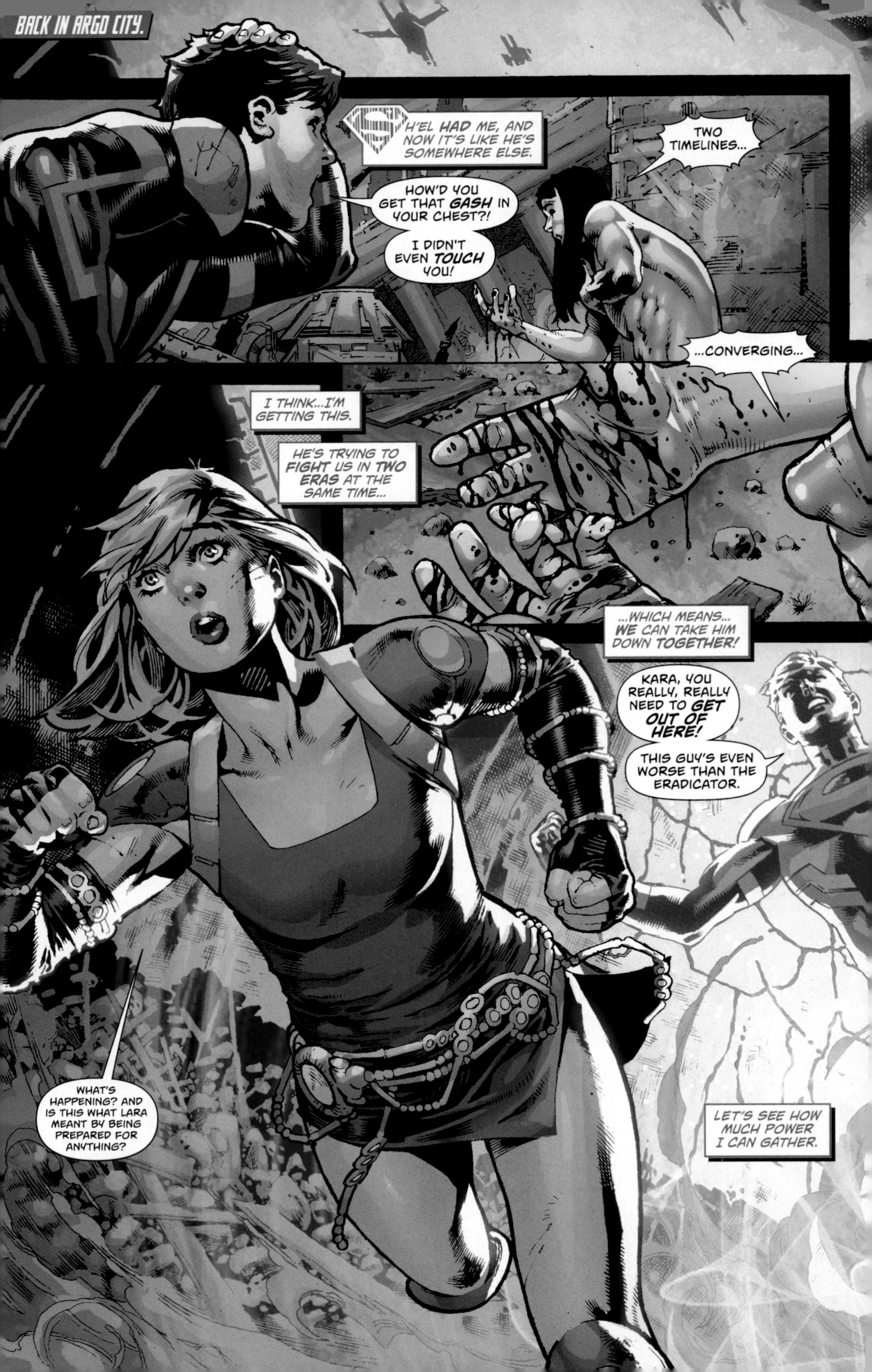
BACK IN ARGO CITY.
H'EL HAD ME, AND NOW IT'S LIKE HE'S SOMEWHERE ELSE.
HOW'D YOU GET THAT GASH IN YOUR CHEST?!
I DIDN'T EVEN TOUCH YOU!
TWO TIMELINES...
...CONVERGING...
I THINK...I'M GETTING THIS.
HE'S TRYING TO FIGHT US IN TWO ERAS AT THE SAME TIME...
...WHICH MEANS... WE CAN TAKE HIM DOWN TOGETHER!
KARA, YOU REALLY, REALLY NEED TO GET OUT OF HERE!
THIS GUY'S EVEN WORSE THAN THE ERADICATOR.
WHAT'S HAPPENING? AND IS THIS WHAT LARA MEANT BY BEING PREPARED FOR ANYTHING?
LET'S SEE HOW MUCH POWER I CAN GATHER.

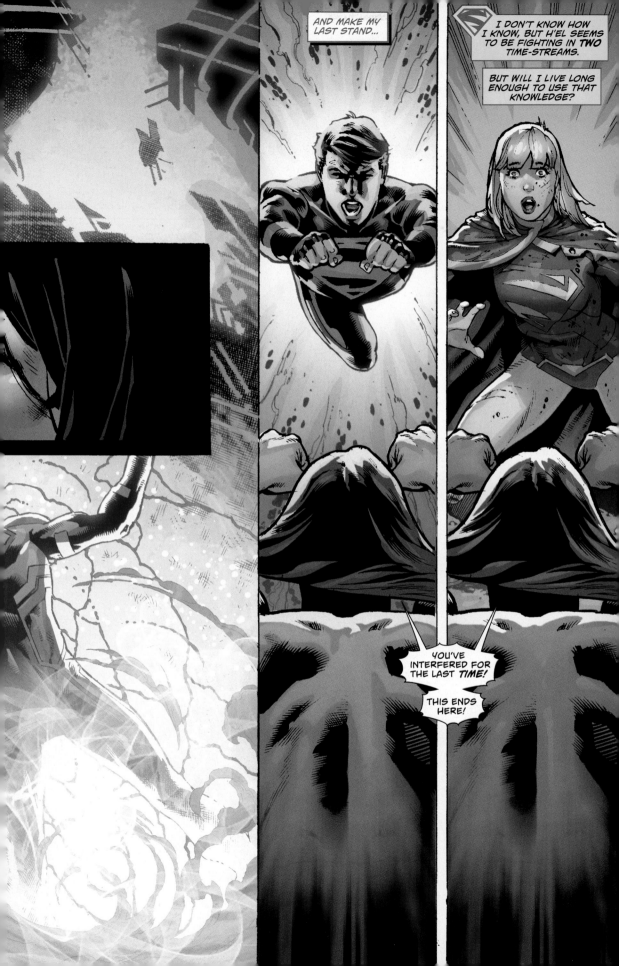

AND MAKE MY
LAST STAND...

I DON'T KNOW HOW
I KNOW, BUT H'EL SEEMS
TO BE FIGHTING IN TWO
TIME-STREAMS.

BUT WILL I LIVE LONG
ENOUGH TO USE THAT
KNOWLEDGE?

YOU'VE
INTERFERED FOR
THE LAST TIME!

THIS ENDS
HERE!

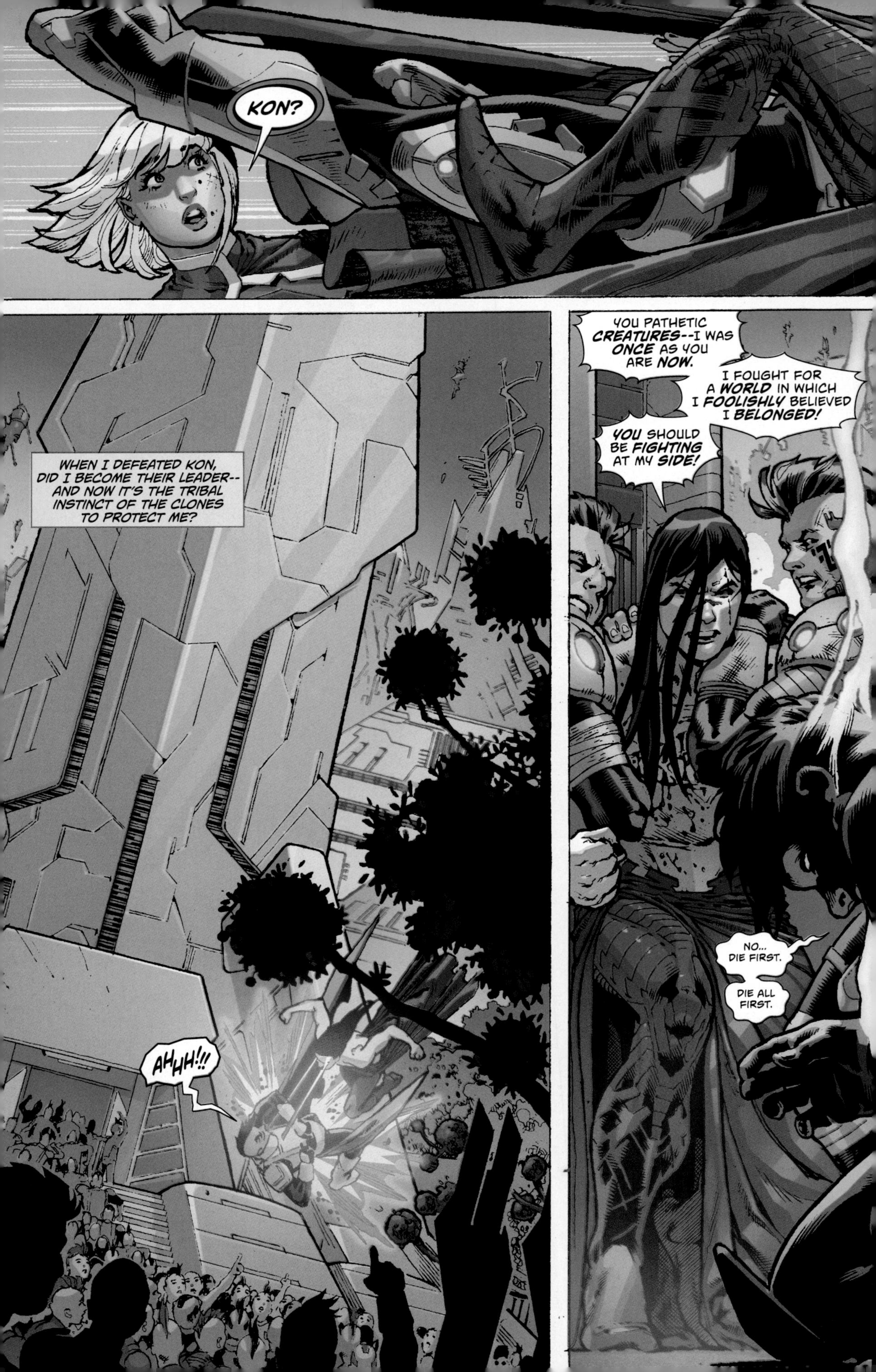
KON?
WHEN I DEFEATED KON, DID I BECOME THEIR LEADER-- AND NOW IT'S THE TRIBAL INSTINCT OF THE CLONES TO PROTECT ME?
AHHH!!!
YOU PATHETIC CREATURES--I WAS ONCE AS YOU ARE NOW.
I FOUGHT FOR A WORLD IN WHICH I FOOLISHLY BELIEVED I BELONGED!
YOU SHOULD BE FIGHTING AT MY SIDE!
NO... DIE FIRST.
DIE ALL FIRST.

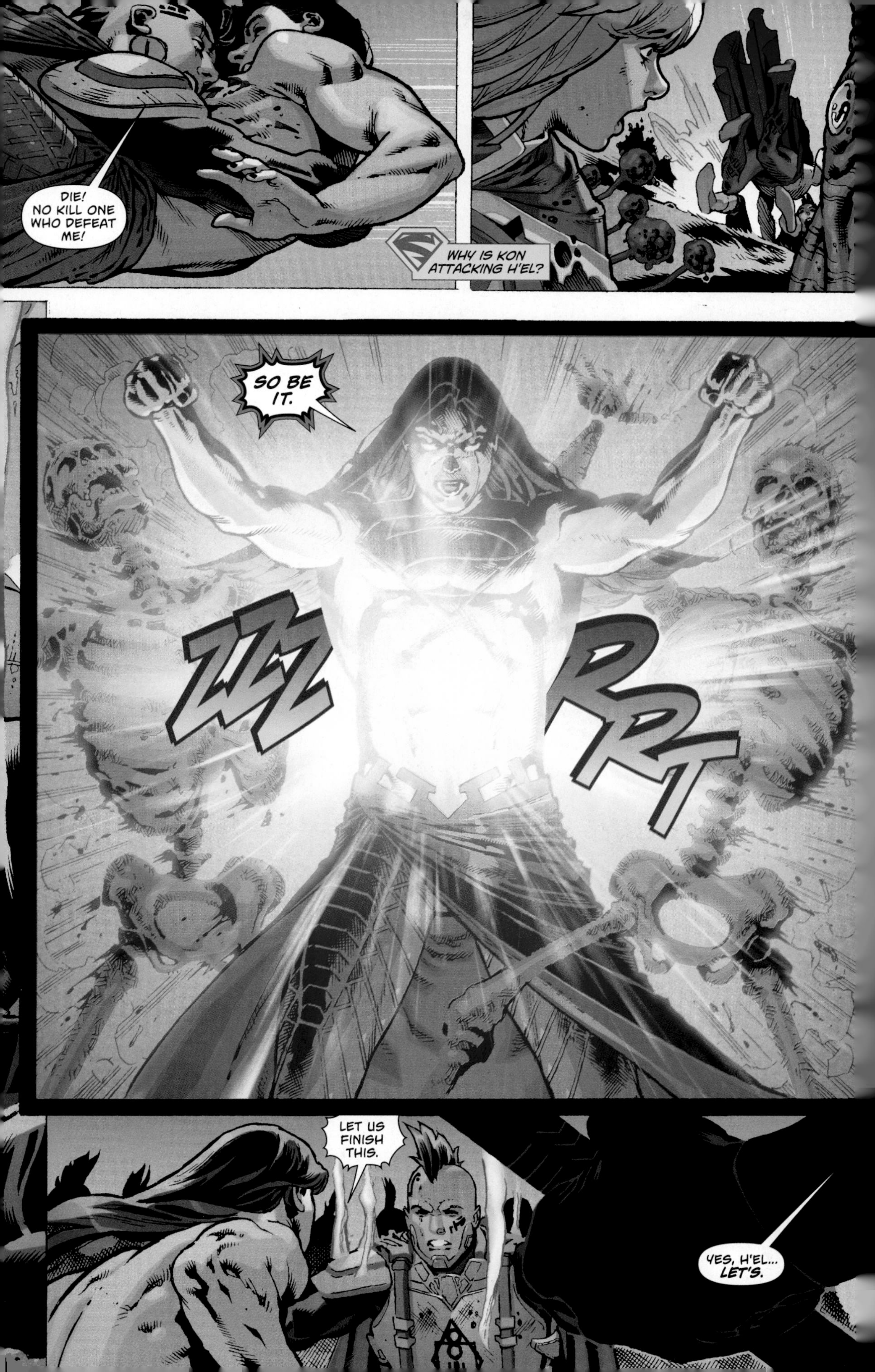
DIE! NO KILL ONE WHO DEFEAT ME!
WHY IS KON ATTACKING H'EL?
SO BE IT.
ZZZRRT
LET US FINISH THIS.
YES, H'EL... LET'S.

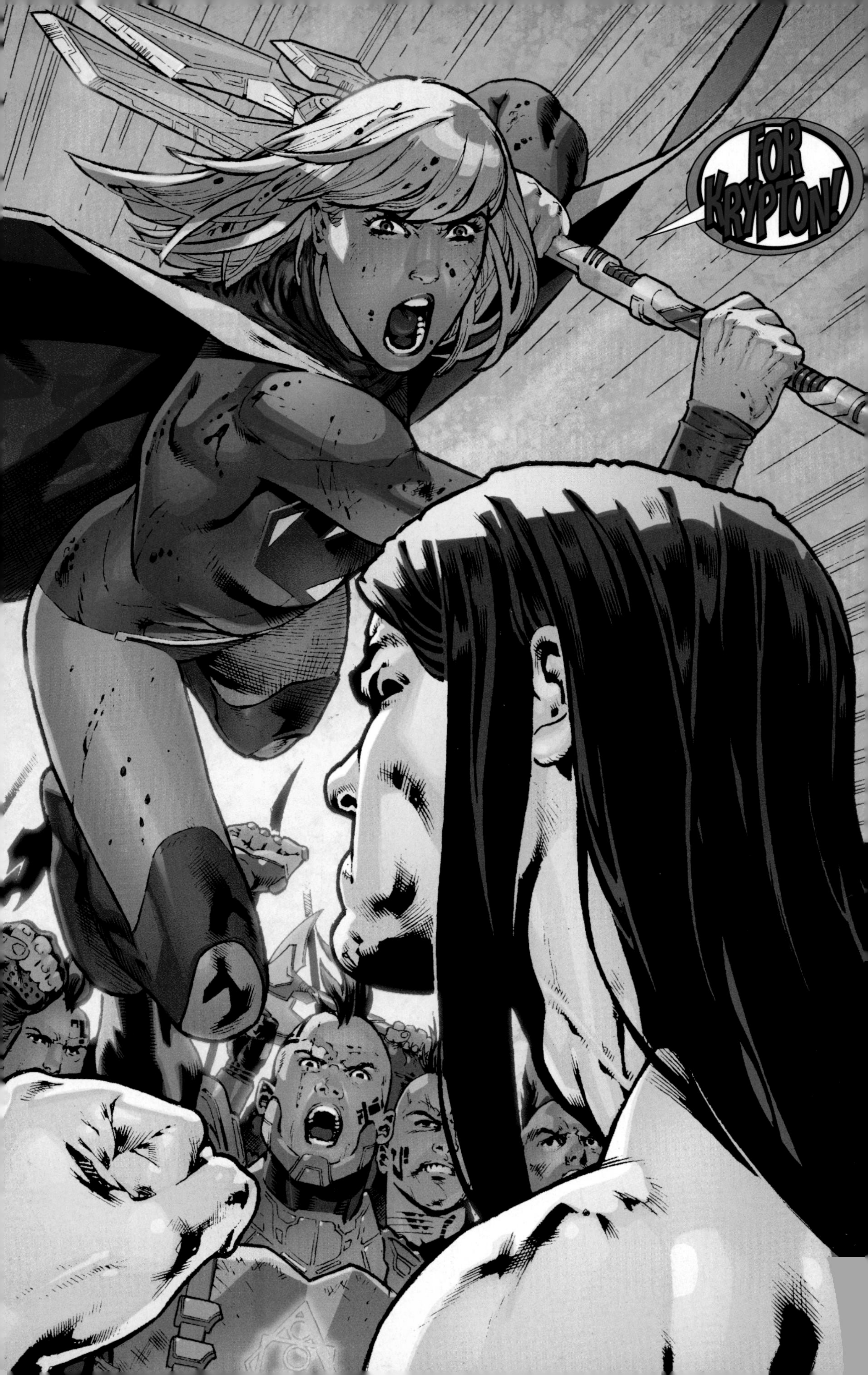
FOR KRYPTON!

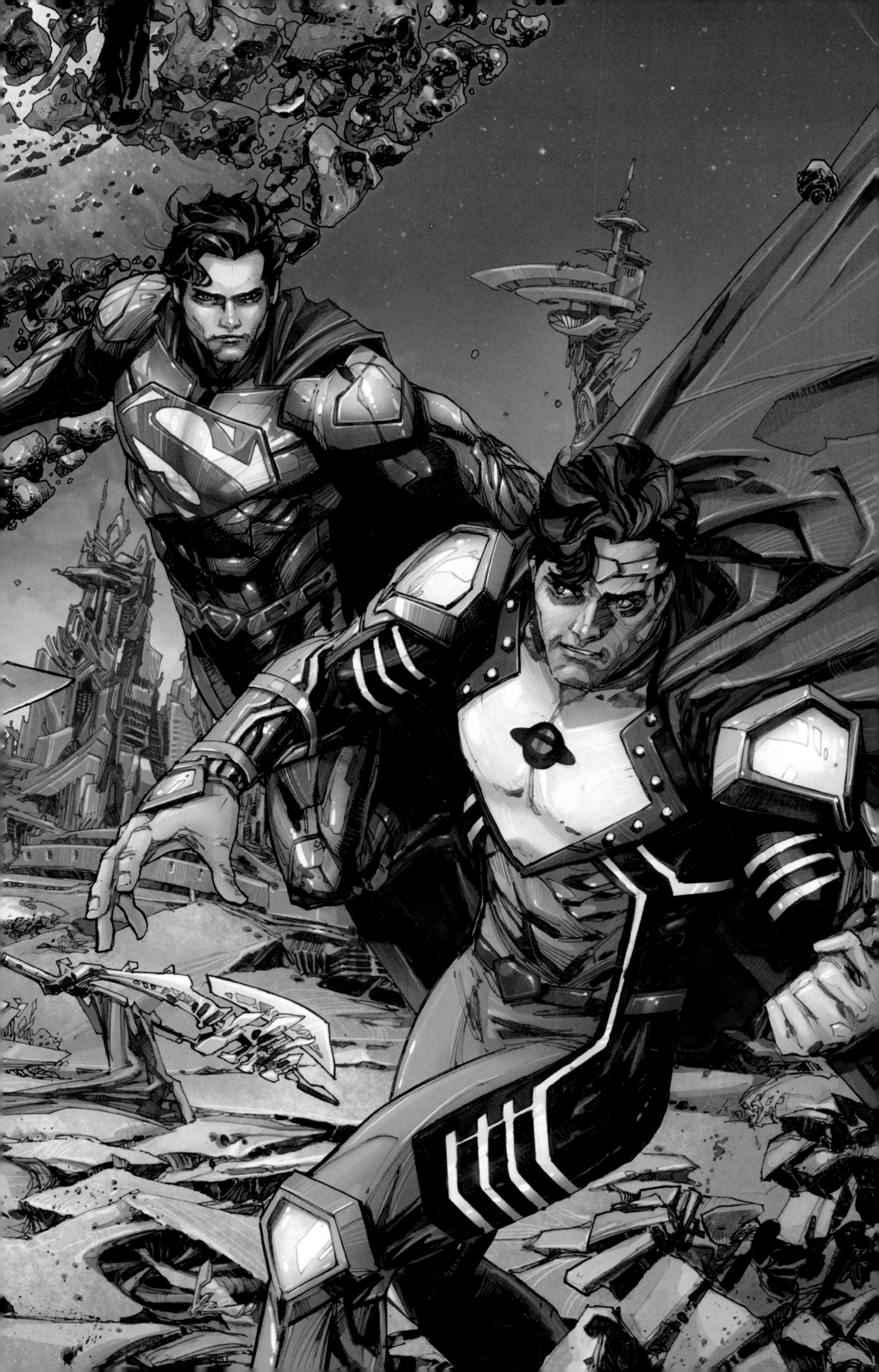

KRYPTON RETURNS: PART 4

SCOTT LOBDELL writer **KENNETH ROCAFORT** artist cover art by **KENNETH ROCAFORT**

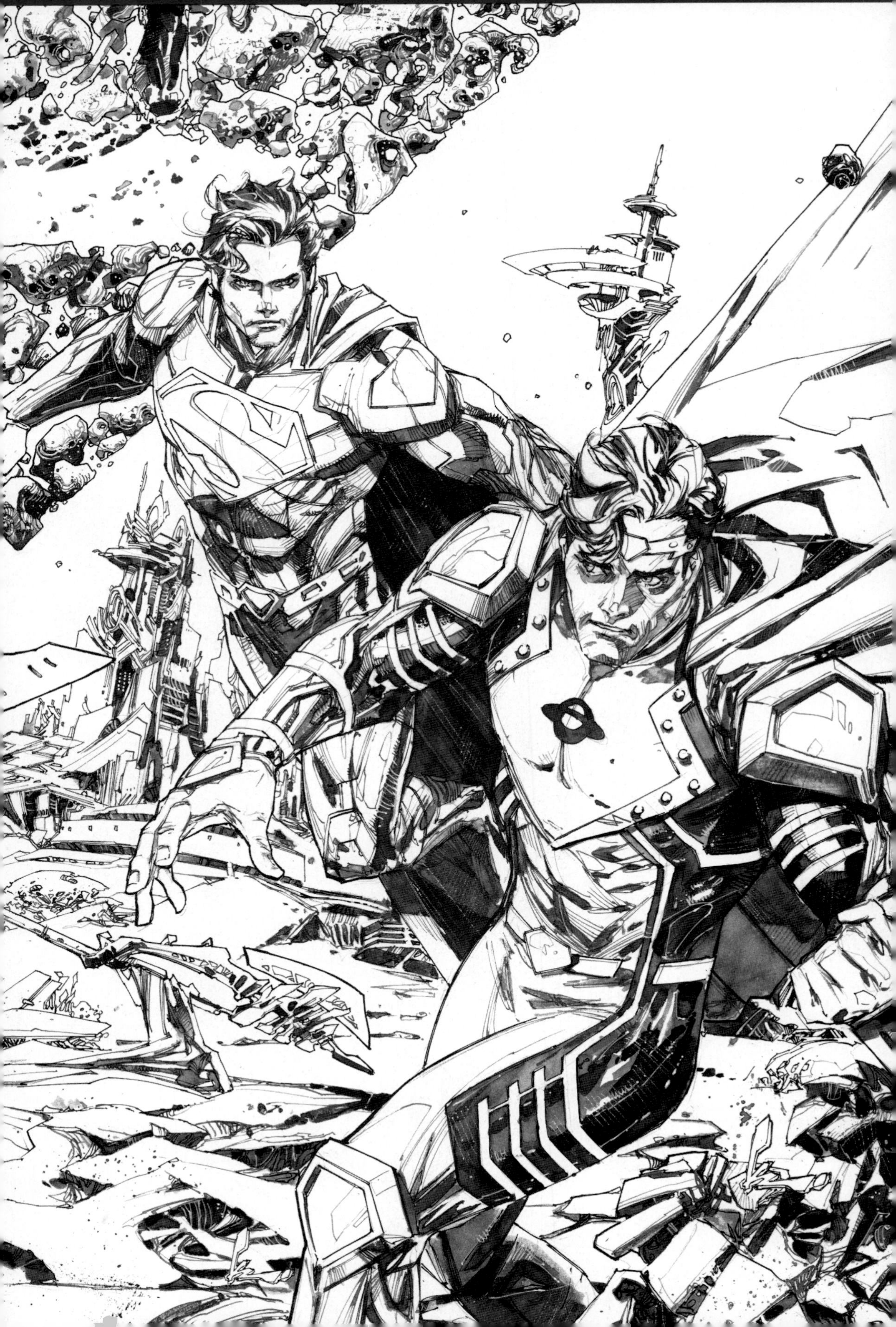

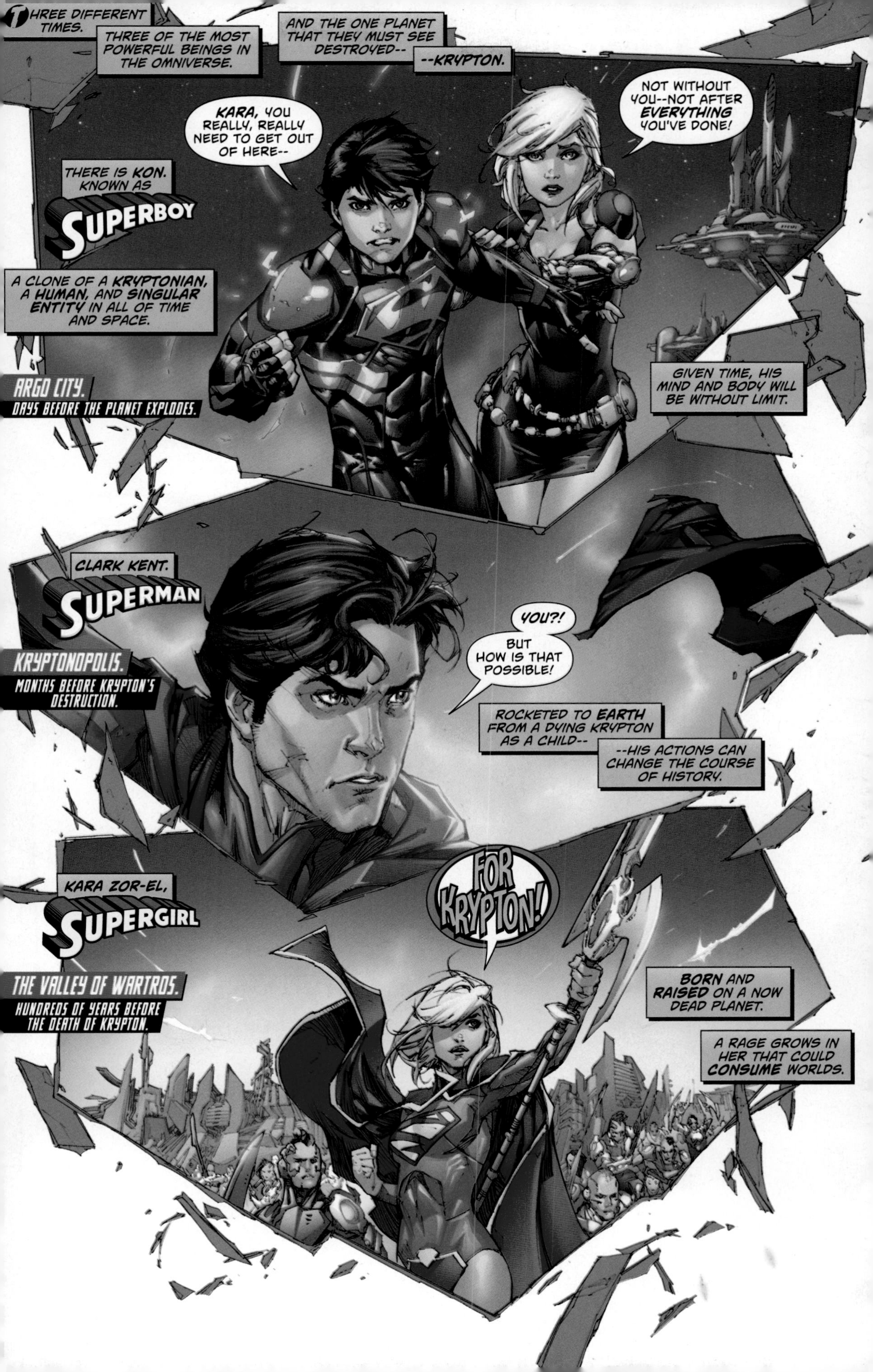
THREE DIFFERENT TIMES.
THREE OF THE MOST POWERFUL BEINGS IN THE OMNIVERSE.
AND THE ONE PLANET THAT THEY MUST SEE DESTROYED--
--KRYPTON.
KARA, YOU REALLY, REALLY NEED TO GET OUT OF HERE--
NOT WITHOUT YOU--NOT AFTER EVERYTHING YOU'VE DONE!
THERE IS KON. KNOWN AS
SUPERBOY
A CLONE OF A KRYPTONIAN, A HUMAN, AND SINGULAR ENTITY IN ALL OF TIME AND SPACE.
ARGO CITY.
DAYS BEFORE THE PLANET EXPLODES.
GIVEN TIME, HIS MIND AND BODY WILL BE WITHOUT LIMIT.
CLARK KENT.
SUPERMAN
KRYPTONOPOLIS.
MONTHS BEFORE KRYPTON'S DESTRUCTION.
YOU?!
BUT HOW IS THAT POSSIBLE!
ROCKETED TO EARTH FROM A DYING KRYPTON AS A CHILD--
--HIS ACTIONS CAN CHANGE THE COURSE OF HISTORY.
KARA ZOR-EL,
SUPERGIRL
FOR KRYPTON!
THE VALLEY OF WARTROS.
HUNDREDS OF YEARS BEFORE THE DEATH OF KRYPTON.
BORN AND RAISED ON A NOW DEAD PLANET.
A RAGE GROWS IN HER THAT COULD CONSUME WORLDS.

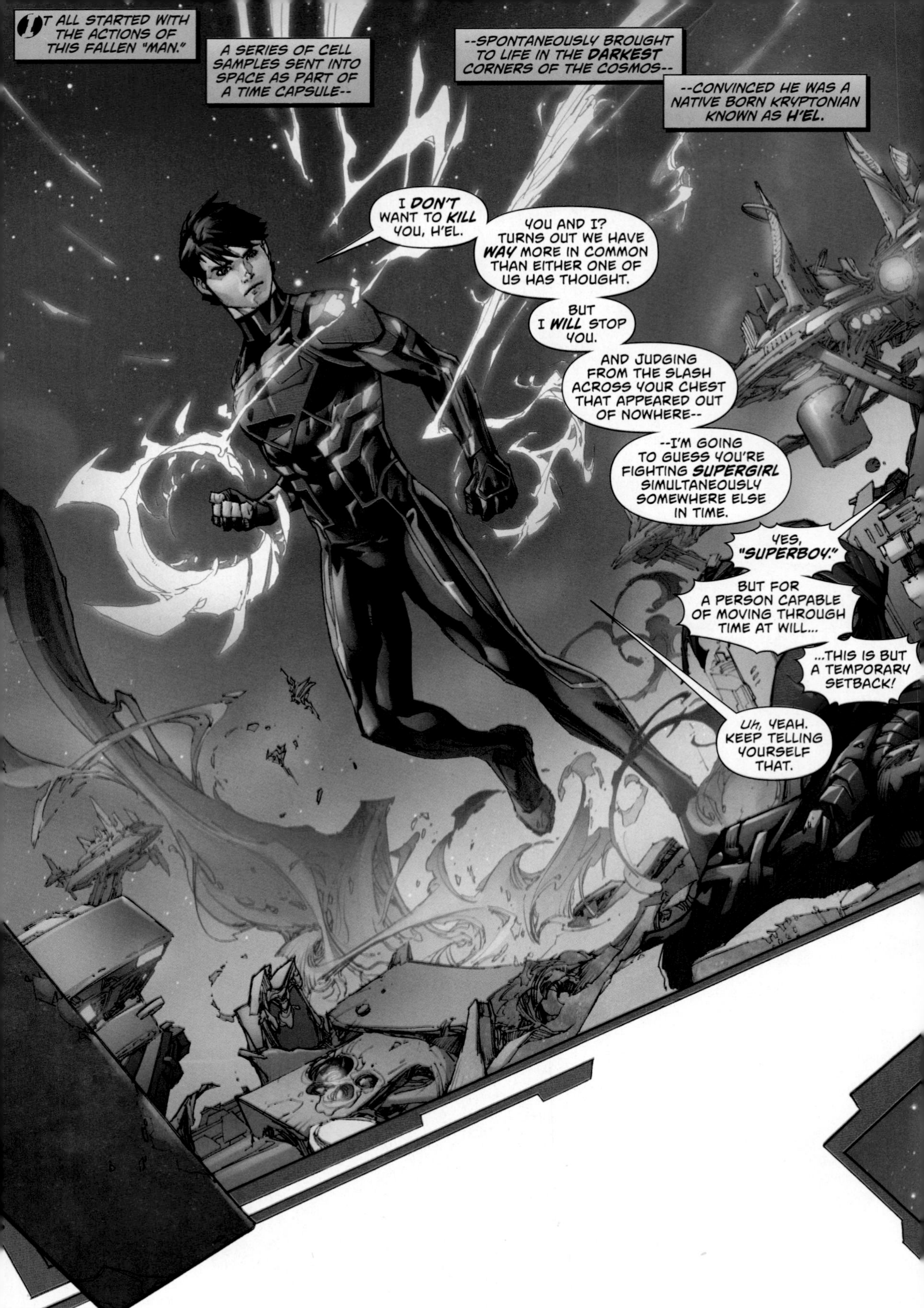
IT ALL STARTED WITH THE ACTIONS OF THIS FALLEN "MAN."
A SERIES OF CELL SAMPLES SENT INTO SPACE AS PART OF A TIME CAPSULE--
--SPONTANEOUSLY BROUGHT TO LIFE IN THE DARKEST CORNERS OF THE COSMOS--
--CONVINCED HE WAS A NATIVE BORN KRYPTONIAN KNOWN AS H'EL.
I DON'T WANT TO KILL YOU, H'EL.
YOU AND I? TURNS OUT WE HAVE WAY MORE IN COMMON THAN EITHER ONE OF US HAS THOUGHT.
BUT I WILL STOP YOU.
AND JUDGING FROM THE SLASH ACROSS YOUR CHEST THAT APPEARED OUT OF NOWHERE--
--I'M GOING TO GUESS YOU'RE FIGHTING SUPERGIRL SIMULTANEOUSLY SOMEWHERE ELSE IN TIME.
YES, "SUPERBOY."
BUT FOR A PERSON CAPABLE OF MOVING THROUGH TIME AT WILL...
...THIS IS BUT A TEMPORARY SETBACK!
Uh, YEAH. KEEP TELLING YOURSELF THAT.

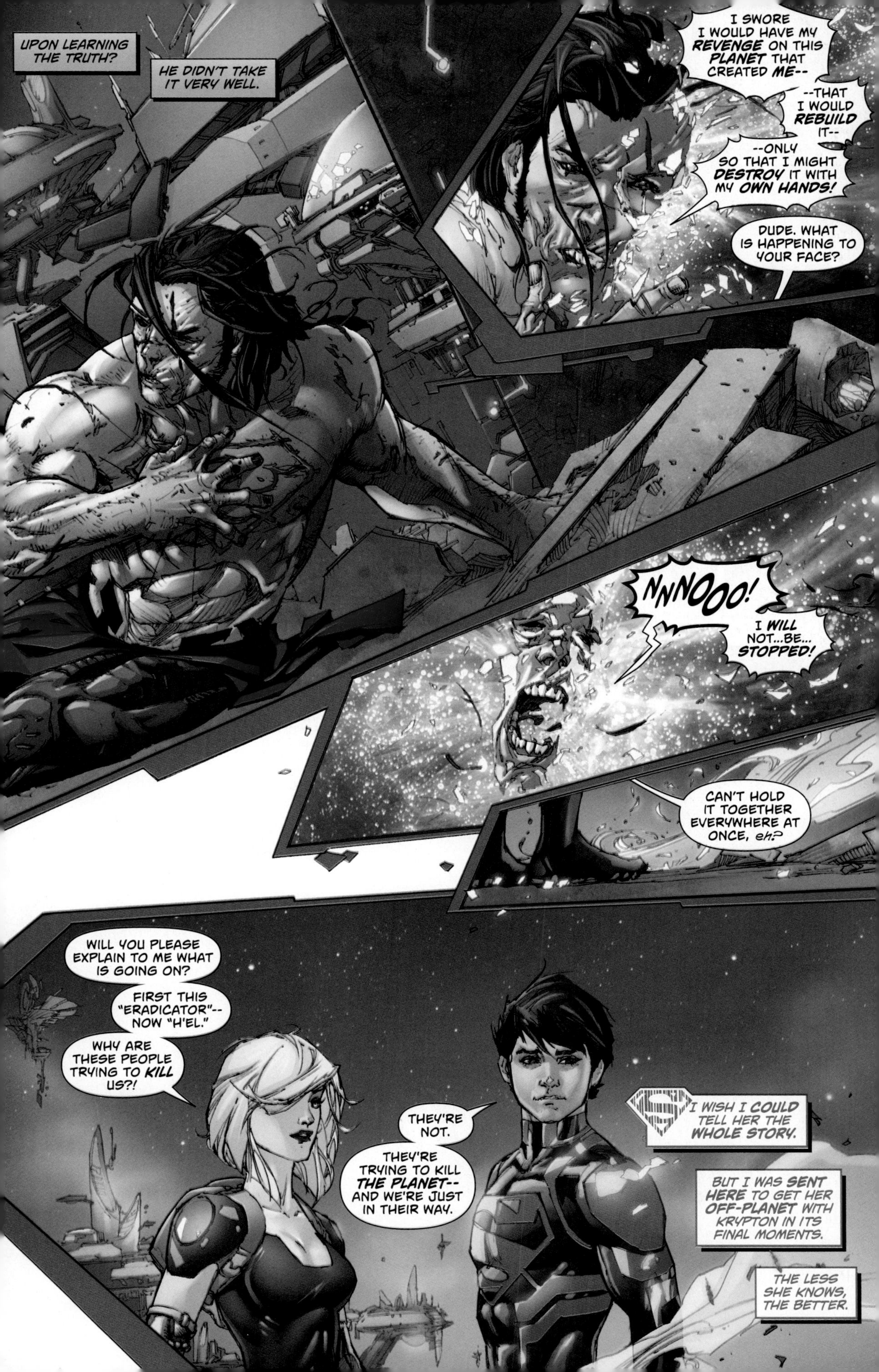
UPON LEARNING THE TRUTH?
HE DIDN'T TAKE IT VERY WELL.
I SWORE I WOULD HAVE MY REVENGE ON THIS PLANET THAT CREATED ME--
--THAT I WOULD REBUILD IT--
--ONLY SO THAT I MIGHT DESTROY IT WITH MY OWN HANDS!
DUDE. WHAT IS HAPPENING TO YOUR FACE?
NNNOOO!
I WILL NOT...BE... STOPPED!
CAN'T HOLD IT TOGETHER EVERYWHERE AT ONCE, eh?
WILL YOU PLEASE EXPLAIN TO ME WHAT IS GOING ON?
FIRST THIS "ERADICATOR"-- NOW "H'EL."
WHY ARE THESE PEOPLE TRYING TO KILL US?!
THEY'RE NOT.
THEY'RE TRYING TO KILL THE PLANET-- AND WE'RE JUST IN THEIR WAY.
I WISH I COULD TELL HER THE WHOLE STORY.
BUT I WAS SENT HERE TO GET HER OFF-PLANET WITH KRYPTON IN ITS FINAL MOMENTS.
THE LESS SHE KNOWS, THE BETTER.

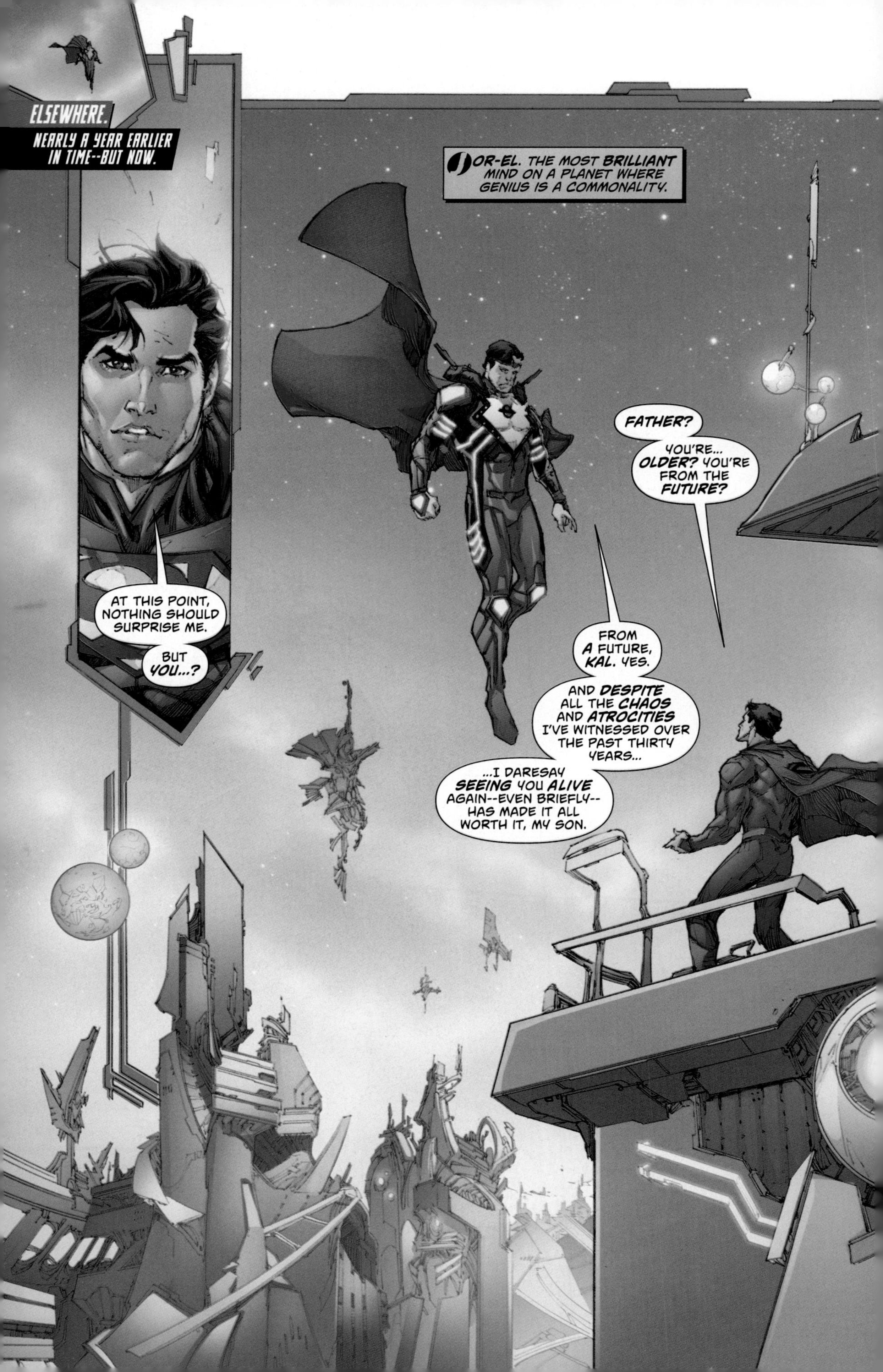
ELSEWHERE.
NEARLY A YEAR EARLIER IN TIME--BUT NOW.
JOR-EL. THE MOST BRILLIANT MIND ON A PLANET WHERE GENIUS IS A COMMONALITY.
AT THIS POINT, NOTHING SHOULD SURPRISE ME.
BUT YOU...?
FATHER?
YOU'RE... OLDER? YOU'RE FROM THE FUTURE?
FROM A FUTURE, KAL. YES.
AND DESPITE ALL THE CHAOS AND ATROCITIES I'VE WITNESSED OVER THE PAST THIRTY YEARS...
...I DARESAY SEEING YOU ALIVE AGAIN--EVEN BRIEFLY--HAS MADE IT ALL WORTH IT, MY SON.

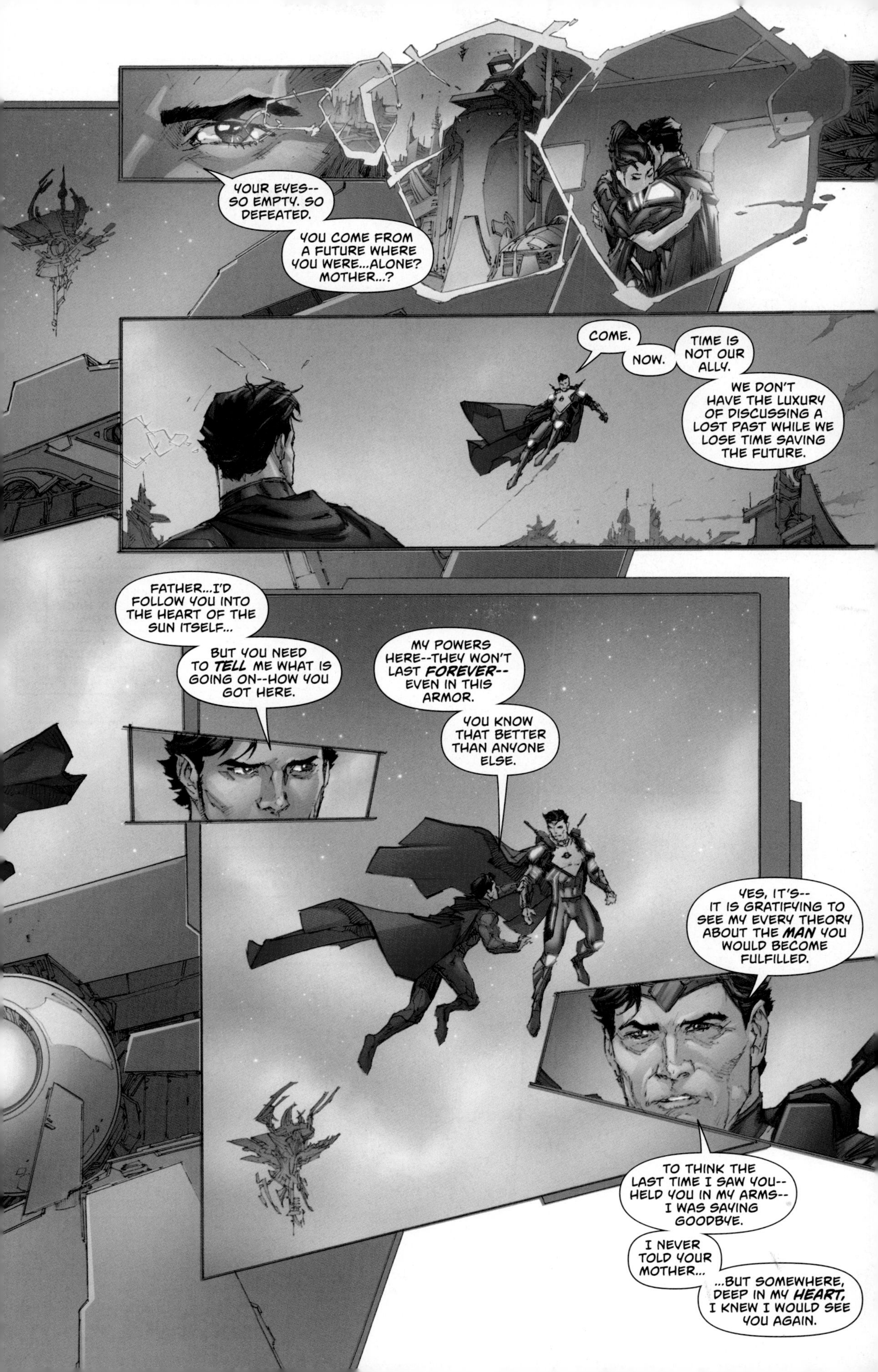
YOUR EYES-- SO EMPTY. SO DEFEATED.
YOU COME FROM A FUTURE WHERE YOU WERE...ALONE? MOTHER...?
COME.
NOW.
TIME IS NOT OUR ALLY.
WE DON'T HAVE THE LUXURY OF DISCUSSING A LOST PAST WHILE WE LOSE TIME SAVING THE FUTURE.
FATHER...I'D FOLLOW YOU INTO THE HEART OF THE SUN ITSELF...
BUT YOU NEED TO TELL ME WHAT IS GOING ON--HOW YOU GOT HERE.
MY POWERS HERE--THEY WON'T LAST FOREVER-- EVEN IN THIS ARMOR.
YOU KNOW THAT BETTER THAN ANYONE ELSE.
YES, IT'S-- IT IS GRATIFYING TO SEE MY EVERY THEORY ABOUT THE MAN YOU WOULD BECOME FULFILLED.
TO THINK THE LAST TIME I SAW YOU-- HELD YOU IN MY ARMS-- I WAS SAYING GOODBYE.
I NEVER TOLD YOUR MOTHER...
...BUT SOMEWHERE, DEEP IN MY HEART, I KNEW I WOULD SEE YOU AGAIN.

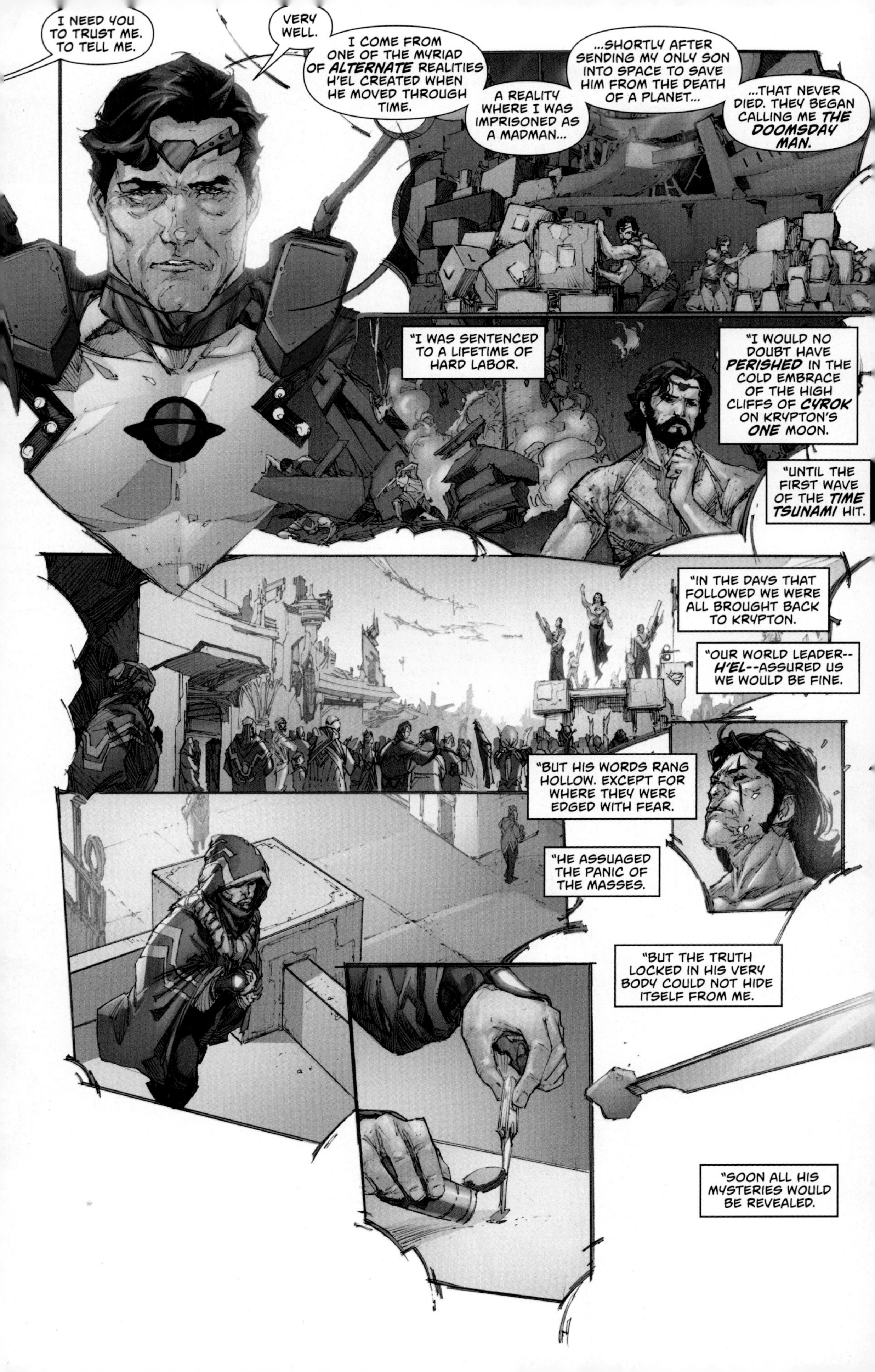
I NEED YOU TO TRUST ME. TO TELL ME.
VERY WELL.
I COME FROM ONE OF THE MYRIAD OF ALTERNATE REALITIES H'EL CREATED WHEN HE MOVED THROUGH TIME.
A REALITY WHERE I WAS IMPRISONED AS A MADMAN...
...SHORTLY AFTER SENDING MY ONLY SON INTO SPACE TO SAVE HIM FROM THE DEATH OF A PLANET...
...THAT NEVER DIED. THEY BEGAN CALLING ME THE DOOMSDAY MAN.
"I WAS SENTENCED TO A LIFETIME OF HARD LABOR.
"I WOULD NO DOUBT HAVE PERISHED IN THE COLD EMBRACE OF THE HIGH CLIFFS OF CYROK ON KRYPTON'S ONE MOON.
"UNTIL THE FIRST WAVE OF THE TIME TSUNAMI HIT.
"IN THE DAYS THAT FOLLOWED WE WERE ALL BROUGHT BACK TO KRYPTON.
"OUR WORLD LEADER--H'EL--ASSURED US WE WOULD BE FINE.
"BUT HIS WORDS RANG HOLLOW. EXCEPT FOR WHERE THEY WERE EDGED WITH FEAR.
"HE ASSUAGED THE PANIC OF THE MASSES.
"BUT THE TRUTH LOCKED IN HIS VERY BODY COULD NOT HIDE ITSELF FROM ME.
"SOON ALL HIS MYSTERIES WOULD BE REVEALED.

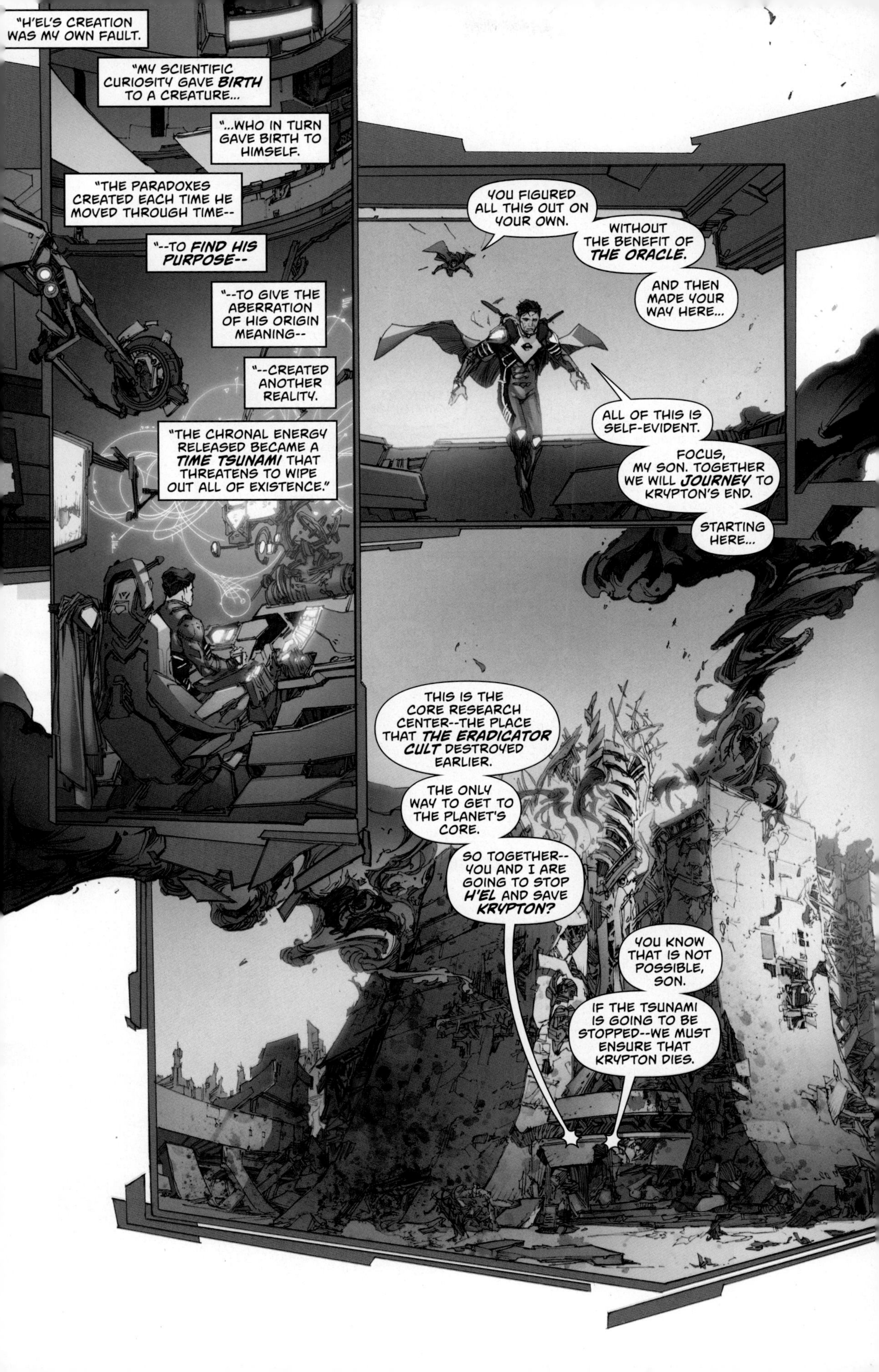
"H'EL'S CREATION WAS MY OWN FAULT.
"MY SCIENTIFIC CURIOSITY GAVE BIRTH TO A CREATURE...
"...WHO IN TURN GAVE BIRTH TO HIMSELF.
"THE PARADOXES CREATED EACH TIME HE MOVED THROUGH TIME--
"--TO FIND HIS PURPOSE--
"--TO GIVE THE ABERRATION OF HIS ORIGIN MEANING--
"--CREATED ANOTHER REALITY.
"THE CHRONAL ENERGY RELEASED BECAME A TIME TSUNAMI THAT THREATENS TO WIPE OUT ALL OF EXISTENCE."
YOU FIGURED ALL THIS OUT ON YOUR OWN.
WITHOUT THE BENEFIT OF THE ORACLE.
AND THEN MADE YOUR WAY HERE...
ALL OF THIS IS SELF-EVIDENT.
FOCUS, MY SON. TOGETHER WE WILL JOURNEY TO KRYPTON'S END.
STARTING HERE...
THIS IS THE CORE RESEARCH CENTER--THE PLACE THAT THE ERADICATOR CULT DESTROYED EARLIER.
THE ONLY WAY TO GET TO THE PLANET'S CORE.
SO TOGETHER--YOU AND I ARE GOING TO STOP H'EL AND SAVE KRYPTON?
YOU KNOW THAT IS NOT POSSIBLE, SON.
IF THE TSUNAMI IS GOING TO BE STOPPED--WE MUST ENSURE THAT KRYPTON DIES.

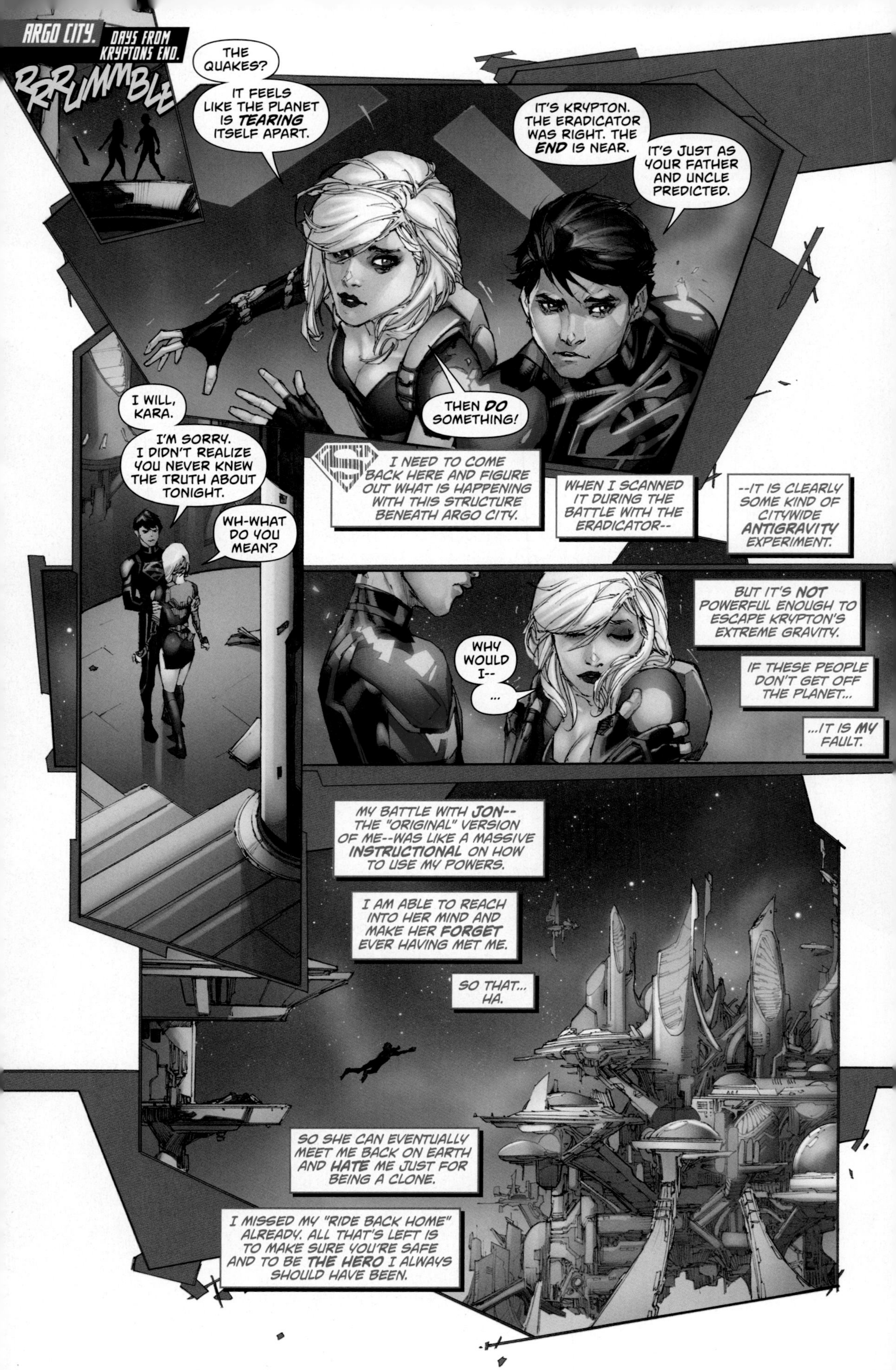
ARGO CITY.
DAYS FROM KRYPTONS END.
RRRUMMBLE
THE QUAKES?
IT FEELS LIKE THE PLANET IS TEARING ITSELF APART.
IT'S KRYPTON. THE ERADICATOR WAS RIGHT. THE END IS NEAR.
IT'S JUST AS YOUR FATHER AND UNCLE PREDICTED.
THEN DO SOMETHING!
I WILL, KARA.
I'M SORRY. I DIDN'T REALIZE YOU NEVER KNEW THE TRUTH ABOUT TONIGHT.
WH-WHAT DO YOU MEAN?
I NEED TO COME BACK HERE AND FIGURE OUT WHAT IS HAPPENING WITH THIS STRUCTURE BENEATH ARGO CITY.
WHEN I SCANNED IT DURING THE BATTLE WITH THE ERADICATOR--
--IT IS CLEARLY SOME KIND OF CITYWIDE ANTIGRAVITY EXPERIMENT.
BUT IT'S NOT POWERFUL ENOUGH TO ESCAPE KRYPTON'S EXTREME GRAVITY.
WHY WOULD I--
...
IF THESE PEOPLE DON'T GET OFF THE PLANET...
...IT IS MY FAULT.
MY BATTLE WITH JON--THE "ORIGINAL" VERSION OF ME--WAS LIKE A MASSIVE INSTRUCTIONAL ON HOW TO USE MY POWERS.
I AM ABLE TO REACH INTO HER MIND AND MAKE HER FORGET EVER HAVING MET ME.
SO THAT... HA.
SO SHE CAN EVENTUALLY MEET ME BACK ON EARTH AND HATE ME JUST FOR BEING A CLONE.
I MISSED MY "RIDE BACK HOME" ALREADY. ALL THAT'S LEFT IS TO MAKE SURE YOU'RE SAFE AND TO BE THE HERO I ALWAYS SHOULD HAVE BEEN.

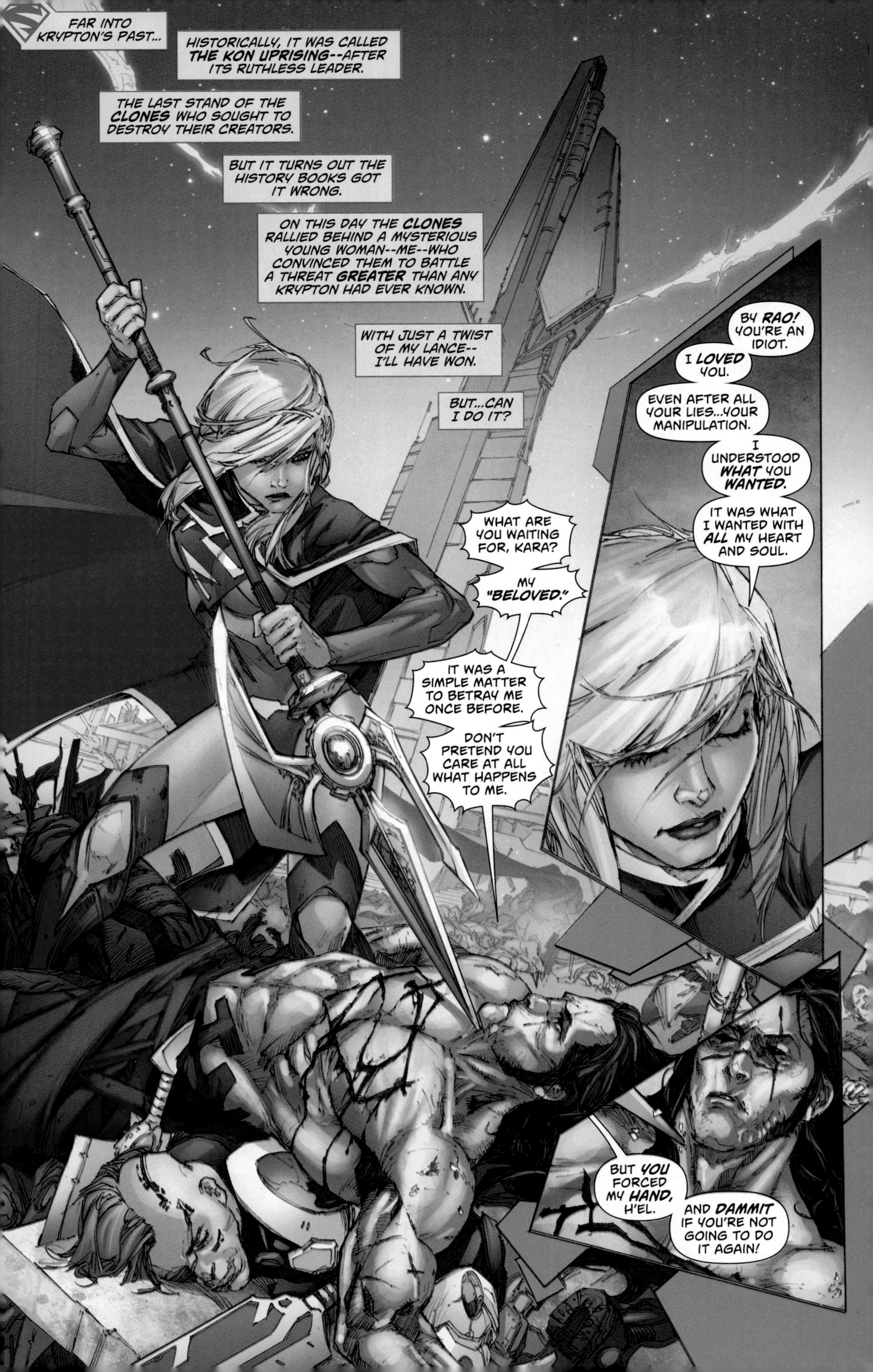

FAR INTO KRYPTON'S PAST...
HISTORICALLY, IT WAS CALLED THE KON UPRISING--AFTER ITS RUTHLESS LEADER.
THE LAST STAND OF THE CLONES WHO SOUGHT TO DESTROY THEIR CREATORS.
BUT IT TURNS OUT THE HISTORY BOOKS GOT IT WRONG.
ON THIS DAY THE CLONES RALLIED BEHIND A MYSTERIOUS YOUNG WOMAN--ME--WHO CONVINCED THEM TO BATTLE A THREAT GREATER THAN ANY KRYPTON HAD EVER KNOWN.
WITH JUST A TWIST OF MY LANCE-- I'LL HAVE WON.
BUT...CAN I DO IT?
WHAT ARE YOU WAITING FOR, KARA?
MY "BELOVED."
IT WAS A SIMPLE MATTER TO BETRAY ME ONCE BEFORE.
DON'T PRETEND YOU CARE AT ALL WHAT HAPPENS TO ME.
BY RAO! YOU'RE AN IDIOT.
I LOVED YOU.
EVEN AFTER ALL YOUR LIES...YOUR MANIPULATION.
I UNDERSTOOD WHAT YOU WANTED.
IT WAS WHAT I WANTED WITH ALL MY HEART AND SOUL.
BUT YOU FORCED MY HAND, H'EL.
AND DAMMIT IF YOU'RE NOT GOING TO DO IT AGAIN!

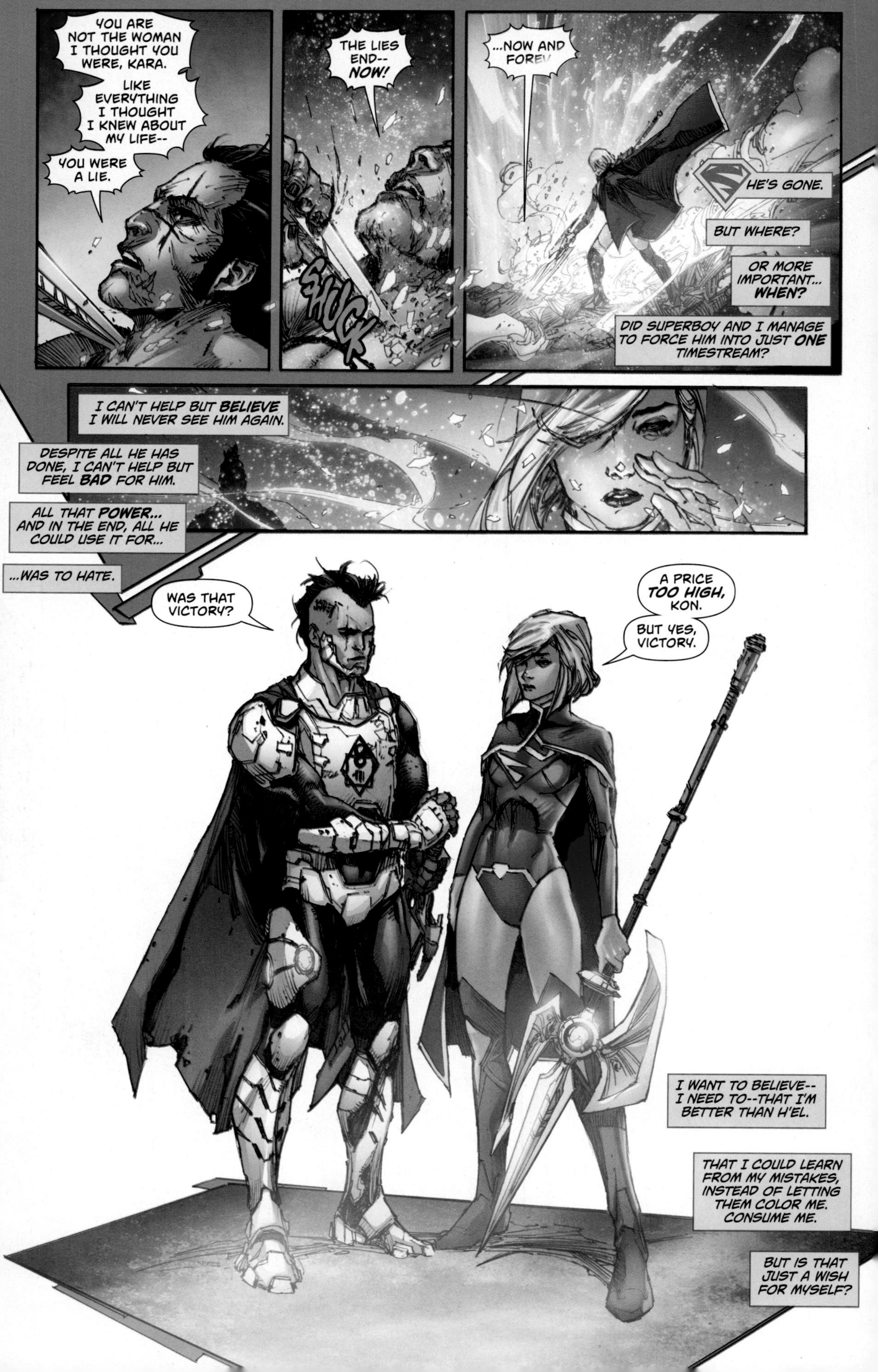

YOU ARE NOT THE WOMAN I THOUGHT YOU WERE, KARA.
LIKE EVERYTHING I THOUGHT I KNEW ABOUT MY LIFE--
YOU WERE A LIE.
THE LIES END-- NOW!
SHUCK
...NOW AND FOREV
HE'S GONE.
BUT WHERE?
OR MORE IMPORTANT... WHEN?
DID SUPERBOY AND I MANAGE TO FORCE HIM INTO JUST ONE TIMESTREAM?
I CAN'T HELP BUT BELIEVE I WILL NEVER SEE HIM AGAIN.
DESPITE ALL HE HAS DONE, I CAN'T HELP BUT FEEL BAD FOR HIM.
ALL THAT POWER... AND IN THE END, ALL HE COULD USE IT FOR...
...WAS TO HATE.
WAS THAT VICTORY?
A PRICE TOO HIGH, KON.
BUT YES, VICTORY.
I WANT TO BELIEVE-- I NEED TO--THAT I'M BETTER THAN H'EL.
THAT I COULD LEARN FROM MY MISTAKES, INSTEAD OF LETTING THEM COLOR ME. CONSUME ME.
BUT IS THAT JUST A WISH FOR MYSELF?

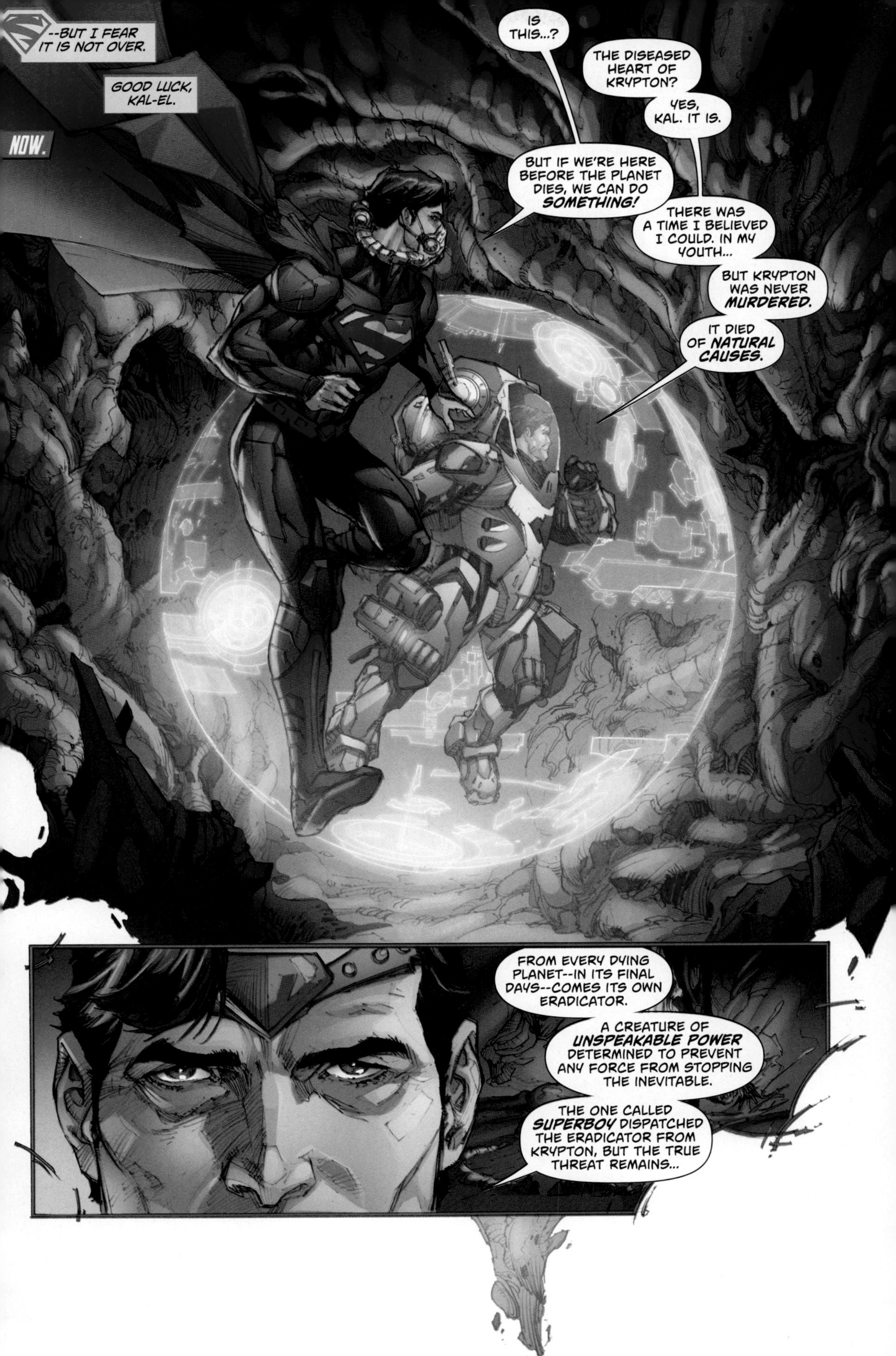
--BUT I FEAR IT IS NOT OVER.
GOOD LUCK, KAL-EL.
NOW.
IS THIS...?
THE DISEASED HEART OF KRYPTON?
YES, KAL. IT IS.
BUT IF WE'RE HERE BEFORE THE PLANET DIES, WE CAN DO SOMETHING!
THERE WAS A TIME I BELIEVED I COULD. IN MY YOUTH...
BUT KRYPTON WAS NEVER MURDERED.
IT DIED OF NATURAL CAUSES.
FROM EVERY DYING PLANET--IN ITS FINAL DAYS--COMES ITS OWN ERADICATOR.
A CREATURE OF UNSPEAKABLE POWER DETERMINED TO PREVENT ANY FORCE FROM STOPPING THE INEVITABLE.
THE ONE CALLED SUPERBOY DISPATCHED THE ERADICATOR FROM KRYPTON, BUT THE TRUE THREAT REMAINS...

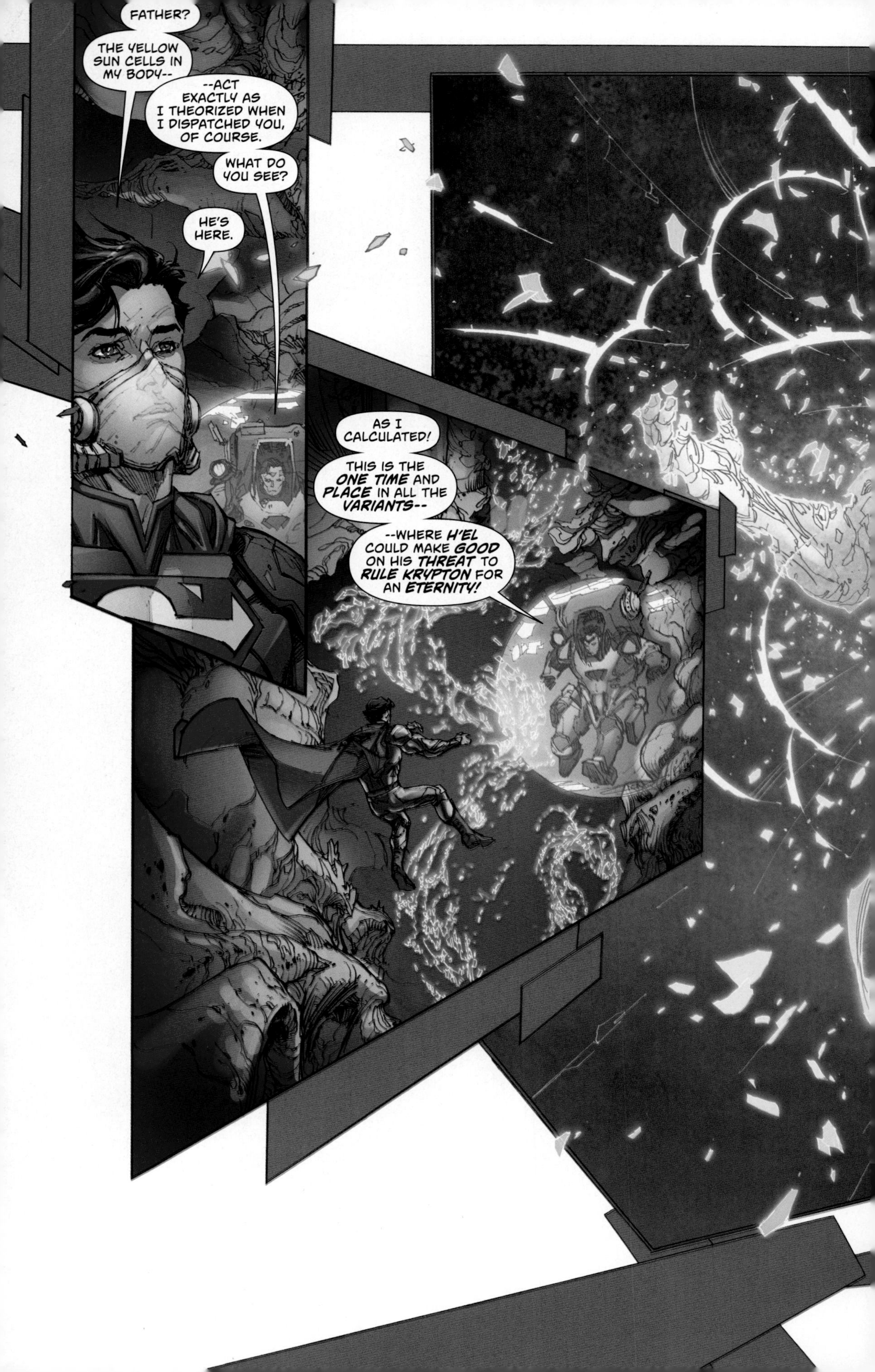
FATHER?
THE YELLOW SUN CELLS IN MY BODY--
--ACT EXACTLY AS I THEORIZED WHEN I DISPATCHED YOU, OF COURSE.
WHAT DO YOU SEE?
HE'S HERE.
AS I CALCULATED!
THIS IS THE ONE TIME AND PLACE IN ALL THE VARIANTS--
--WHERE H'EL COULD MAKE GOOD ON HIS THREAT TO RULE KRYPTON FOR AN ETERNITY!

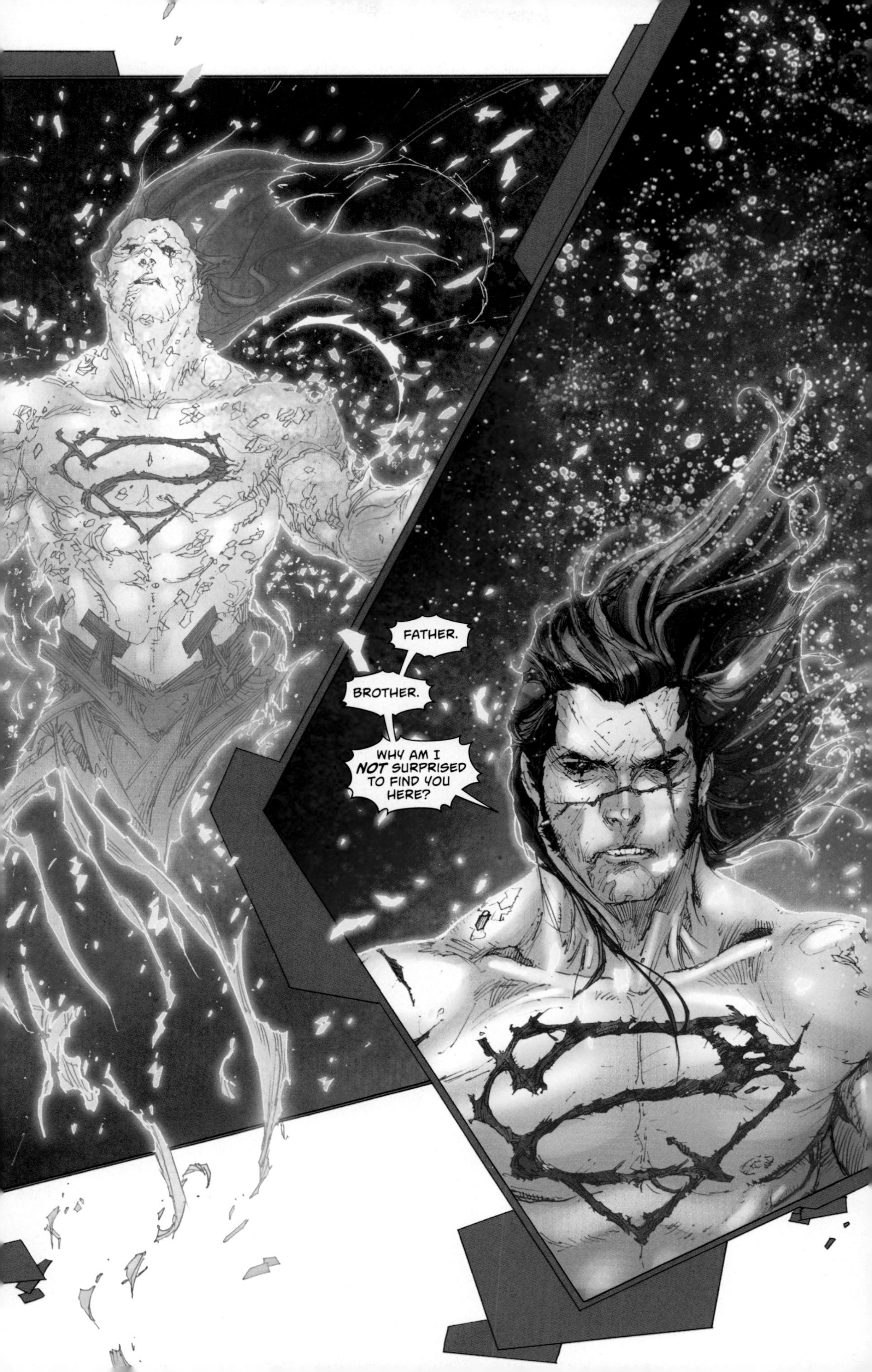
FATHER.
BROTHER.
WHY AM I NOT SURPRISED TO FIND YOU HERE?

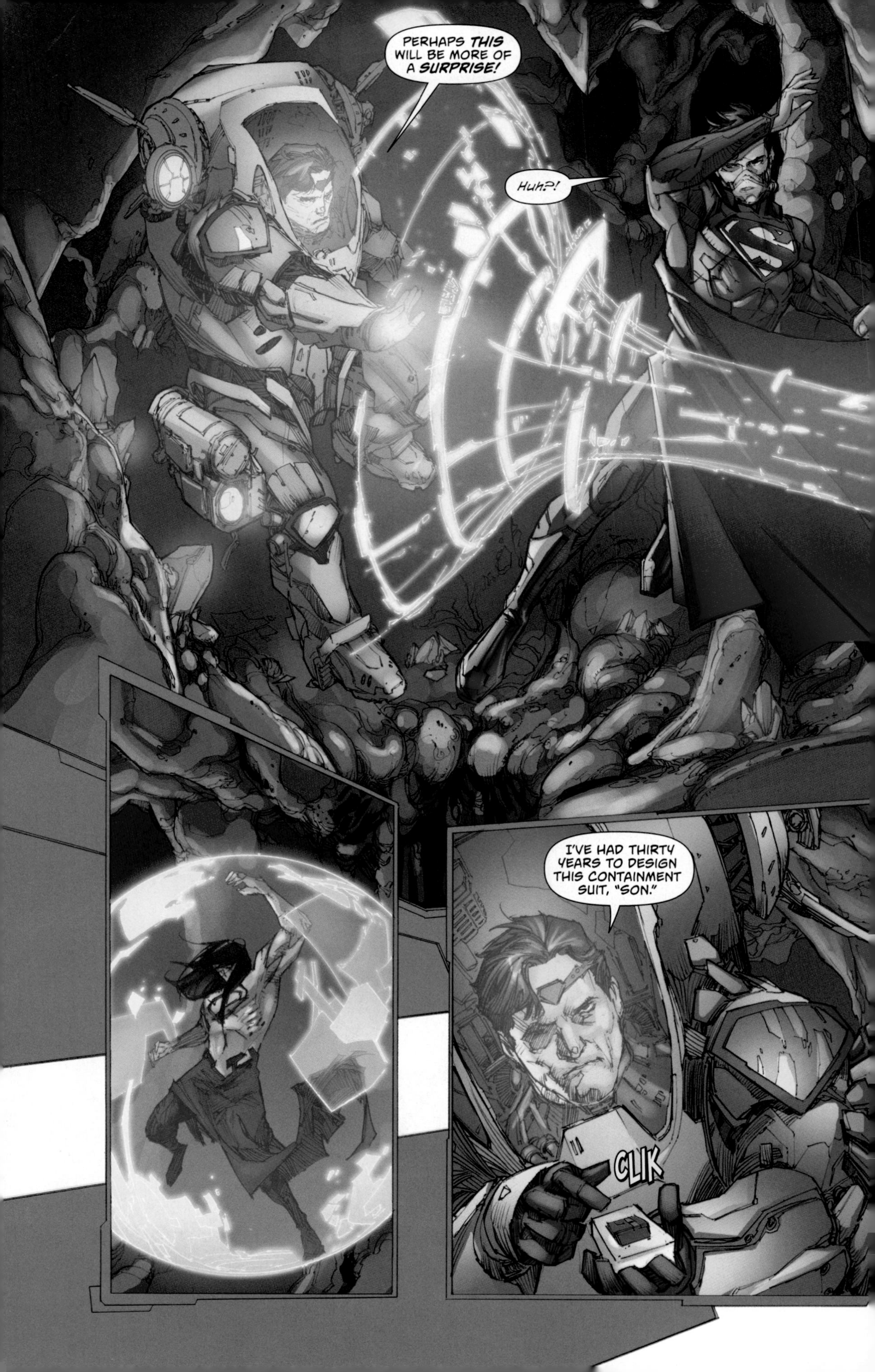
PERHAPS THIS WILL BE MORE OF A SURPRISE!
Huh?!
I'VE HAD THIRTY YEARS TO DESIGN THIS CONTAINMENT SUIT, "SON."
CLIK

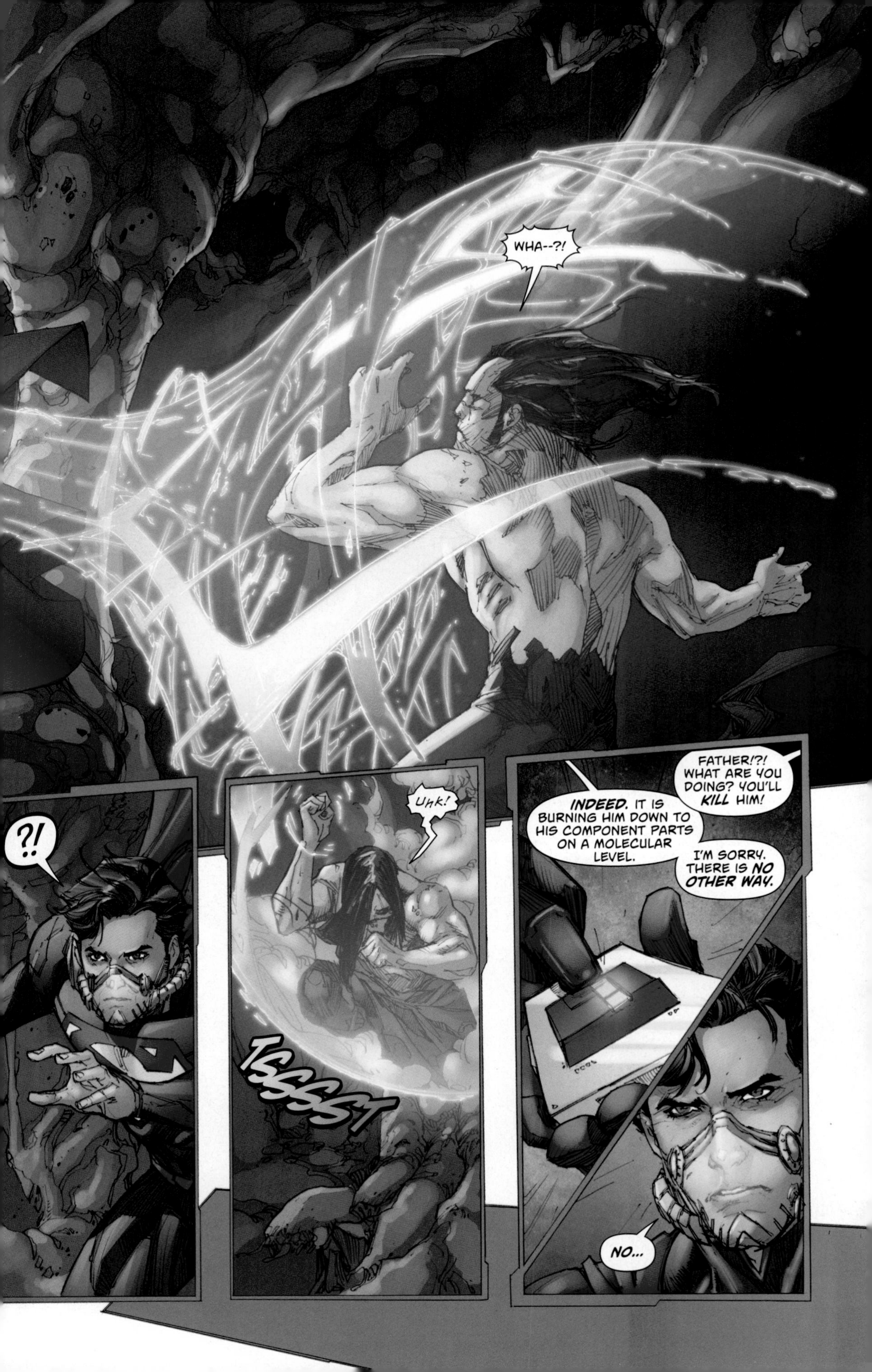
WHA--?!
?!
Uhk!
TSSSSST
FATHER!?! WHAT ARE YOU DOING? YOU'LL KILL HIM!
INDEED. IT IS BURNING HIM DOWN TO HIS COMPONENT PARTS ON A MOLECULAR LEVEL.
I'M SORRY. THERE IS NO OTHER WAY.
NO...

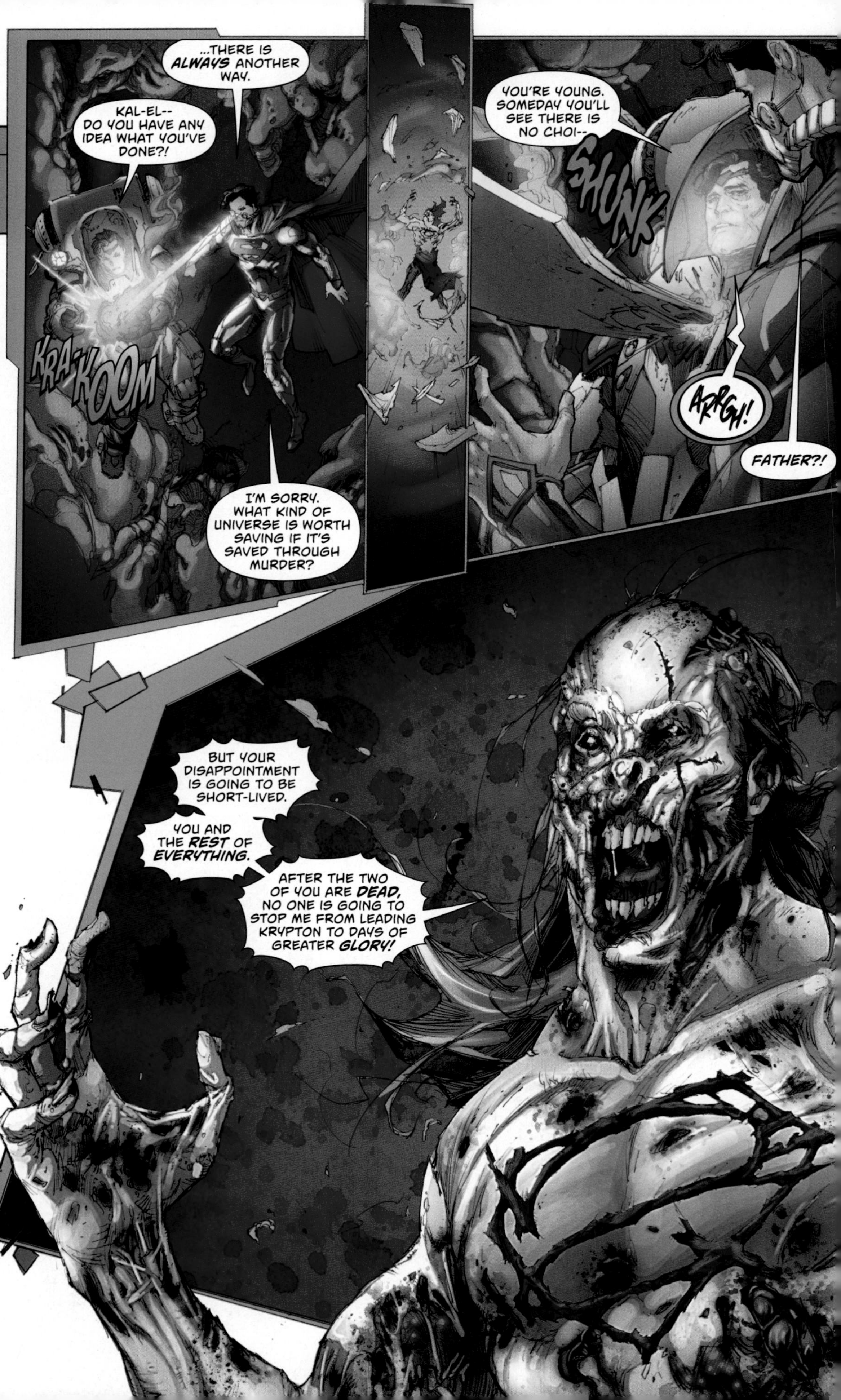
...THERE IS ALWAYS ANOTHER WAY.
KAL-EL-- DO YOU HAVE ANY IDEA WHAT YOU'VE DONE?!
KRA-KOOM
I'M SORRY. WHAT KIND OF UNIVERSE IS WORTH SAVING IF IT'S SAVED THROUGH MURDER?
YOU'RE YOUNG. SOMEDAY YOU'LL SEE THERE IS NO CHOI--
SHUNK
ARRGH!
FATHER?!
BUT YOUR DISAPPOINTMENT IS GOING TO BE SHORT-LIVED.
YOU AND THE REST OF EVERYTHING.
AFTER THE TWO OF YOU ARE DEAD, NO ONE IS GOING TO STOP ME FROM LEADING KRYPTON TO DAYS OF GREATER GLORY!

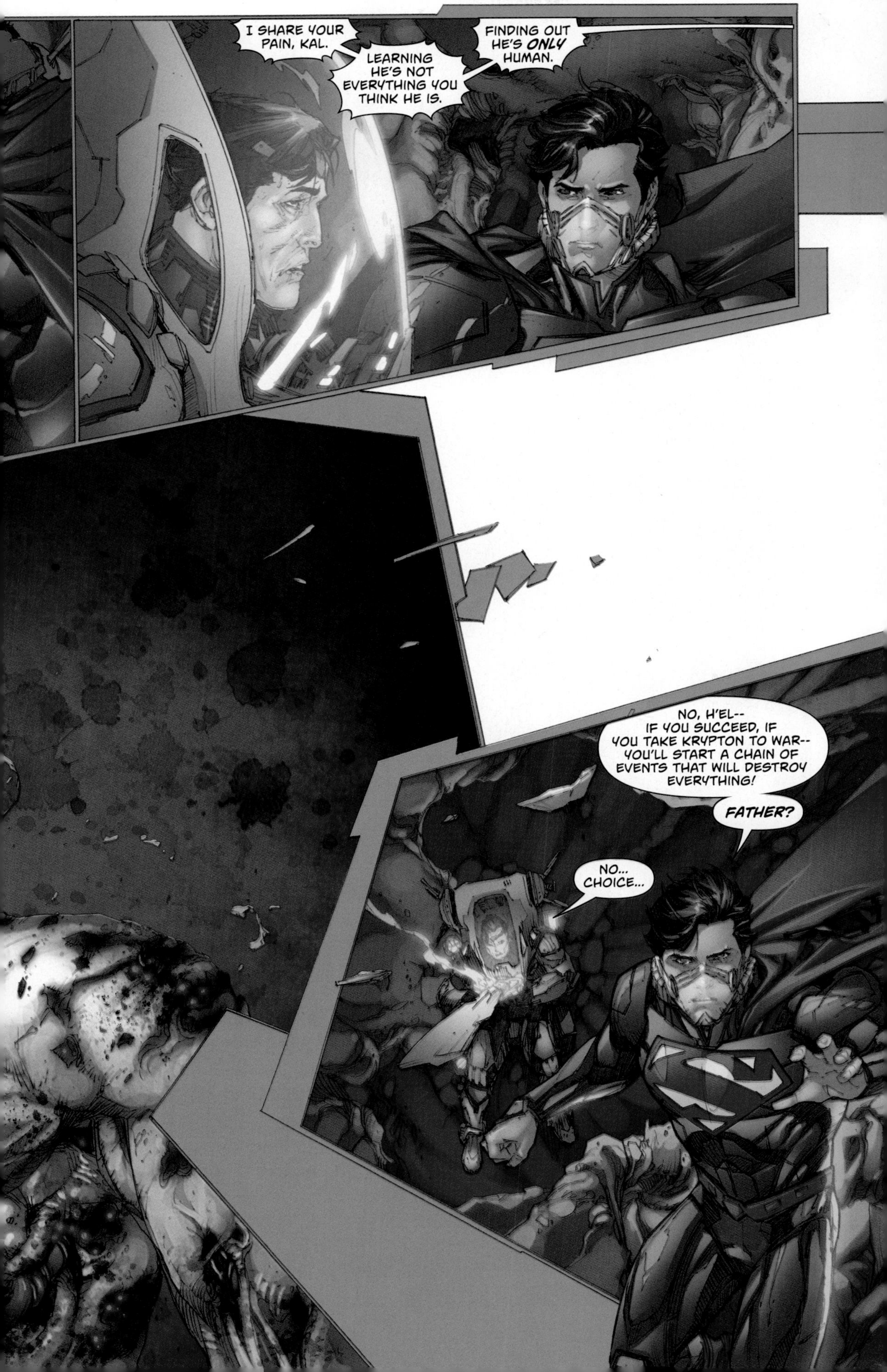

I SHARE YOUR PAIN, KAL.
LEARNING HE'S NOT EVERYTHING YOU THINK HE IS.
FINDING OUT HE'S *ONLY* HUMAN.
NO, H'EL-- IF YOU SUCCEED, IF YOU TAKE KRYPTON TO WAR-- YOU'LL START A CHAIN OF EVENTS THAT WILL DESTROY EVERYTHING!
FATHER?
NO... CHOICE...

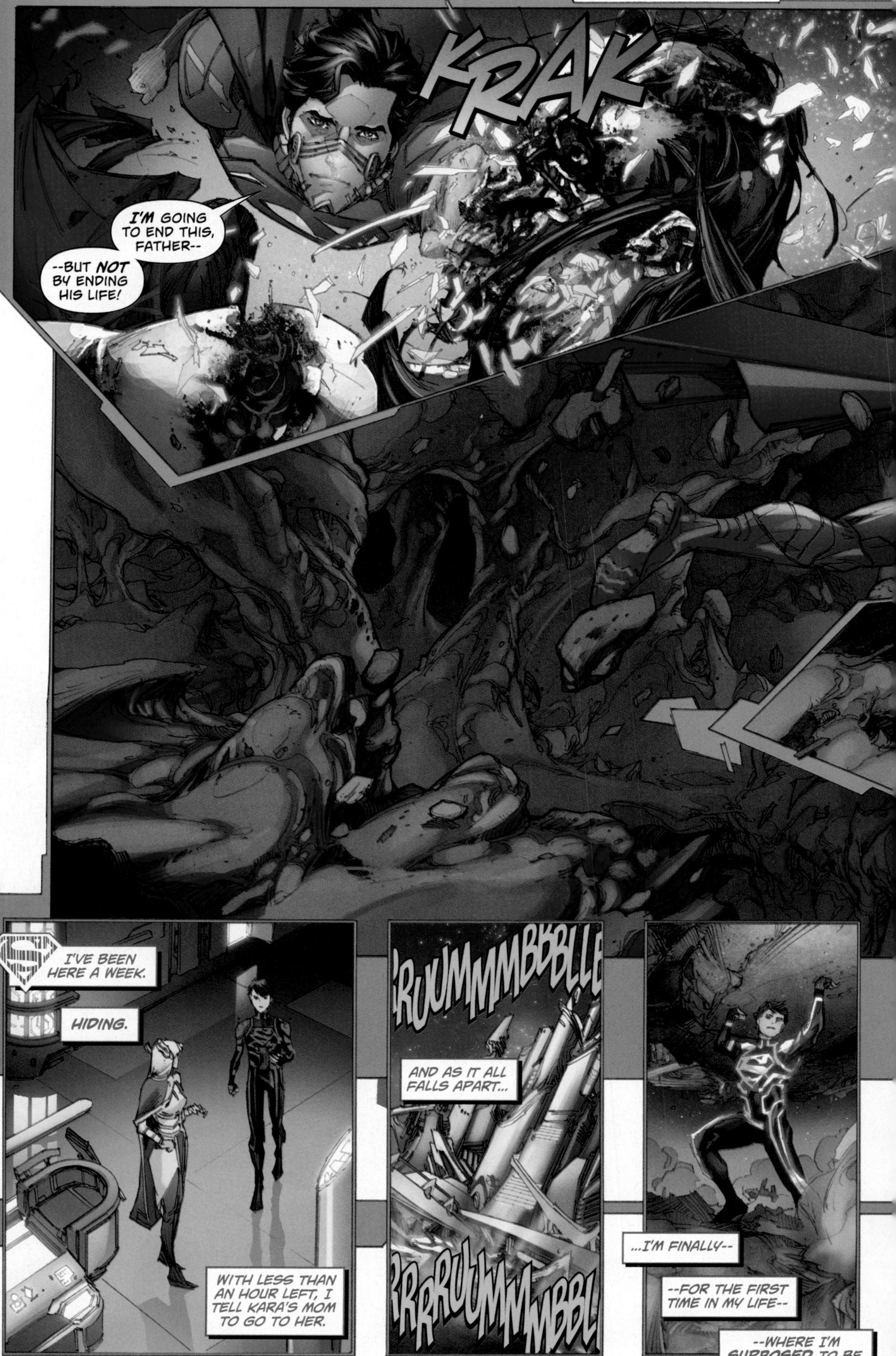
KRAK
I'M GOING TO END THIS, FATHER--
--BUT NOT BY ENDING HIS LIFE!
I'VE BEEN HERE A WEEK.
HIDING.
WITH LESS THAN AN HOUR LEFT, I TELL KARA'S MOM TO GO TO HER.
RRUUMMMBBBLLE
AND AS IT ALL FALLS APART...
RRRRUUMMMBBL
...I'M FINALLY--
--FOR THE FIRST TIME IN MY LIFE--
--WHERE I'M SUPPOSED TO BE.

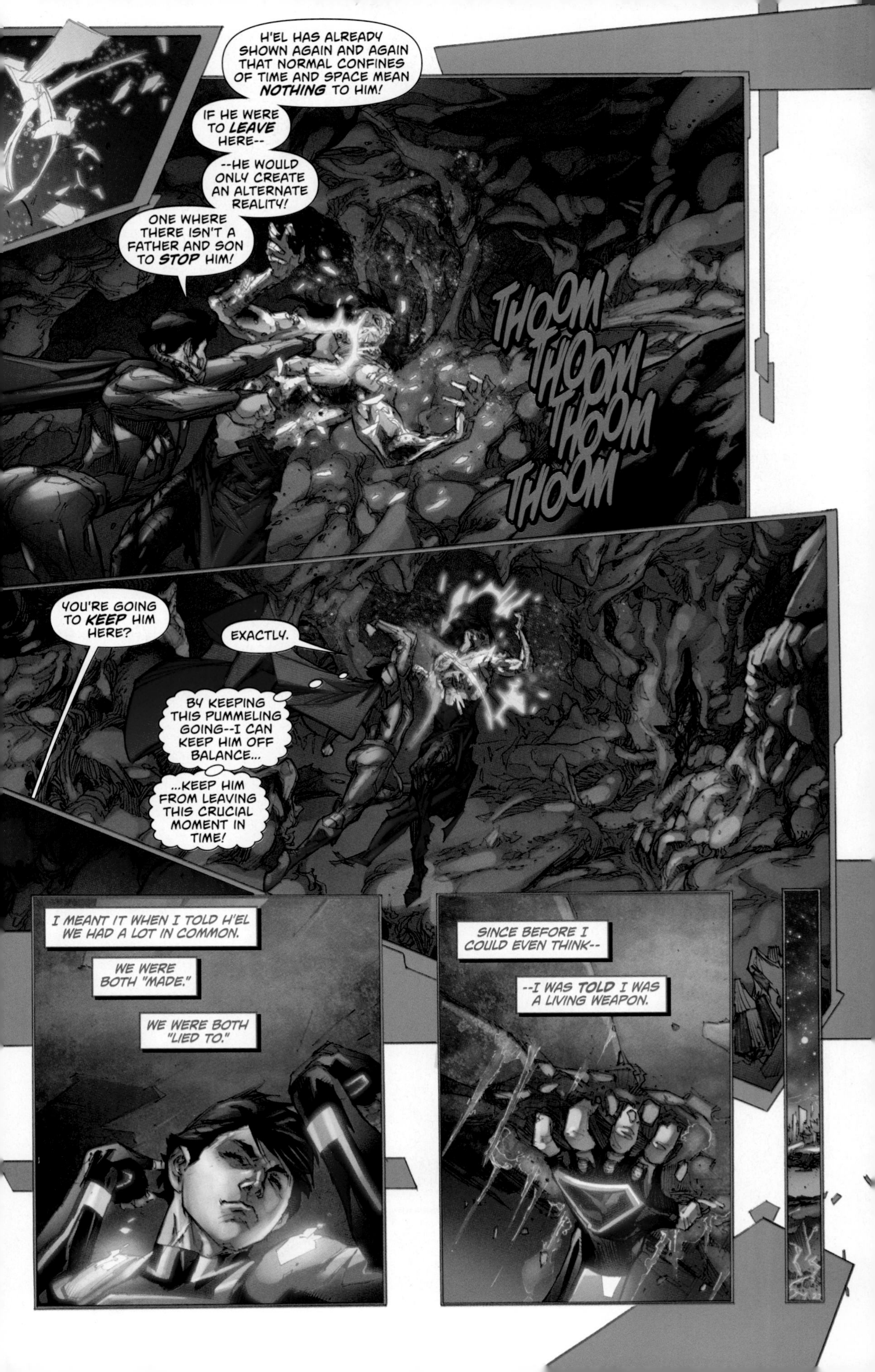
H'EL HAS ALREADY SHOWN AGAIN AND AGAIN THAT NORMAL CONFINES OF TIME AND SPACE MEAN NOTHING TO HIM!
IF HE WERE TO LEAVE HERE--
--HE WOULD ONLY CREATE AN ALTERNATE REALITY!
ONE WHERE THERE ISN'T A FATHER AND SON TO STOP HIM!
THOOM THOOM THOOM THOOM
YOU'RE GOING TO KEEP HIM HERE?
EXACTLY.
BY KEEPING THIS PUMMELING GOING--I CAN KEEP HIM OFF BALANCE...
...KEEP HIM FROM LEAVING THIS CRUCIAL MOMENT IN TIME!
I MEANT IT WHEN I TOLD H'EL WE HAD A LOT IN COMMON.
WE WERE BOTH "MADE."
WE WERE BOTH "LIED TO."
SINCE BEFORE I COULD EVEN THINK--
--I WAS TOLD I WAS A LIVING WEAPON.

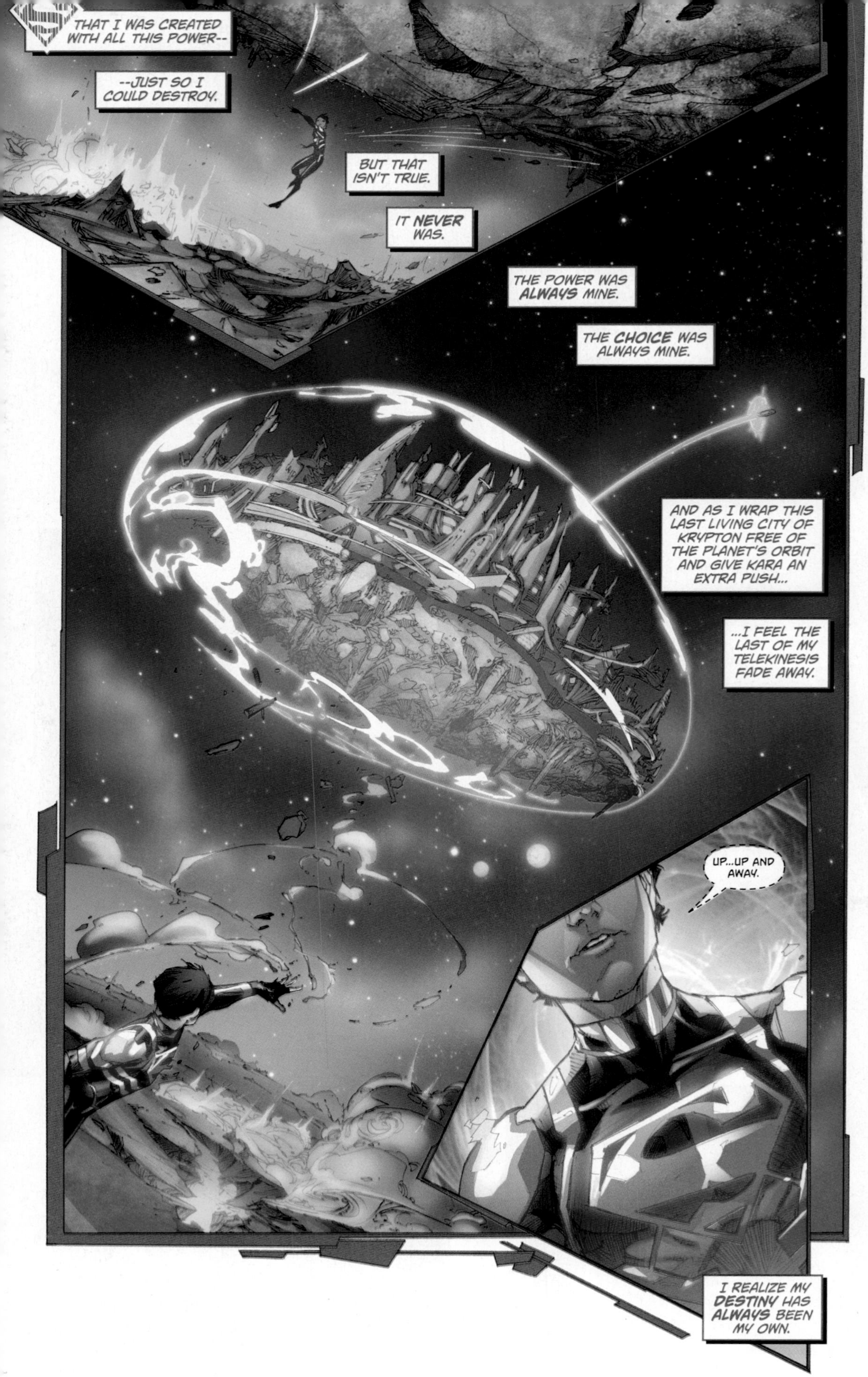
THAT I WAS CREATED WITH ALL THIS POWER--
--JUST SO I COULD DESTROY.
BUT THAT ISN'T TRUE.
IT NEVER WAS.
THE POWER WAS ALWAYS MINE.
THE CHOICE WAS ALWAYS MINE.
AND AS I WRAP THIS LAST LIVING CITY OF KRYPTON FREE OF THE PLANET'S ORBIT AND GIVE KARA AN EXTRA PUSH...
...I FEEL THE LAST OF MY TELEKINESIS FADE AWAY.
UP...UP AND AWAY.
I REALIZE MY DESTINY HAS ALWAYS BEEN MY OWN.

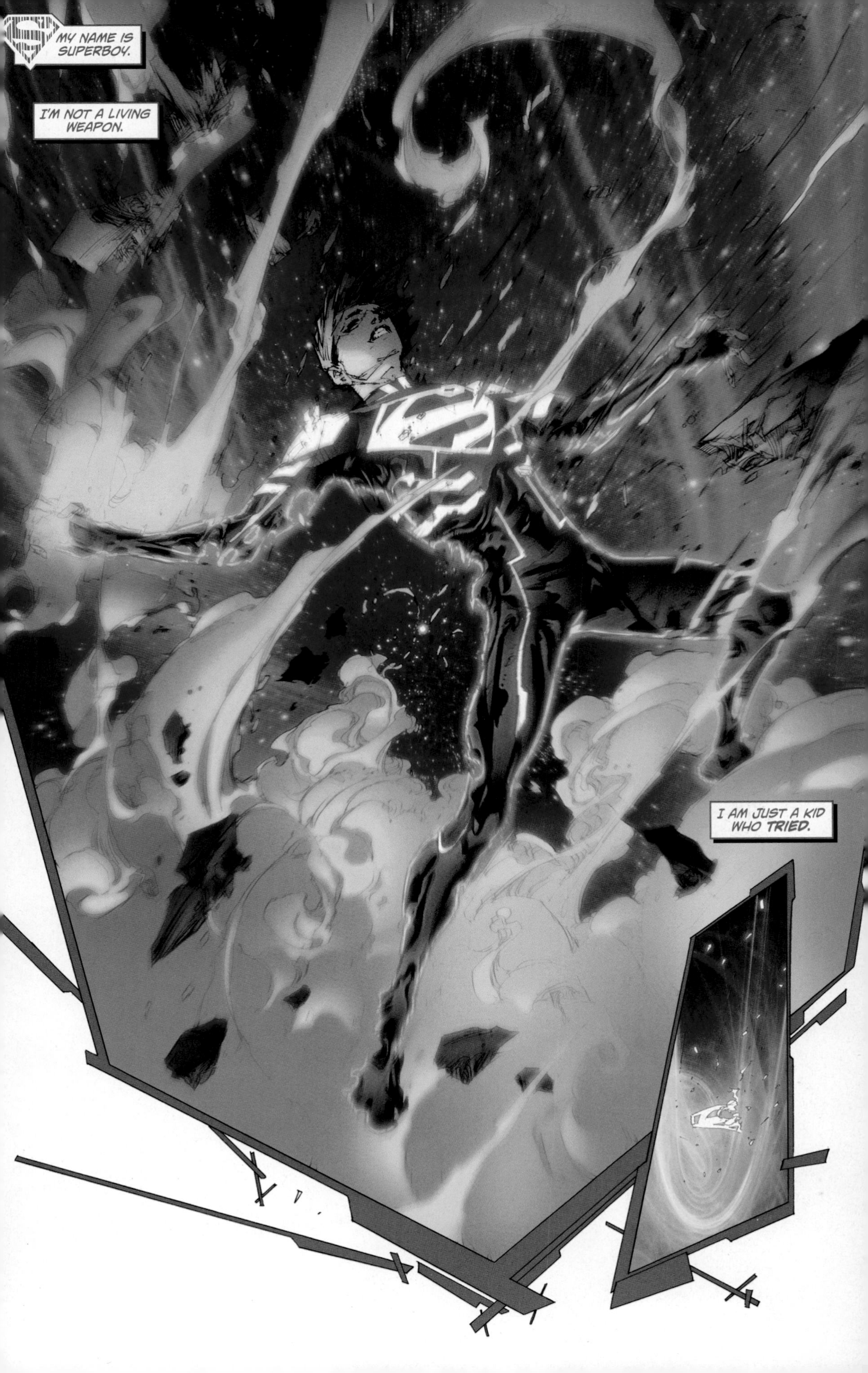
MY NAME IS SUPERBOY.
I'M NOT A LIVING WEAPON.
I AM JUST A KID WHO TRIED.

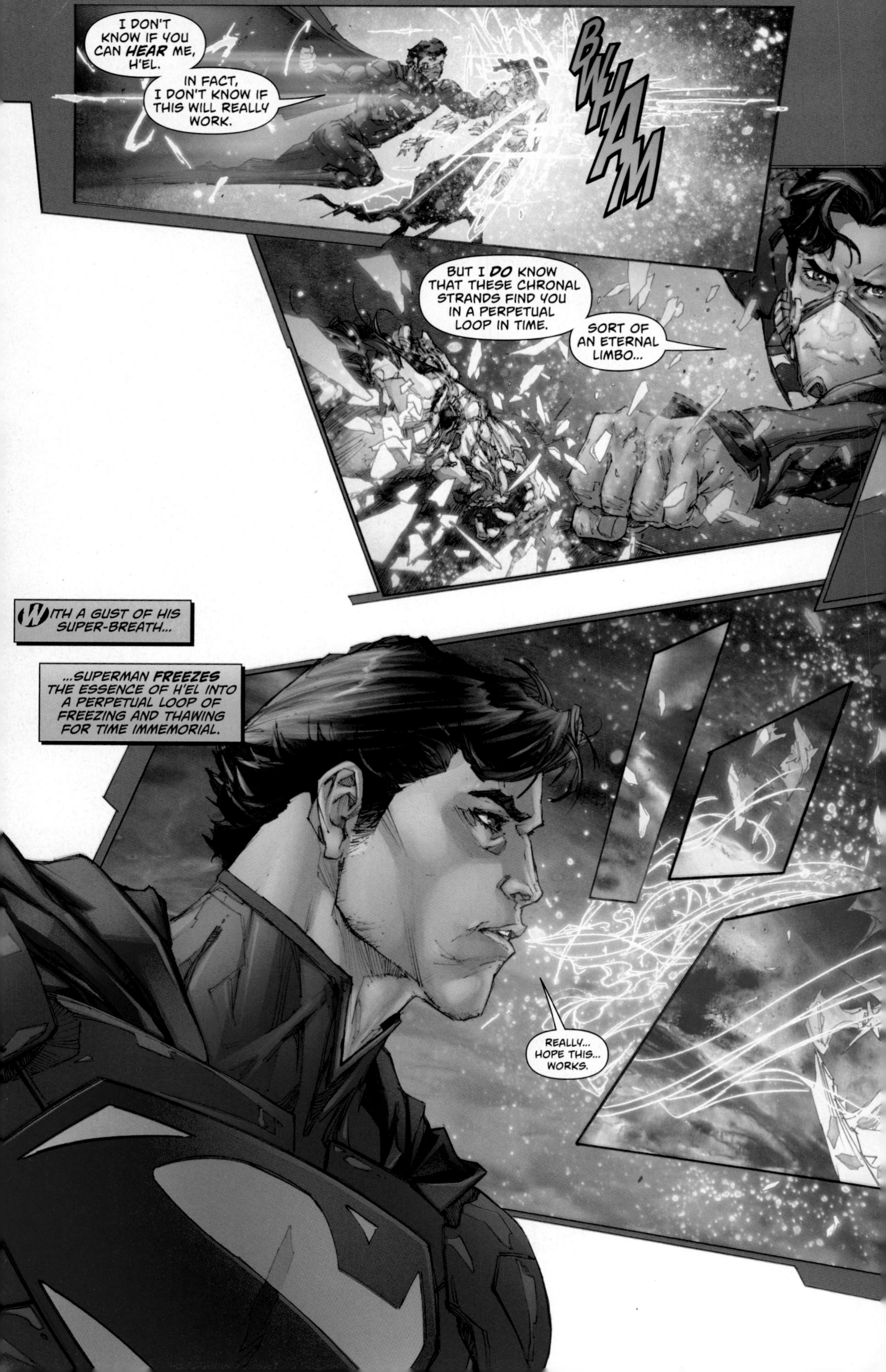

I DON'T KNOW IF YOU CAN HEAR ME, H'EL.
IN FACT, I DON'T KNOW IF THIS WILL REALLY WORK.
BWHAM
BUT I DO KNOW THAT THESE CHRONAL STRANDS FIND YOU IN A PERPETUAL LOOP IN TIME.
SORT OF AN ETERNAL LIMBO...
WITH A GUST OF HIS SUPER-BREATH...
...SUPERMAN FREEZES THE ESSENCE OF H'EL INTO A PERPETUAL LOOP OF FREEZING AND THAWING FOR TIME IMMEMORIAL.
REALLY... HOPE THIS... WORKS.

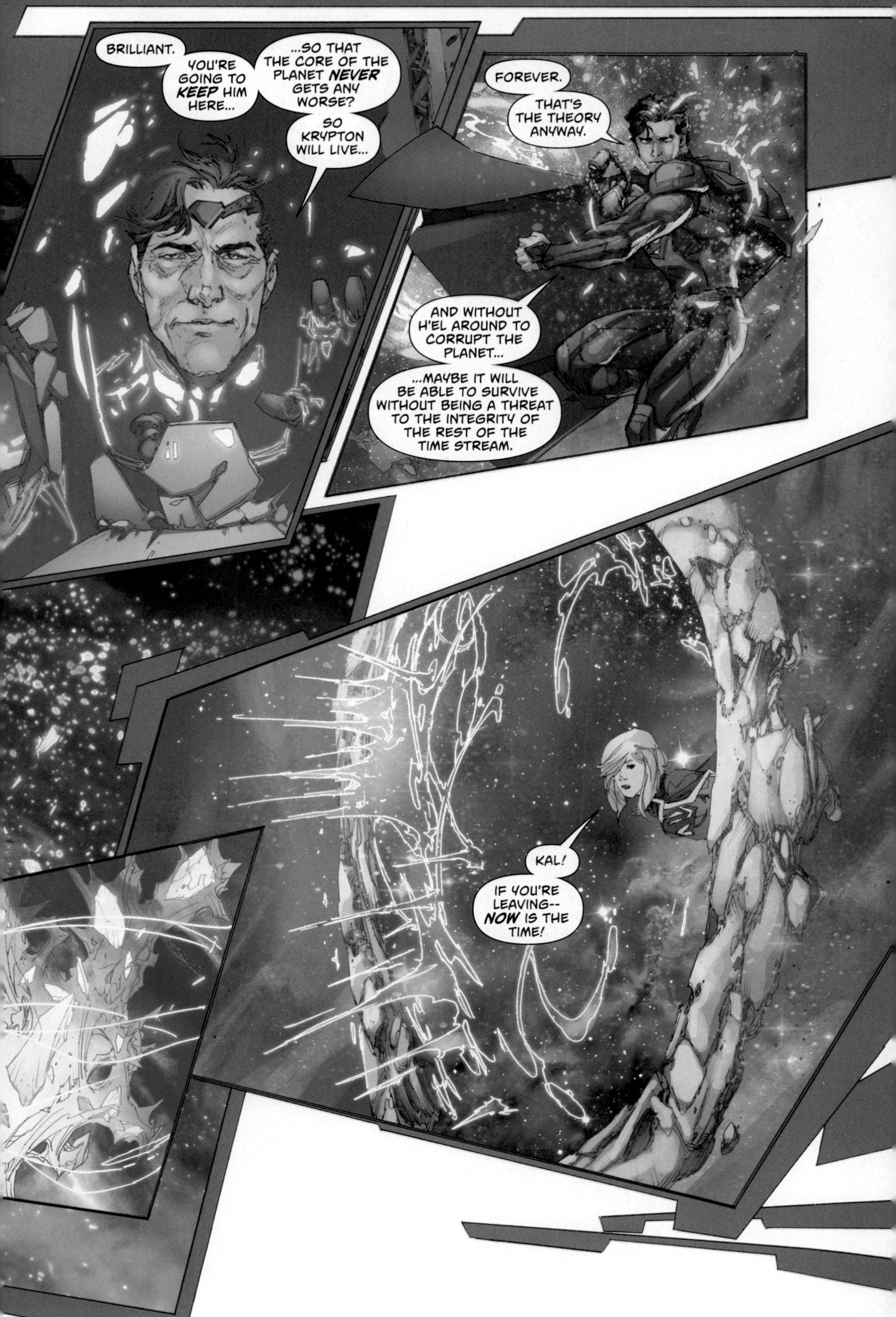
BRILLIANT.
YOU'RE GOING TO **KEEP** HIM HERE...
...SO THAT THE CORE OF THE PLANET **NEVER** GETS ANY WORSE?
SO KRYPTON WILL LIVE...
FOREVER.
THAT'S THE THEORY ANYWAY.
AND WITHOUT H'EL AROUND TO CORRUPT THE PLANET...
...MAYBE IT WILL BE ABLE TO SURVIVE WITHOUT BEING A THREAT TO THE INTEGRITY OF THE REST OF THE TIME STREAM.
KAL!
IF YOU'RE LEAVING-- **NOW** IS THE TIME!

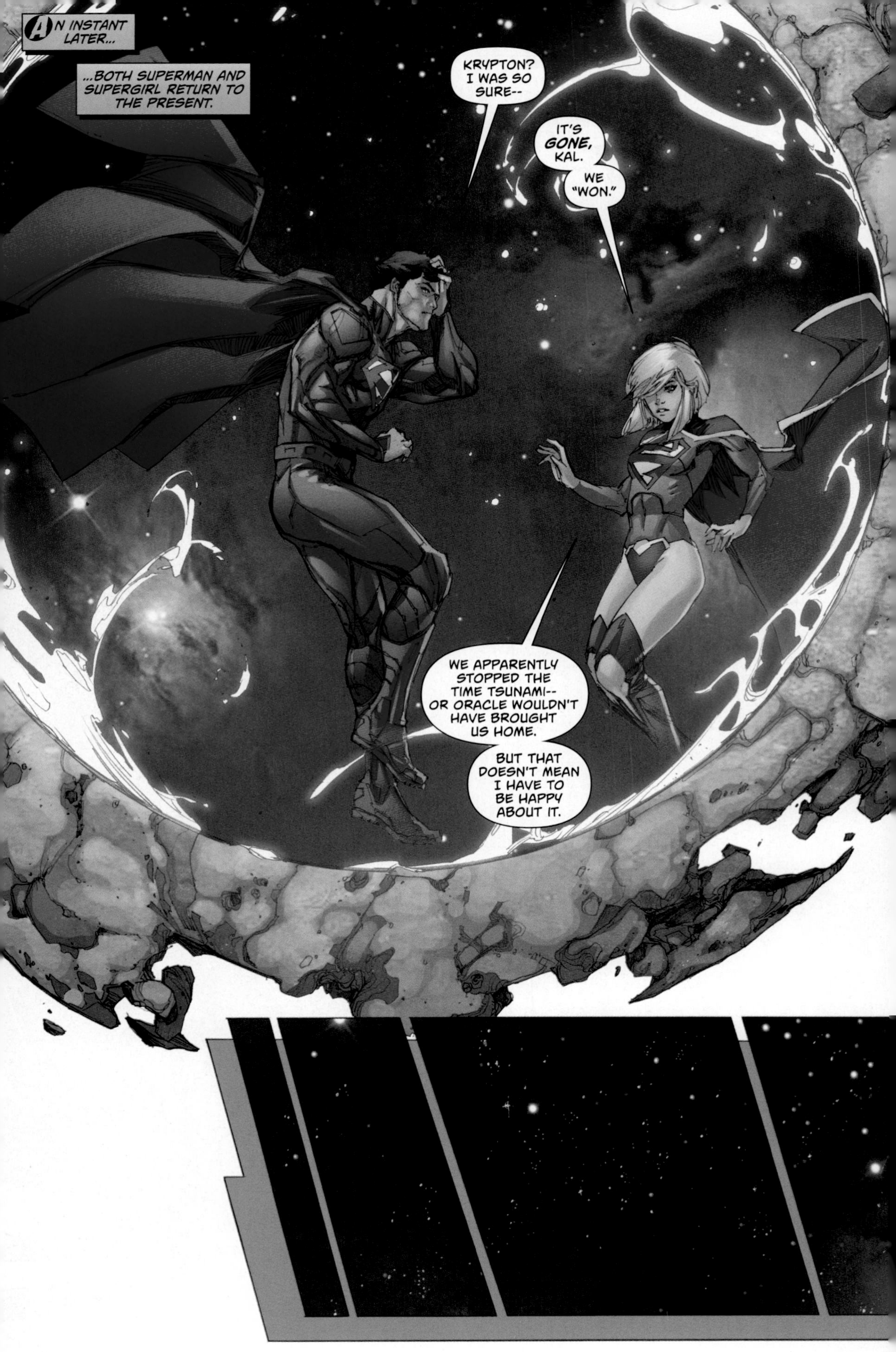
AN INSTANT LATER...
...BOTH SUPERMAN AND SUPERGIRL RETURN TO THE PRESENT.
KRYPTON? I WAS SO SURE--
IT'S GONE, KAL.
WE "WON."
WE APPARENTLY STOPPED THE TIME TSUNAMI-- OR ORACLE WOULDN'T HAVE BROUGHT US HOME.
BUT THAT DOESN'T MEAN I HAVE TO BE HAPPY ABOUT IT.

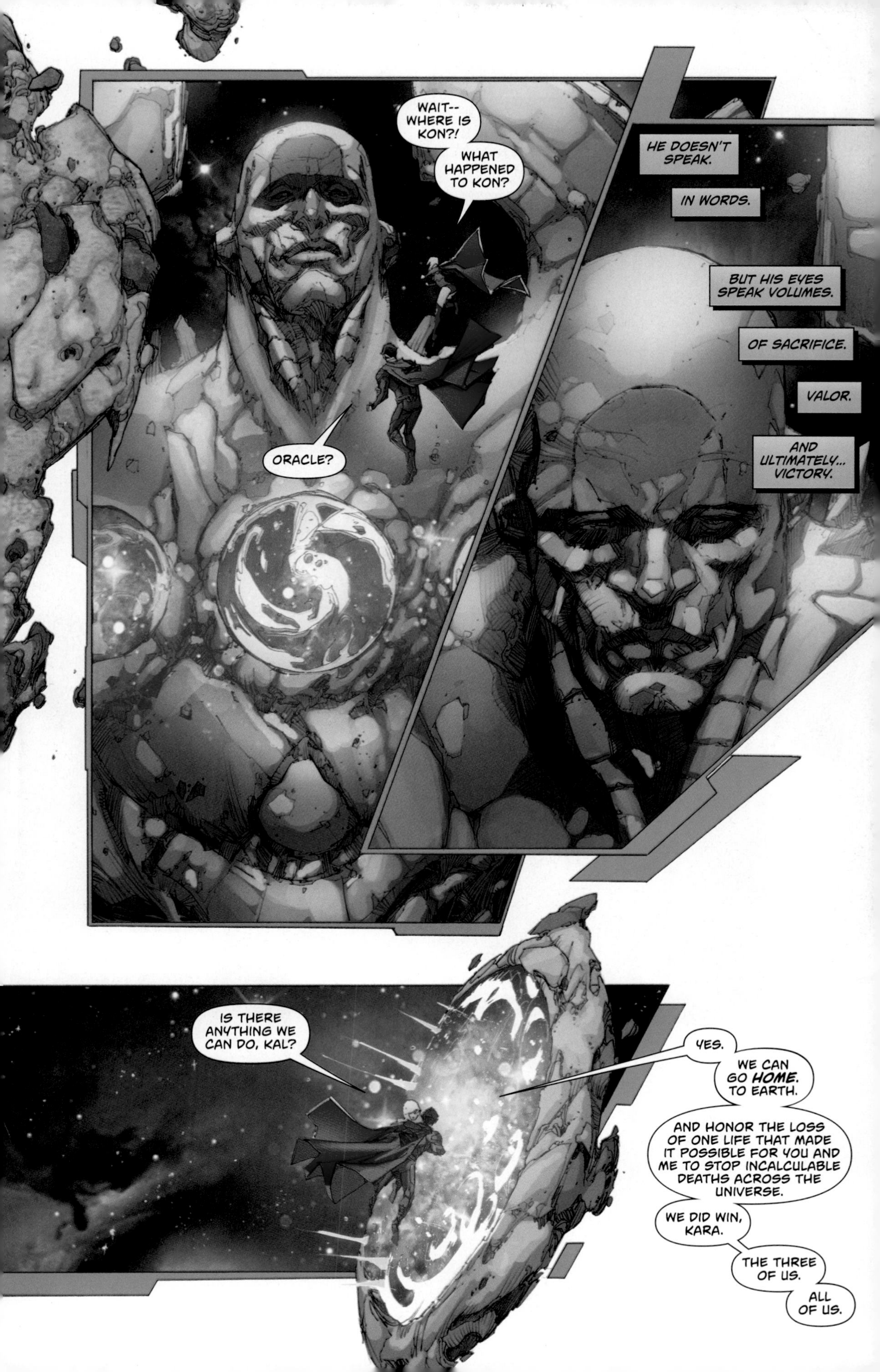
WAIT-- WHERE IS KON?!
WHAT HAPPENED TO KON?
ORACLE?
HE DOESN'T SPEAK.
IN WORDS.
BUT HIS EYES SPEAK VOLUMES.
OF SACRIFICE.
VALOR.
AND ULTIMATELY... VICTORY.
IS THERE ANYTHING WE CAN DO, KAL?
YES.
WE CAN GO HOME. TO EARTH.
AND HONOR THE LOSS OF ONE LIFE THAT MADE IT POSSIBLE FOR YOU AND ME TO STOP INCALCULABLE DEATHS ACROSS THE UNIVERSE.
WE DID WIN, KARA.
THE THREE OF US.
ALL OF US.

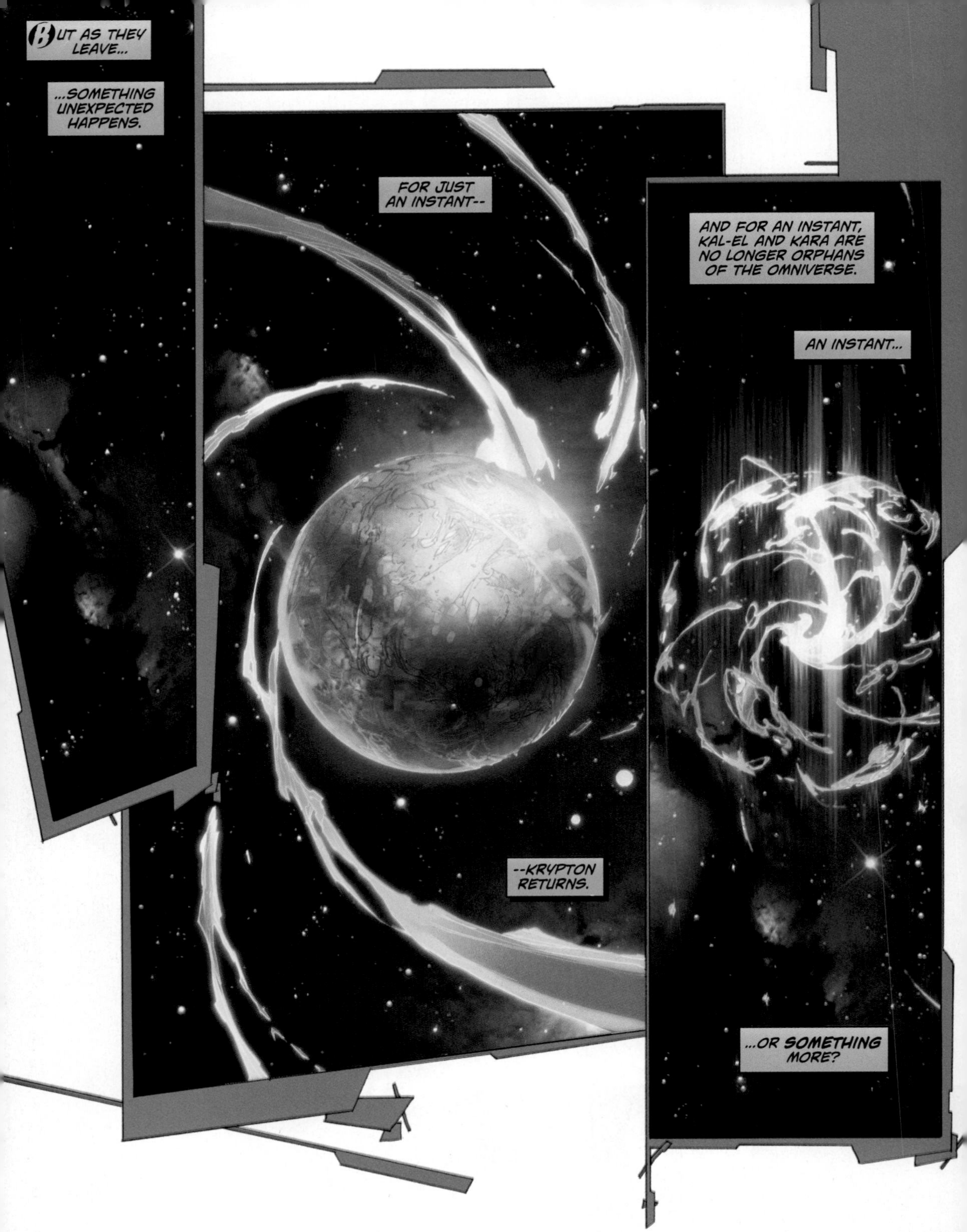
BUT AS THEY LEAVE...
...SOMETHING UNEXPECTED HAPPENS.
FOR JUST AN INSTANT--
--KRYPTON RETURNS.
AND FOR AN INSTANT, KAL-EL AND KARA ARE NO LONGER ORPHANS OF THE OMNIVERSE.
AN INSTANT...
...OR SOMETHING MORE?

"ACTION COMICS has successfully carved its own territory and continued exploring Morrison's familiar themes about heroism and ideas."—IGN

"Casts the character in a new light, opens up fresh storytelling possibilities, and pushes it all forward with dynamic Rags Morales art. I loved it."—THE ONION/AV CLUB

START AT THE BEGINNING!

SUPERMAN: ACTION COMICS VOLUME 1: SUPERMAN AND THE MEN OF STEEL

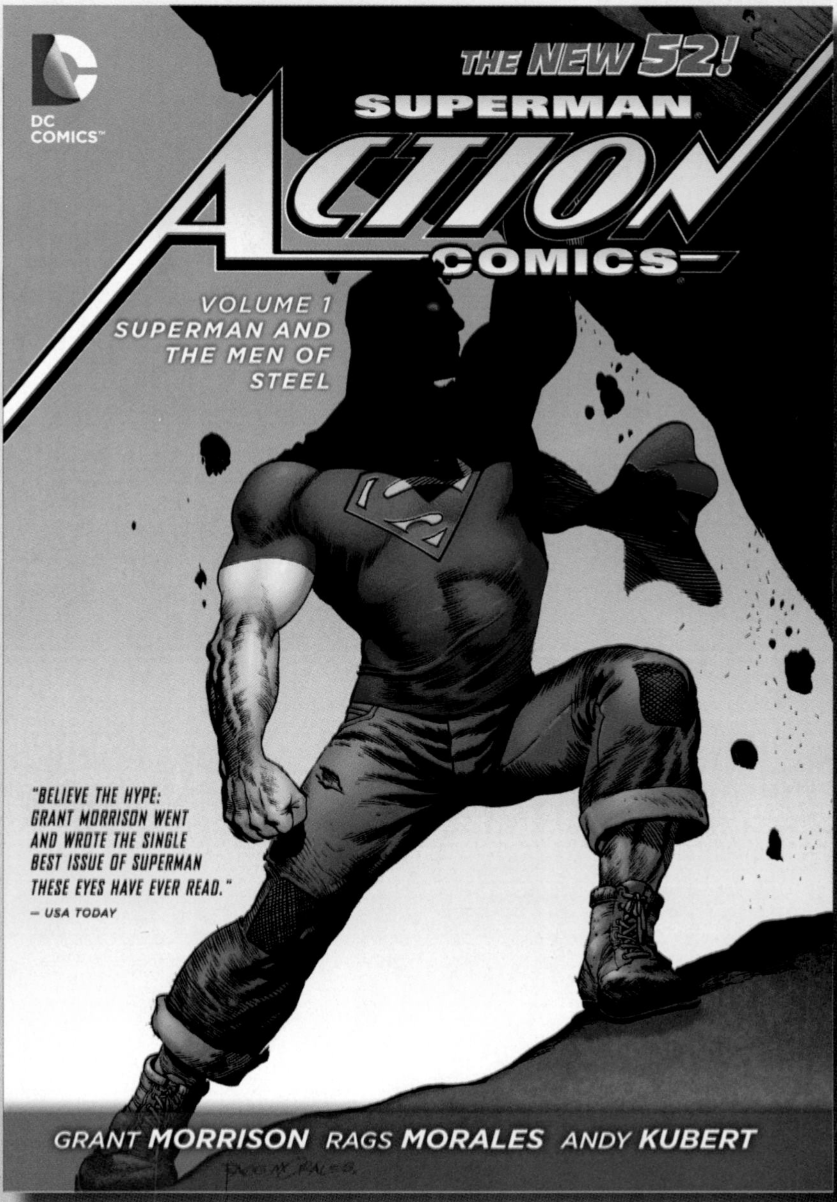
DC COMICS
THE NEW 52!
SUPERMAN
ACTION COMICS
VOLUME 1 SUPERMAN AND THE MEN OF STEEL
"BELIEVE THE HYPE: GRANT MORRISON WENT AND WROTE THE SINGLE BEST ISSUE OF SUPERMAN THESE EYES HAVE EVER READ."
– USA TODAY
GRANT MORRISON RAGS MORALES ANDY KUBERT

SUPERMAN: ACTION COMICS VOL. 2: BULLETPROOF

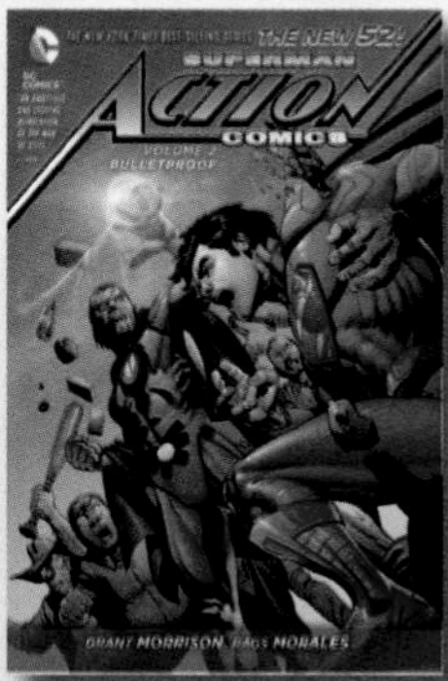
THE NEW 52!
SUPERMAN
ACTION COMICS

with GRANT MORRISON and RAGS MORALES

SUPERMAN: ACTION COMICS VOL. 3: AT THE END OF DAYS

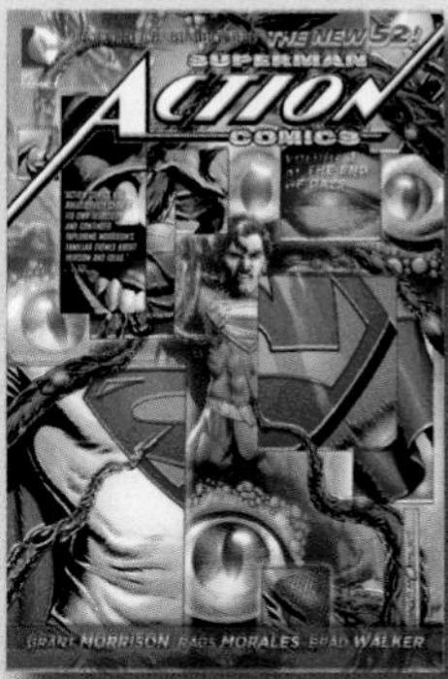
THE NEW 52!
SUPERMAN
ACTION COMICS

with GRANT MORRISON and RAGS MORALES

SUPERBOY VOL. 1: INCUBATION

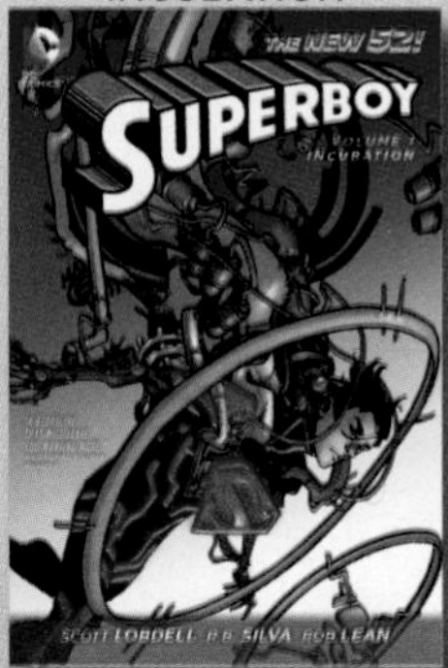
THE NEW 52!
SUPERBOY

DC COMICS™

DC COMICS™

"Superman is still super."
—WALL STREET JOURNAL

"The SUPERMAN world is also one now where fans new and old, young and not-so-young, can come to a common ground to talk about the superhero that started it all."
—CRAVE ONLINE

START AT THE BEGINNING!

SUPERMAN VOLUME 1: WHAT PRICE TOMORROW?

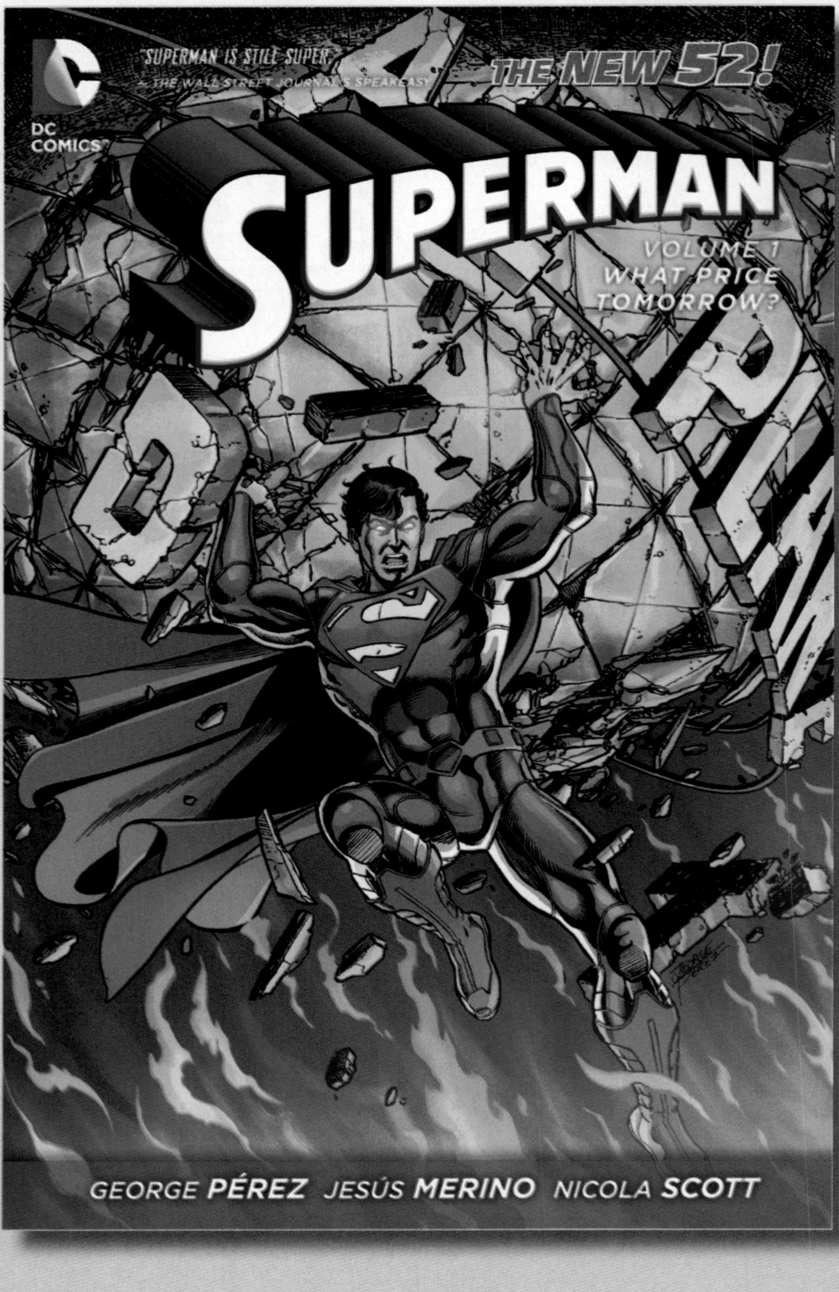

DC COMICS
"SUPERMAN IS STILL SUPER."
— THE WALL STREET JOURNAL'S SPEAKEASY
THE NEW 52!
SUPERMAN
VOLUME 1
WHAT PRICE
TOMORROW?
GEORGE PÉREZ JESÚS MERINO NICOLA SCOTT

SUPERMAN VOL. 2: SECRETS & LIES

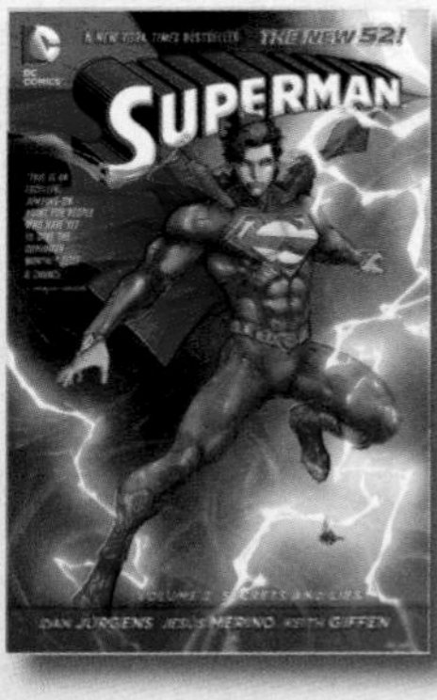

THE NEW 52!
SUPERMAN
DAN JURGENS JESÚS MERINO KEITH GIFFEN

SUPERMAN VOL. 3: FURY AT WORLD'S END

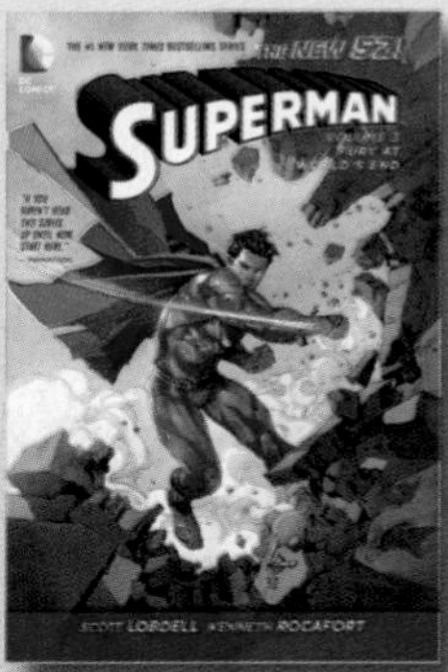

THE NEW 52!
SUPERMAN
SCOTT LOBDELL KENNETH ROCAFORT

SUPERMAN: H'EL ON EARTH

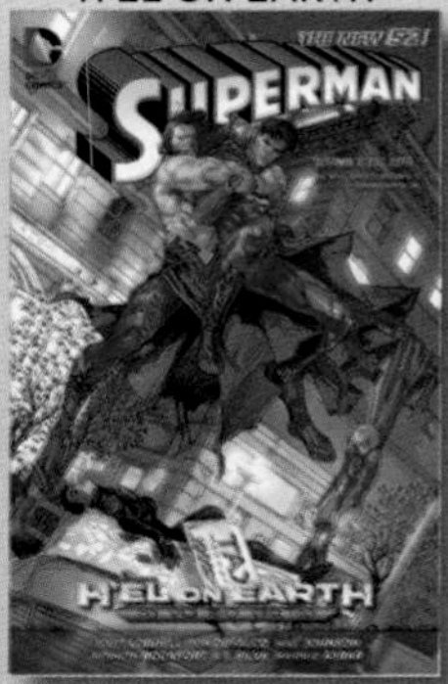

THE NEW 52!
SUPERMAN
H'EL ON EARTH

"Drips with energy."—IGN

"Grade A."—USA TODAY

START AT THE BEGINNING!

TEEN TITANS
VOLUME 1: IT'S OUR RIGHT TO FIGHT

TEEN TITANS VOL. 2: THE CULLING

TEEN TITANS VOL. 3: DEATH OF THE FAMILY

THE CULLING: RISE OF THE RAVAGERS

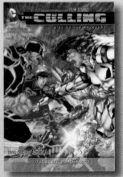

DC COMICS™

"Simone and artist Ardian Syaf not only do justice to Babs' legacy, but build in a new complexity that is the starting point for a future full of new storytelling possibilities. A hell of a ride."—IGN

START AT THE BEGINNING!

BATGIRL

VOLUME 1: THE DARKEST REFLECTION

DC COMICS™
"THIS IS A MUST-BUY SERIES."
— THE NEW YORK TIMES
THE NEW 52!
BATGIRL
VOLUME 1
THE DARKEST
REFLECTION
GAIL SIMONE ARDIAN SYAF VICENTE CIFUENTES

BATGIRL VOL. 2:
KNIGHTFALL DESCENDS

THE NEW 52!
BATGIRL
VOLUME 2
KNIGHTFALL DESCENDS
GAIL SIMONE ARDIAN SYAF ED BENES VICENTE CIFUENTES

BATGIRL VOL. 3:
DEATH OF THE FAMILY

THE NEW 52!
BATGIRL
VOLUME 3
DEATH OF THE FAMILY
GAIL SIMONE DANIEL SAMPERE

BATWOMAN VOL. 1:
HYDROLOGY

THE NEW 52!
BATWOMAN
VOLUME 1 HYDROLOGY
J.H. WILLIAMS III W. HADEN BLACKMAN

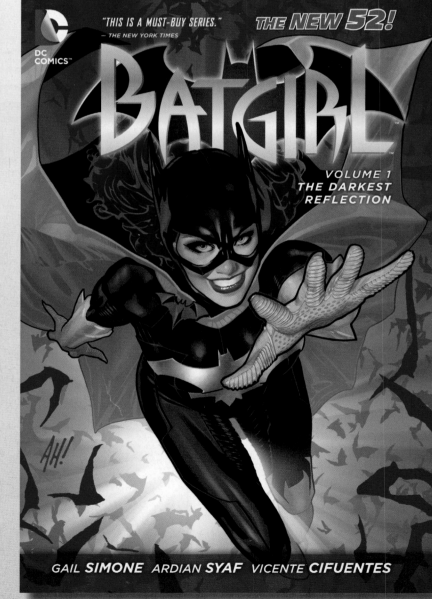